YOU ARE READING IN THE WRONG DIRECTION!!

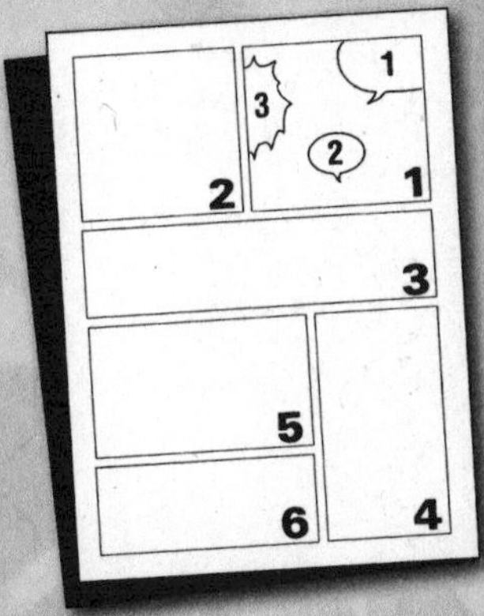
1
2
3
1
2
3
4
5
6

Whoops!
Guess what?
You're starting at the wrong end of the comic!

...It's true! In keeping with the original Japanese format, *Yu-Gi-Oh! 5Ds* is meant to be read from right to left, starting in the upper-right corner.

Unlike English, which is read from left to right, Japanese is read from right to left, meaning that action, sound effects and word-balloon order are completely reversed... something which can make readers unfamiliar with Japanese feel pretty backwards themselves. For this reason, manga or Japanese comics published in the U.S. in English have sometimes been published "flopped"—that is, printed in exact reverse order, as though seen from the other side of a mirror.

By flopping pages, U.S. publishers can avoid confusing readers, but the compromise is not without its downside. For one thing, a character in a flopped manga series who once wore in the original Japanese version a T-shirt emblazoned with "M A Y" (as in "the merry month of") now wears one which reads "Y A M"! Additionally, many manga creators in Japan are themselves unhappy with the process, as some feel the mirror-imaging of their art alters their original intentions.

We are proud to bring you Masahiro Hikokubo and Masashi Sato's *Yu-Gi-Oh! 5D's* in the original unflopped format. For now, though, turn to the other side of the book and let the duel begin...!

–Editor

IN THE NEXT VOLUME...

Yusei fights to save his friend Sect from the clutches of the Skeleton Knight's curse. But can Yusei's loyalty overcome Sect's thirst for power?

COMING SOON!!

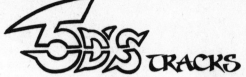

5D's Tracks

The 31st

By Satomasa

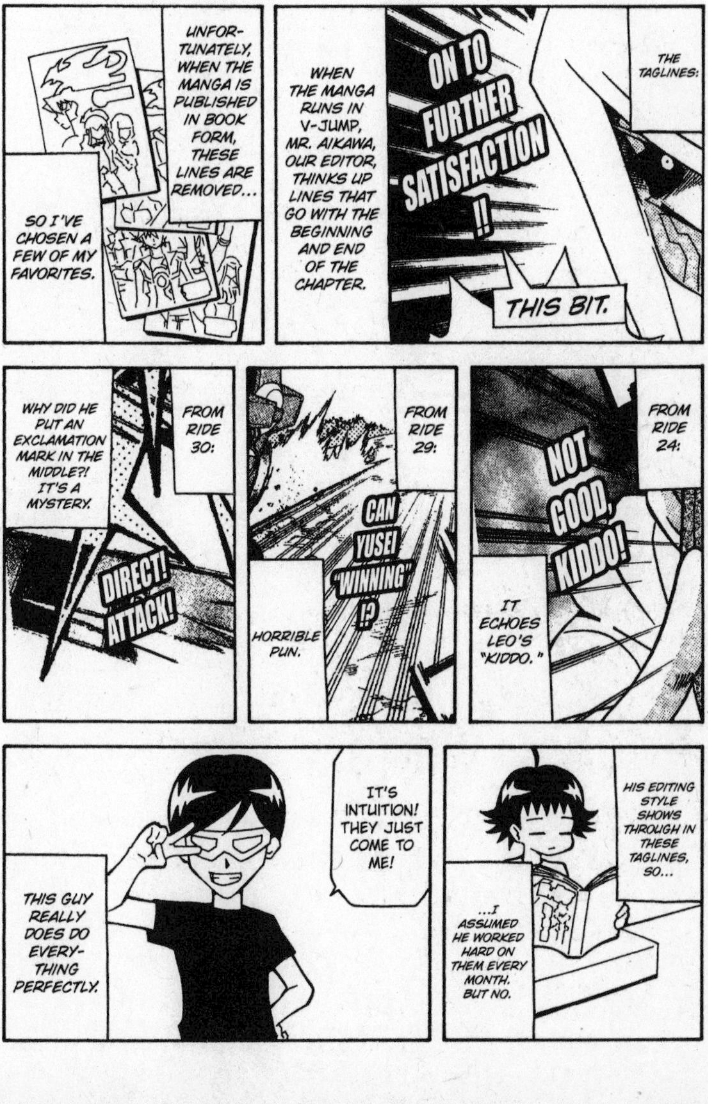

THE TAGLINES:
ON TO FURTHER SATISFACTION!!
WHEN THE MANGA RUNS IN V-JUMP, MR. AIKAWA, OUR EDITOR, THINKS UP LINES THAT GO WITH THE BEGINNING AND END OF THE CHAPTER.
THIS BIT.
UNFOR-TUNATELY, WHEN THE MANGA IS PUBLISHED IN BOOK FORM, THESE LINES ARE REMOVED...
SO I'VE CHOSEN A FEW OF MY FAVORITES.
FROM RIDE 24:
NOT GOOD, KIDDO!
IT ECHOES LEO'S "KIDDO."
FROM RIDE 29:
CAN YUSEI "WINNING"!?
HORRIBLE PUN.
FROM RIDE 30:
WHY DID HE PUT AN EXCLAMATION MARK IN THE MIDDLE?! IT'S A MYSTERY.
DIRECT! ATTACK!
HIS EDITING STYLE SHOWS THROUGH IN THESE TAGLINES, SO...
...I ASSUMED HE WORKED HARD ON THEM EVERY MONTH. BUT NO.
IT'S INTUITION! THEY JUST COME TO ME!
THIS GUY REALLY DOES DO EVERY-THING PERFECTLY.

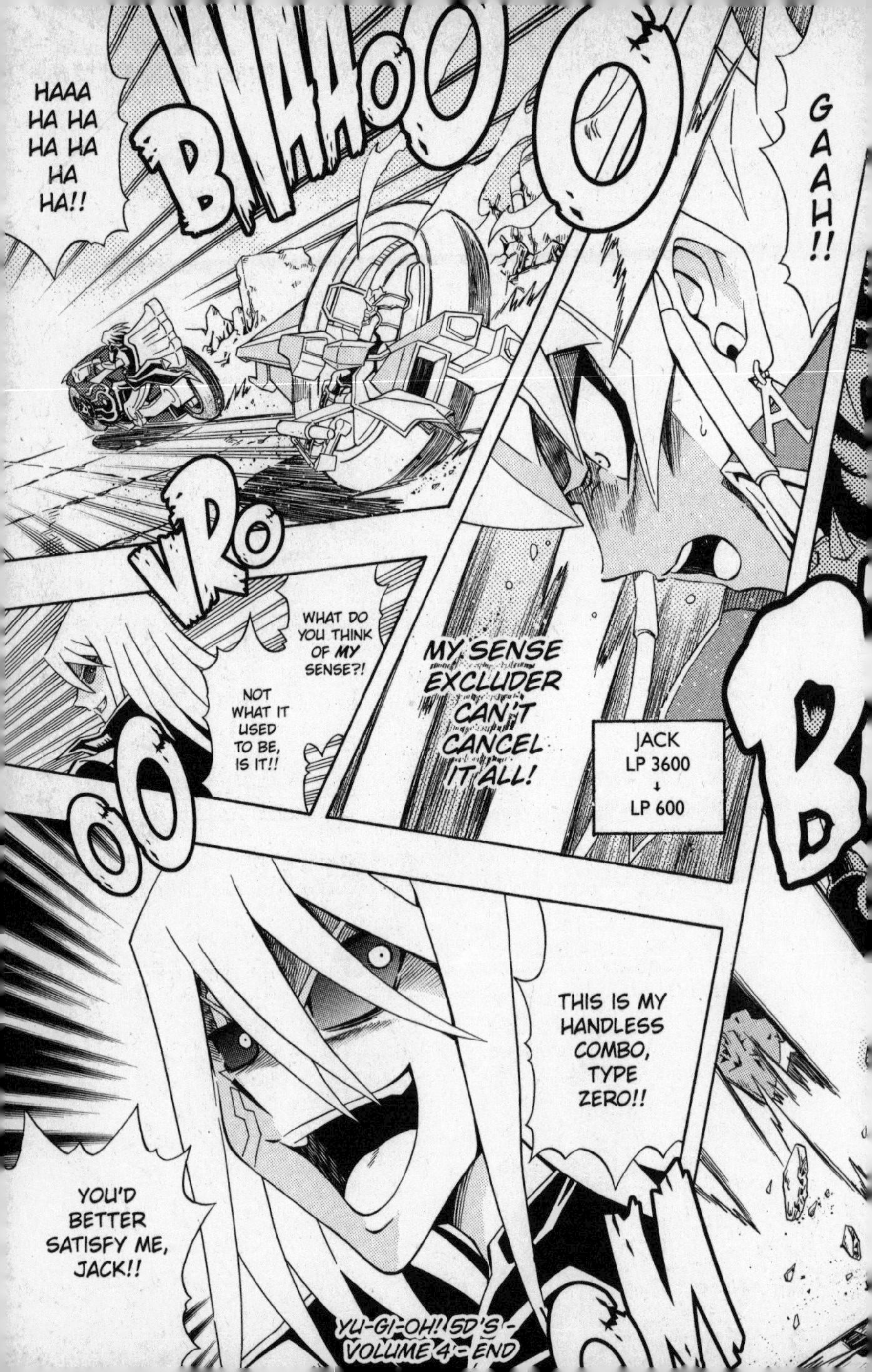
GAAAH!!
BWAHOOO
HAAAA HA HA HA HA HA HA!!
JACK LP 3600 → LP 600
MY SENSE EXCLUDER CAN'T CANCEL IT ALL!
VROOO
WHAT DO YOU THINK OF MY SENSE?!
NOT WHAT IT USED TO BE, IS IT!!
THIS IS MY HANDLESS COMBO, TYPE ZERO!!
YOU'D BETTER SATISFY ME, JACK!!
YU-GI-OH! 5D'S - VOLUME 4 - END

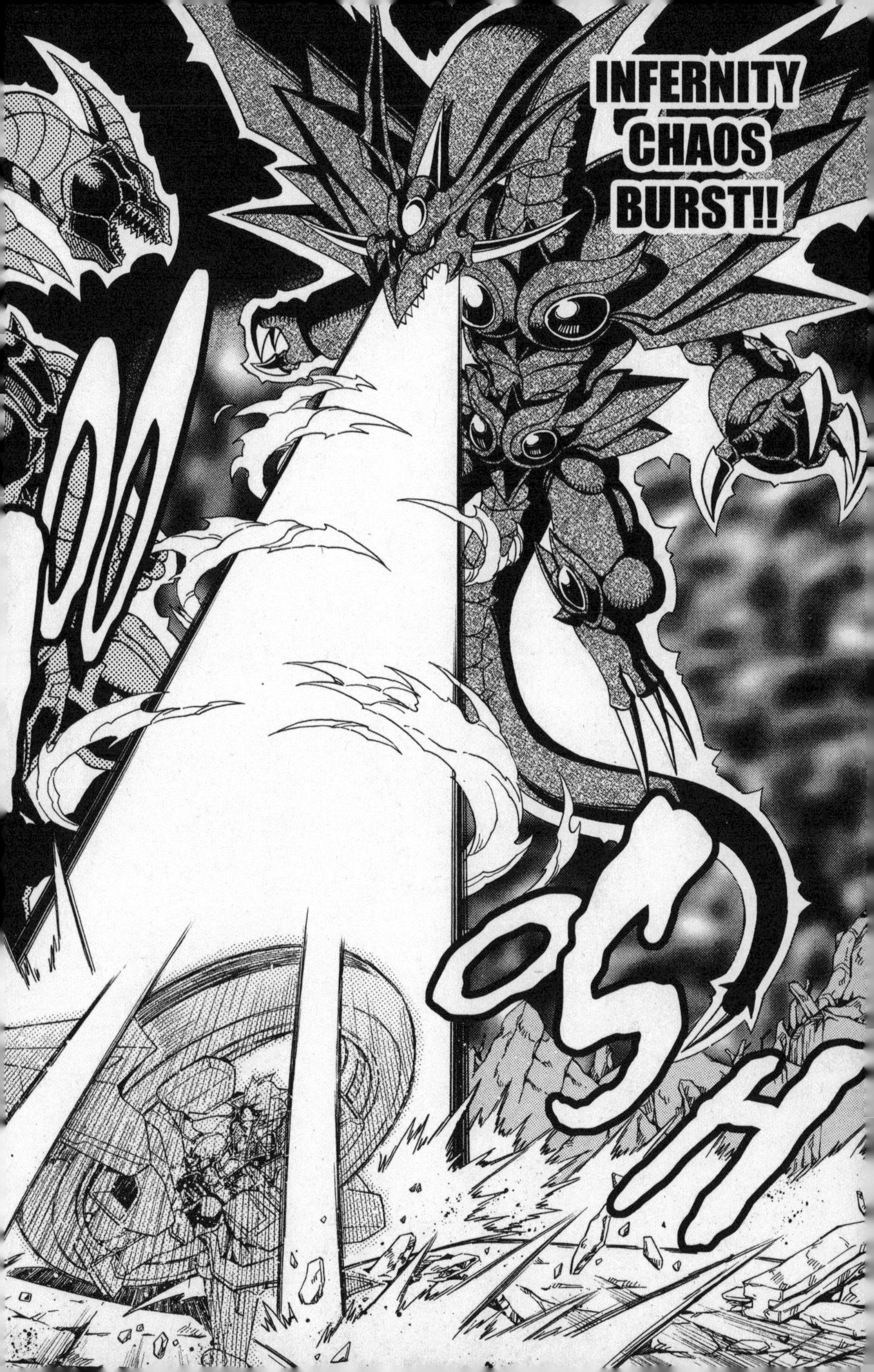
INFERNITY CHAOS BURST!!

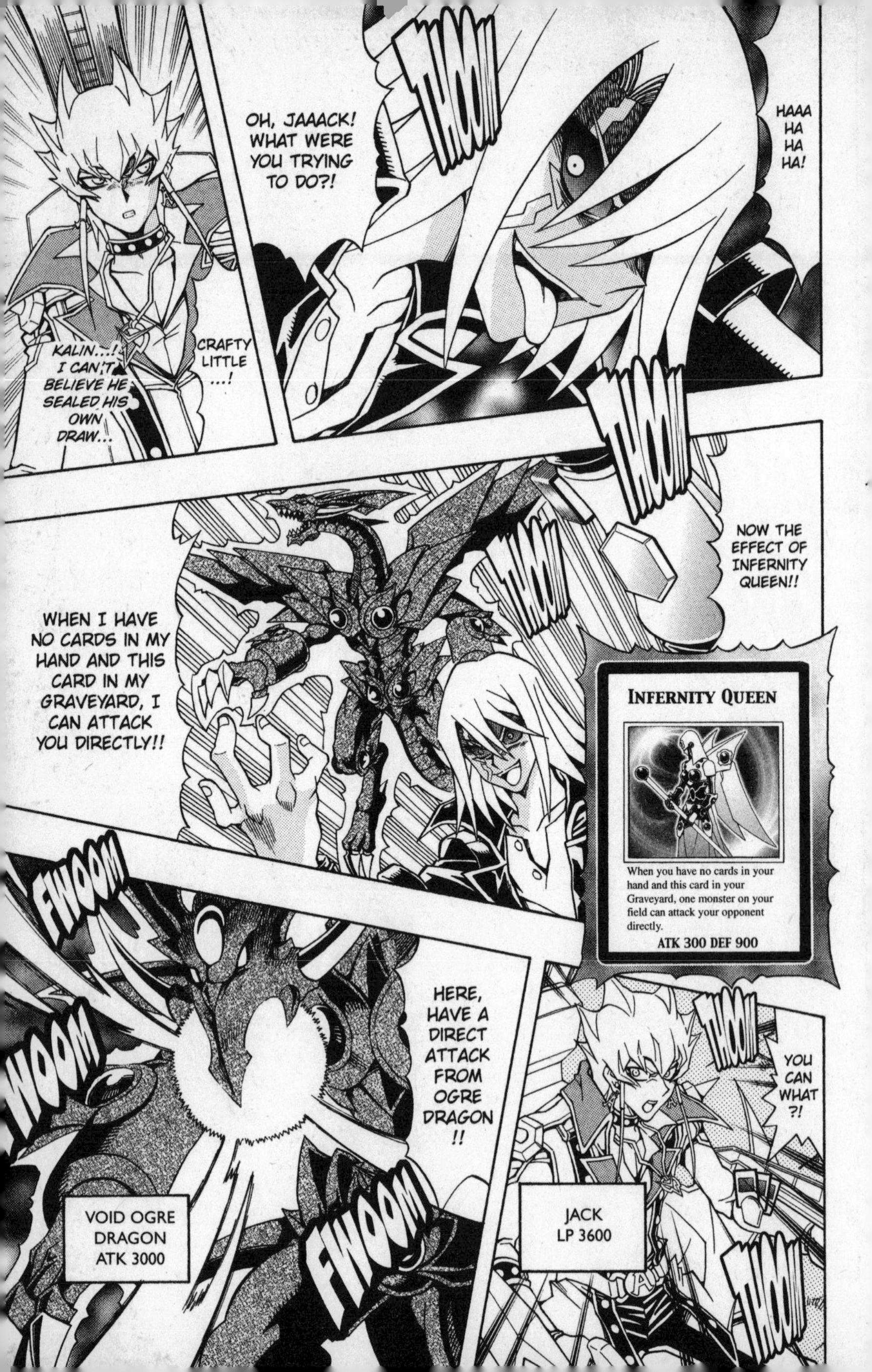
HAAA HA HA HA!
THOOM
OH, JAAACK! WHAT WERE YOU TRYING TO DO?!
THOOM
CRAFTY LITTLE ...!
KALIN...! I CAN'T BELIEVE HE SEALED HIS OWN DRAW...
NOW THE EFFECT OF INFERNITY QUEEN!!
THOOM
INFERNITY QUEEN
When you have no cards in your hand and this card in your Graveyard, one monster on your field can attack your opponent directly.
ATK 300 DEF 900
WHEN I HAVE NO CARDS IN MY HAND AND THIS CARD IN MY GRAVEYARD, I CAN ATTACK YOU DIRECTLY!!
THOOM
YOU CAN WHAT ?!
JACK LP 3600
THOOM
HERE, HAVE A DIRECT ATTACK FROM OGRE DRAGON !!
FWOOM
WOOM
VOID OGRE DRAGON ATK 3000
FWOOM

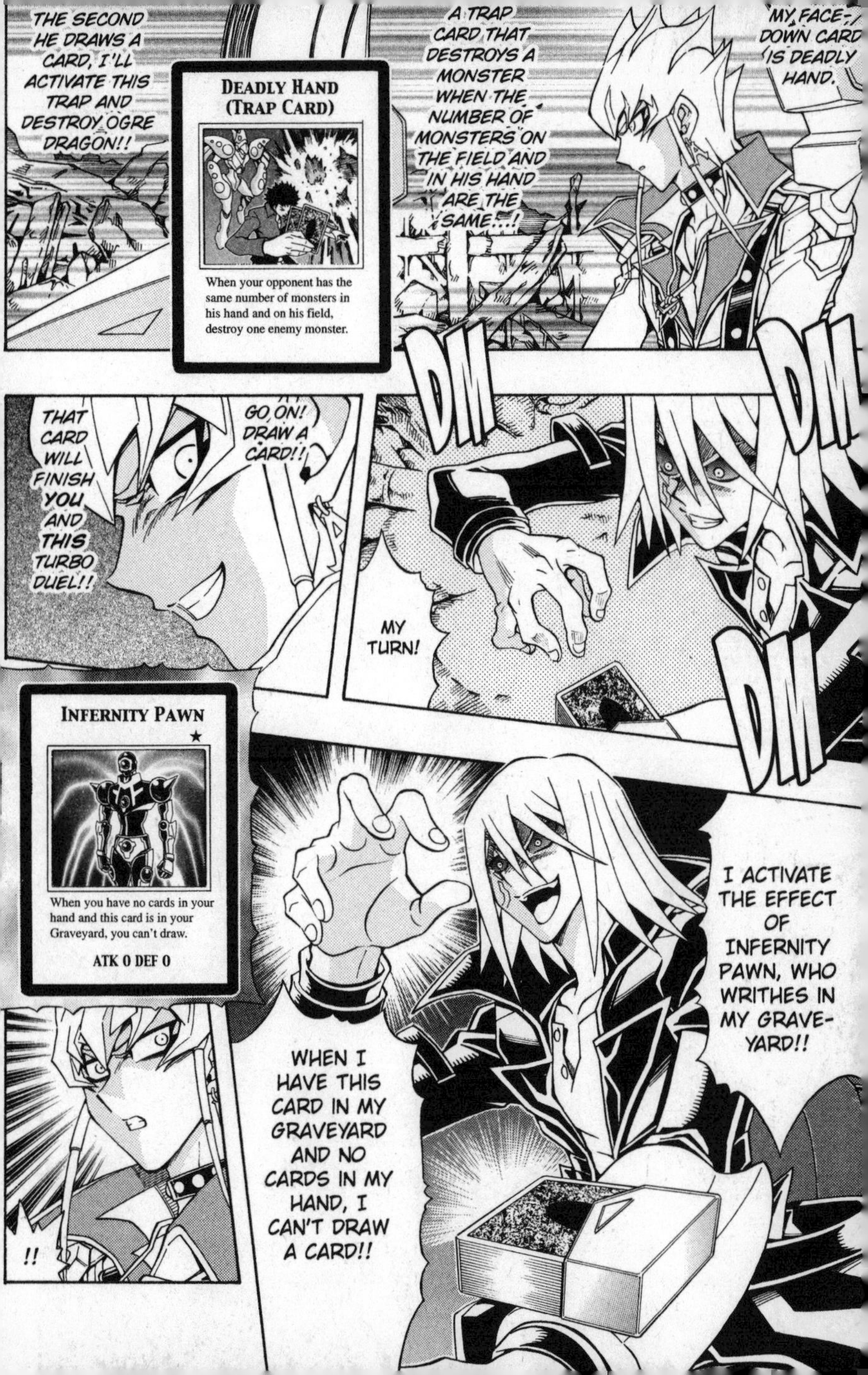
MY FACE-DOWN CARD IS DEADLY HAND.
A TRAP CARD THAT DESTROYS A MONSTER WHEN THE NUMBER OF MONSTERS ON THE FIELD AND IN HIS HAND ARE THE SAME...!
THE SECOND HE DRAWS A CARD, I'LL ACTIVATE THIS TRAP AND DESTROY OGRE DRAGON!!
DEADLY HAND (TRAP CARD)
When your opponent has the same number of monsters in his hand and on his field, destroy one enemy monster.
DM
DM
MY TURN!
GO ON! DRAW A CARD!!
THAT CARD WILL FINISH YOU AND THIS TURBO DUEL!!
DM
I ACTIVATE THE EFFECT OF INFERNITY PAWN, WHO WRITHES IN MY GRAVEYARD!!
WHEN I HAVE THIS CARD IN MY GRAVEYARD AND NO CARDS IN MY HAND, I CAN'T DRAW A CARD!!
INFERNITY PAWN
★
When you have no cards in your hand and this card is in your Graveyard, you can't draw.
ATK 0 DEF 0
!!

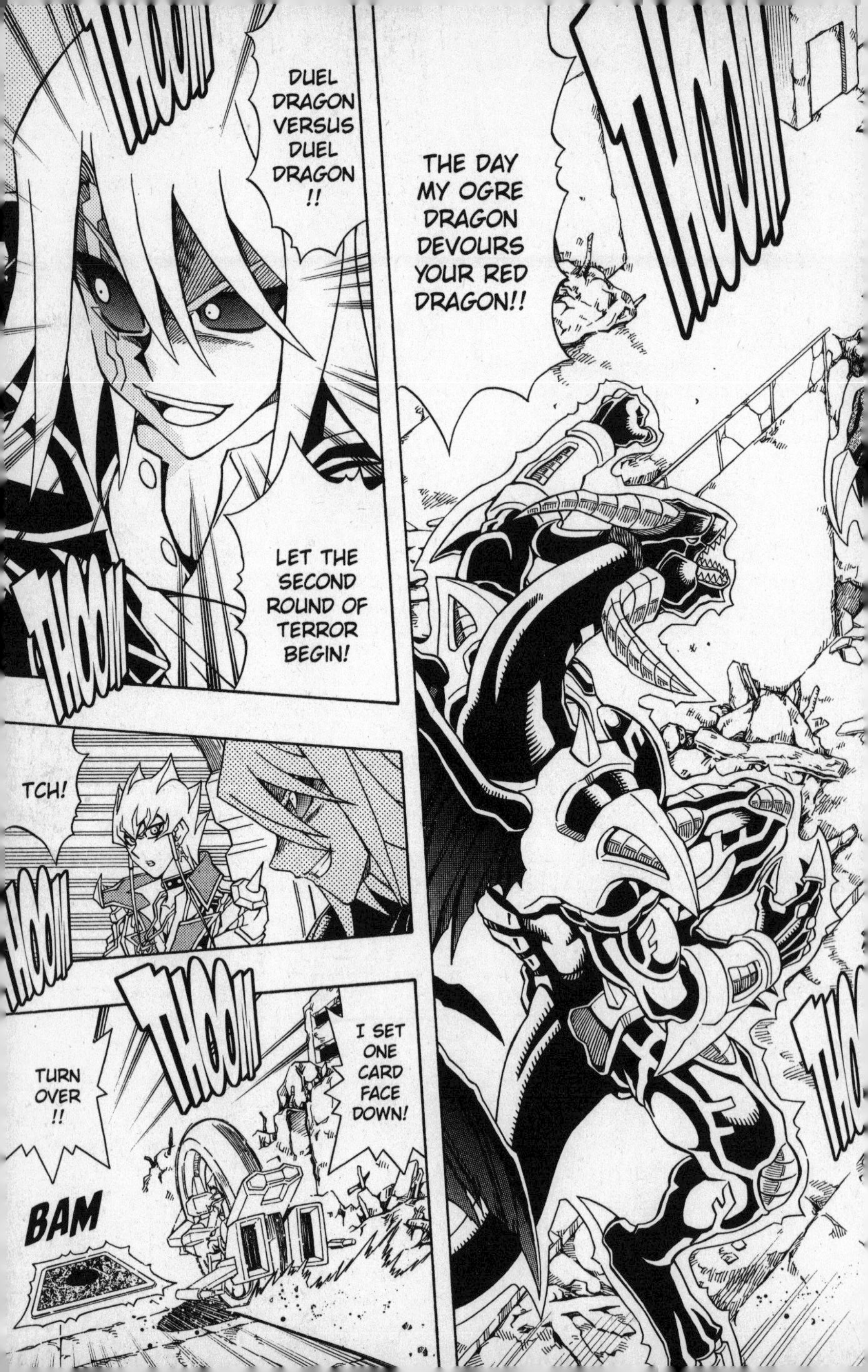
THOOM
THE DAY MY OGRE DRAGON DEVOURS YOUR RED DRAGON!!
THOOM
THOOM
DUEL DRAGON VERSUS DUEL DRAGON!!
LET THE SECOND ROUND OF TERROR BEGIN!
THOOM
TCH!
THOOM
I SET ONE CARD FACE DOWN!
THOOM
TURN OVER!!
BAM

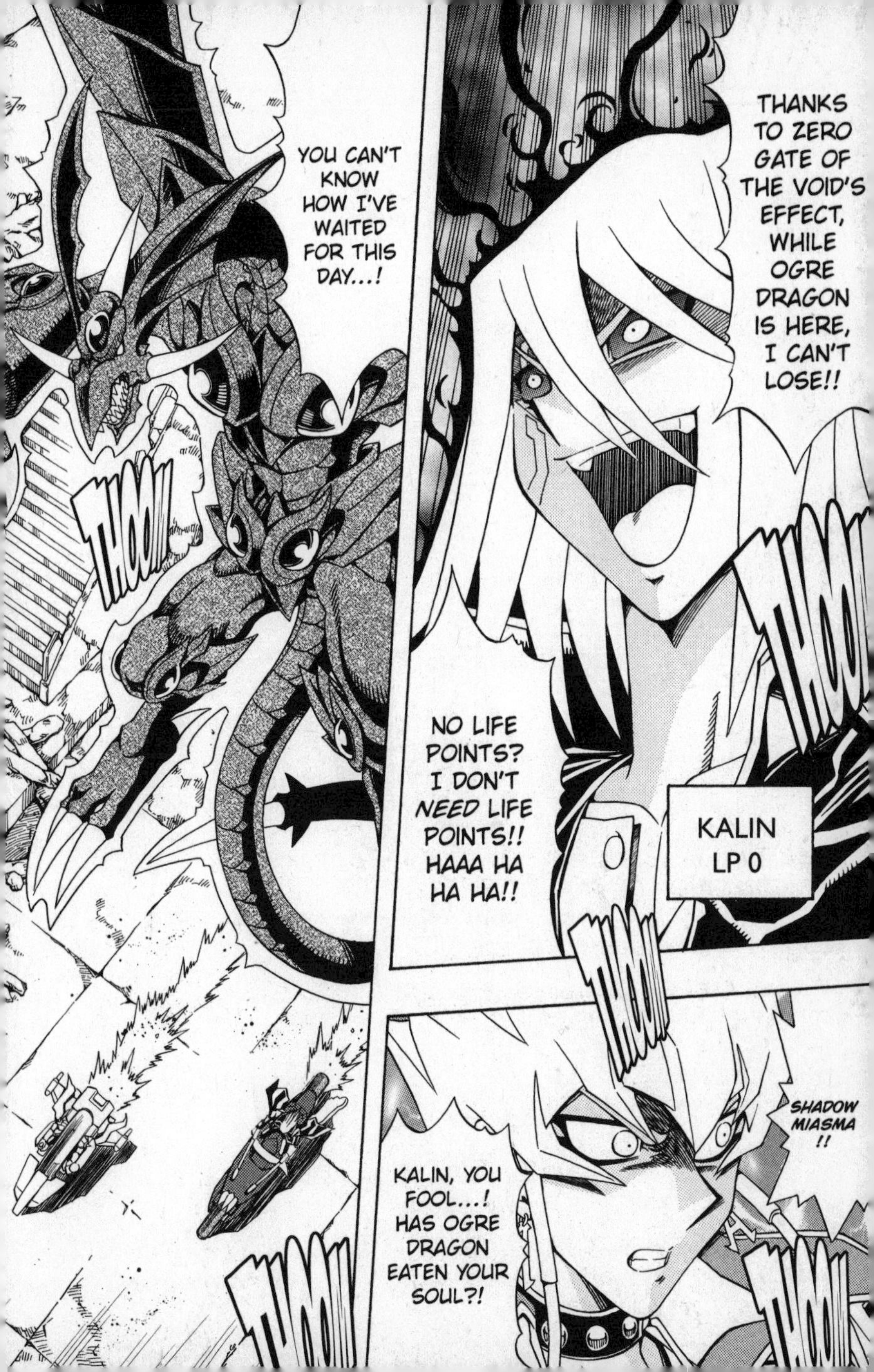
THANKS TO ZERO GATE OF THE VOID'S EFFECT, WHILE OGRE DRAGON IS HERE, I CAN'T LOSE!!
THOOM
NO LIFE POINTS? I DON'T *NEED* LIFE POINTS!! HAAA HA HA HA!!
KALIN LP 0
THOOM
SHADOW MIASMA!!
KALIN, YOU FOOL...! HAS OGRE DRAGON EATEN YOUR SOUL?!
THOOM
YOU CAN'T KNOW HOW I'VE WAITED FOR THIS DAY...!
THOOM

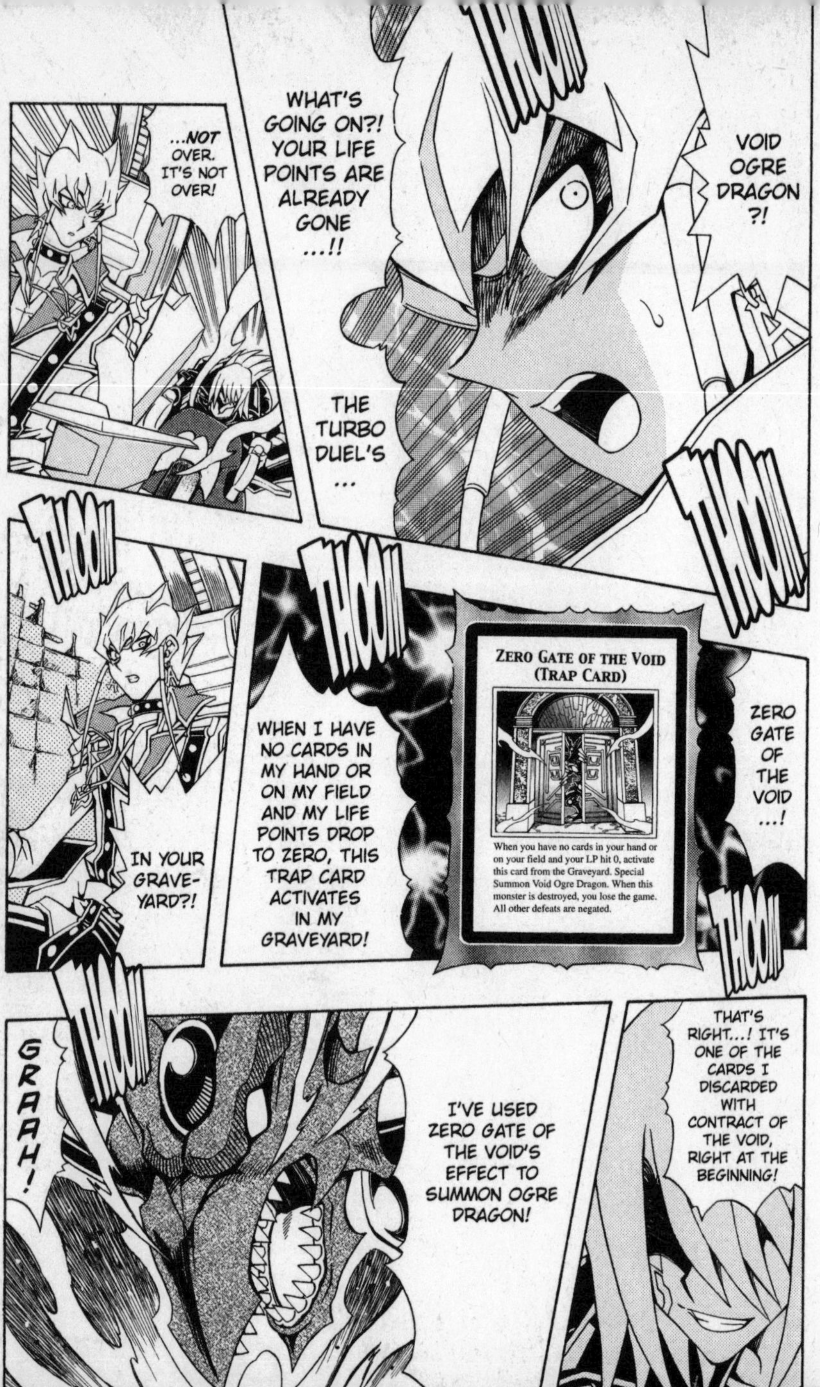
THOOM
VOID OGRE DRAGON ?!
WHAT'S GOING ON?! YOUR LIFE POINTS ARE ALREADY GONE ...!!
THE TURBO DUEL'S ...
THOOM
...NOT OVER. IT'S NOT OVER!
ZERO GATE OF THE VOID ...!
ZERO GATE OF THE VOID (TRAP CARD)
When you have no cards in your hand or on your field and your LP hit 0, activate this card from the Graveyard. Special Summon Void Ogre Dragon. When this monster is destroyed, you lose the game. All other defeats are negated.
THOOM
THOOM
WHEN I HAVE NO CARDS IN MY HAND OR ON MY FIELD AND MY LIFE POINTS DROP TO ZERO, THIS TRAP CARD ACTIVATES IN MY GRAVEYARD!
THOOM
IN YOUR GRAVE-YARD?!
THAT'S RIGHT...! IT'S ONE OF THE CARDS I DISCARDED WITH CONTRACT OF THE VOID, RIGHT AT THE BEGINNING!
I'VE USED ZERO GATE OF THE VOID'S EFFECT TO SUMMON OGRE DRAGON!
THOOM
GRAAH!

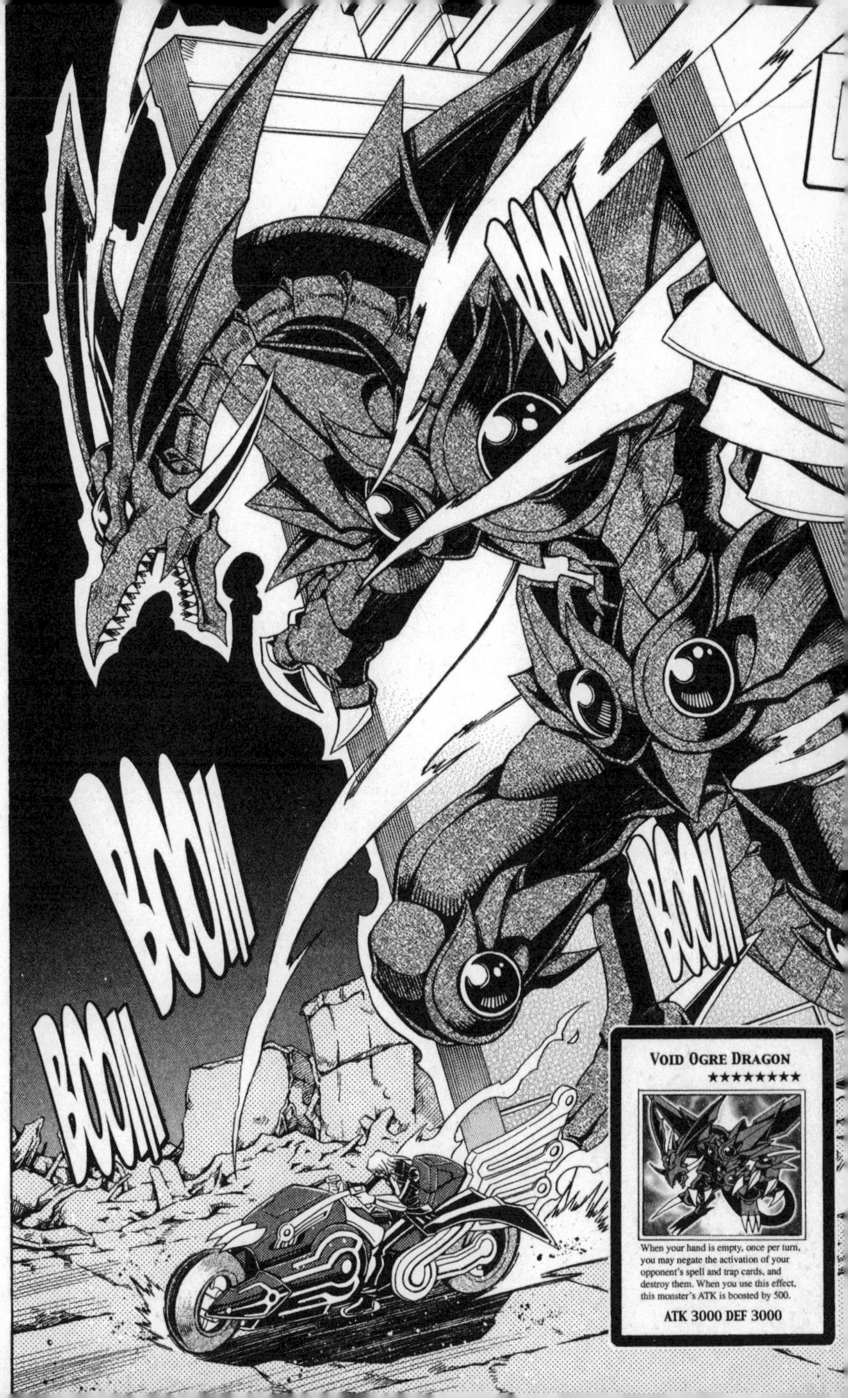
BOOM
BOOM
BOOM
BOOM
VOID OGRE DRAGON
★★★★★★★★
When your hand is empty, once per turn, you may negate the activation of your opponent's spell and trap cards, and destroy them. When you use this effect, this monster's ATK is boosted by 500.
ATK 3000 DEF 3000

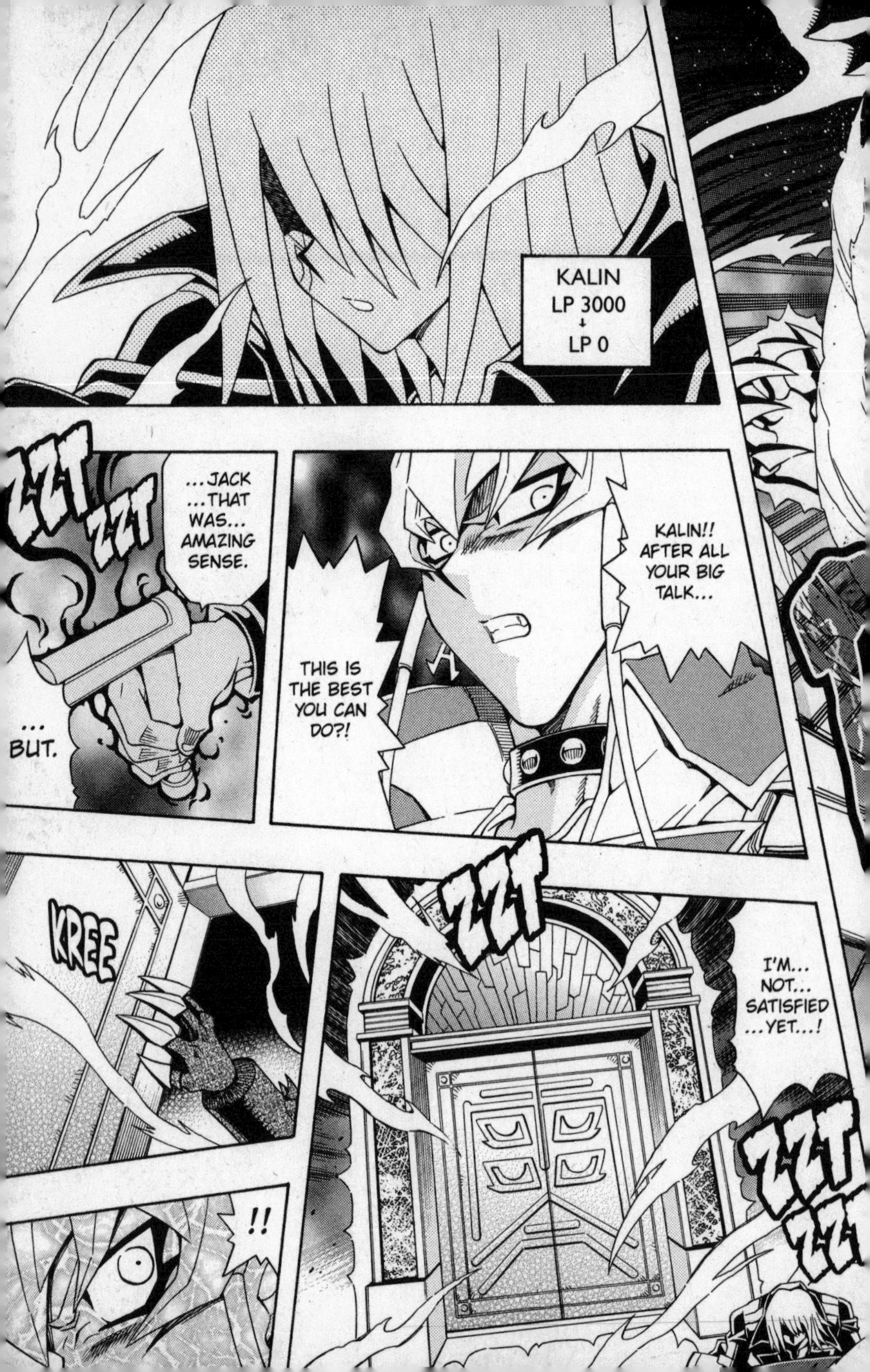
KALIN
LP 3000
↓
LP 0
KALIN!! AFTER ALL YOUR BIG TALK...
THIS IS THE BEST YOU CAN DO?!
Z-Z-T
Z-Z-T
...JACK ...THAT WAS... AMAZING SENSE.
... BUT.
Z-Z-T
I'M... NOT... SATISFIED ...YET...!
Z-Z-T
Z-Z-
KREE
!!

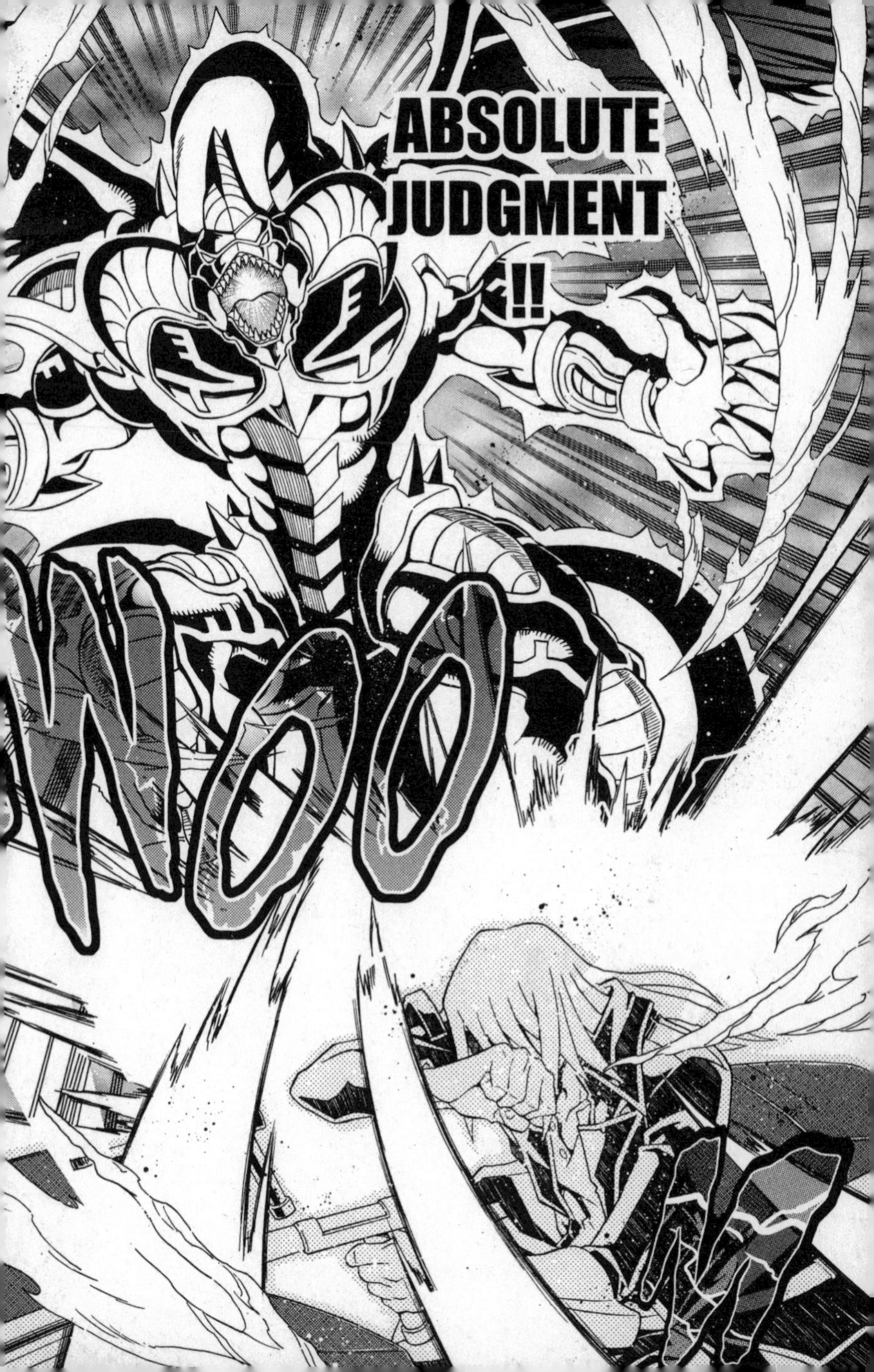
ABSOLUTE JUDGMENT!!
WHOOO

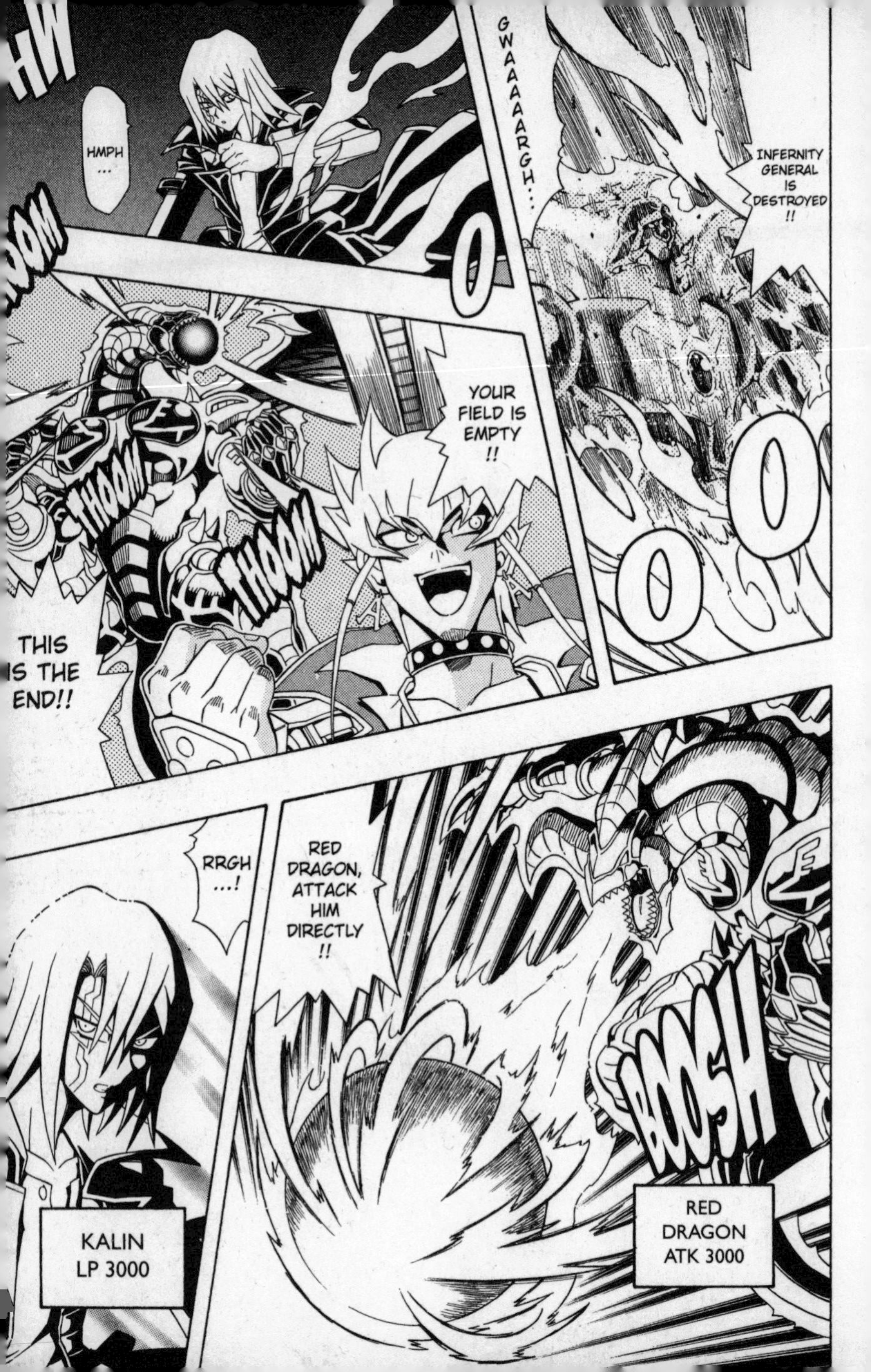
GWAAAAARGH...
INFERNITY GENERAL IS DESTROYED!!
HMPH...
YOUR FIELD IS EMPTY!!
THOOM
THOOM
THIS IS THE END!!
RED DRAGON, ATTACK HIM DIRECTLY!!
BOOSH
RED DRAGON ATK 3000
RRGH...!
KALIN LP 3000

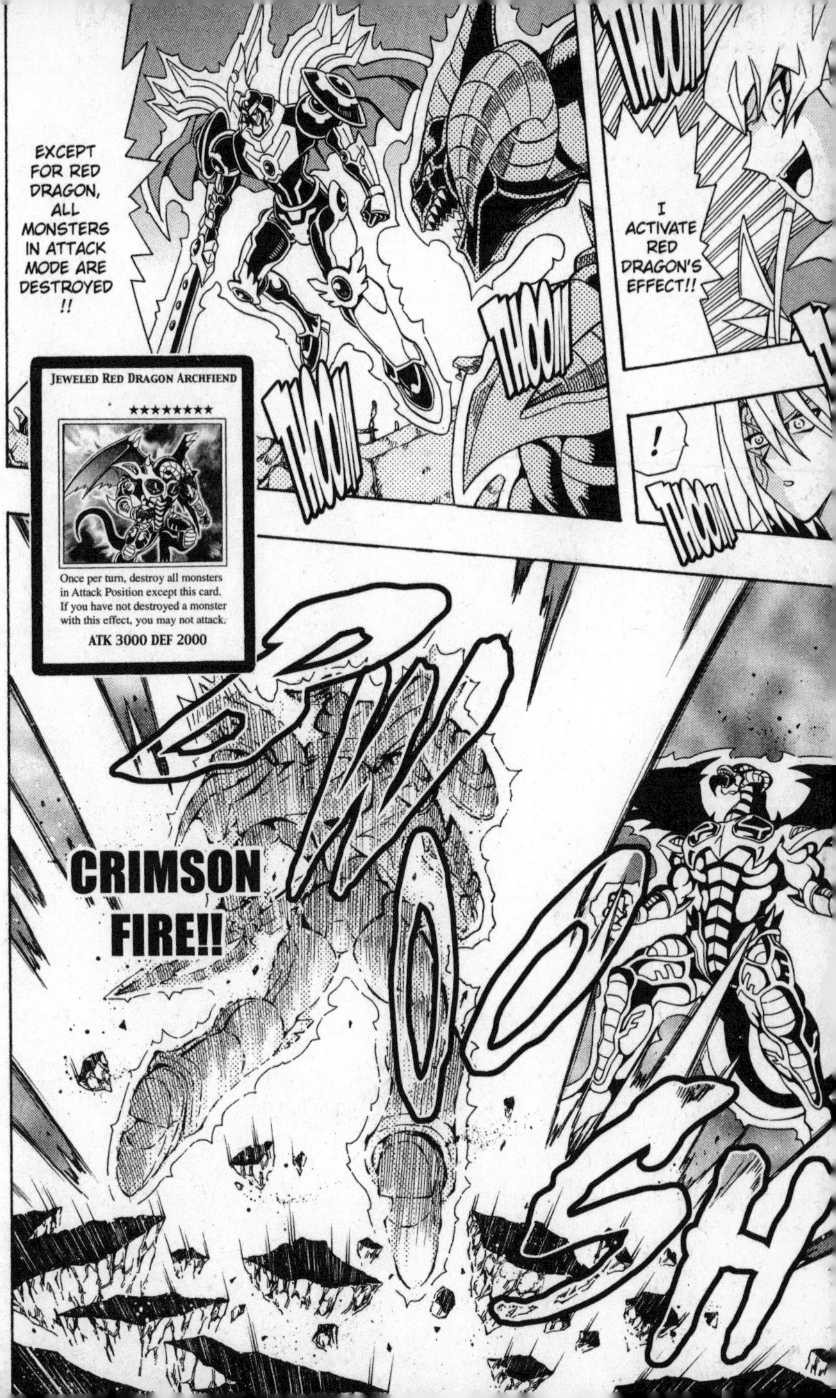
THOOM
I ACTIVATE RED DRAGON'S EFFECT!!
!
THOOM
EXCEPT FOR RED DRAGON, ALL MONSTERS IN ATTACK MODE ARE DESTROYED !!
THOOM
THOOM
JEWELED RED DRAGON ARCHFIEND
Once per turn, destroy all monsters in Attack Position except this card. If you have not destroyed a monster with this effect, you may not attack.
ATK 3000 DEF 2000
CRIMSON FIRE!!

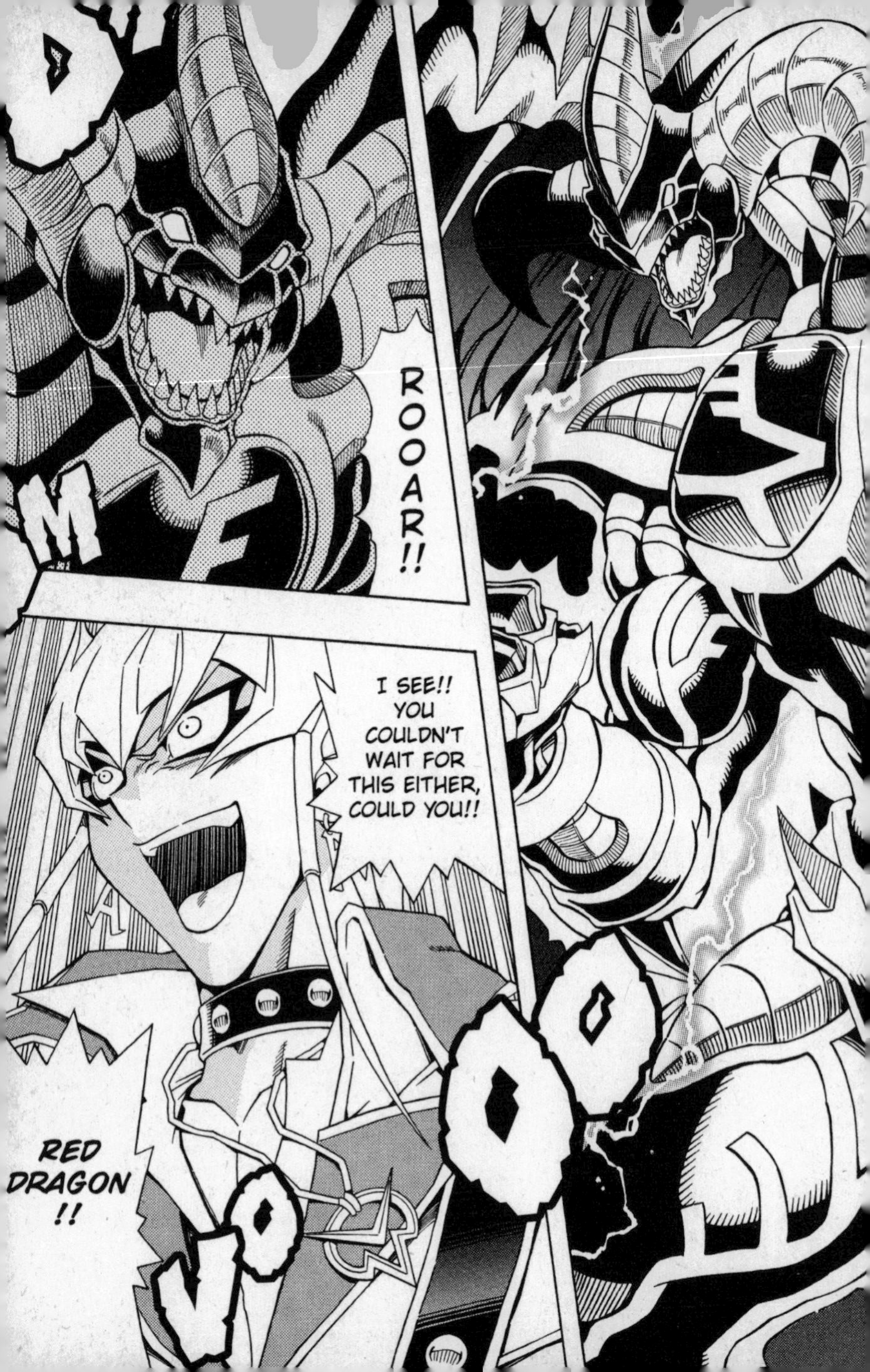
ROOOAR!!
I SEE!! YOU COULDN'T WAIT FOR THIS EITHER, COULD YOU!!
RED DRAGON!!

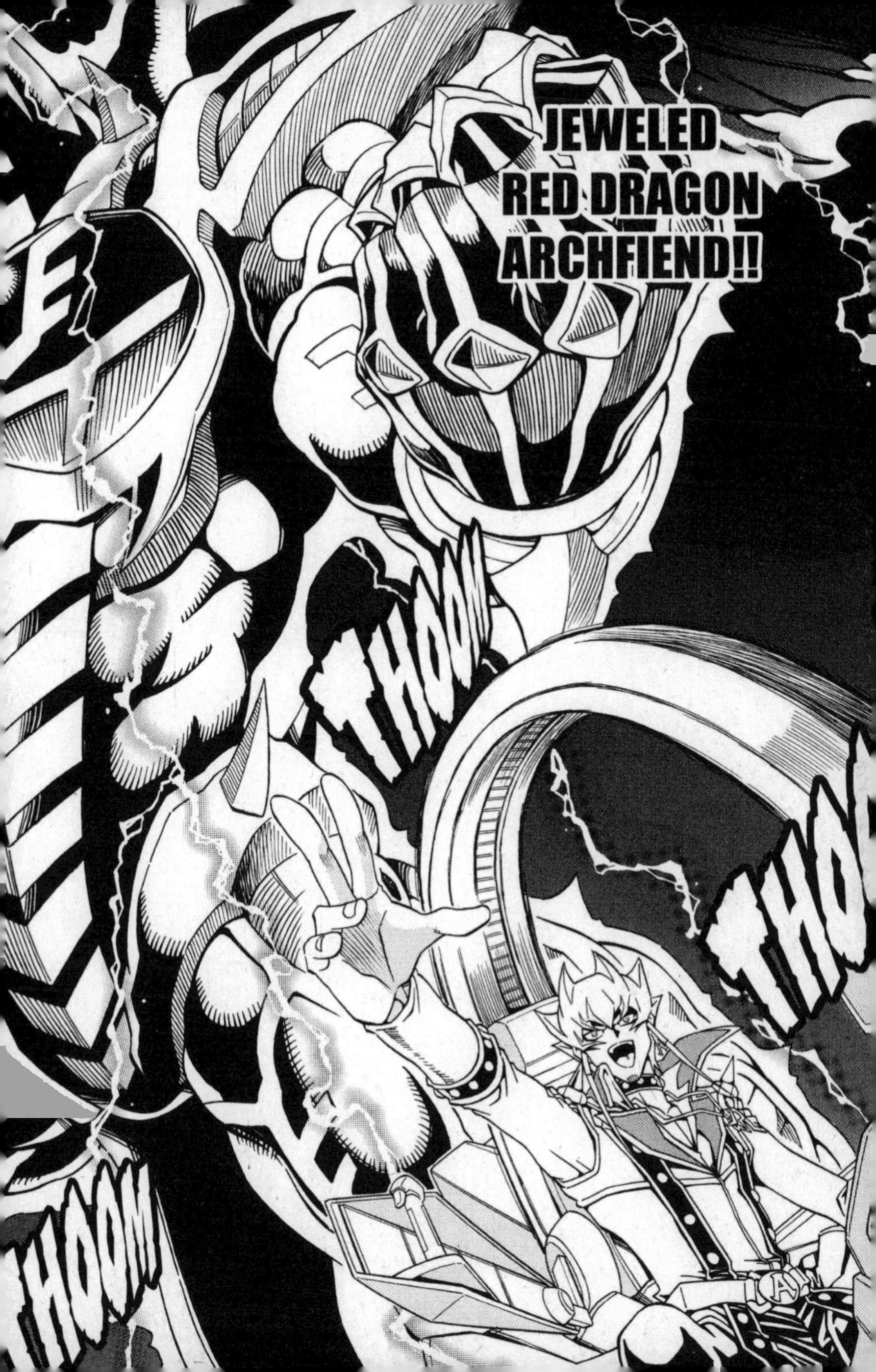
JEWELED RED DRAGON ARCHFIEND!!
THOOM
THO
HOOM

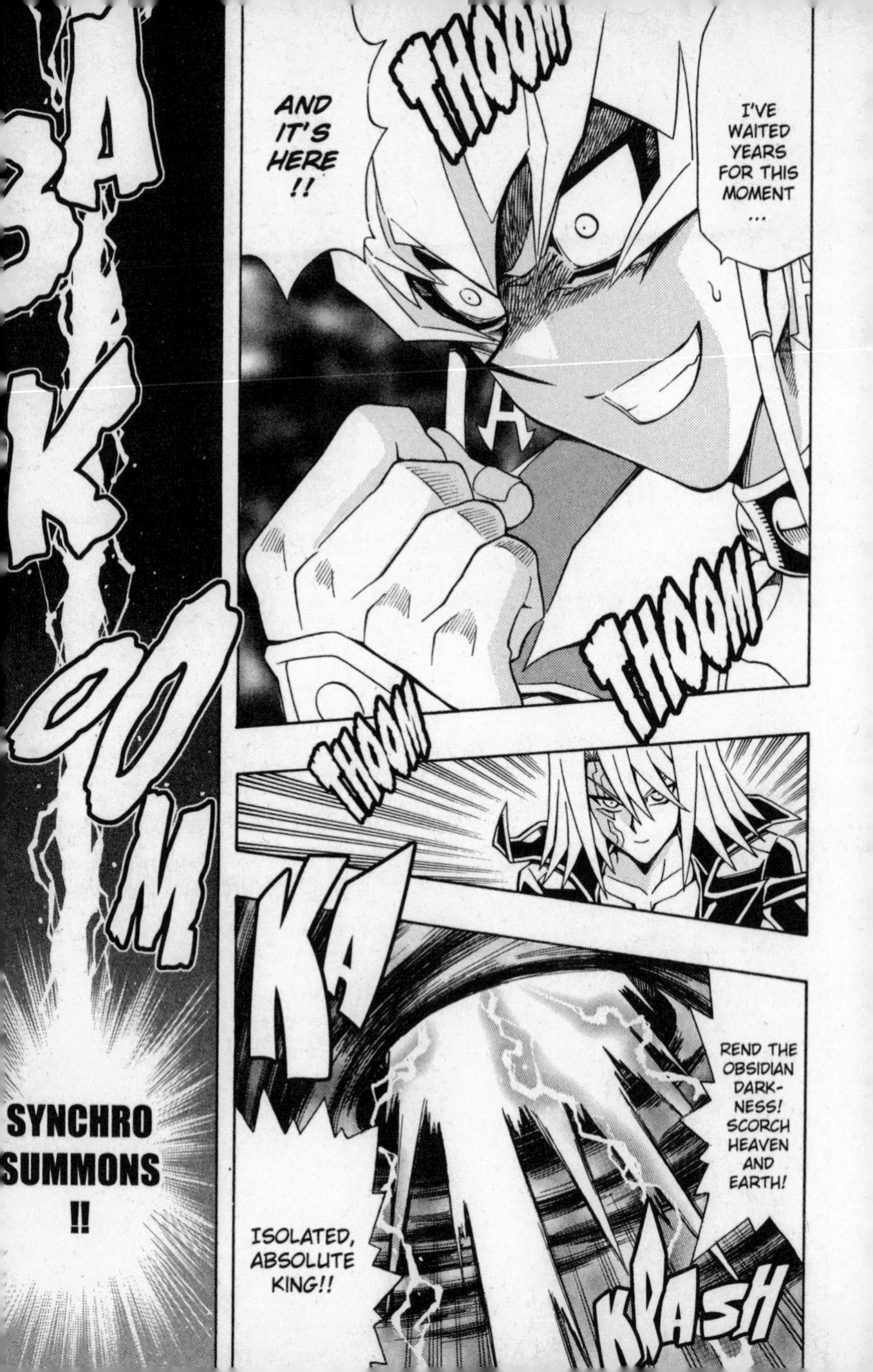
I'VE WAITED YEARS FOR THIS MOMENT ...
AND IT'S HERE!!
THOOM
THOOM
THOOM
KA
REND THE OBSIDIAN DARKNESS! SCORCH HEAVEN AND EARTH!
ISOLATED, ABSOLUTE KING!!
KRASH
BAKOOM
SYNCHRO SUMMONS!!

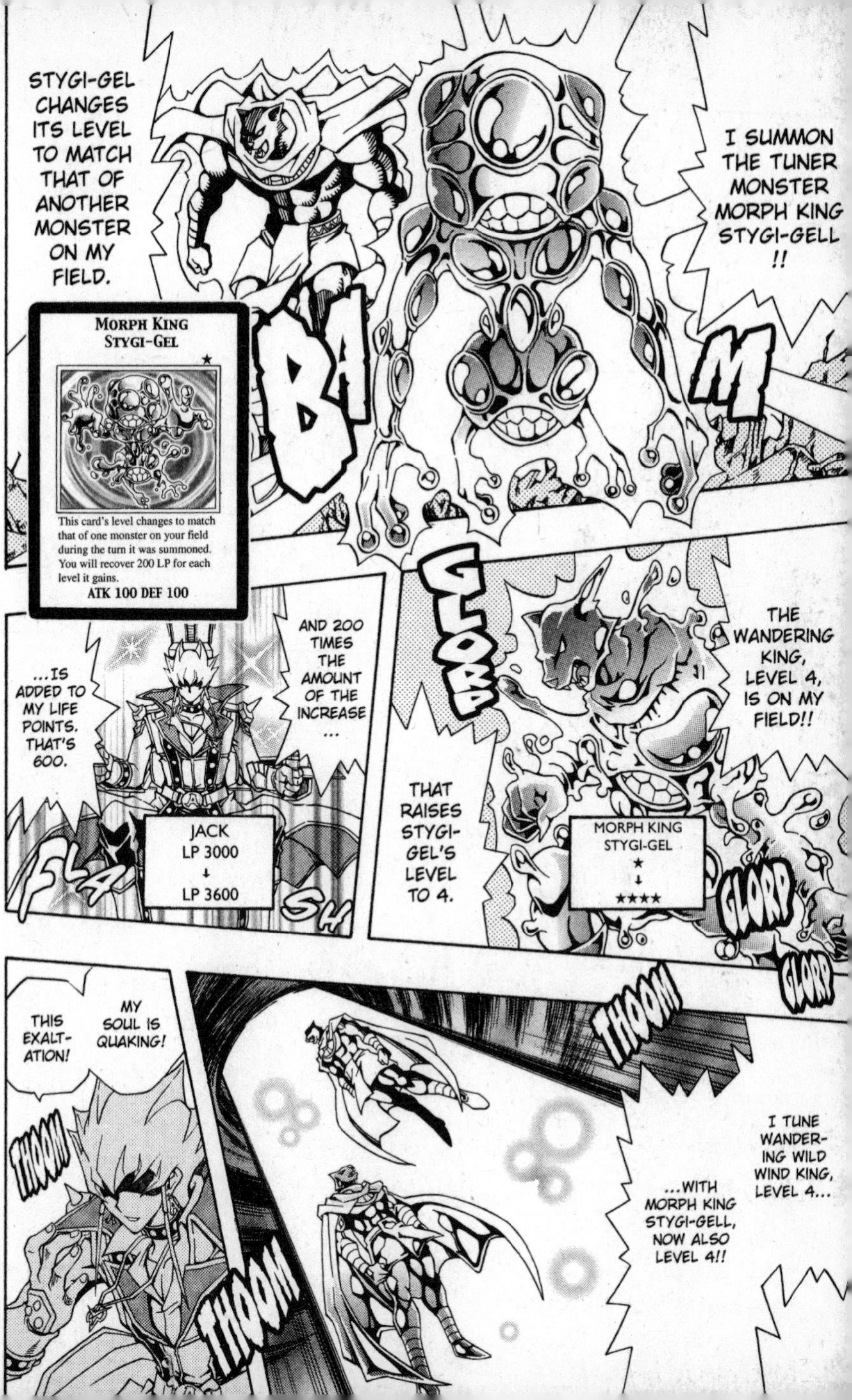
I SUMMON THE TUNER MONSTER MORPH KING STYGI-GELL !!
BAM
STYGI-GEL CHANGES ITS LEVEL TO MATCH THAT OF ANOTHER MONSTER ON MY FIELD.
MORPH KING STYGI-GEL
★
This card's level changes to match that of one monster on your field during the turn it was summoned. You will recover 200 LP for each level it gains.
ATK 100 DEF 100
THE WANDERING KING, LEVEL 4, IS ON MY FIELD!!
GLORP
THAT RAISES STYGI-GEL'S LEVEL TO 4.
MORPH KING STYGI-GEL ★ ↓ ★★★★
GLORP
GLORP
AND 200 TIMES THE AMOUNT OF THE INCREASE...
...IS ADDED TO MY LIFE POINTS. THAT'S 600.
JACK LP 3000 ↓ LP 3600
FLASH
THOOM
I TUNE WANDERING WILD WIND KING, LEVEL 4...
...WITH MORPH KING STYGI-GELL, NOW ALSO LEVEL 4!!
MY SOUL IS QUAKING!
THIS EXALTATION!
THOOM
THOOM

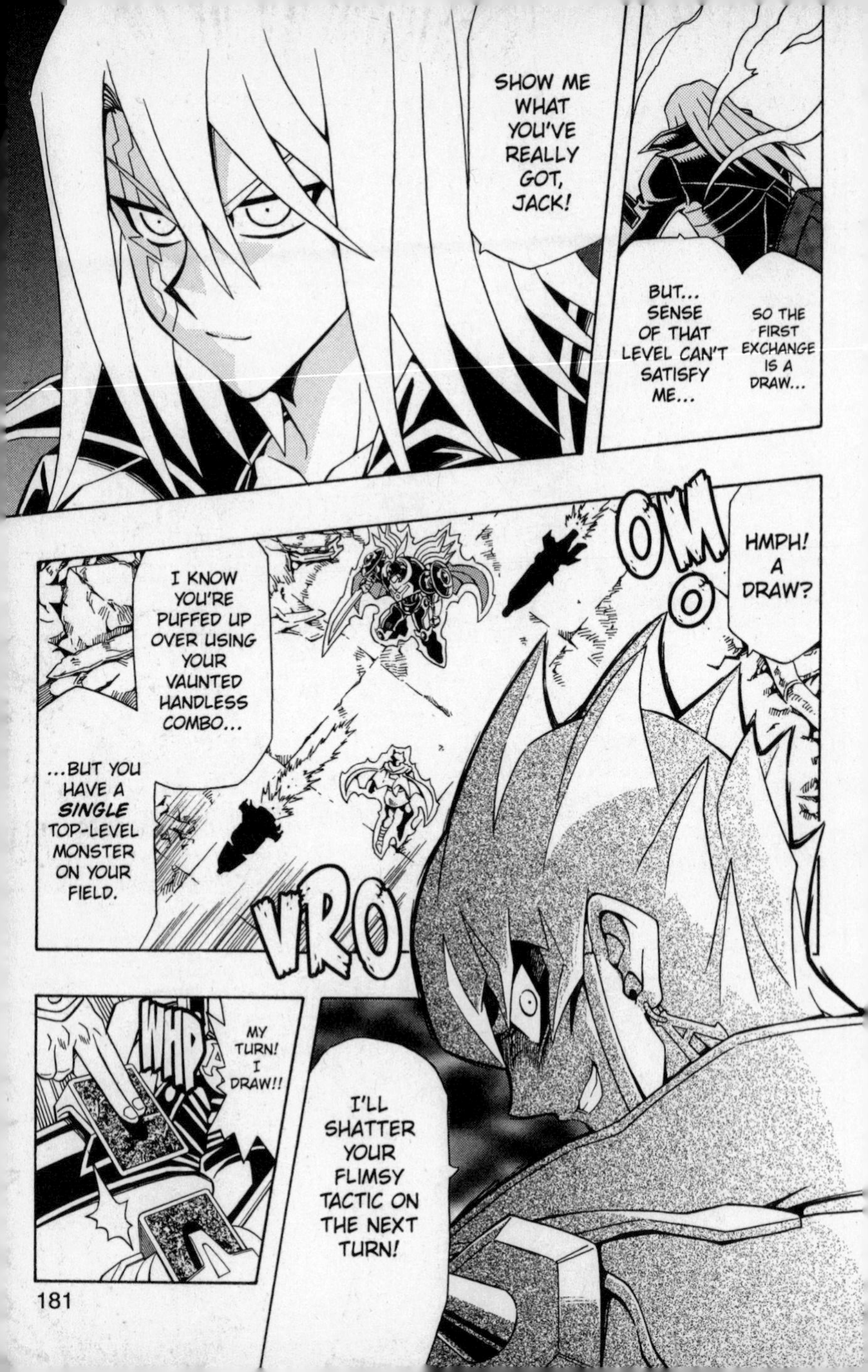
SO THE FIRST EXCHANGE IS A DRAW...
BUT... SENSE OF THAT LEVEL CAN'T SATISFY ME...
SHOW ME WHAT YOU'VE REALLY GOT, JACK!
HMPH! A DRAW?
OM
O
I KNOW YOU'RE PUFFED UP OVER USING YOUR VAUNTED HANDLESS COMBO...
...BUT YOU HAVE A ***SINGLE*** TOP-LEVEL MONSTER ON YOUR FIELD.
VRO
I'LL SHATTER YOUR FLIMSY TACTIC ON THE NEXT TURN!
WHD
MY TURN! I DRAW!!

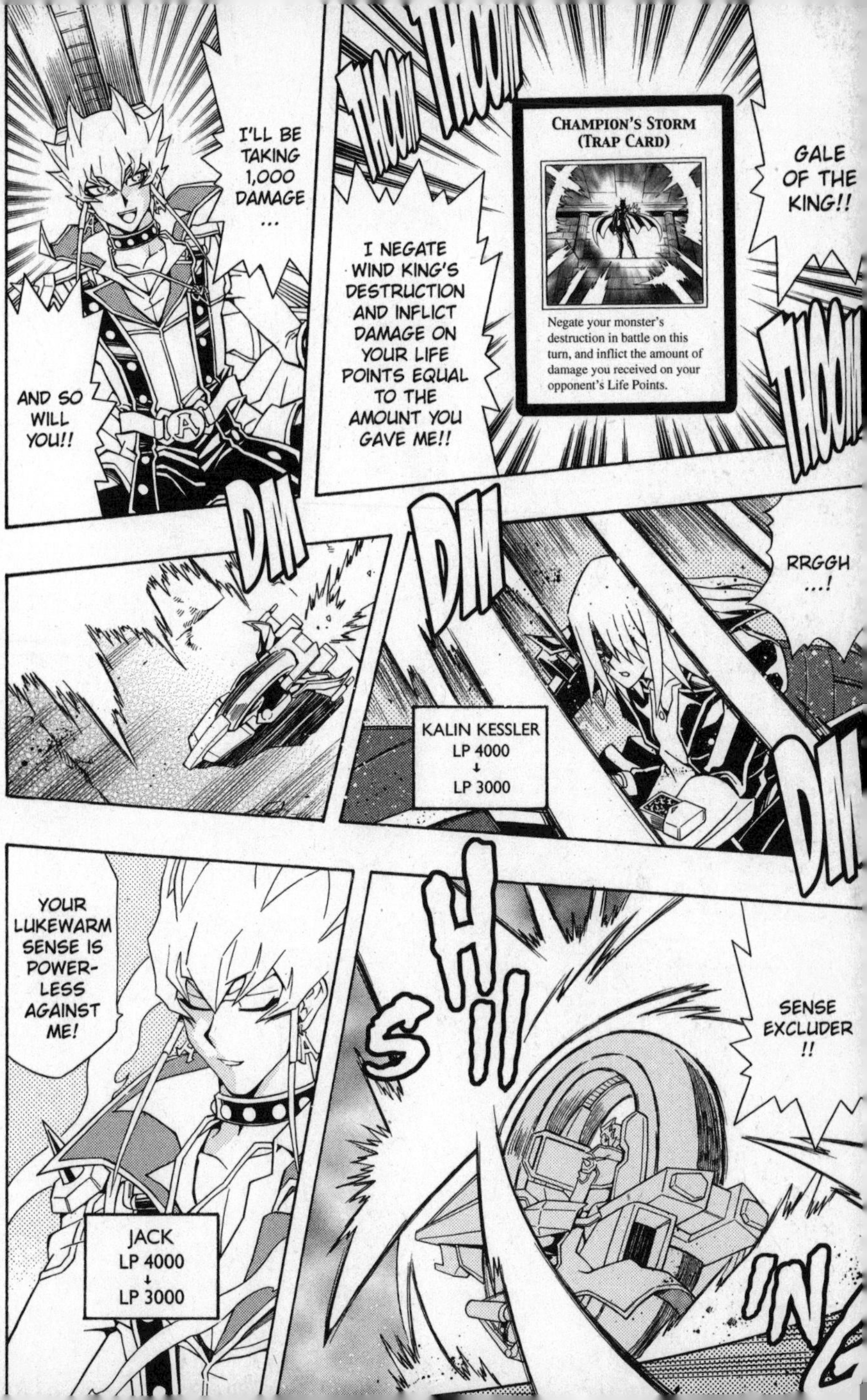
GALE OF THE KING!!
THOOM
CHAMPION'S STORM (TRAP CARD)
Negate your monster's destruction in battle on this turn, and inflict the amount of damage you received on your opponent's Life Points.
THOOM THOOM
I NEGATE WIND KING'S DESTRUCTION AND INFLICT DAMAGE ON YOUR LIFE POINTS EQUAL TO THE AMOUNT YOU GAVE ME!!
I'LL BE TAKING 1,000 DAMAGE ...
AND SO WILL YOU!!
RRGGH ...!
DM
KALIN KESSLER LP 4000 ↓ LP 3000
DM
SENSE EXCLUDER !!
SHH
YOUR LUKEWARM SENSE IS POWERLESS AGAINST ME!
JACK LP 4000 ↓ LP 3000

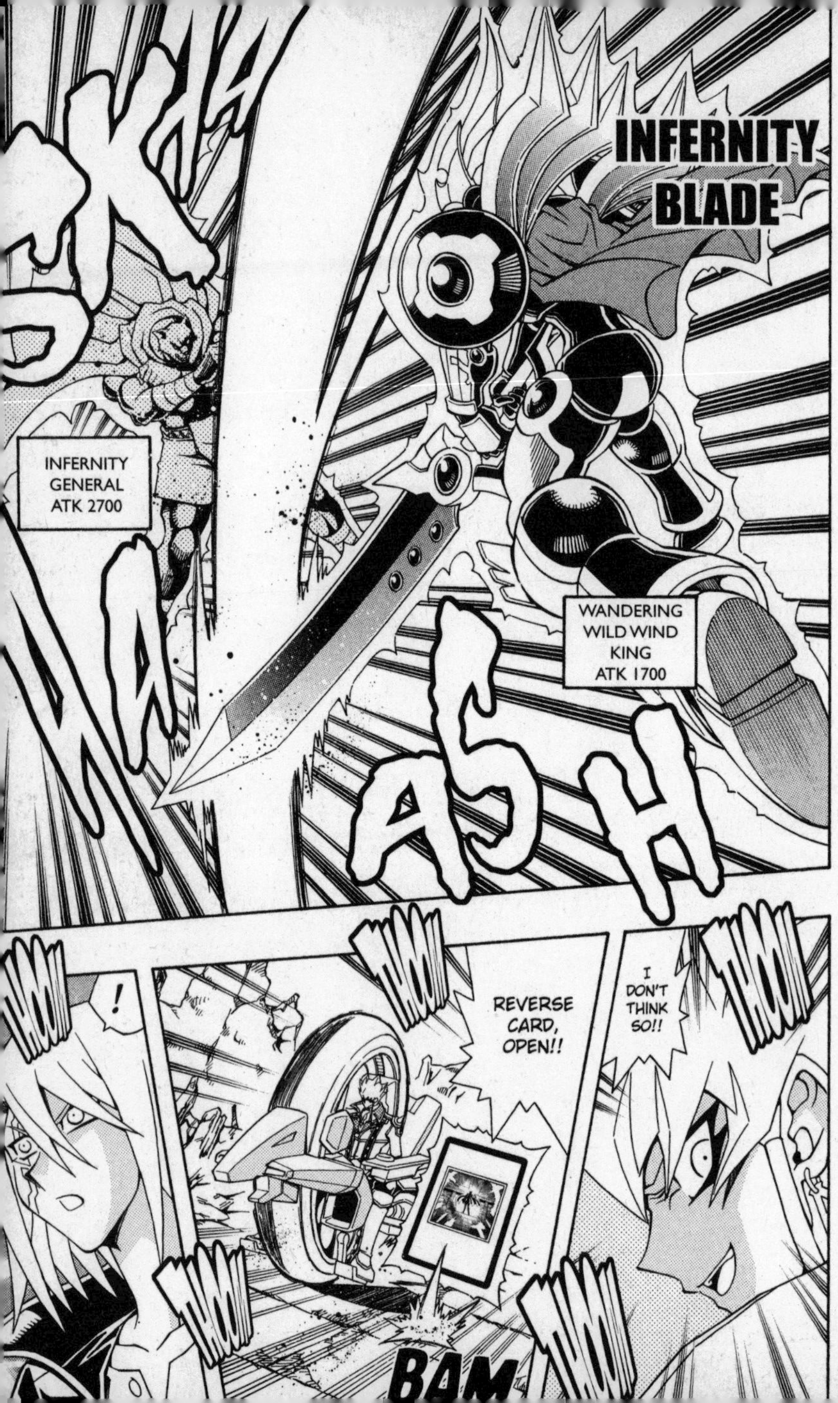
INFERNITY BLADE
WANDERING WILD WIND KING ATK 1700
INFERNITY GENERAL ATK 2700
I DON'T THINK SO!!
REVERSE CARD, OPEN!!
BAM
!

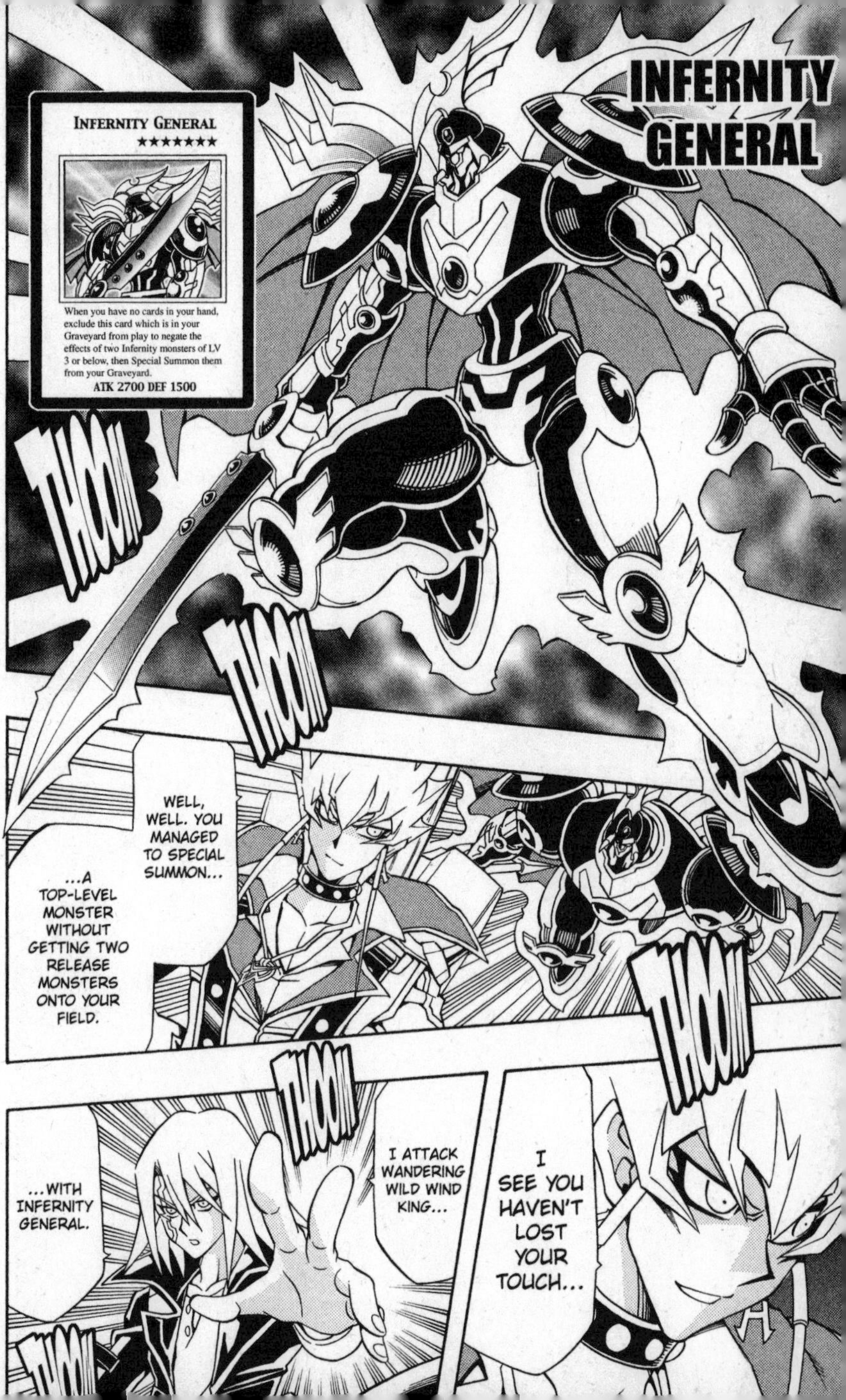

INFERNITY GENERAL
INFERNITY GENERAL
★★★★★★★
When you have no cards in your hand, exclude this card which is in your Graveyard from play to negate the effects of two Infernity monsters of LV 3 or below, then Special Summon them from your Graveyard.
ATK 2700 DEF 1500
THOOM
THOOM
THOOM
WELL, WELL. YOU MANAGED TO SPECIAL SUMMON...
...A TOP-LEVEL MONSTER WITHOUT GETTING TWO RELEASE MONSTERS ONTO YOUR FIELD.
THOOM
I SEE YOU HAVEN'T LOST YOUR TOUCH...
I ATTACK WANDERING WILD WIND KING...
...WITH INFERNITY GENERAL.

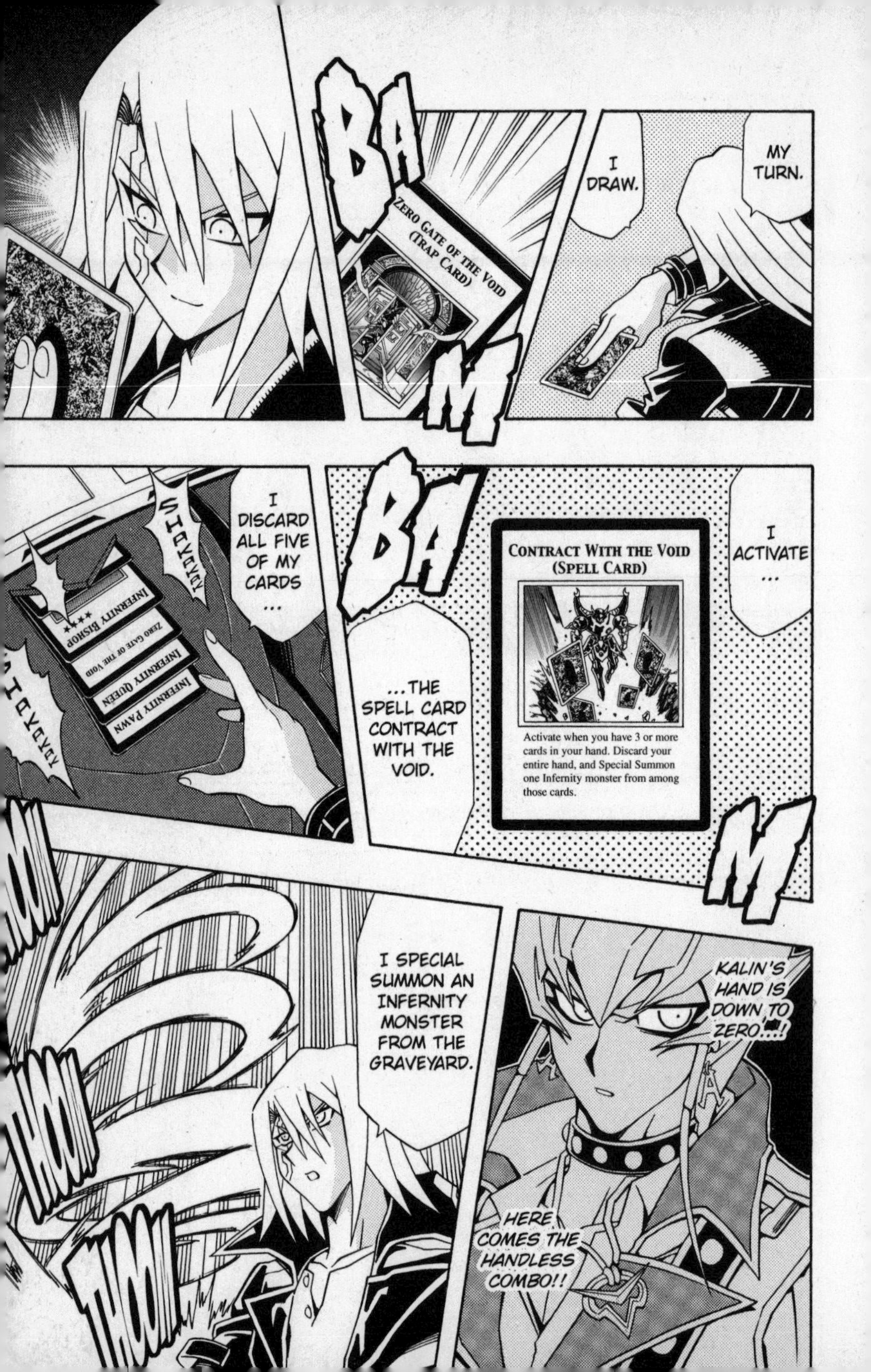
MY TURN.
I DRAW.
BAM
ZERO GATE OF THE VOID (TRAP CARD)
I ACTIVATE ...
CONTRACT WITH THE VOID (SPELL CARD)
Activate when you have 3 or more cards in your hand. Discard your entire hand, and Special Summon one Infernity monster from among those cards.
...THE SPELL CARD CONTRACT WITH THE VOID.
BAM
I DISCARD ALL FIVE OF MY CARDS ...
INFERNITY BISHOP
ZERO GATE OF THE VOID
INFERNITY QUEEN
INFERNITY PAWN
KALIN'S HAND IS DOWN TO ZERO...!
HERE COMES THE HANDLESS COMBO!!
I SPECIAL SUMMON AN INFERNITY MONSTER FROM THE GRAVEYARD.

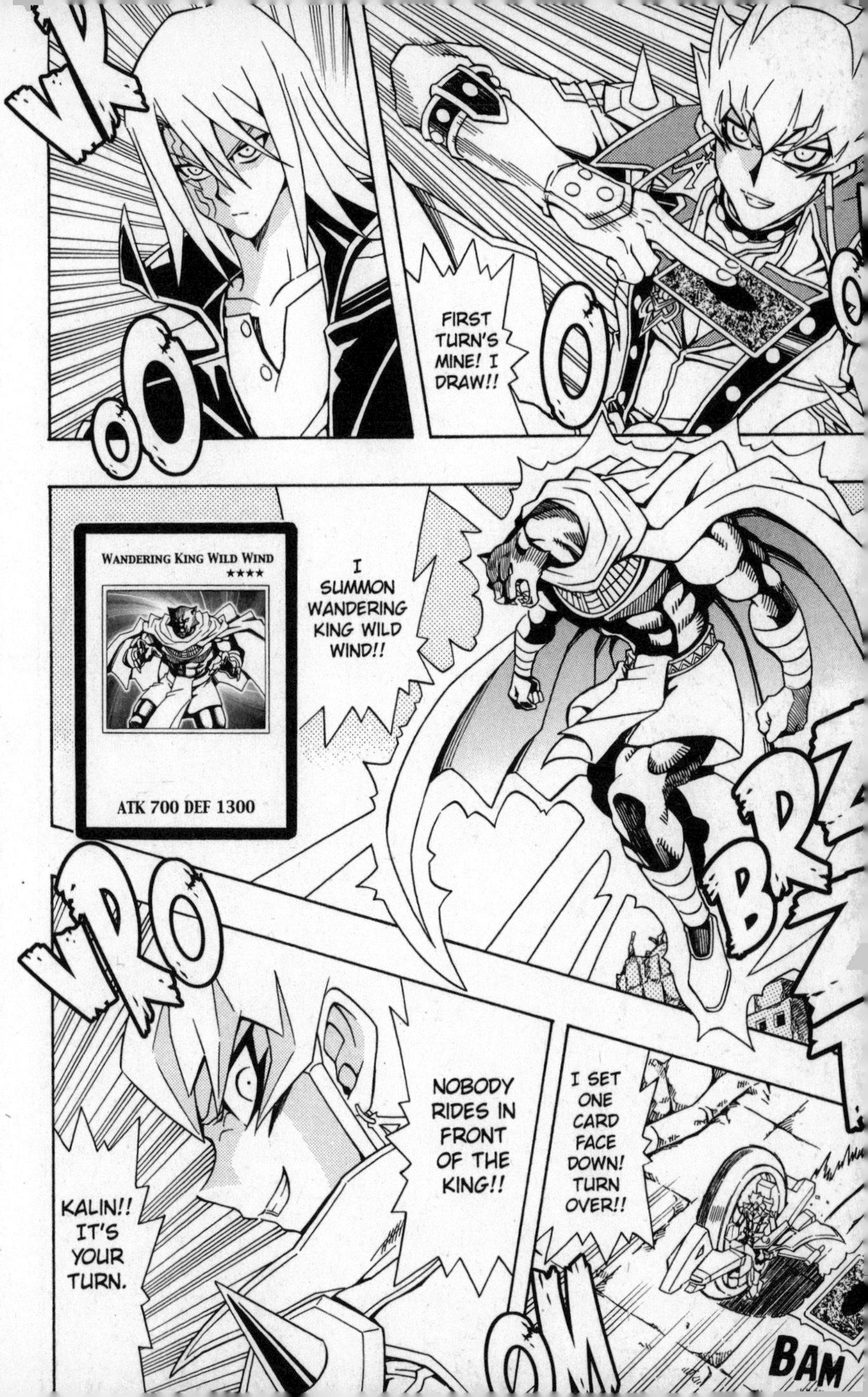
FIRST TURN'S MINE! I DRAW!!
I SUMMON WANDERING KING WILD WIND!!
WANDERING KING WILD WIND
ATK 700 DEF 1300
I SET ONE CARD FACE DOWN! TURN OVER!!
BAM
NOBODY RIDES IN FRONT OF THE KING!!
KALIN!! IT'S YOUR TURN.

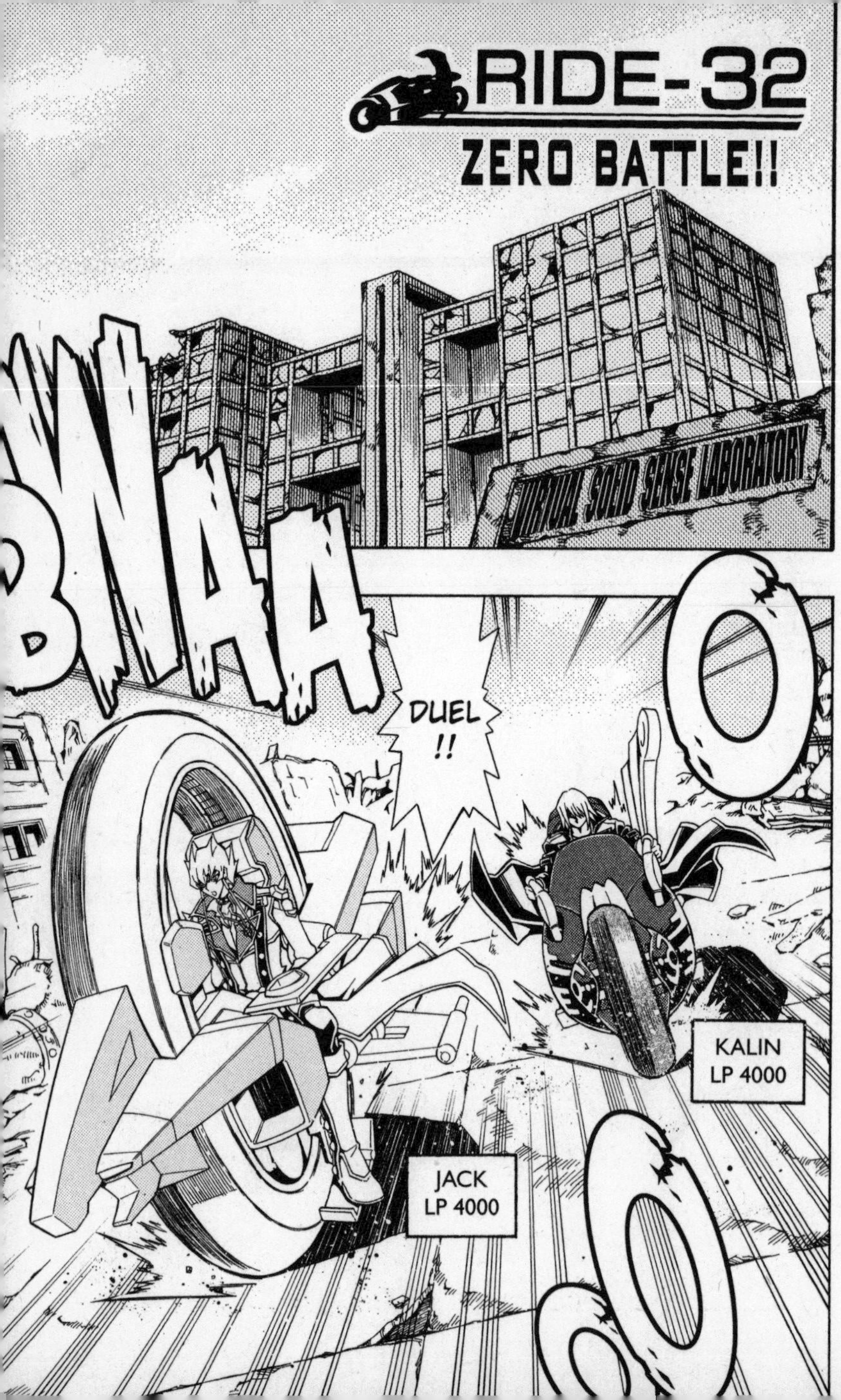
RIDE-32
ZERO BATTLE!!
VIRTUAL SOLID SENSE LABORATORY
DUEL !!
KALIN LP 4000
JACK LP 4000

5D's TRACKS

THE 30TH

BY SATOMASA

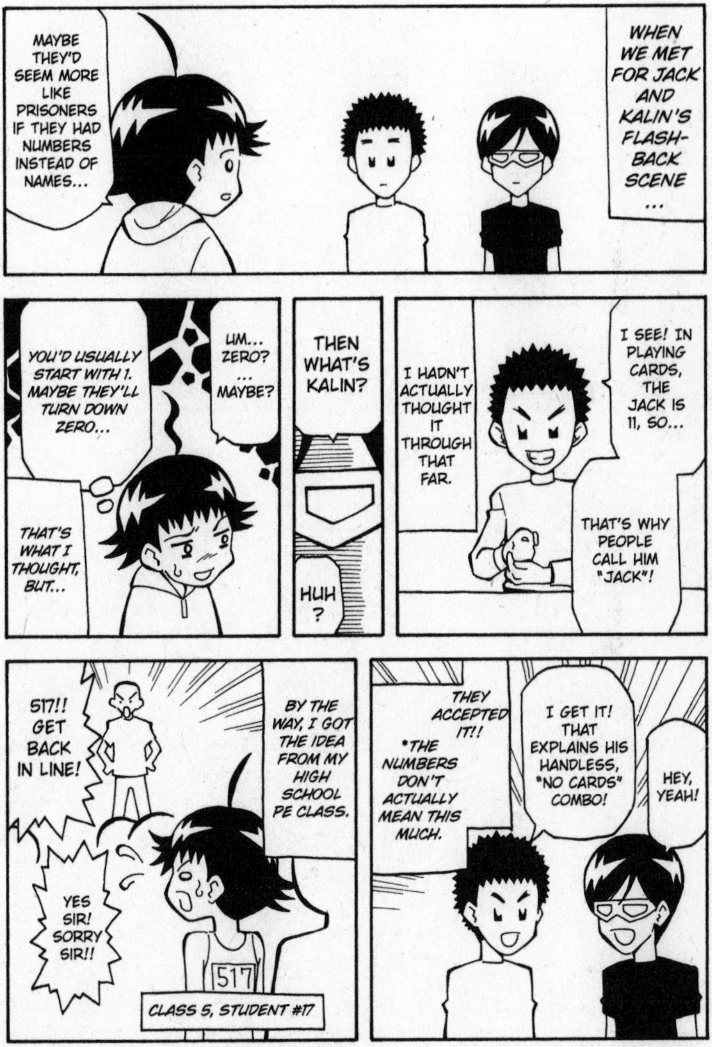
WHEN WE MET FOR JACK AND KALIN'S FLASH-BACK SCENE ...
MAYBE THEY'D SEEM MORE LIKE PRISONERS IF THEY HAD NUMBERS INSTEAD OF NAMES...
I SEE! IN PLAYING CARDS, THE JACK IS 11, SO...
THAT'S WHY PEOPLE CALL HIM "JACK"!
I HADN'T ACTUALLY THOUGHT IT THROUGH THAT FAR.
THEN WHAT'S KALIN?
HUH?
UM... ZERO? ... MAYBE?
YOU'D USUALLY START WITH 1. MAYBE THEY'LL TURN DOWN ZERO...
THAT'S WHAT I THOUGHT, BUT...
HEY, YEAH!
I GET IT! THAT EXPLAINS HIS HANDLESS, "NO CARDS" COMBO!
THEY ACCEPTED IT!!
*THE NUMBERS DON'T ACTUALLY MEAN THIS MUCH.
BY THE WAY, I GOT THE IDEA FROM MY HIGH SCHOOL PE CLASS.
517!! GET BACK IN LINE!
YES SIR! SORRY SIR!!
517
CLASS 5, STUDENT #17

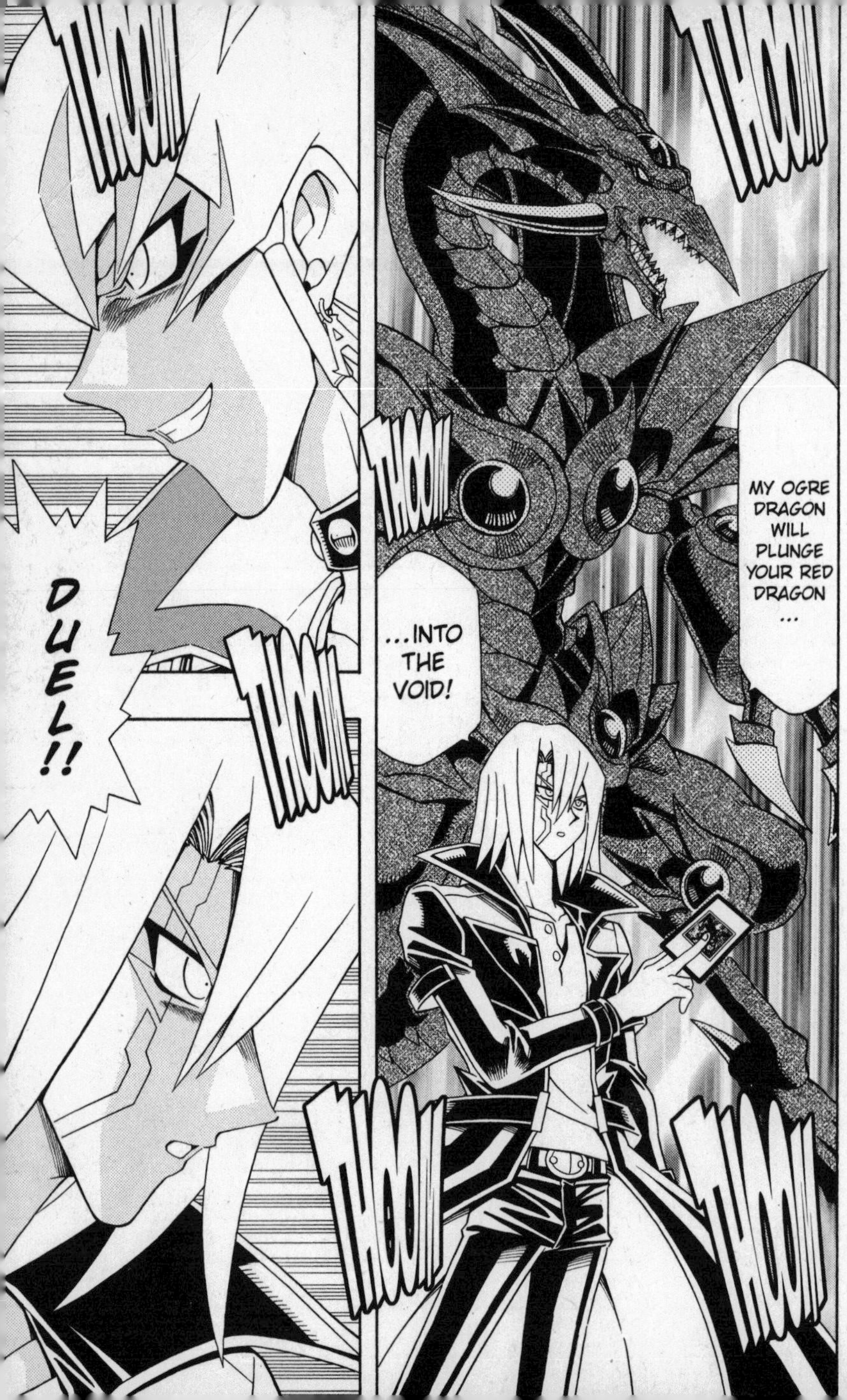
THOOM
THOOM
MY OGRE DRAGON WILL PLUNGE YOUR RED DRAGON ...
...INTO THE VOID!
THOOM
THOOM
THOOM
THOOM
DUEL!!
THOOM

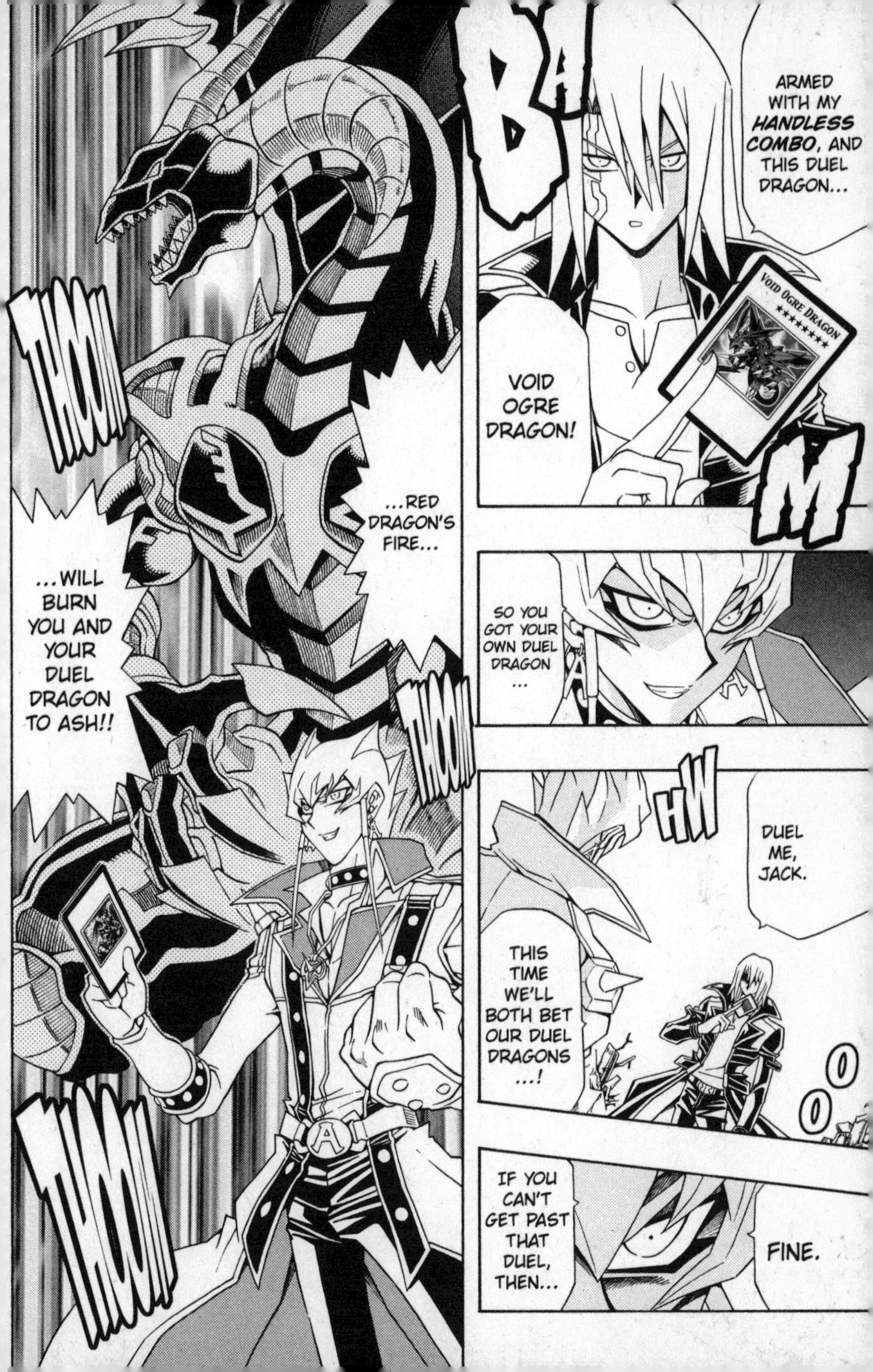
BA
ARMED WITH MY HANDLESS COMBO, AND THIS DUEL DRAGON...
VOID OGRE DRAGON!
Void Ogre Dragon
M
SO YOU GOT YOUR OWN DUEL DRAGON...
HW
DUEL ME, JACK.
THIS TIME WE'LL BOTH BET OUR DUEL DRAGONS...!
FINE.
IF YOU CAN'T GET PAST THAT DUEL, THEN...
...RED DRAGON'S FIRE...
THOOM
...WILL BURN YOU AND YOUR DUEL DRAGON TO ASH!!
THOOM
THOOM

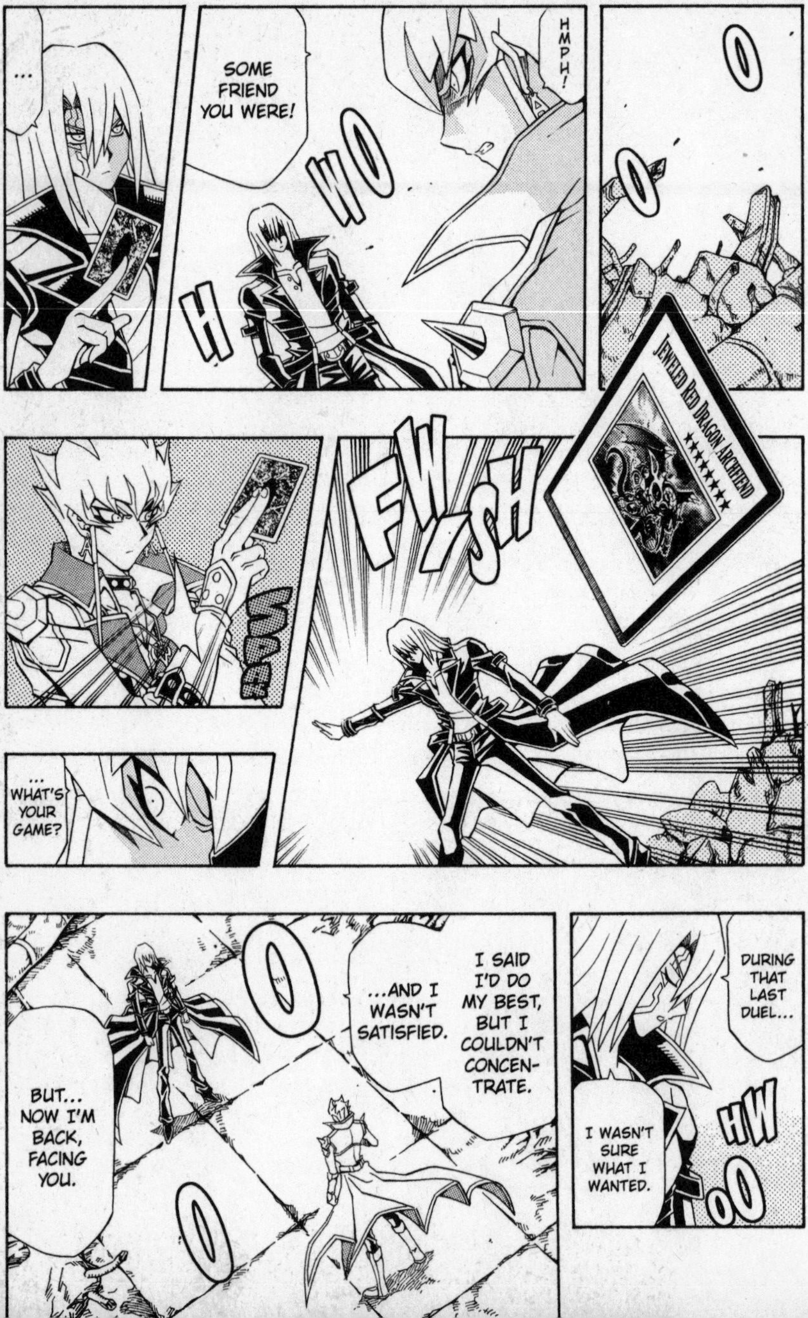
O
O
HMPH!
SOME FRIEND YOU WERE!
WO
H
...
JEWELED RED DRAGON ARCHFIEND
FW ISH
... WHAT'S YOUR GAME?
DURING THAT LAST DUEL...
I WASN'T SURE WHAT I WANTED.
HW
OO
I SAID I'D DO MY BEST, BUT I COULDN'T CONCENTRATE.
...AND I WASN'T SATISFIED.
O
BUT... NOW I'M BACK, FACING YOU.
O

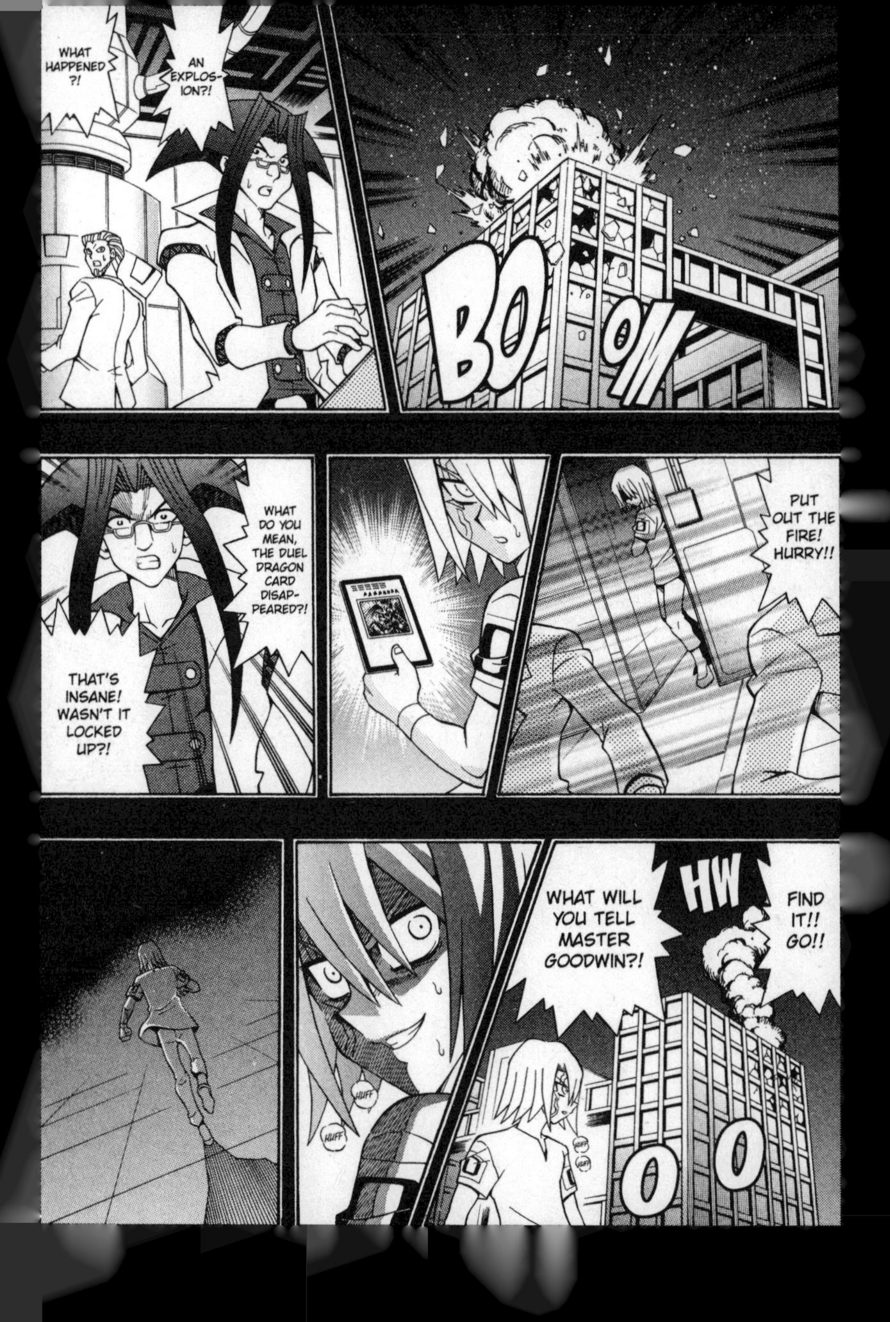
BOOM
AN EXPLOSION?!
WHAT HAPPENED?!
PUT OUT THE FIRE! HURRY!!
WHAT DO YOU MEAN, THE DUEL DRAGON CARD DISAPPEARED?!
THAT'S INSANE! WASN'T IT LOCKED UP?!
FIND IT!! GO!!
HW
WHAT WILL YOU TELL MASTER GOODWIN?!
HUFF
HUFF
OO
HUFF
HUFF

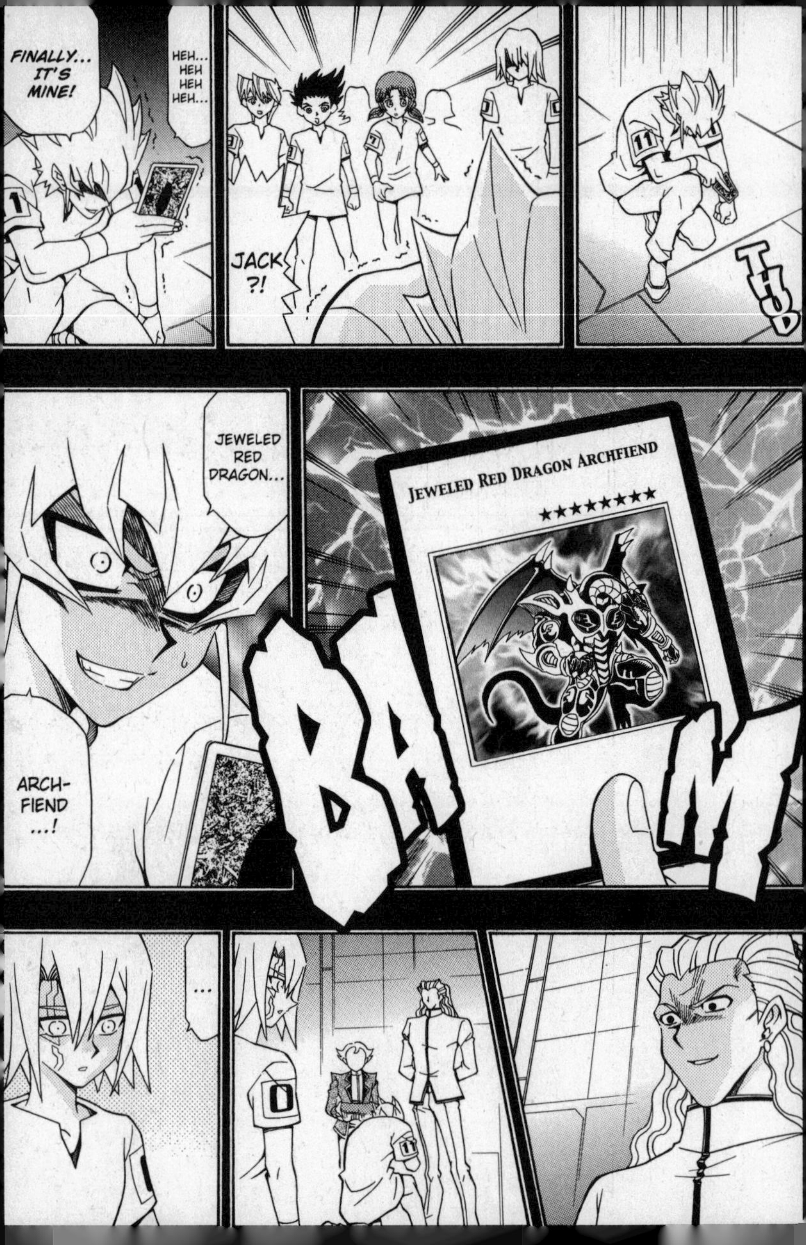
THUD
JACK ?!
HEH... HEH HEH HEH...
FINALLY... IT'S MINE!
JEWELED RED DRAGON ARCHFIEND
BAM
JEWELED RED DRAGON...
ARCH-FIEND ...!
...

MASAHIRO HIKOKUBO

It's the volume you've all been waiting for! That Duel Dragon (yes, THAT one!) finally takes the stage!! The Turbo Duel called "fate" is spinning into action for Yusei and company. Enjoy the ride!!

MASASHI SATO

Volume 4 goes on sale on *6/4, which just happens to be Sect's birthday!! They must've bugged my studio! Oh, but don't let that bug you!! Hope you like the manga!!

Note: *Refers to the Japanese release.

Volume 4
SHONEN JUMP Manga Edition

Story by **MASAHIRO HIKOKUBO**
Art by **MASASHI SATO**
Production Assistance **STUDIO DICE**

Translation & English Adaptation **TAYLOR ENGEL AND IAN REID, HC LANGUAGE SOLUTIONS**
Touch-up Art & Lettering **JOHN HUNT**
Designer **SHAWN CARRICO**
Editor **MIKE MONTESA**

Published by VIZ Media, LLC
P.O. Box 77010
San Francisco, CA 94107

10 9 8 7 6 5 4 3 2 1
First printing, April 2013

www.viz.com

PARENTAL ADVISORY
YU-GI-OH! 5D's is rated T for Teen and
is recommended for ages 13 and up.
This volume contains fantasy violence.
ratings.viz.com

www.shonenjump.com

VOLUME 4
SYNCHRO VS. SYNCHRO!!

Story by MASAHIRO HIKOKUBO
Art by MASASHI SATO
Production Assistance STUDIO DICE

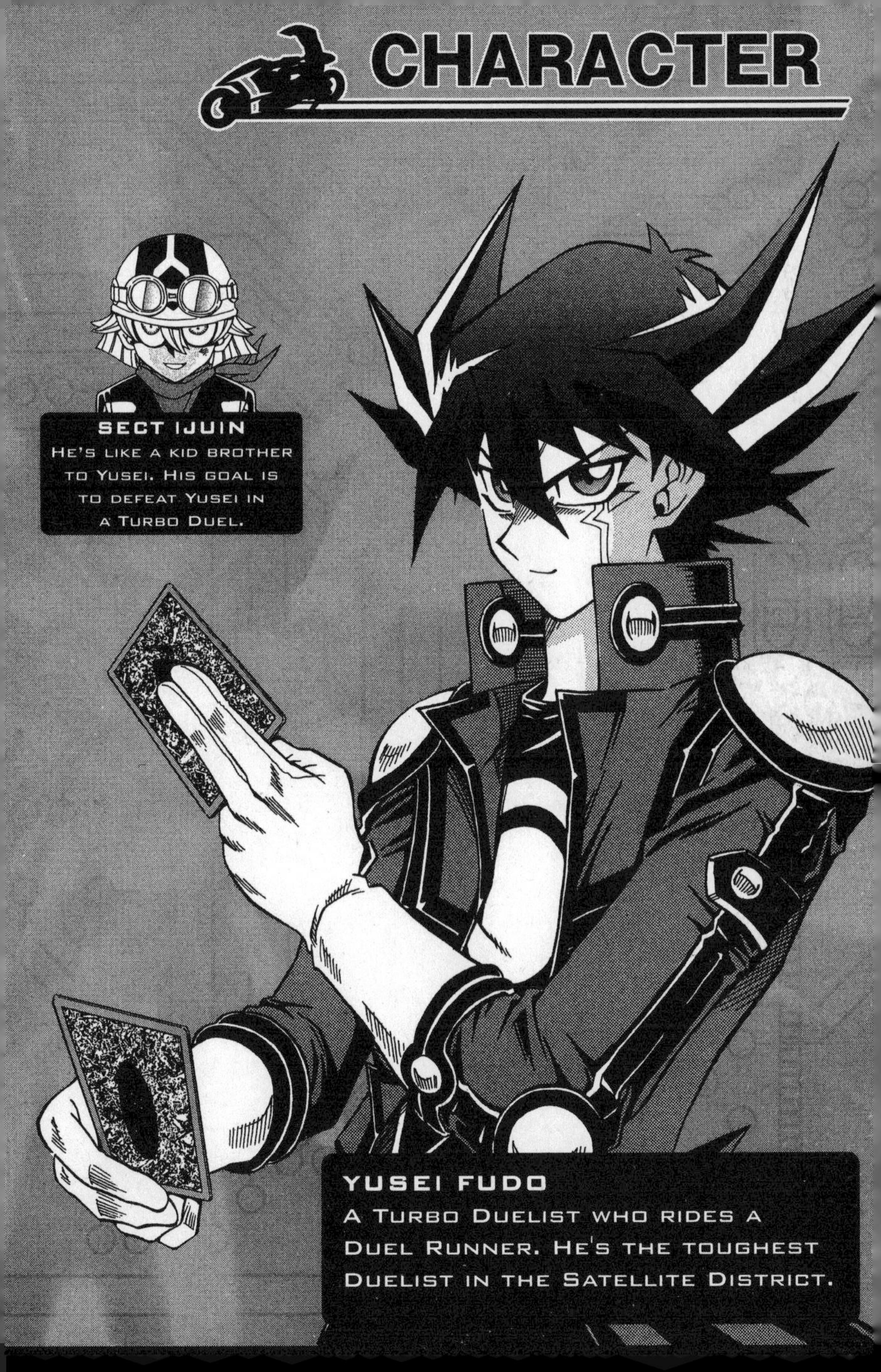
CHARACTER
SECT IJUIN
He's like a kid brother to Yusei. His goal is to defeat Yusei in a Turbo Duel.
YUSEI FUDO
A Turbo Duelist who rides a Duel Runner. He's the toughest Duelist in the Satellite District.

KALIN KESSLER
A FIENDISHLY STRONG TURBO DUELIST WHOSE SPECIALTY IS HIS "HANDLESS COMBO."

JACK ATLAS
A TURBO DUELIST KNOWN AS "THE KING," AND FEARED BY ALL AROUND.

AKIZA IZINSKI
A TURBO DUELIST WHO HOLDS THE TITLE "QUEEN OF QUEENS."

LEO (RIGHT) & LUNA (LEFT)
EACH OF THESE TWIN TURBO DUELISTS HAS A DUEL DRAGON. GOODWIN, THE TOURNAMENT HOST, HAS TOLD THEM TO FIND DUELISTS COMPATIBLE WITH THE DUEL DRAGONS.

CROW HOGAN
A SUPER HIGH-SPEED SYNCHRO-USER, NICKNAMED "THE BLACK WHIRLWIND."

STORY

IN NEW DOMINO CITY, IN THE YEAR 20XX, TURBO DUELS FOUGHT FROM THE SEATS OF MOTORCYCLE-SHAPED DUEL DISKS, CALLED "DUEL RUNNERS," ARE THE HOTTEST GAME IN TOWN.

AS THE STRONGMEN OF THE DUELING WORLD SLUG IT OUT, YUSEI WINS HIS SECOND ROUND OF THE D1 GRAND PRIX IN STYLE! MEANWHILE, SECT ACQUIRED A DUEL DRAGON AND HAS FALLEN INTO DARKNESS AND DISAPPEARED ALONG WITH THE SKELETON KNIGHT. SEARCHING FOR A WAY TO SAVE SECT, YUSEI BEGINS A DUEL WITH LEO AND LUNA, TWIN TURBO DUELISTS WHO BOTH HOLD DUEL DRAGONS!

VOLUME 4
SYNCHRO VS. SYNCHRO!!

RIDE-25

SENSE UPON SENSE!!

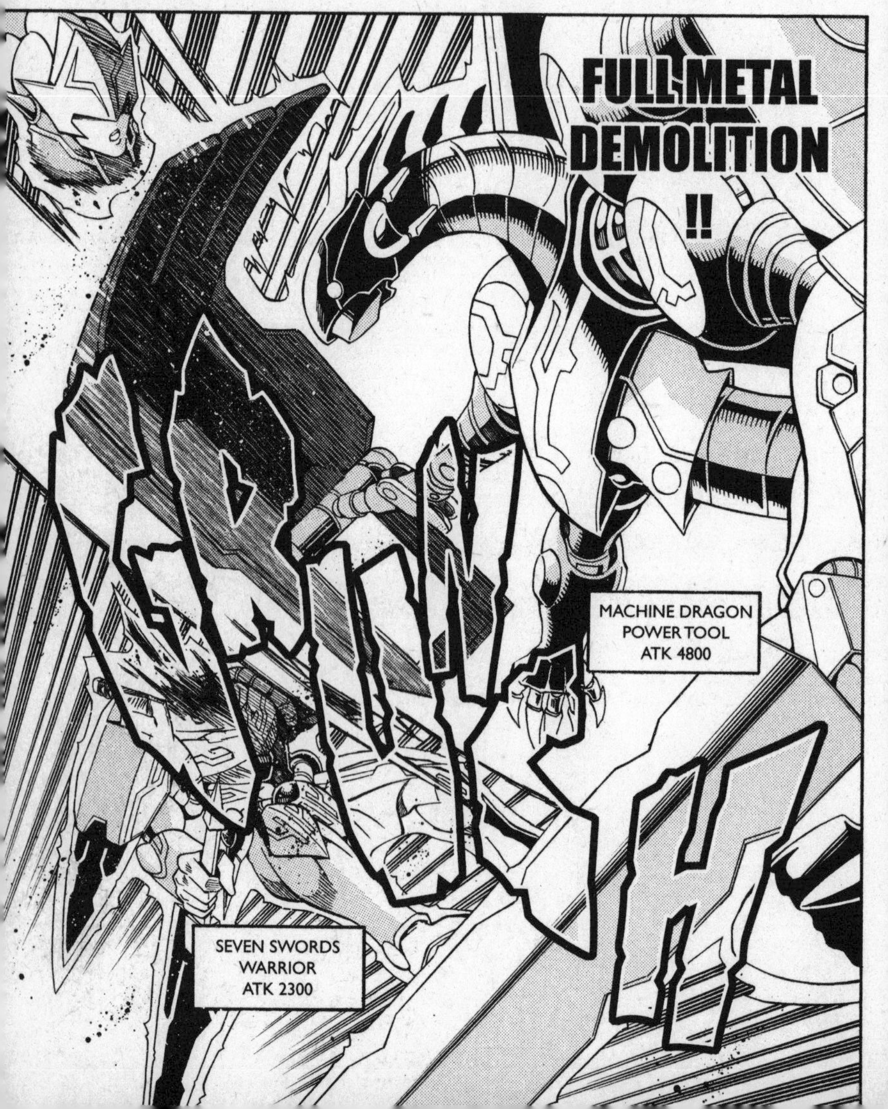
FULL METAL DEMOLITION !!
MACHINE DRAGON POWER TOOL ATK 4800
SEVEN SWORDS WARRIOR ATK 2300

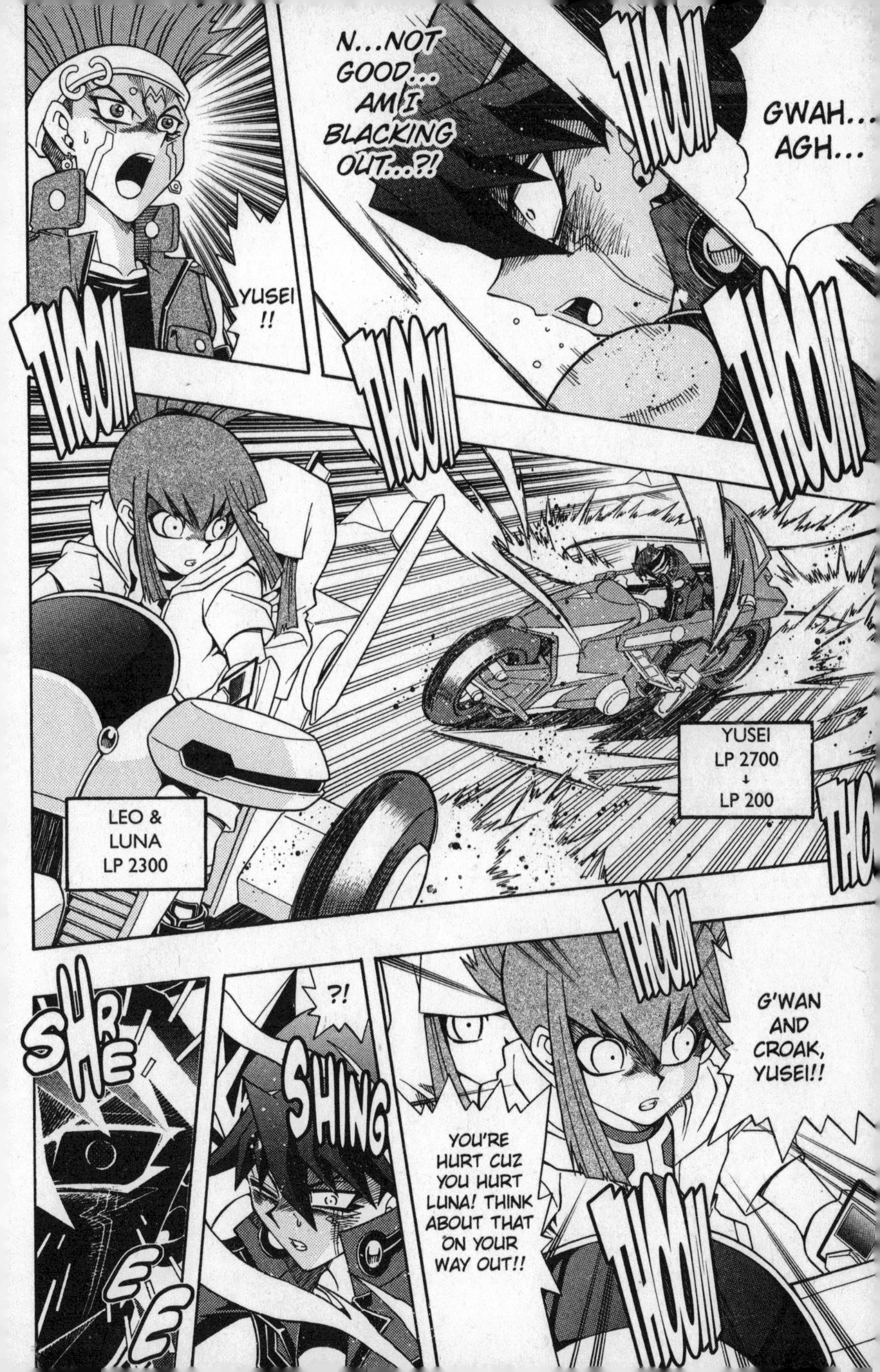
GWAH... AGH...
THOOM
N...NOT GOOD... AM I BLACKING OUT...?!
YUSEI !!
THOOM
THOOM
THOOM
THOOM
THO
YUSEI LP 2700 ↓ LP 200
LEO & LUNA LP 2300
THOOM
G'WAN AND CROAK, YUSEI!!
YOU'RE HURT CUZ YOU HURT LUNA! THINK ABOUT THAT ON YOUR WAY OUT!!
THOOM
?!
SHING
SHREE

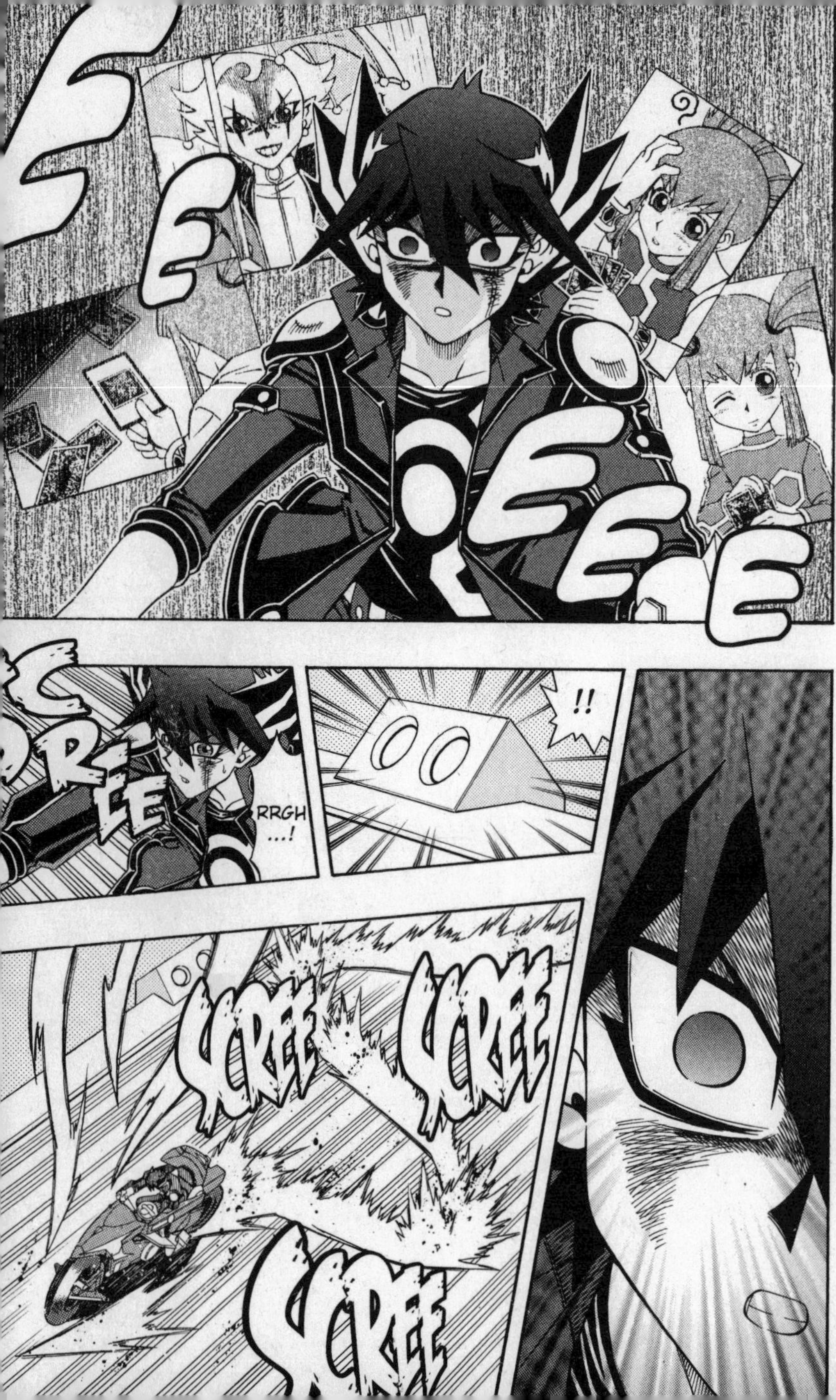
EEEEE
!!
SCREE
RRGH ...!
SCREE
SCREE
SCREE

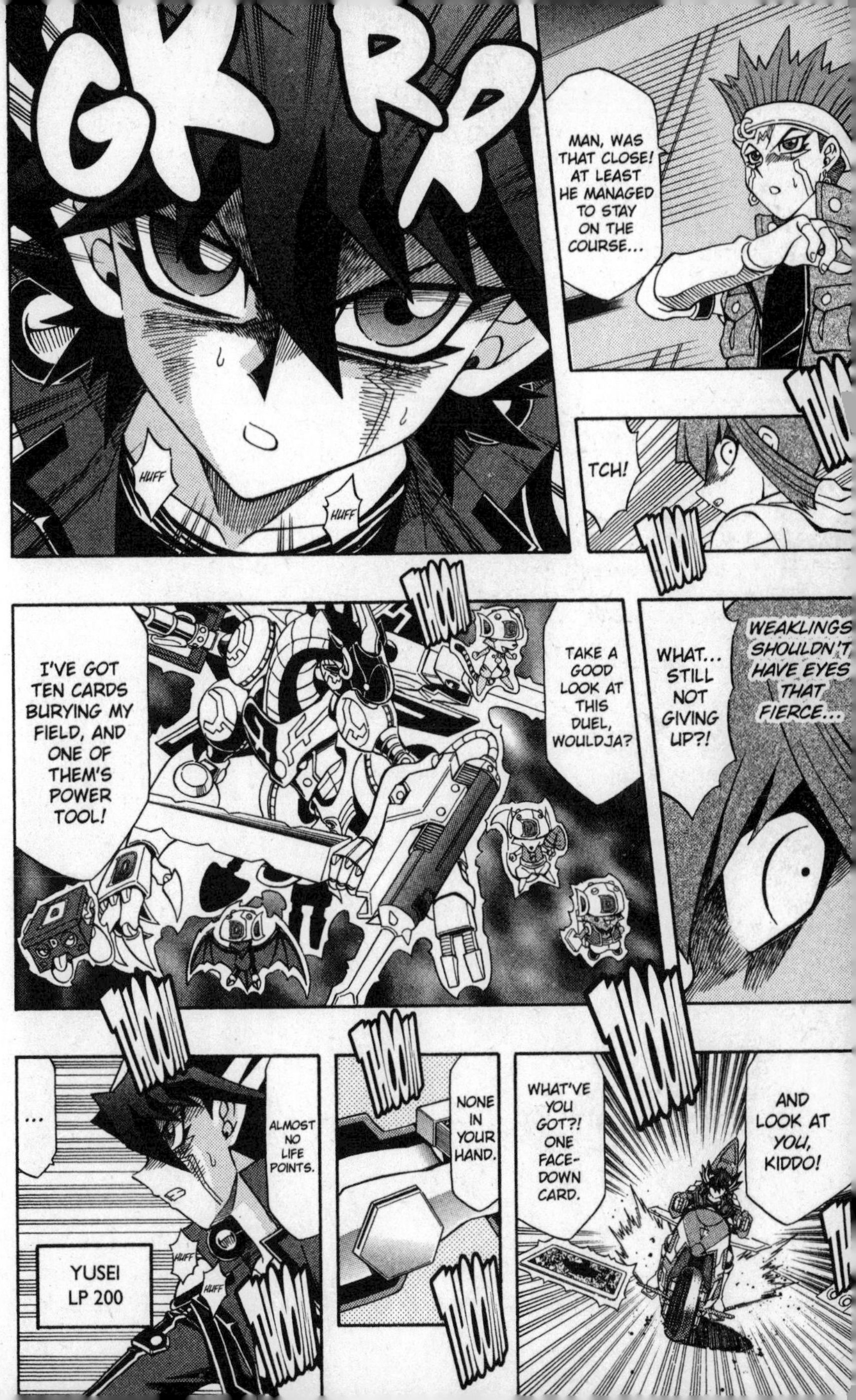
MAN, WAS THAT CLOSE! AT LEAST HE MANAGED TO STAY ON THE COURSE...
THOOM
TCH!
THOOM
GKRR
HUFF
HUFF
WEAKLINGS SHOULDN'T HAVE EYES THAT FIERCE...
WHAT... STILL NOT GIVING UP?!
TAKE A GOOD LOOK AT THIS DUEL, WOULDJA?
THOOM
I'VE GOT TEN CARDS BURYING MY FIELD, AND ONE OF THEM'S POWER TOOL!
THOOM
AND LOOK AT YOU, KIDDO!
WHAT'VE YOU GOT?! ONE FACE-DOWN CARD.
THOOM
NONE IN YOUR HAND.
ALMOST NO LIFE POINTS.
THOOM
...
HUFF
HUFF
YUSEI LP 200

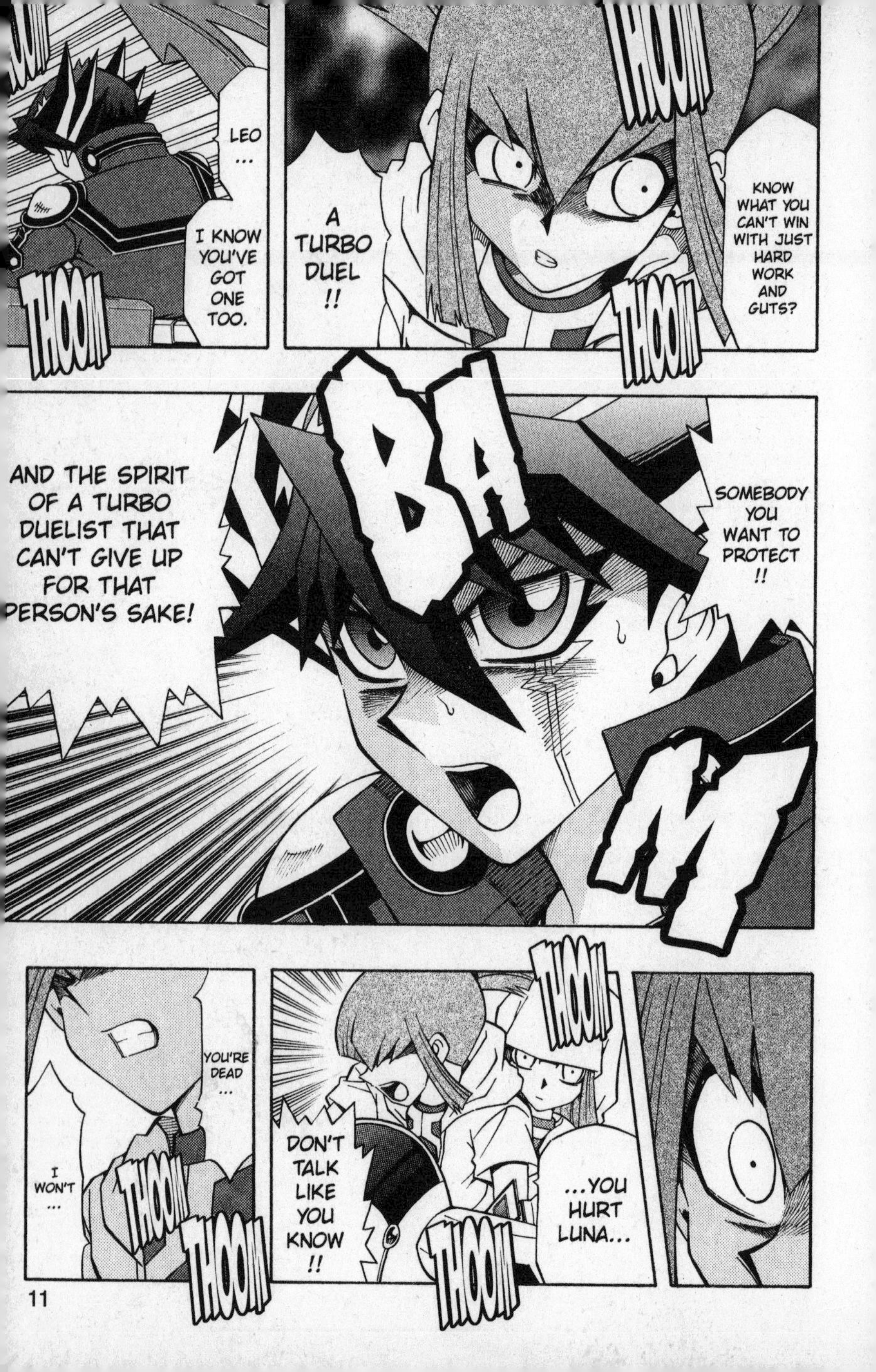
THOOM
KNOW WHAT YOU CAN'T WIN WITH JUST HARD WORK AND GUTS?
A TURBO DUEL !!
THOOM
THOOM
LEO ...
I KNOW YOU'VE GOT ONE TOO.
THOOM
BAM
SOMEBODY YOU WANT TO PROTECT !!
AND THE SPIRIT OF A TURBO DUELIST THAT CAN'T GIVE UP FOR THAT PERSON'S SAKE!
...YOU HURT LUNA...
THOOM
DON'T TALK LIKE YOU KNOW !!
THOOM
YOU'RE DEAD ...
I WON'T ...
THOOM
THOOM

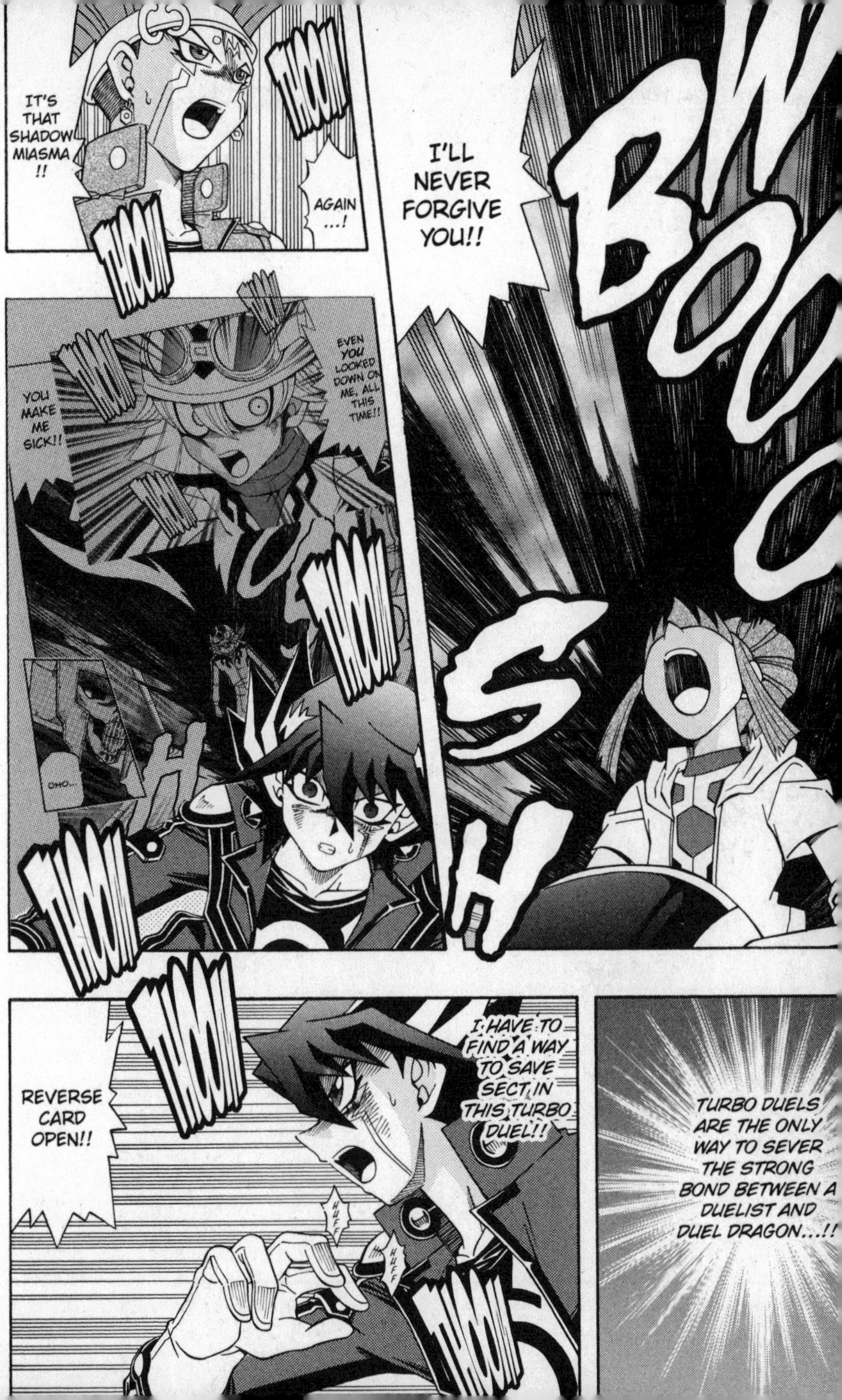
I'LL NEVER FORGIVE YOU!!
IT'S THAT SHADOW MIASMA!!
AGAIN...!
THOOM
THOOM
EVEN YOU LOOKED DOWN ON ME, ALL THIS TIME!!
YOU MAKE ME SICK!!
THOOM
OHO...
THOOM
TURBO DUELS ARE THE ONLY WAY TO SEVER THE STRONG BOND BETWEEN A DUELIST AND DUEL DRAGON...!!
I HAVE TO FIND A WAY TO SAVE SECT IN THIS TURBO DUEL!!
THOOM
REVERSE CARD OPEN!!
HUFF
HUFF
THOOM

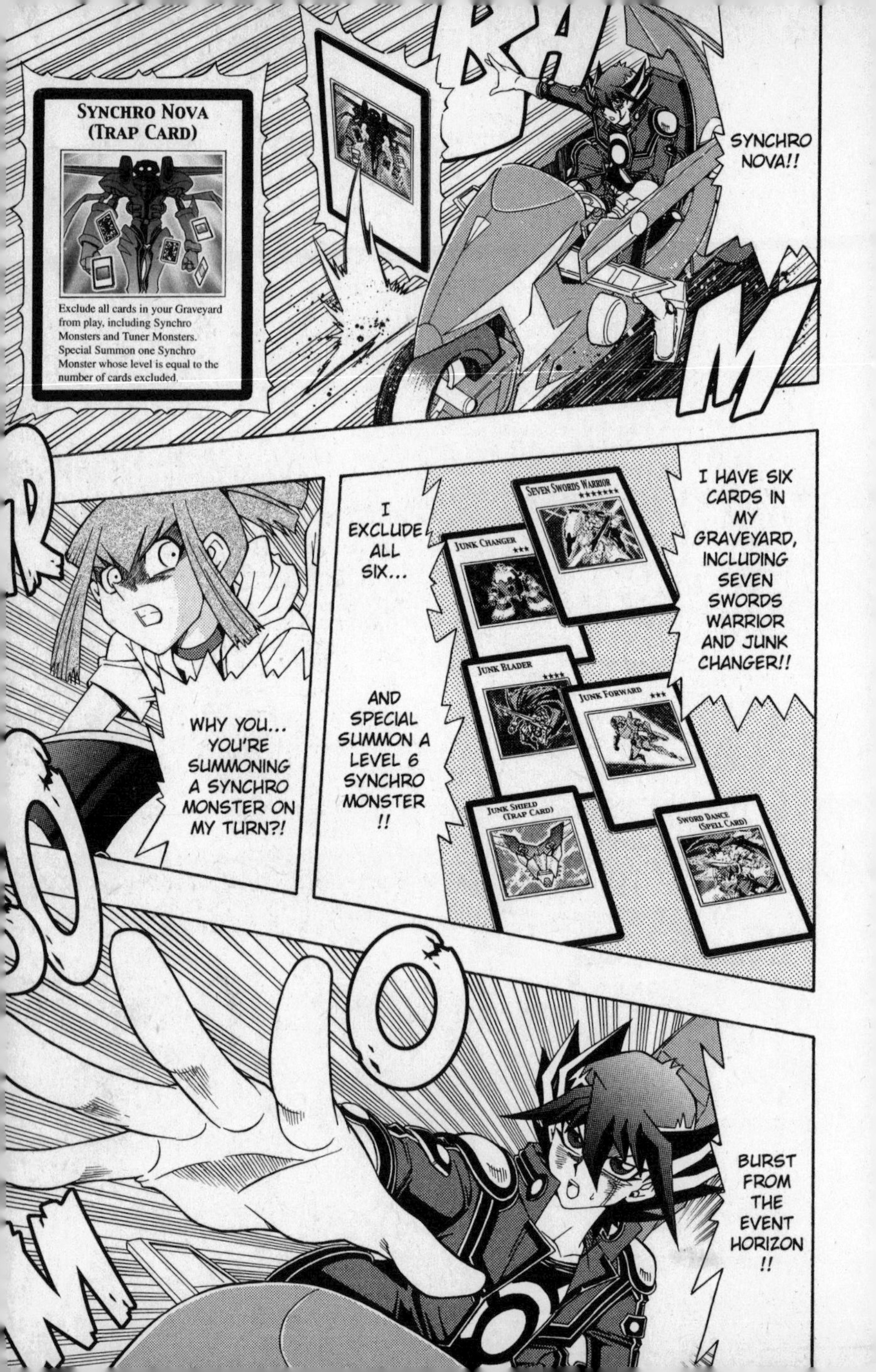
SYNCHRO NOVA!!
SYNCHRO NOVA (TRAP CARD)
Exclude all cards in your Graveyard from play, including Synchro Monsters and Tuner Monsters. Special Summon one Synchro Monster whose level is equal to the number of cards excluded.
I HAVE SIX CARDS IN MY GRAVEYARD, INCLUDING SEVEN SWORDS WARRIOR AND JUNK CHANGER!!
SEVEN SWORDS WARRIOR
JUNK CHANGER
I EXCLUDE ALL SIX...
JUNK BLADER
JUNK FORWARD
SWORD DANCE (SPELL CARD)
JUNK SHIELD (TRAP CARD)
AND SPECIAL SUMMON A LEVEL 6 SYNCHRO MONSTER!!
WHY YOU... YOU'RE SUMMONING A SYNCHRO MONSTER ON MY TURN?!
BURST FROM THE EVENT HORIZON!!

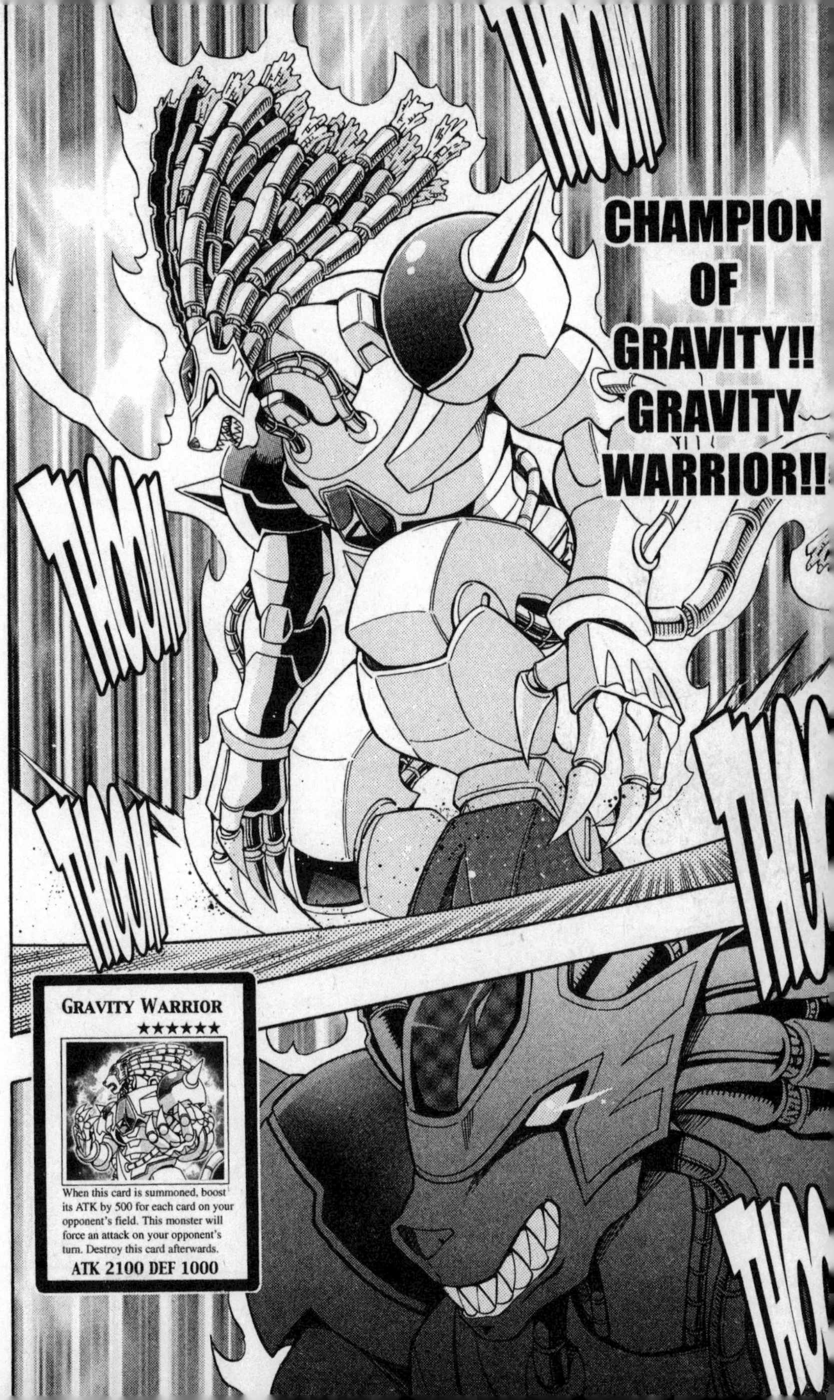
THOOM
CHAMPION OF GRAVITY!! GRAVITY WARRIOR!!
THOOM
THOOM
GRAVITY WARRIOR
★★★★★★
When this card is summoned, boost its ATK by 500 for each card on your opponent's field. This monster will force an attack on your opponent's turn. Destroy this card afterwards.
ATK 2100 DEF 1000

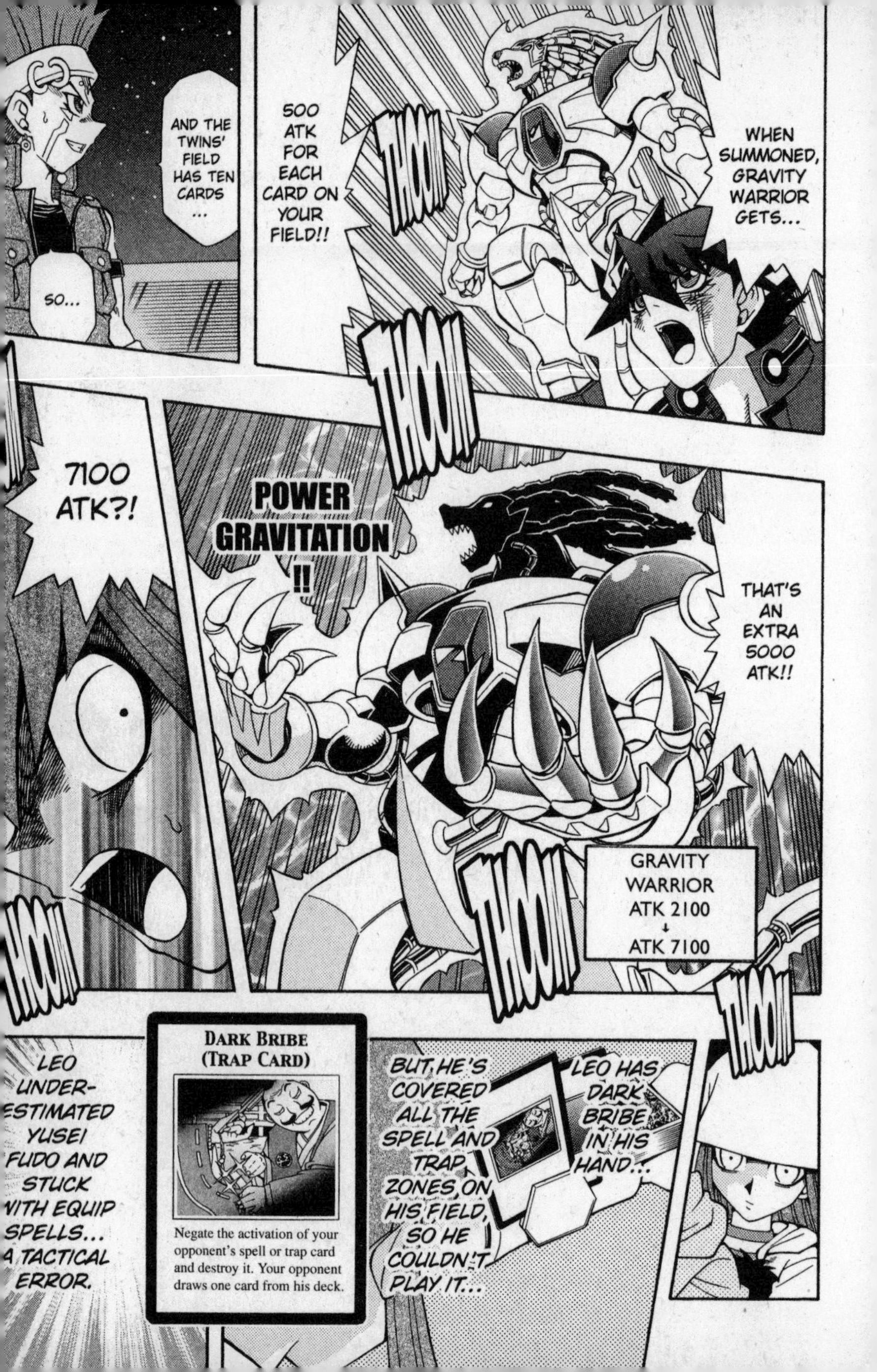
WHEN SUMMONED, GRAVITY WARRIOR GETS...
500 ATK FOR EACH CARD ON YOUR FIELD!!
THOOM
THOOM
AND THE TWINS' FIELD HAS TEN CARDS ...
SO...
THAT'S AN EXTRA 5000 ATK!!
POWER GRAVITATION!!
GRAVITY WARRIOR ATK 2100 ↓ ATK 7100
THOOM
THOOM
7100 ATK?!
THOOM
LEO HAS DARK BRIBE IN HIS HAND...
BUT HE'S COVERED ALL THE SPELL AND TRAP ZONES ON HIS FIELD, SO HE COULDN'T PLAY IT...
DARK BRIBE (TRAP CARD)
Negate the activation of your opponent's spell or trap card and destroy it. Your opponent draws one card from his deck.
LEO UNDER-ESTIMATED YUSEI FUDO AND STUCK WITH EQUIP SPELLS... A TACTICAL ERROR.

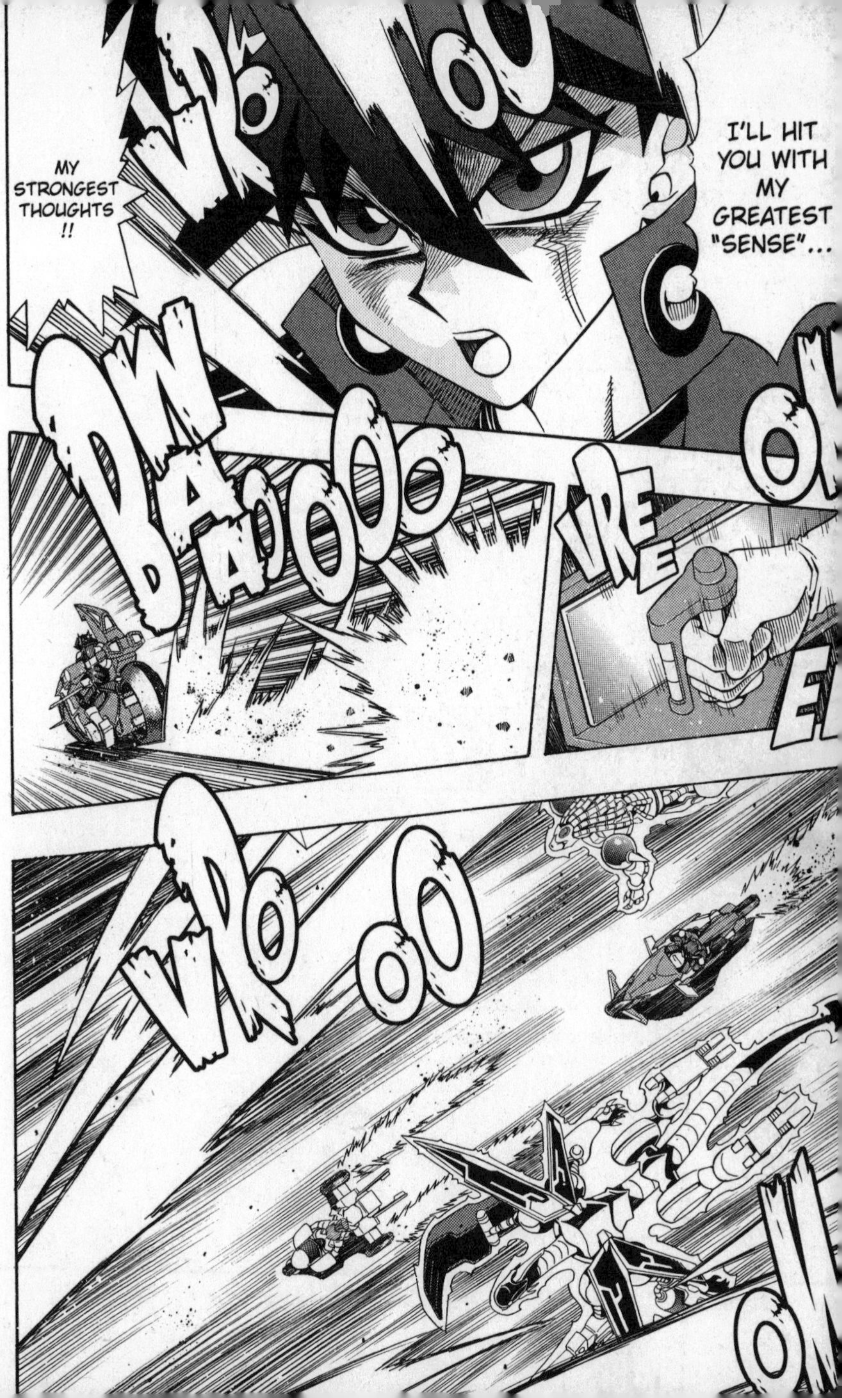
I'LL HIT YOU WITH MY GREATEST "SENSE"...
MY STRONGEST THOUGHTS !!

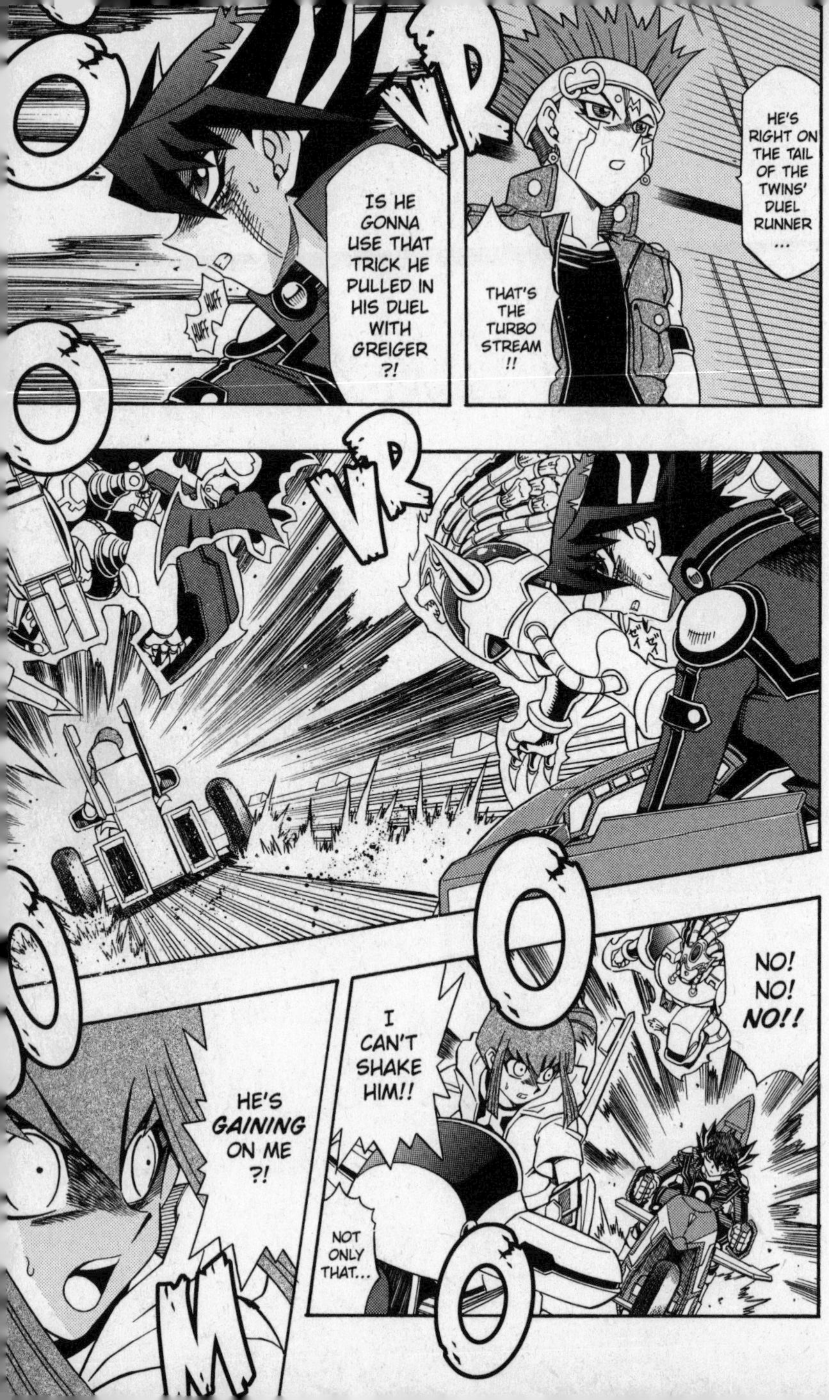
HE'S RIGHT ON THE TAIL OF THE TWINS' DUEL RUNNER ...
THAT'S THE TURBO STREAM !!
IS HE GONNA USE THAT TRICK HE PULLED IN HIS DUEL WITH GREIGER ?!
HUFF
HUFF
NO! NO! NO!!
I CAN'T SHAKE HIM!!
NOT ONLY THAT...
HE'S GAINING ON ME ?!

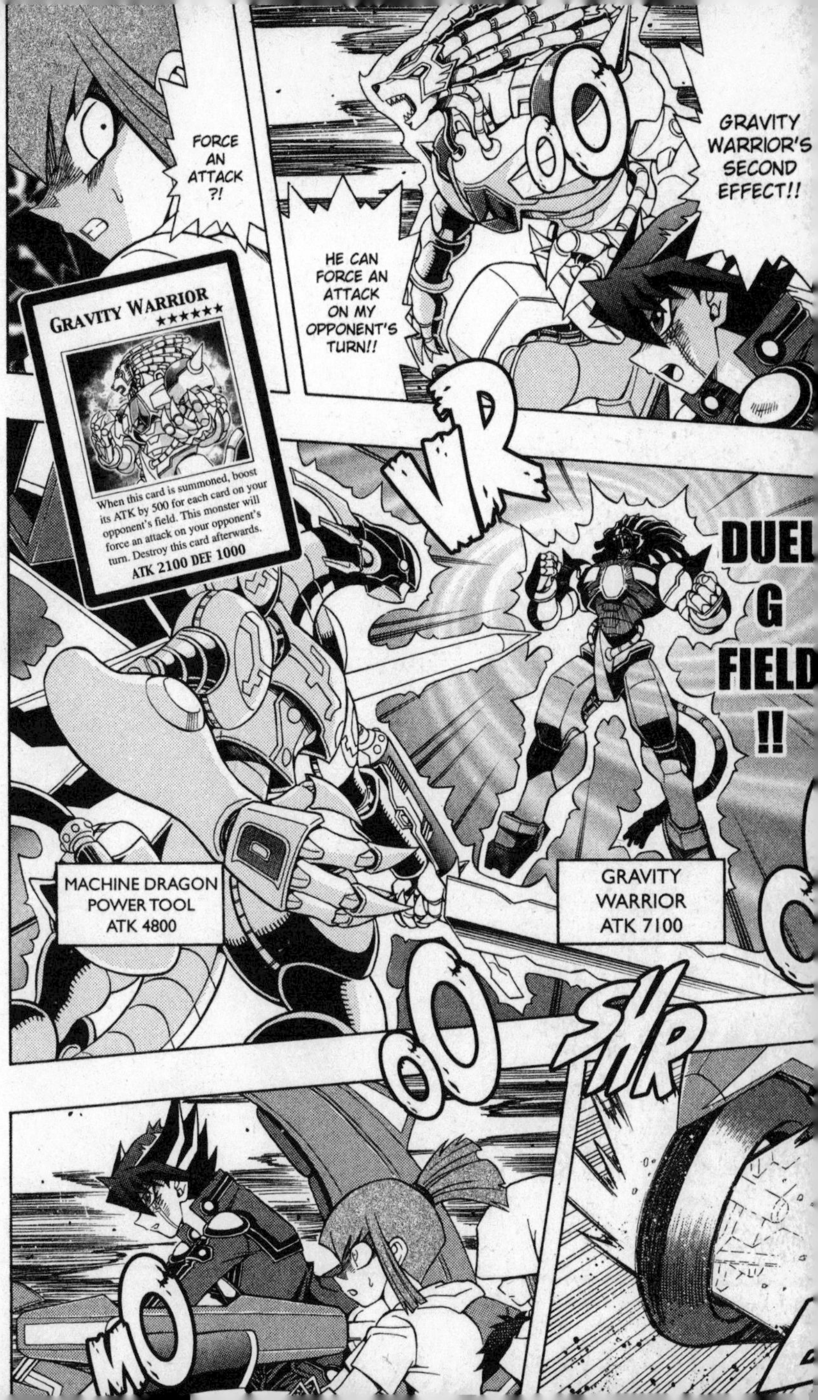
GRAVITY WARRIOR'S SECOND EFFECT!!
HE CAN FORCE AN ATTACK ON MY OPPONENT'S TURN!!
FORCE AN ATTACK ?!
GRAVITY WARRIOR ★★★★★★
When this card is summoned, boost its ATK by 500 for each card on your opponent's field. This monster will force an attack on your opponent's turn. Destroy this card afterwards.
ATK 2100 DEF 1000
VR
DUEL G FIELD !!
GRAVITY WARRIOR ATK 7100
MACHINE DRAGON POWER TOOL ATK 4800
SHR
OO
MO

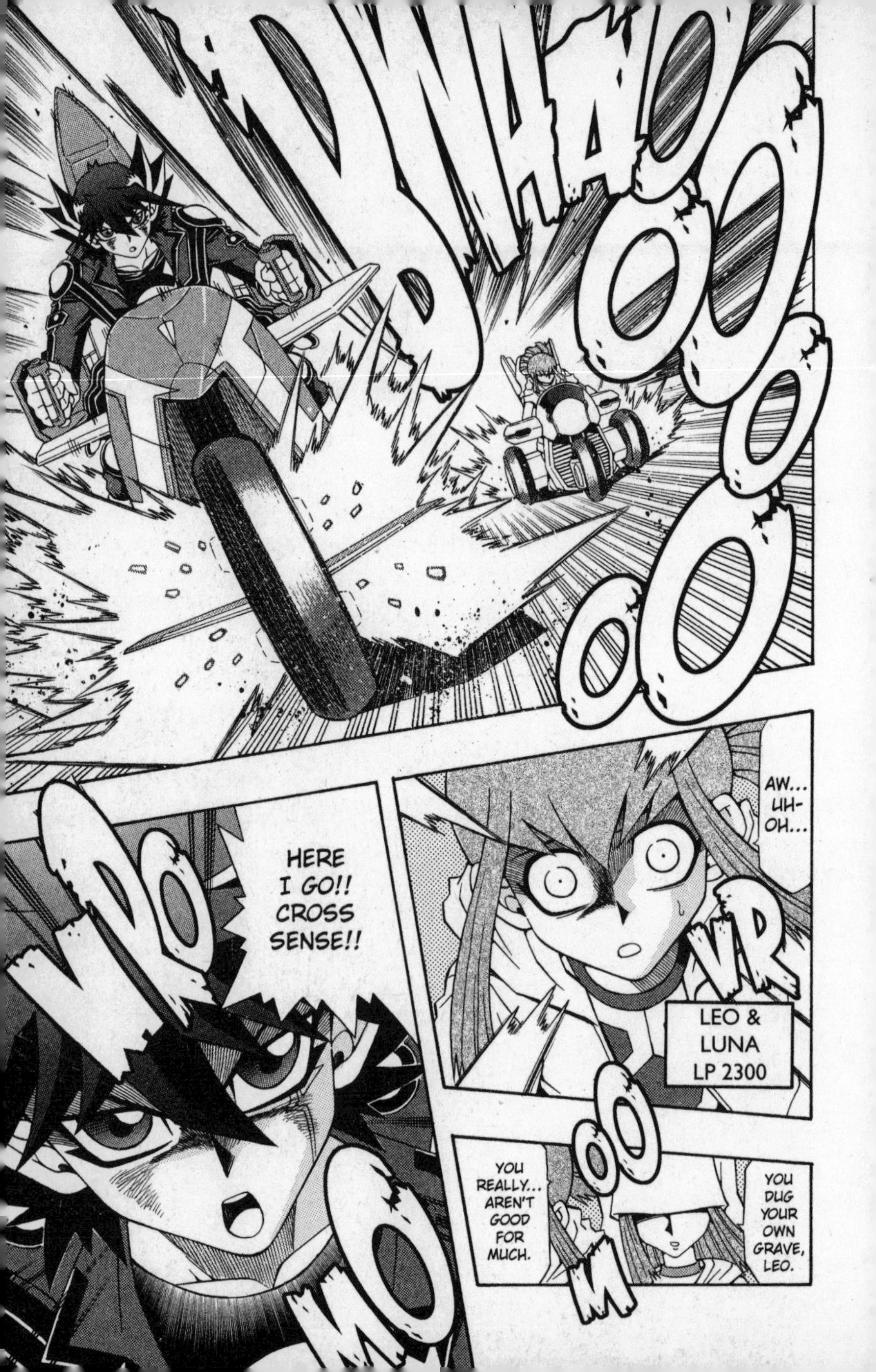

AW... UH-OH...
LEO & LUNA LP 2300
YOU DUG YOUR OWN GRAVE, LEO.
YOU REALLY... AREN'T GOOD FOR MUCH.
HERE I GO!! CROSS SENSE!!

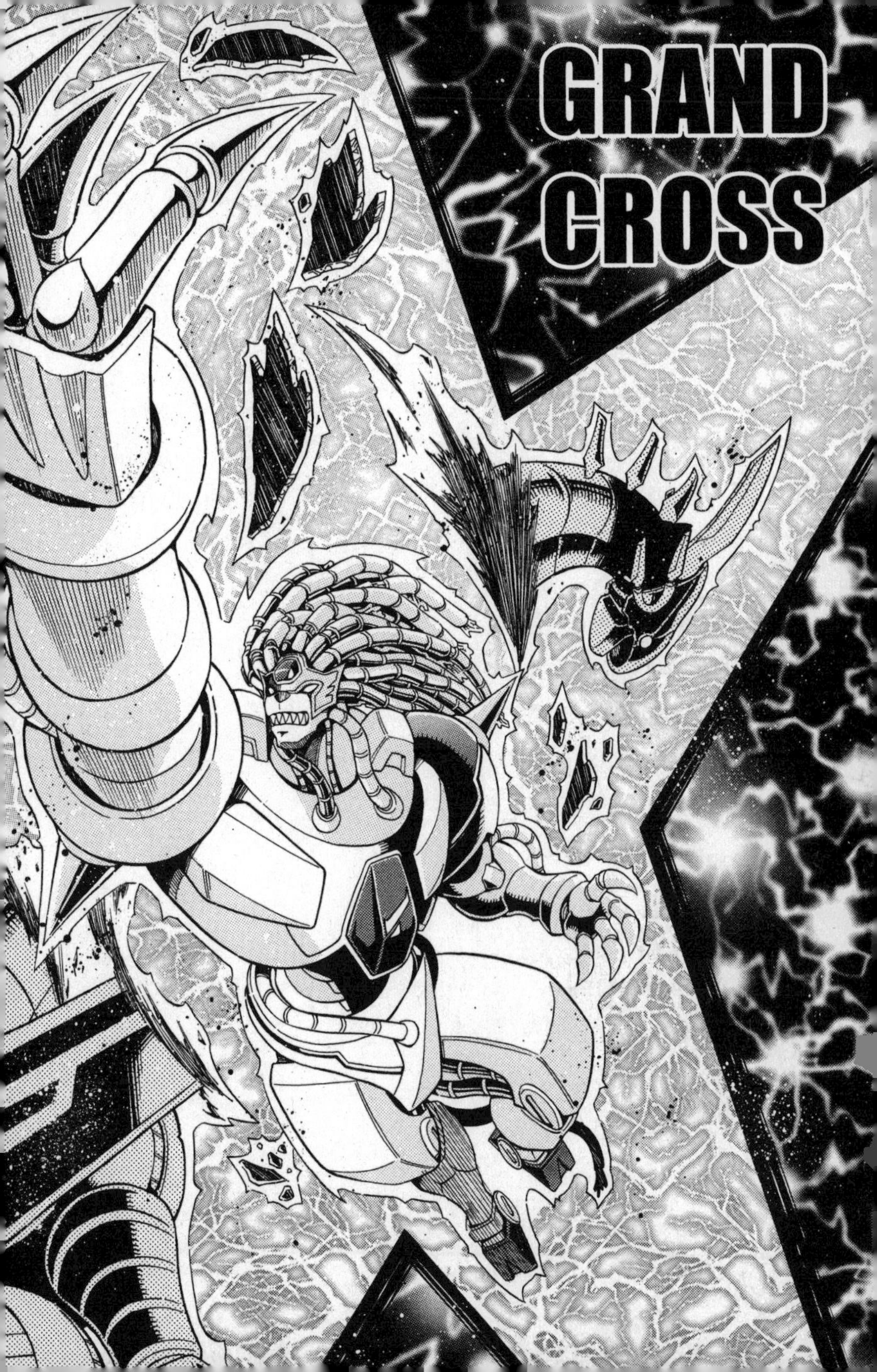
GRAND
CROSS

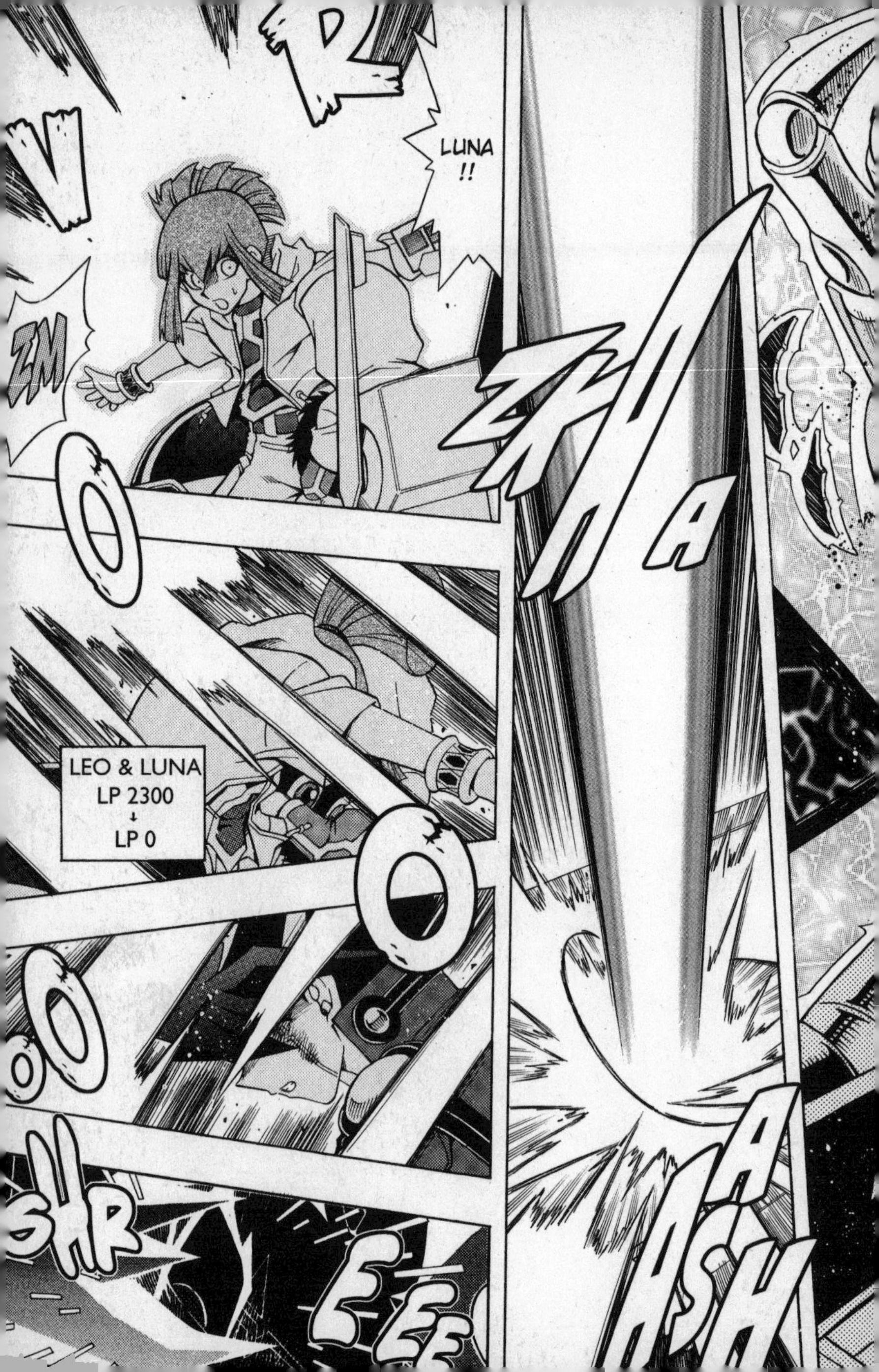
LUNA !!
LEO & LUNA
LP 2300
↓
LP 0

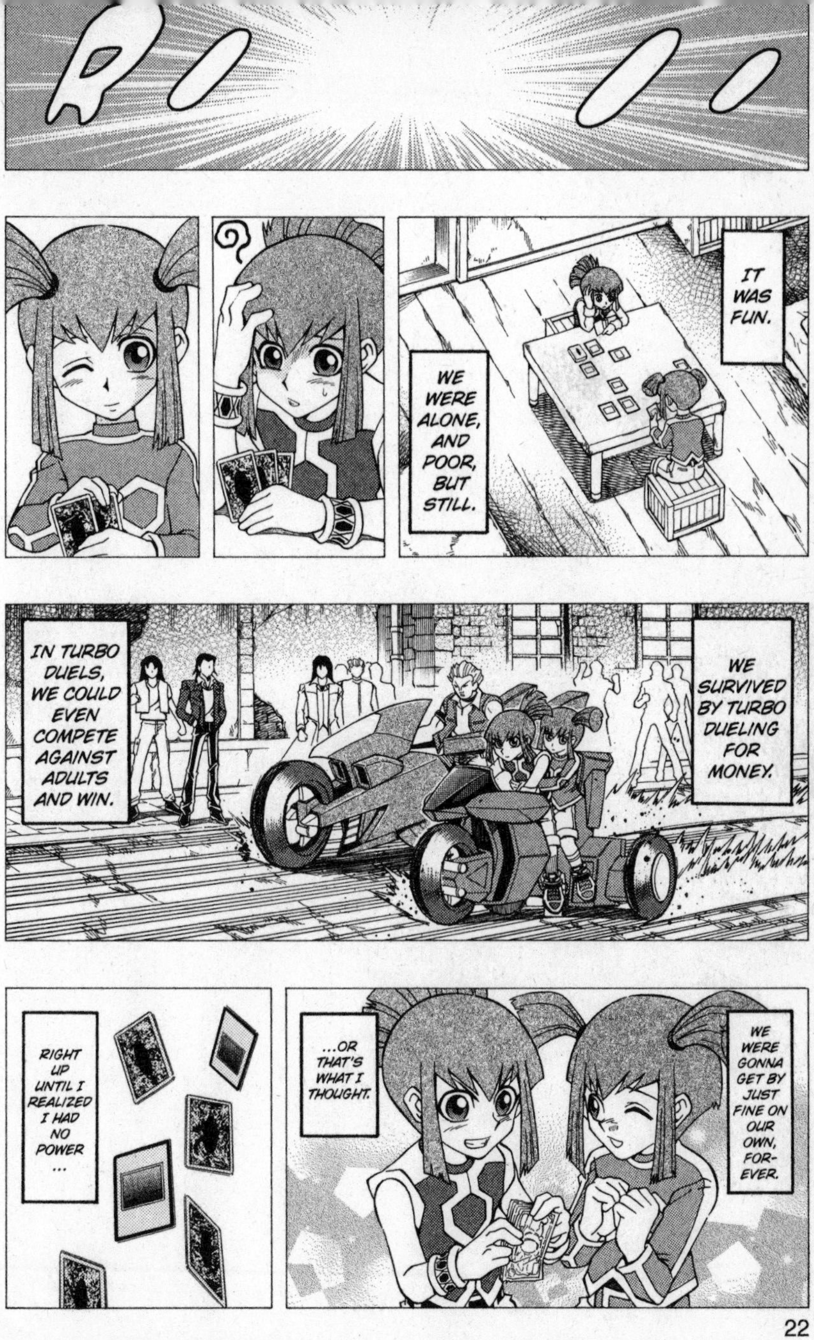

IT WAS FUN.
WE WERE ALONE, AND POOR, BUT STILL.
WE SURVIVED BY TURBO DUELING FOR MONEY.
IN TURBO DUELS, WE COULD EVEN COMPETE AGAINST ADULTS AND WIN.
WE WERE GONNA GET BY JUST FINE ON OUR OWN, FOR-EVER.
...OR THAT'S WHAT I THOUGHT.
RIGHT UP UNTIL I REALIZED I HAD NO POWER ...

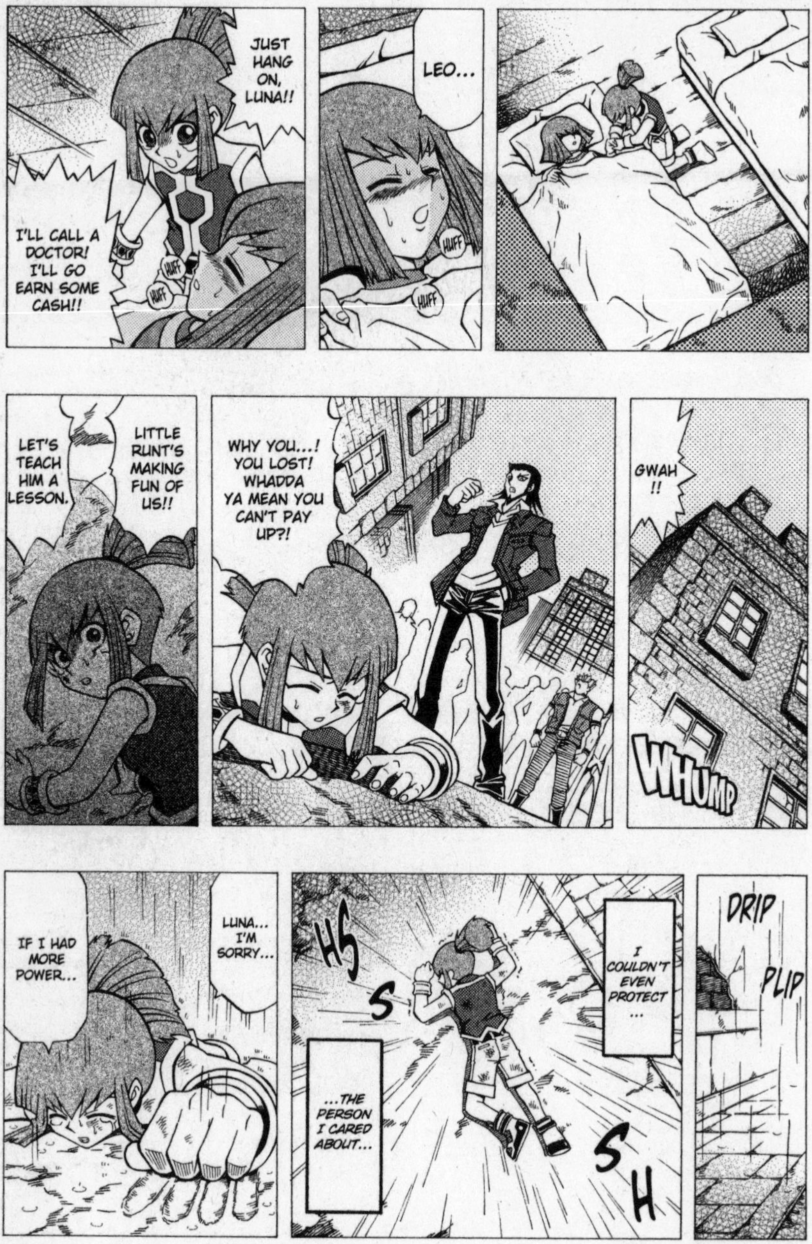
LEO...
HUFF
HUFF
JUST HANG ON, LUNA!!
I'LL CALL A DOCTOR! I'LL GO EARN SOME CASH!!
HUFF
HUFF
GWAH!!
WHUMP
WHY YOU...! YOU LOST! WHADDA YA MEAN YOU CAN'T PAY UP?!
LITTLE RUNT'S MAKING FUN OF US!!
LET'S TEACH HIM A LESSON.
DRIP
PLIP
I COULDN'T EVEN PROTECT...
...THE PERSON I CARED ABOUT...
HS
S
S
H
LUNA... I'M SORRY...
IF I HAD MORE POWER...

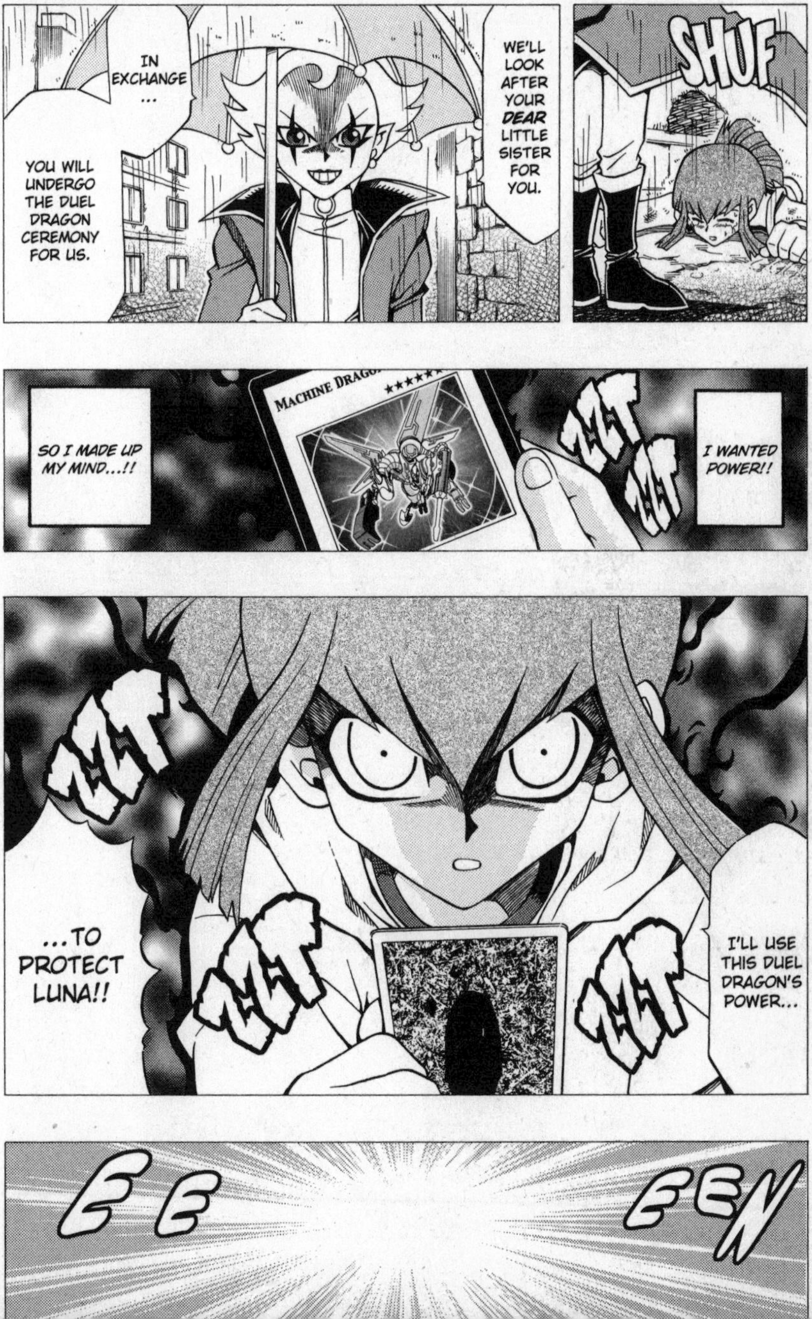
SHUF
WE'LL LOOK AFTER YOUR DEAR LITTLE SISTER FOR YOU.
IN EXCHANGE...
YOU WILL UNDERGO THE DUEL DRAGON CEREMONY FOR US.
I WANTED POWER!!
ZZT ZZT
MACHINE DRAGO
SO I MADE UP MY MIND...!!
I'LL USE THIS DUEL DRAGON'S POWER...
ZZT
ZZT
ZZT
...TO PROTECT LUNA!!
E E EEEN

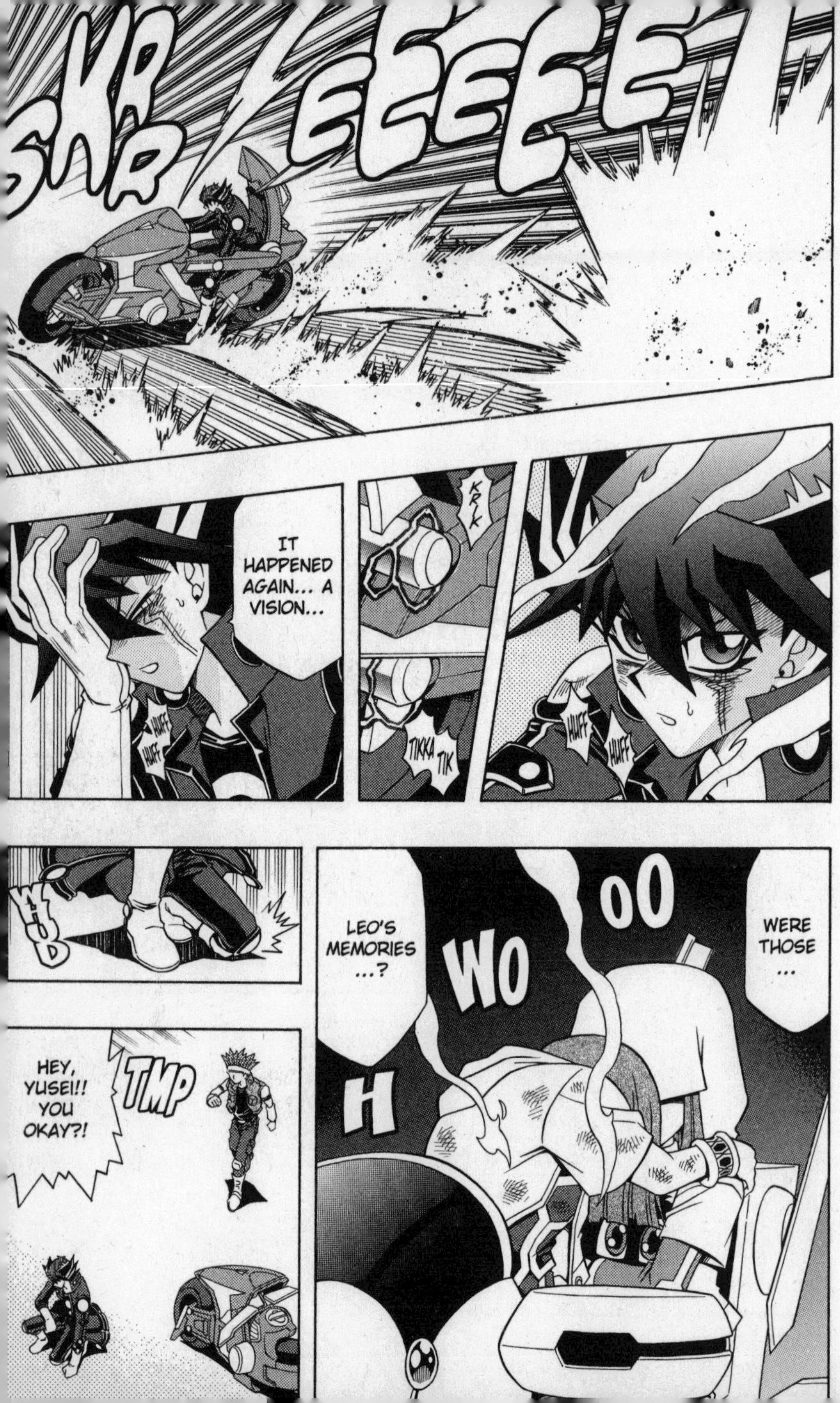
SKR SKR
EEEEEE
HUFF HUFF
KRIK
TIKKA TIK
IT HAPPENED AGAIN... A VISION...
HUFF HUFF
WERE THOSE...
WOOO H
LEO'S MEMORIES...?
WOB
HEY, YUSEI!! YOU OKAY?!
TMP

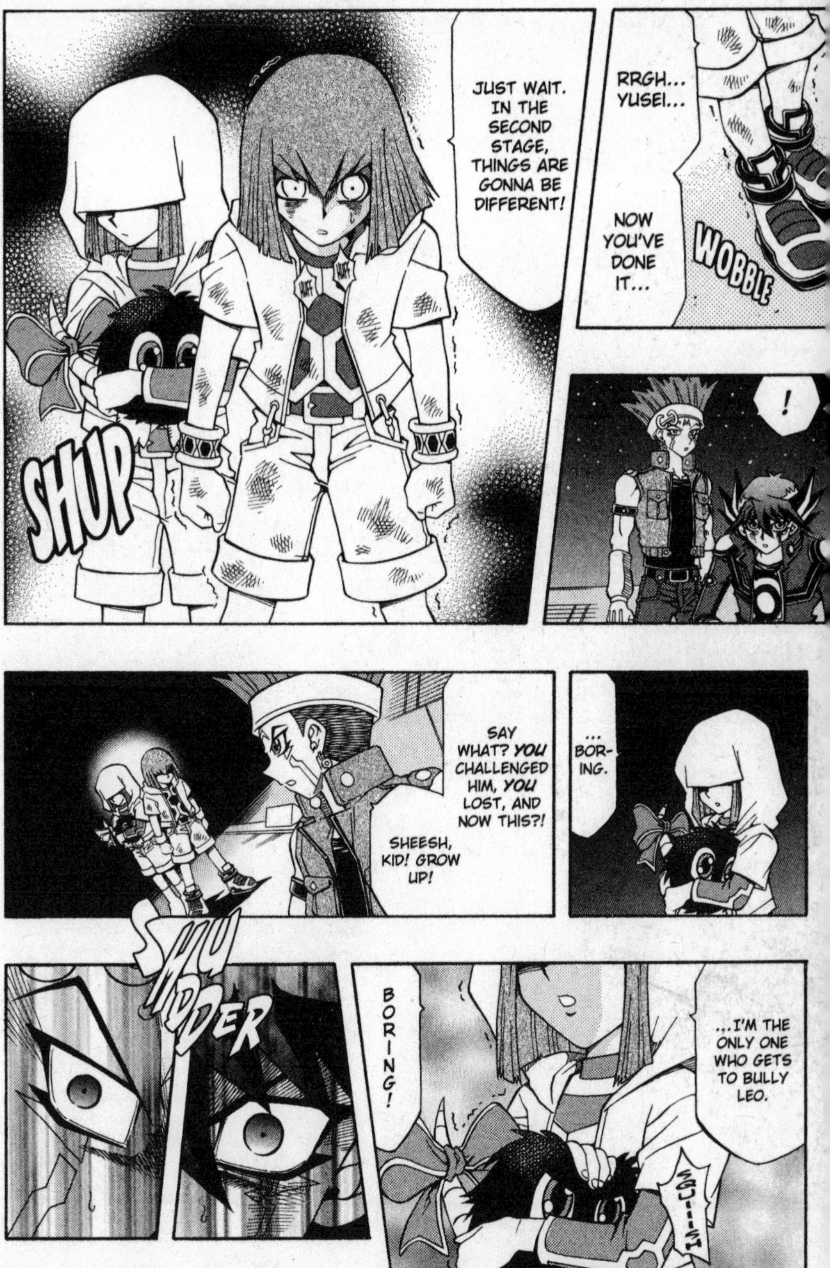
RRGH... YUSEI...
NOW YOU'VE DONE IT...
WOBBLE
!
JUST WAIT. IN THE SECOND STAGE, THINGS ARE GONNA BE DIFFERENT!
HUFF
HUFF
SHUP
...BOR-ING.
SAY WHAT? *YOU* CHALLENGED HIM, *YOU* LOST, AND NOW THIS?!
SHEESH, KID! GROW UP!
...I'M THE ONLY ONE WHO GETS TO BULLY LEO.
BORING!
SQUIISH
SHUDDER

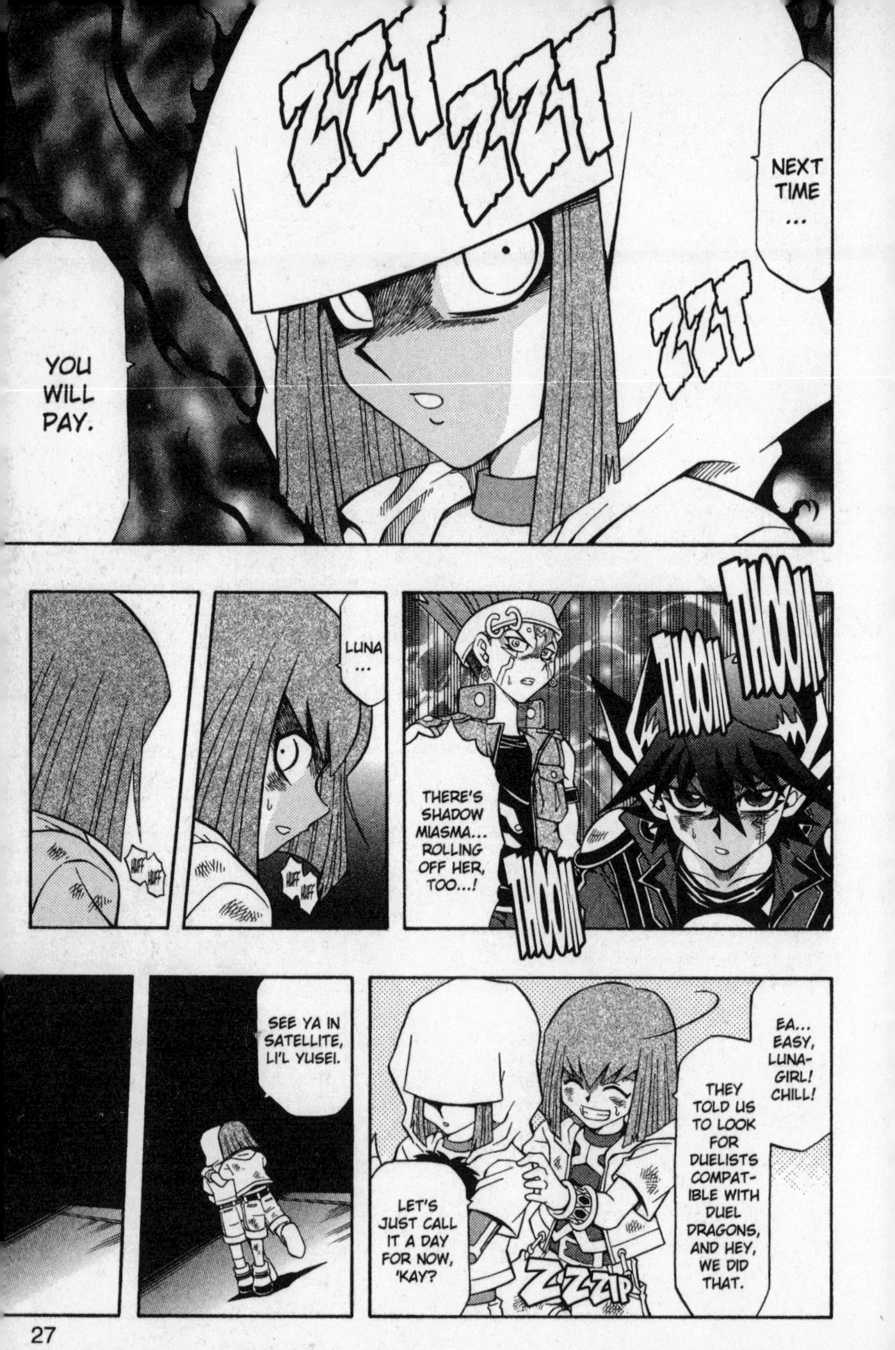
ZZZT ZZZT
NEXT TIME ...
ZZZT
YOU WILL PAY.
THOOM THOOM
THOOM
THERE'S SHADOW MIASMA... ROLLING OFF HER, TOO...!
THOOM
LUNA ...
HUFF HUFF
HUFF HUFF
EA... EASY, LUNA-GIRL! CHILL!
THEY TOLD US TO LOOK FOR DUELISTS COMPATIBLE WITH DUEL DRAGONS, AND HEY, WE DID THAT.
LET'S JUST CALL IT A DAY FOR NOW, 'KAY?
Z-Z-ZZIP
SEE YA IN SATELLITE, LI'L YUSEI.

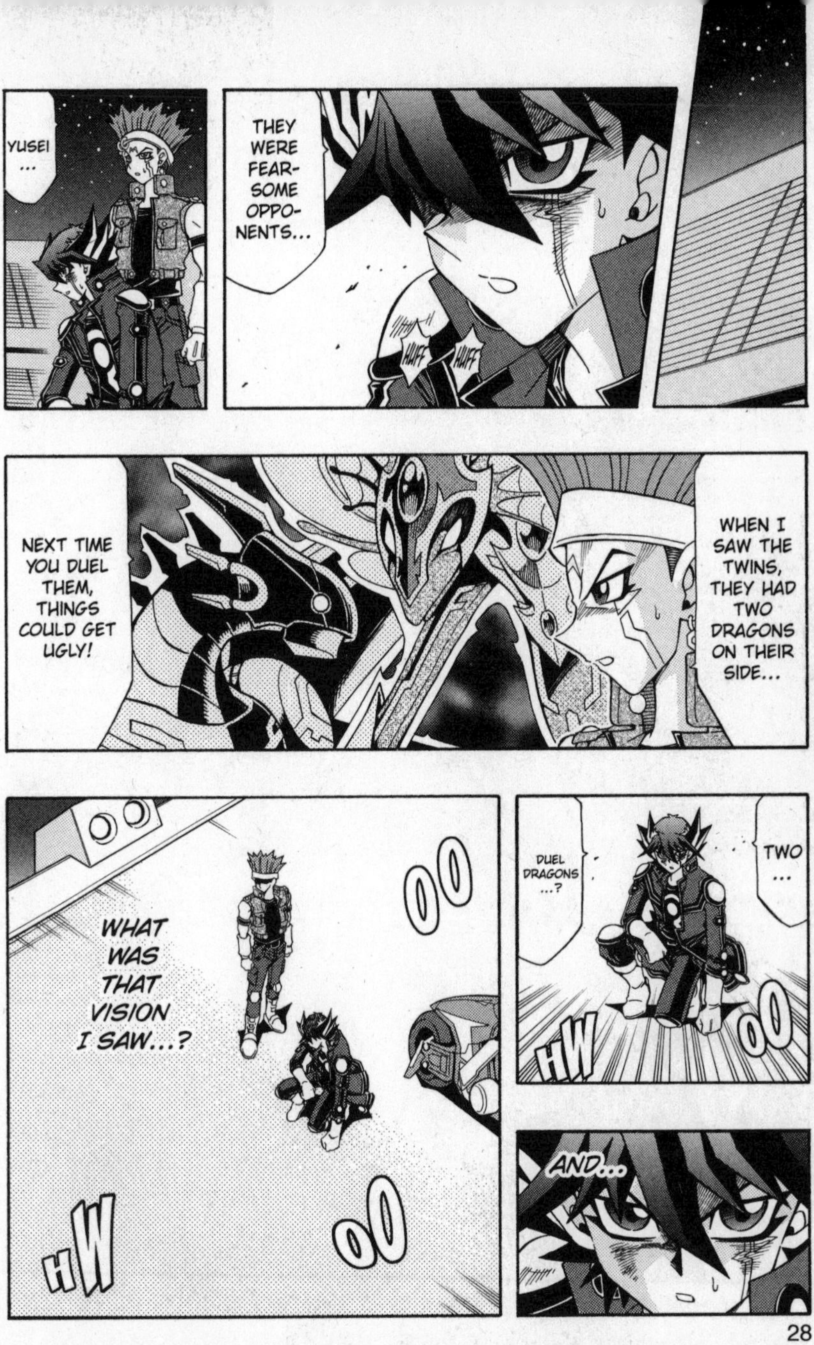
THEY WERE FEAR-SOME OPPO-NENTS...
HUFF HUFF
YUSEI ...
WHEN I SAW THE TWINS, THEY HAD TWO DRAGONS ON THEIR SIDE...
NEXT TIME YOU DUEL THEM, THINGS COULD GET UGLY!
TWO ...
DUEL DRAGONS ...?
HWOO
AND...
WHAT WAS THAT VISION I SAW...?
HWOO

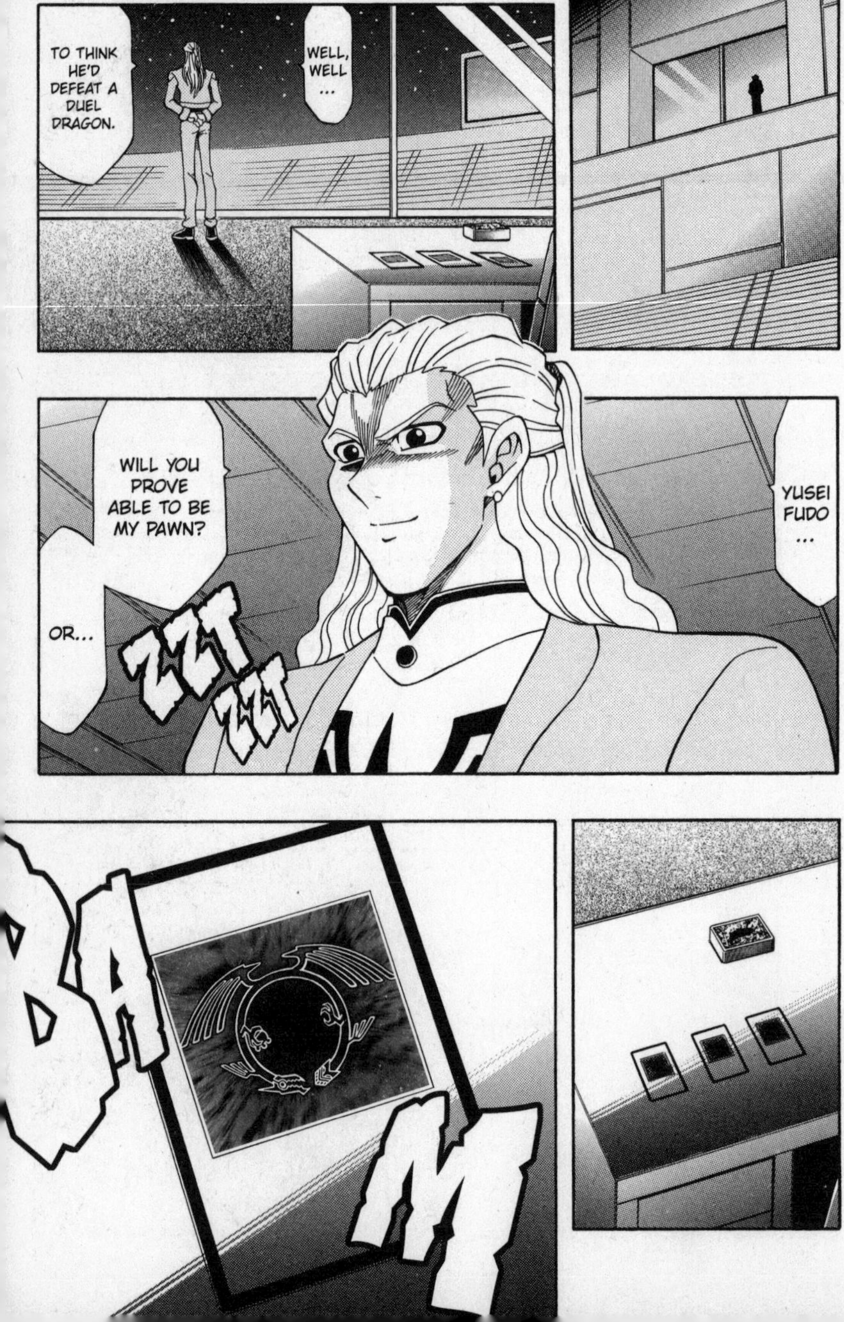
WELL, WELL ...
TO THINK HE'D DEFEAT A DUEL DRAGON.
YUSEI FUDO ...
WILL YOU PROVE ABLE TO BE MY PAWN?
OR...
ZZT ZZT
BAM

5D's TRACKS

THE 25TH

BY SATOMASA

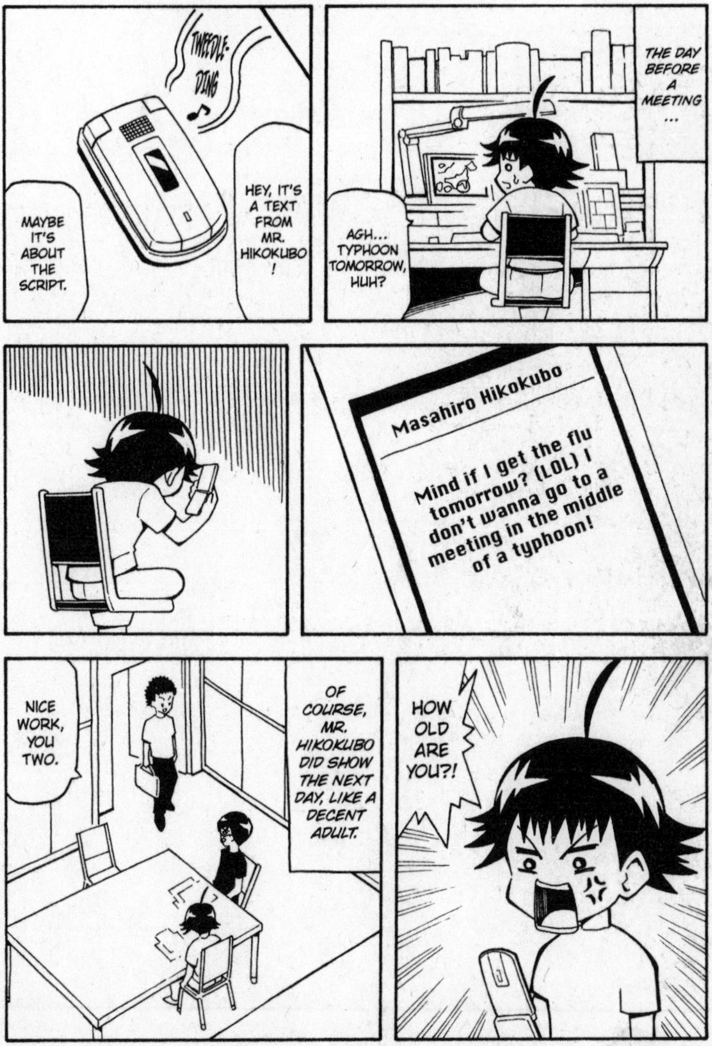
THE DAY BEFORE A MEETING ...
AGH... TYPHOON TOMORROW, HUH?
TWEEDLE-DING
HEY, IT'S A TEXT FROM MR. HIKOKUBO!
MAYBE IT'S ABOUT THE SCRIPT.
Masahiro Hikokubo
Mind if I get the flu tomorrow? (LOL) I don't wanna go to a meeting in the middle of a typhoon!
HOW OLD ARE YOU?!
OF COURSE, MR. HIKOKUBO DID SHOW THE NEXT DAY, LIKE A DECENT ADULT.
NICE WORK, YOU TWO.

RIDE-26

PREMONITION OF A FIERCE FIGHT...!!

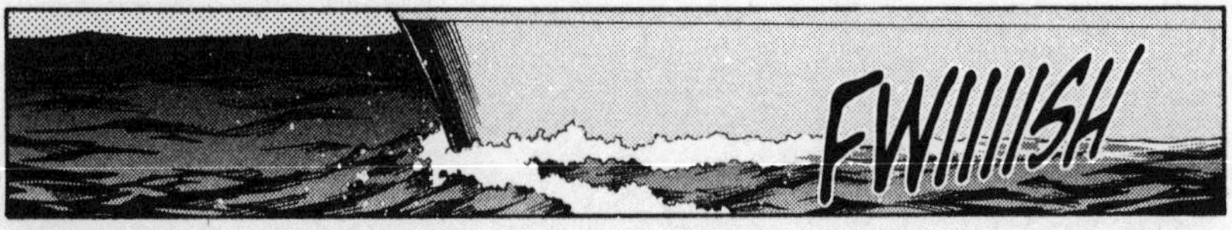
FWIIIISH

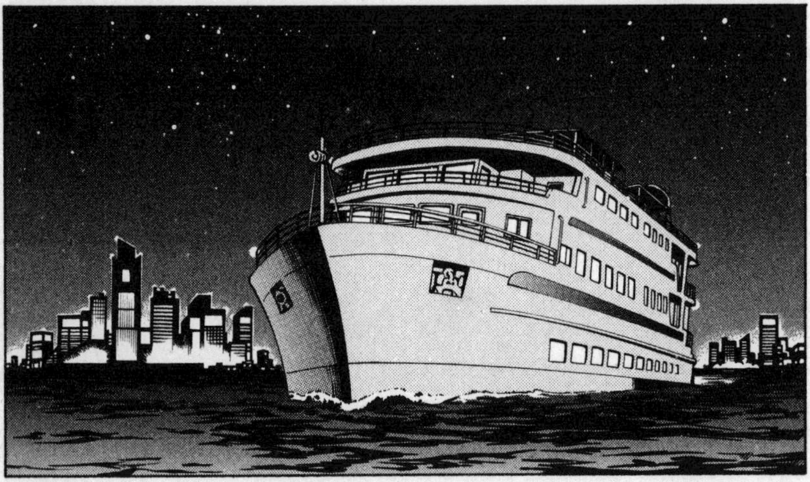

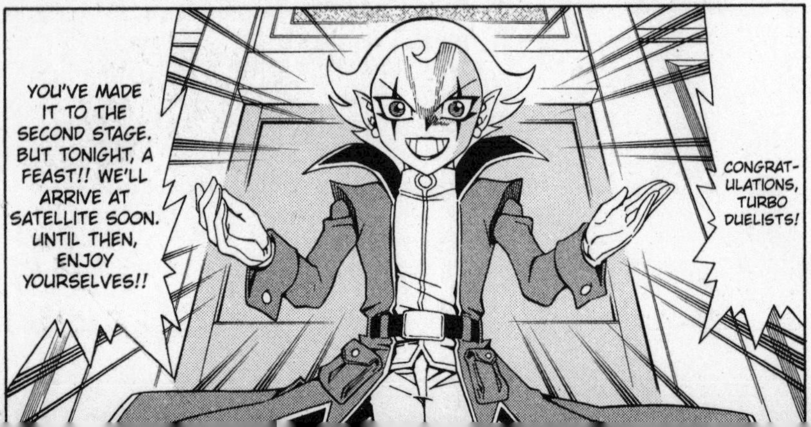
CONGRAT-
ULATIONS,
TURBO
DUELISTS!
YOU'VE MADE IT TO THE SECOND STAGE. BUT TONIGHT, A FEAST!! WE'LL ARRIVE AT SATELLITE SOON. UNTIL THEN, ENJOY YOURSELVES!!

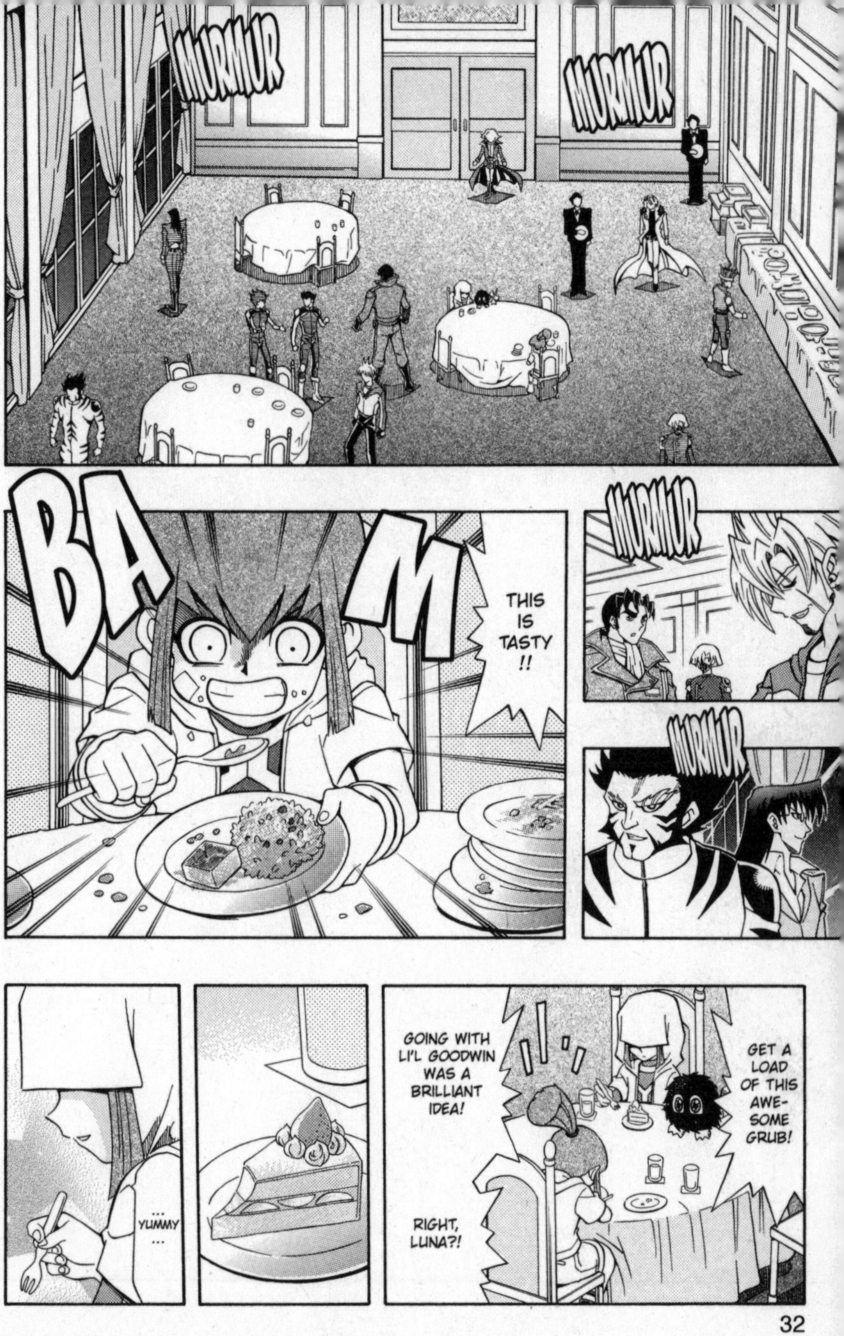
MURMUR
MURMUR
MURMUR
MURMUR
BAM
THIS IS TASTY!!
GET A LOAD OF THIS AWE-SOME GRUB!
GOING WITH LI'L GOODWIN WAS A BRILLIANT IDEA!
RIGHT, LUNA?!
...YUMMY...

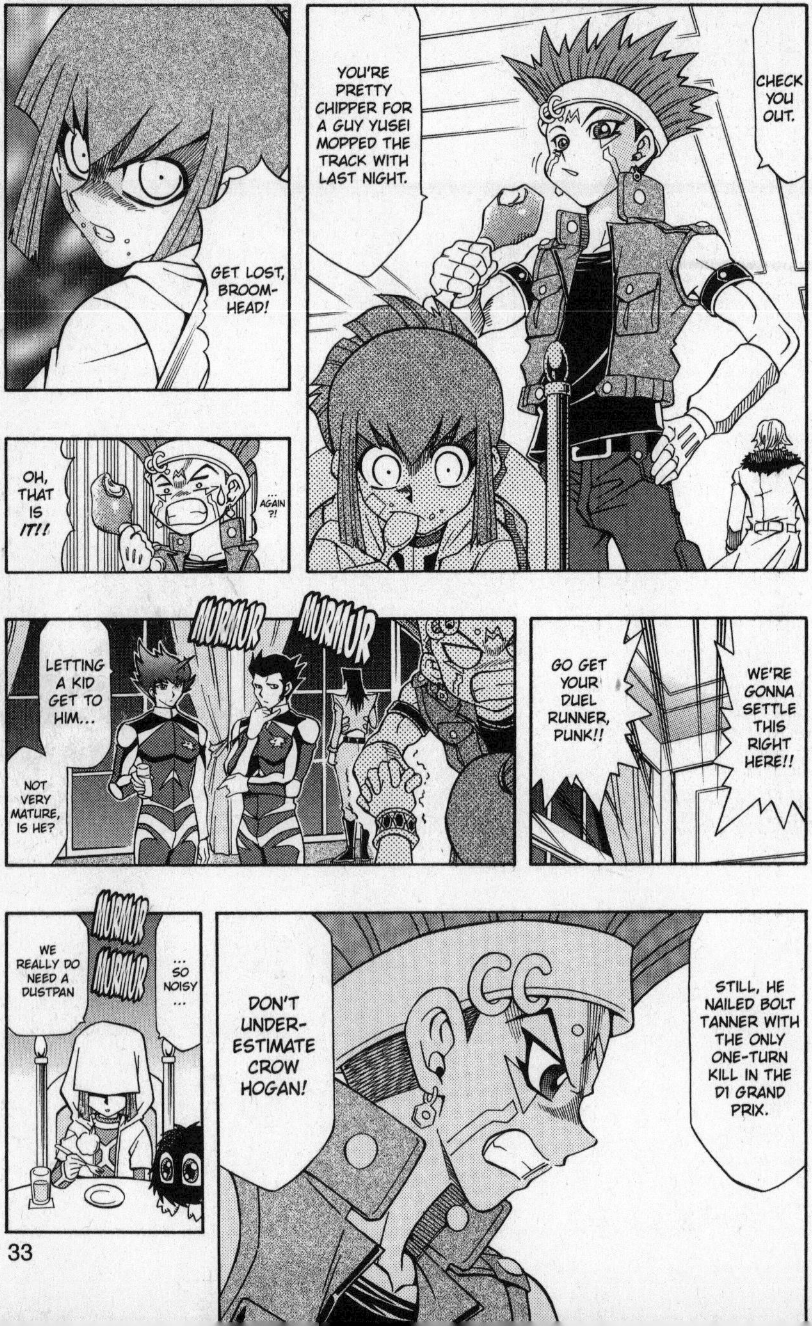
CHECK YOU OUT.
YOU'RE PRETTY CHIPPER FOR A GUY YUSEI MOPPED THE TRACK WITH LAST NIGHT.
GET LOST, BROOM-HEAD!
OH, THAT IS *IT!!*
...AGAIN?!
WE'RE GONNA SETTLE THIS RIGHT HERE!!
GO GET YOUR DUEL RUNNER, PUNK!!
MURMUR
MURMUR
LETTING A KID GET TO HIM...
NOT VERY MATURE, IS HE?
STILL, HE NAILED BOLT TANNER WITH THE ONLY ONE-TURN KILL IN THE D1 GRAND PRIX.
DON'T UNDER-ESTIMATE CROW HOGAN!
MURMUR
MURMUR
...SO NOISY...
WE REALLY DO NEED A DUSTPAN

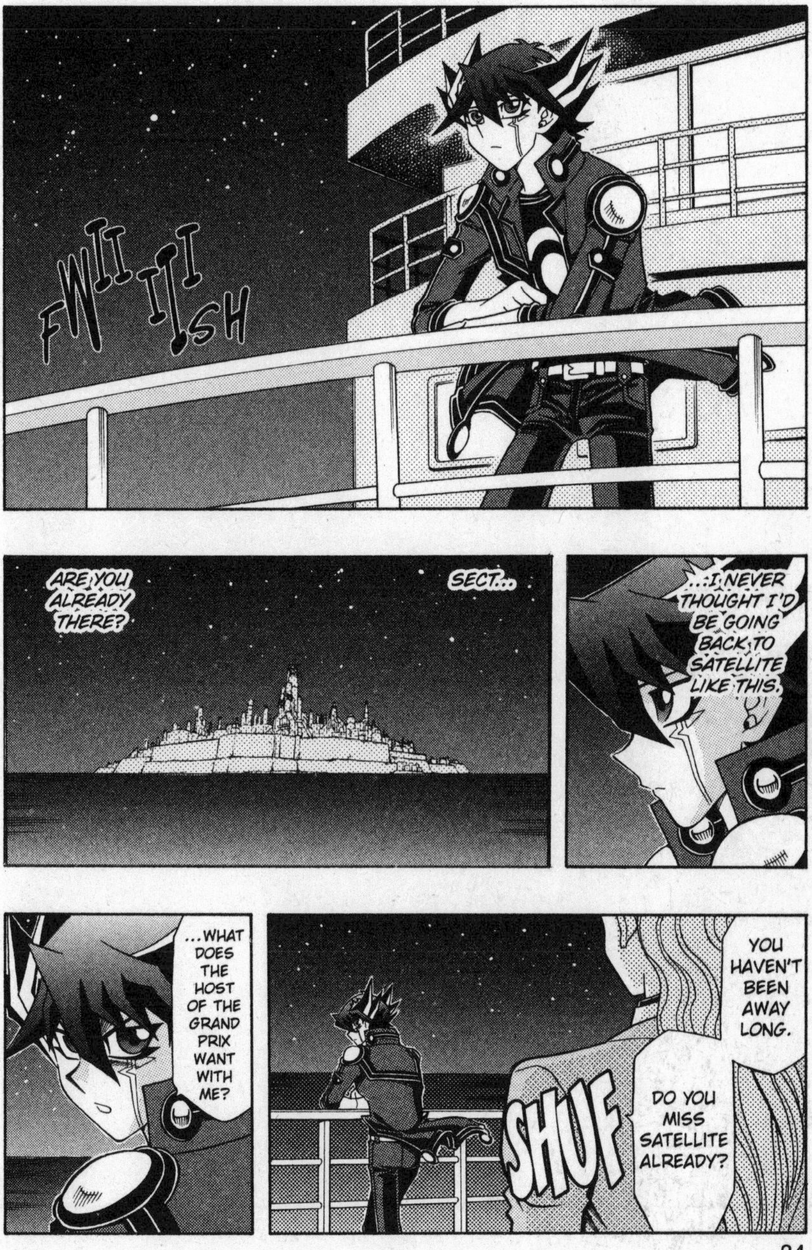
FWIIIISH
...I NEVER THOUGHT I'D BE GOING BACK TO SATELLITE LIKE THIS.
SECT...
ARE YOU ALREADY THERE?
YOU HAVEN'T BEEN AWAY LONG.
SHUF
DO YOU MISS SATELLITE ALREADY?
...WHAT DOES THE HOST OF THE GRAND PRIX WANT WITH ME?

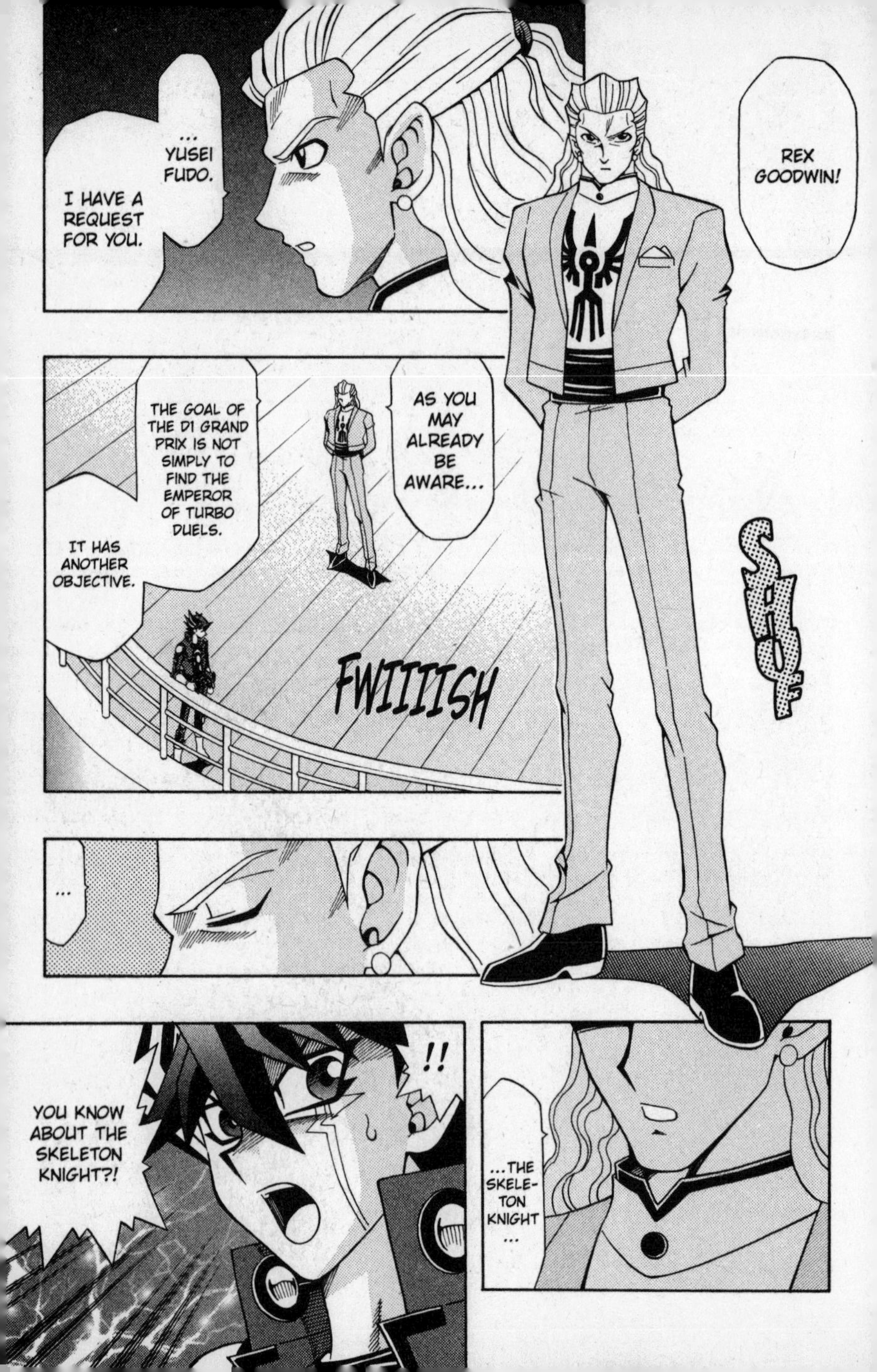
REX GOODWIN!
...YUSEI FUDO.
I HAVE A REQUEST FOR YOU.
AS YOU MAY ALREADY BE AWARE...
THE GOAL OF THE D1 GRAND PRIX IS NOT SIMPLY TO FIND THE EMPEROR OF TURBO DUELS.
IT HAS ANOTHER OBJECTIVE.
FWIIIISH
...
...THE SKELE-TON KNIGHT ...
!!
YOU KNOW ABOUT THE SKELETON KNIGHT?!

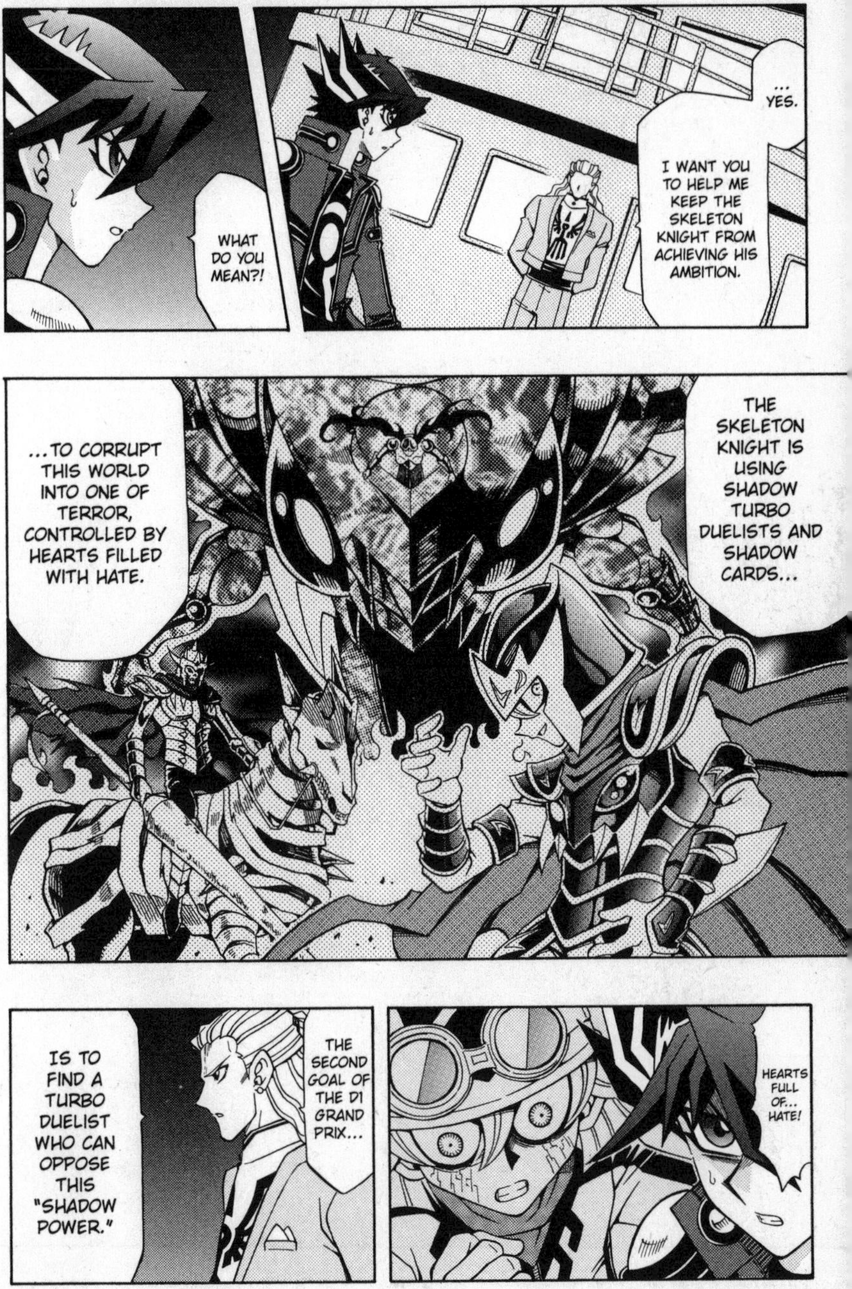
... YES.
I WANT YOU TO HELP ME KEEP THE SKELETON KNIGHT FROM ACHIEVING HIS AMBITION.
WHAT DO YOU MEAN?!
THE SKELETON KNIGHT IS USING SHADOW TURBO DUELISTS AND SHADOW CARDS...
...TO CORRUPT THIS WORLD INTO ONE OF TERROR, CONTROLLED BY HEARTS FILLED WITH HATE.
HEARTS FULL OF... HATE!
THE SECOND GOAL OF THE D1 GRAND PRIX...
IS TO FIND A TURBO DUELIST WHO CAN OPPOSE THIS "SHADOW POWER."

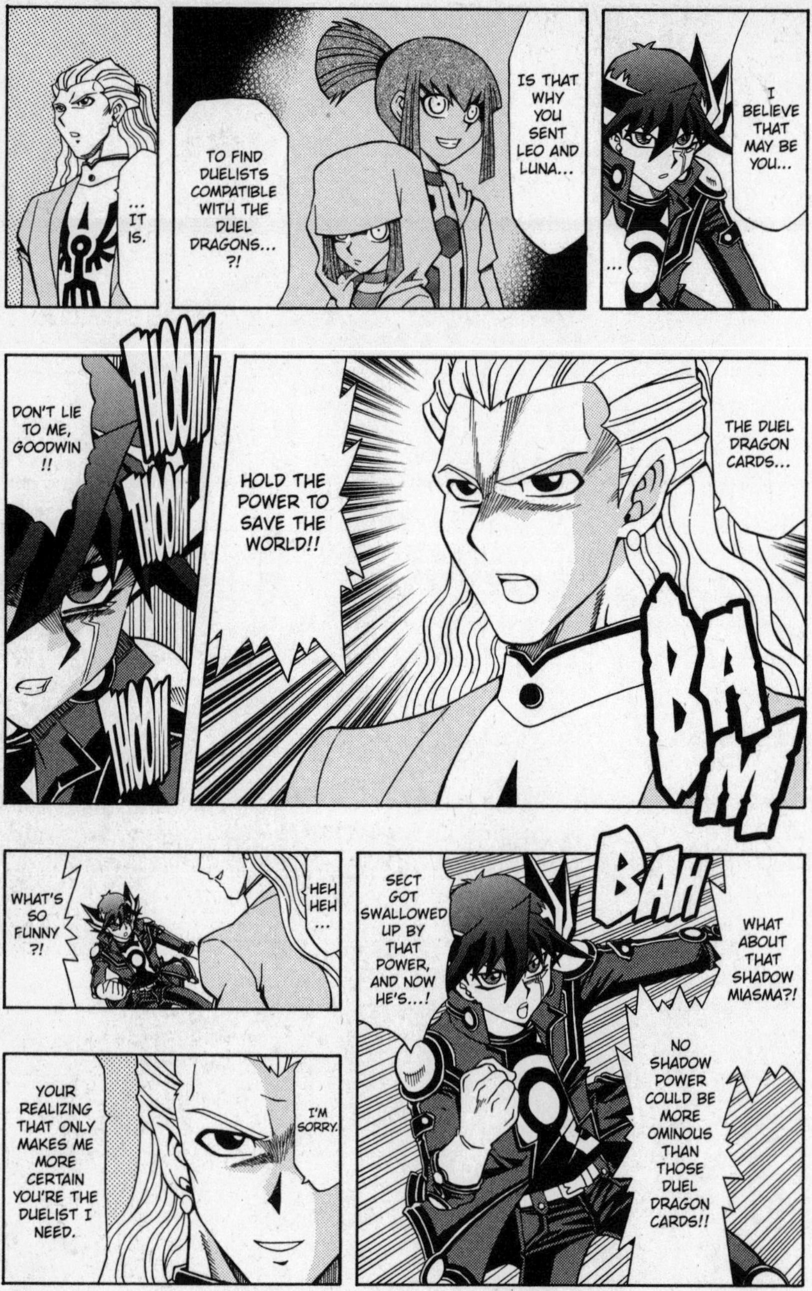
I BELIEVE THAT MAY BE YOU...
...
IS THAT WHY YOU SENT LEO AND LUNA...
TO FIND DUELISTS COMPATIBLE WITH THE DUEL DRAGONS...?!
...IT IS.
THE DUEL DRAGON CARDS...
HOLD THE POWER TO SAVE THE WORLD!!
BAM
DON'T LIE TO ME, GOODWIN!!
THOOM
THOOM
THOOM
BAH
WHAT ABOUT THAT SHADOW MIASMA?!
SECT GOT SWALLOWED UP BY THAT POWER, AND NOW HE'S...!
NO SHADOW POWER COULD BE MORE OMINOUS THAN THOSE DUEL DRAGON CARDS!!
HEH HEH...
WHAT'S SO FUNNY?!
I'M SORRY.
YOUR REALIZING THAT ONLY MAKES ME MORE CERTAIN YOU'RE THE DUELIST I NEED.

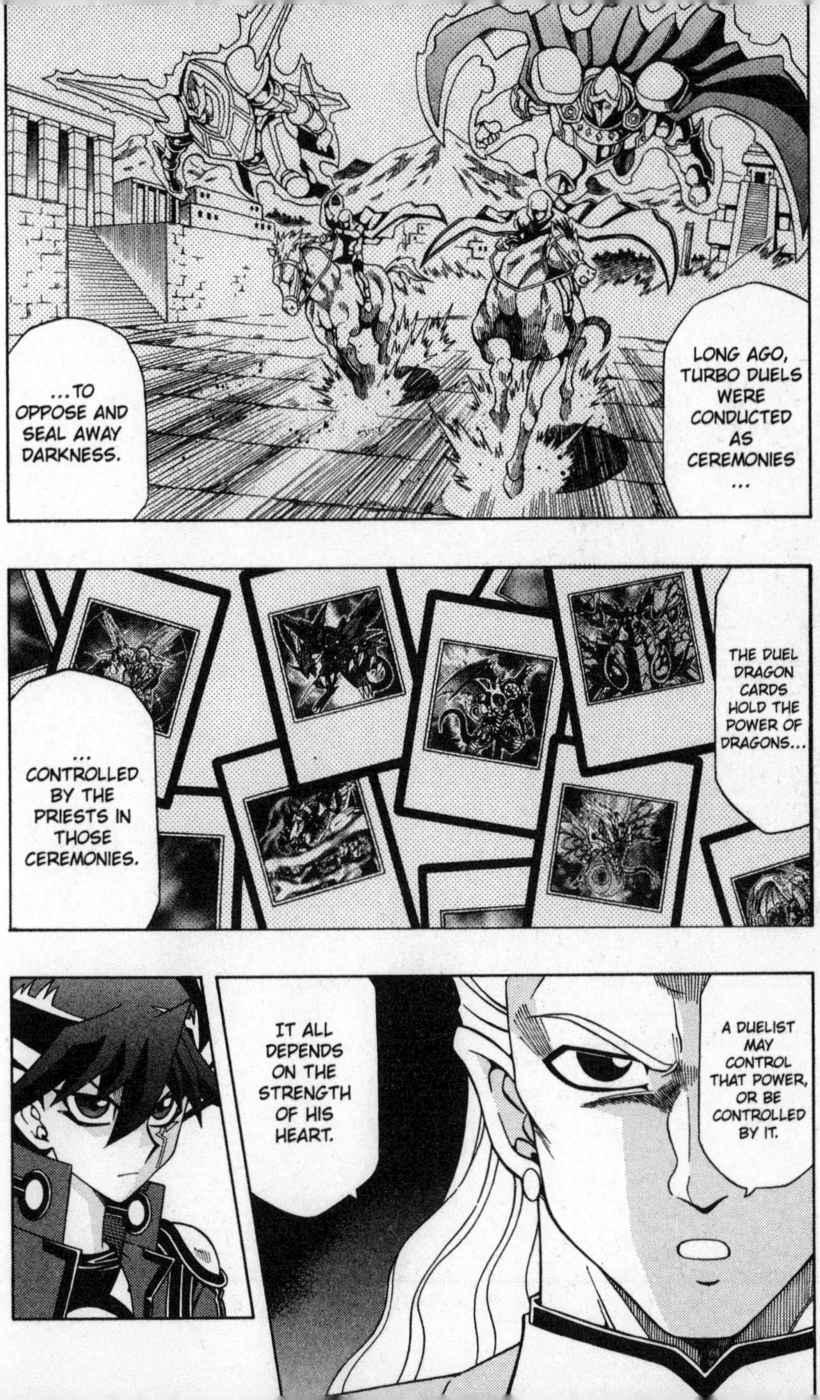
LONG AGO, TURBO DUELS WERE CONDUCTED AS CEREMONIES ...
...TO OPPOSE AND SEAL AWAY DARKNESS.
THE DUEL DRAGON CARDS HOLD THE POWER OF DRAGONS...
... CONTROLLED BY THE PRIESTS IN THOSE CEREMONIES.
A DUELIST MAY CONTROL THAT POWER, OR BE CONTROLLED BY IT.
IT ALL DEPENDS ON THE STRENGTH OF HIS HEART.

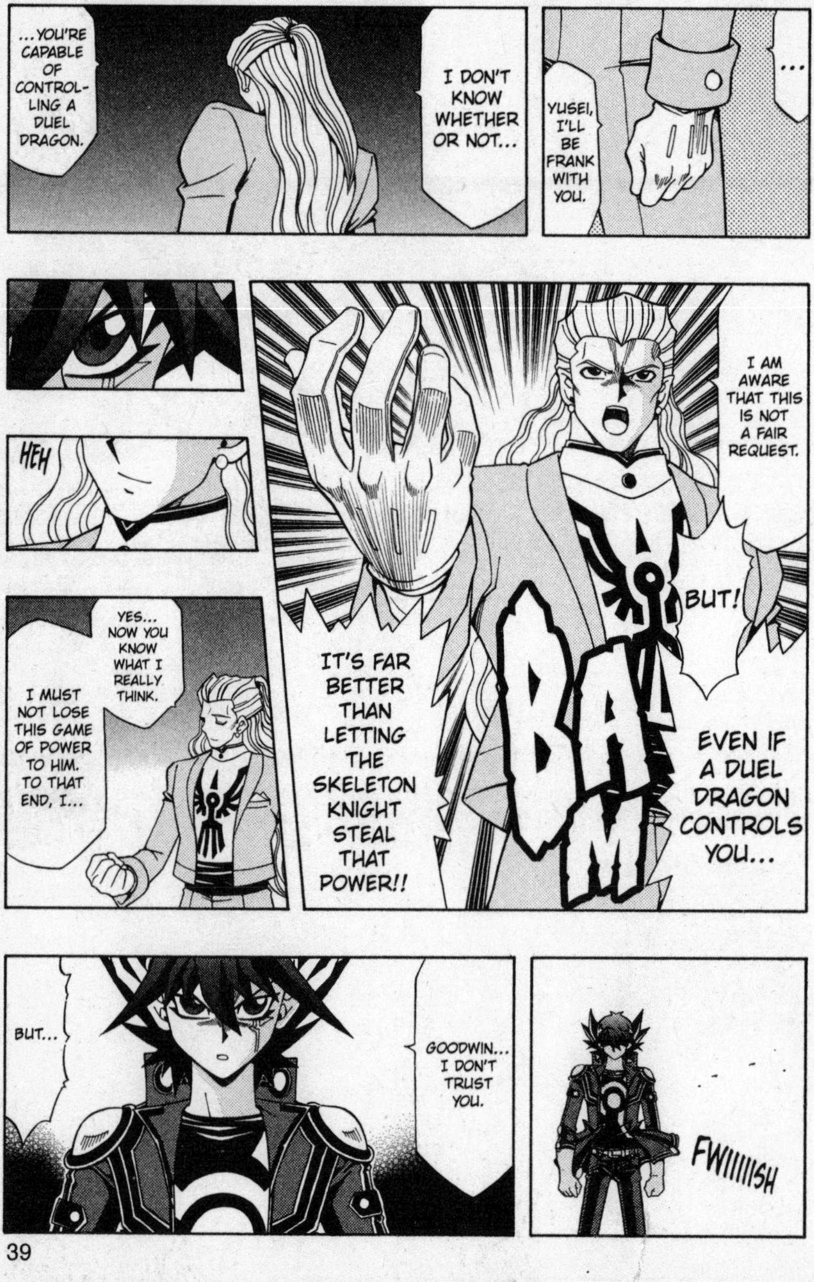
...
YUSEI, I'LL BE FRANK WITH YOU.
I DON'T KNOW WHETHER OR NOT...
...YOU'RE CAPABLE OF CONTROLLING A DUEL DRAGON.
I AM AWARE THAT THIS IS NOT A FAIR REQUEST.
BUT!
BAM
EVEN IF A DUEL DRAGON CONTROLS YOU...
IT'S FAR BETTER THAN LETTING THE SKELETON KNIGHT STEAL THAT POWER!!
HEH
YES... NOW YOU KNOW WHAT I REALLY THINK.
I MUST NOT LOSE THIS GAME OF POWER TO HIM. TO THAT END, I...
FWIIIIISH
GOODWIN... I DON'T TRUST YOU.
BUT...

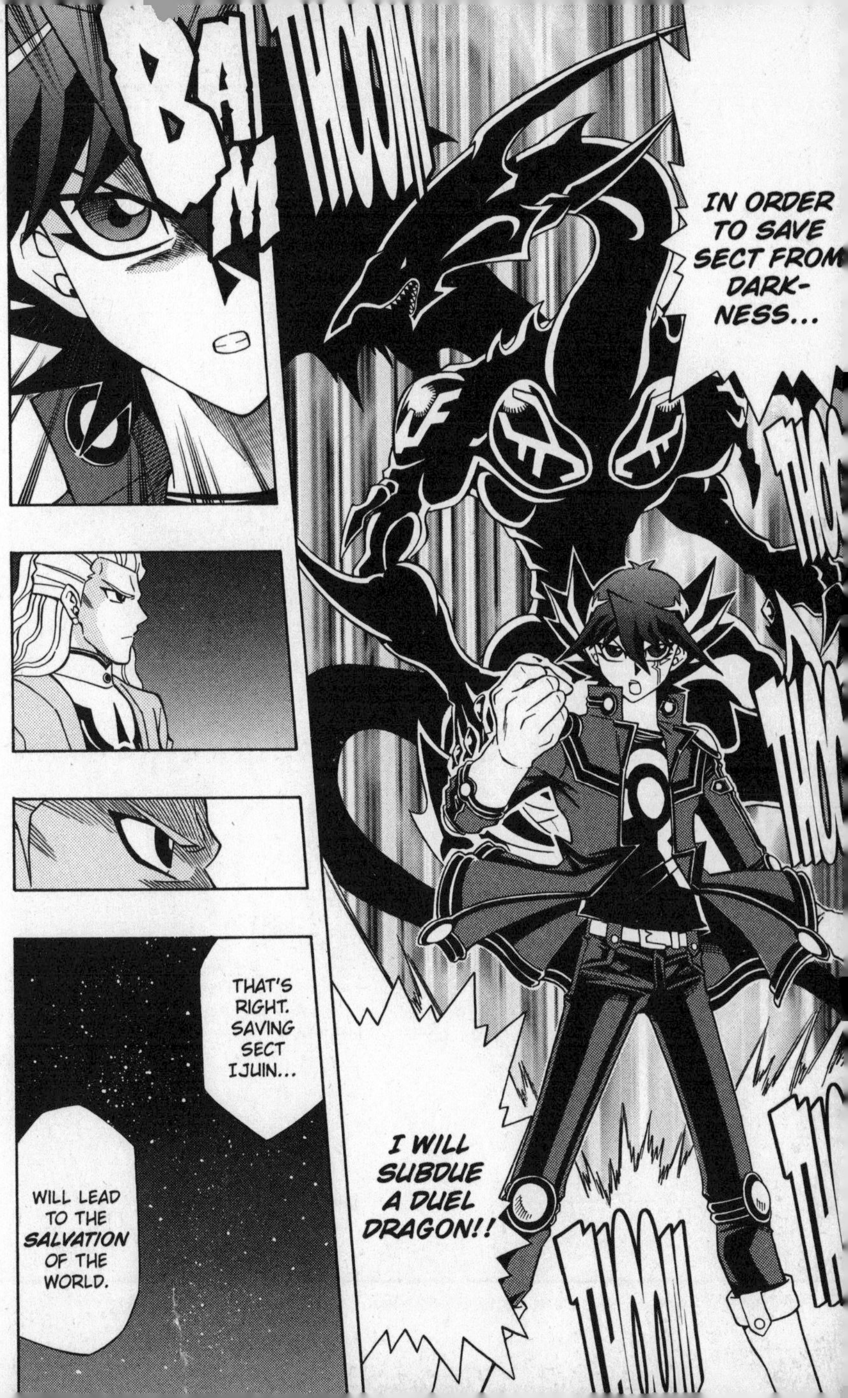
THOOM
IN ORDER TO SAVE SECT FROM DARKNESS...
I WILL SUBDUE A DUEL DRAGON!!
THOOM
BAM
THAT'S RIGHT. SAVING SECT IJUIN...
WILL LEAD TO THE SALVATION OF THE WORLD.

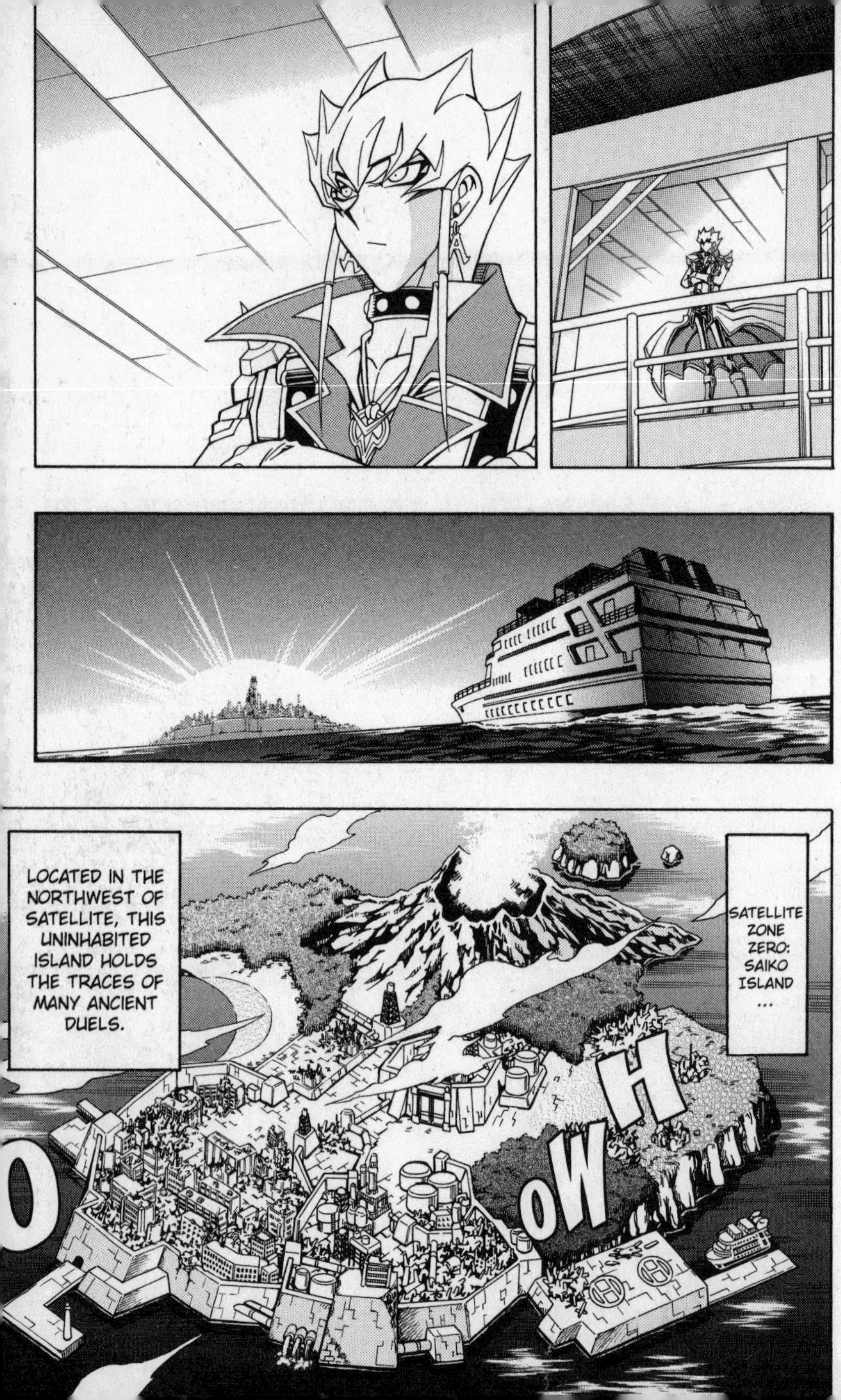
SATELLITE ZONE ZERO: SAIKO ISLAND ...
LOCATED IN THE NORTHWEST OF SATELLITE, THIS UNINHABITED ISLAND HOLDS THE TRACES OF MANY ANCIENT DUELS.
OOWH

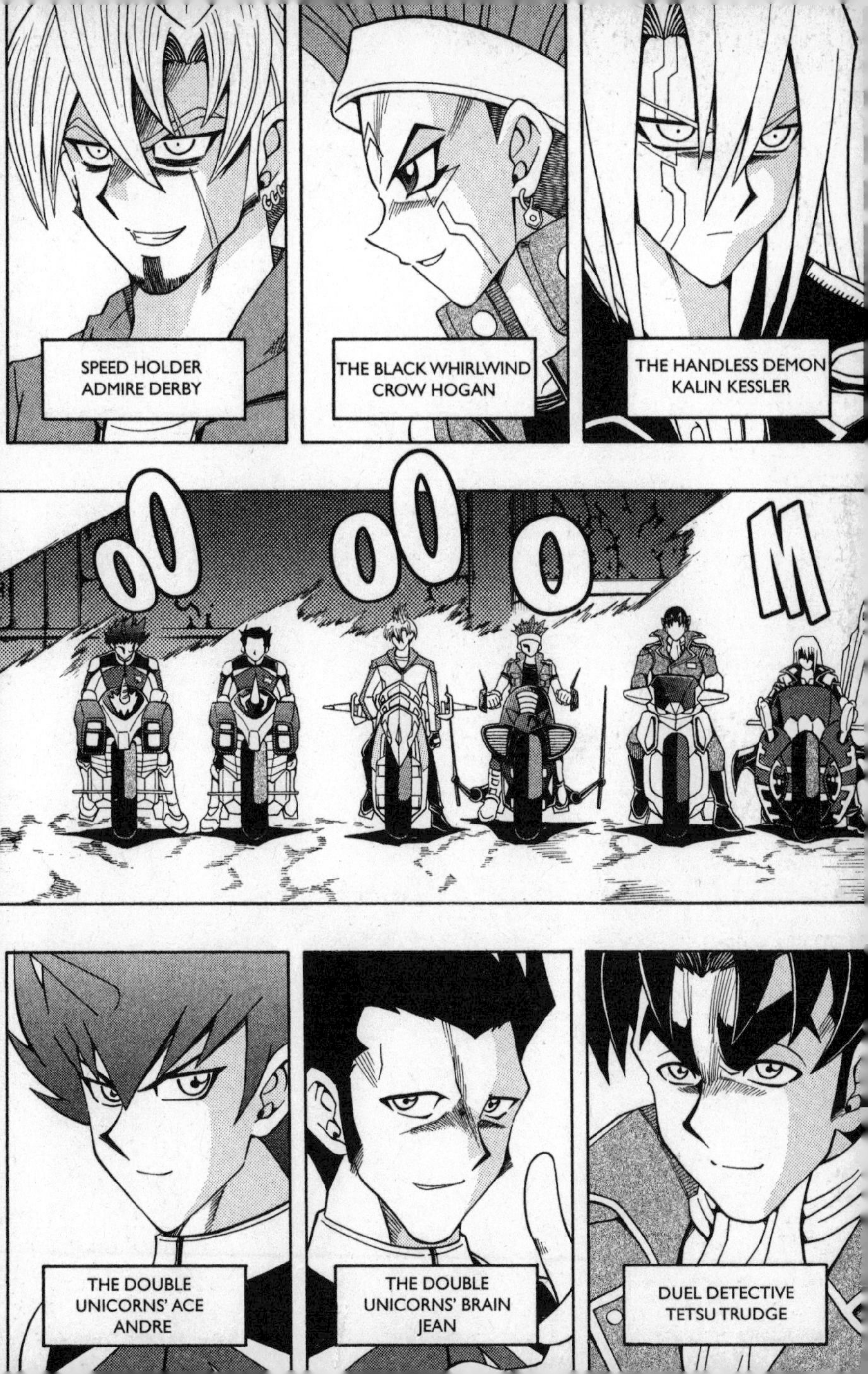
THE HANDLESS DEMON
KALIN KESSLER
THE BLACK WHIRLWIND
CROW HOGAN
SPEED HOLDER
ADMIRE DERBY
OOOOOM
DUEL DETECTIVE
TETSU TRUDGE
THE DOUBLE
UNICORNS' BRAIN
JEAN
THE DOUBLE
UNICORNS' ACE
ANDRE

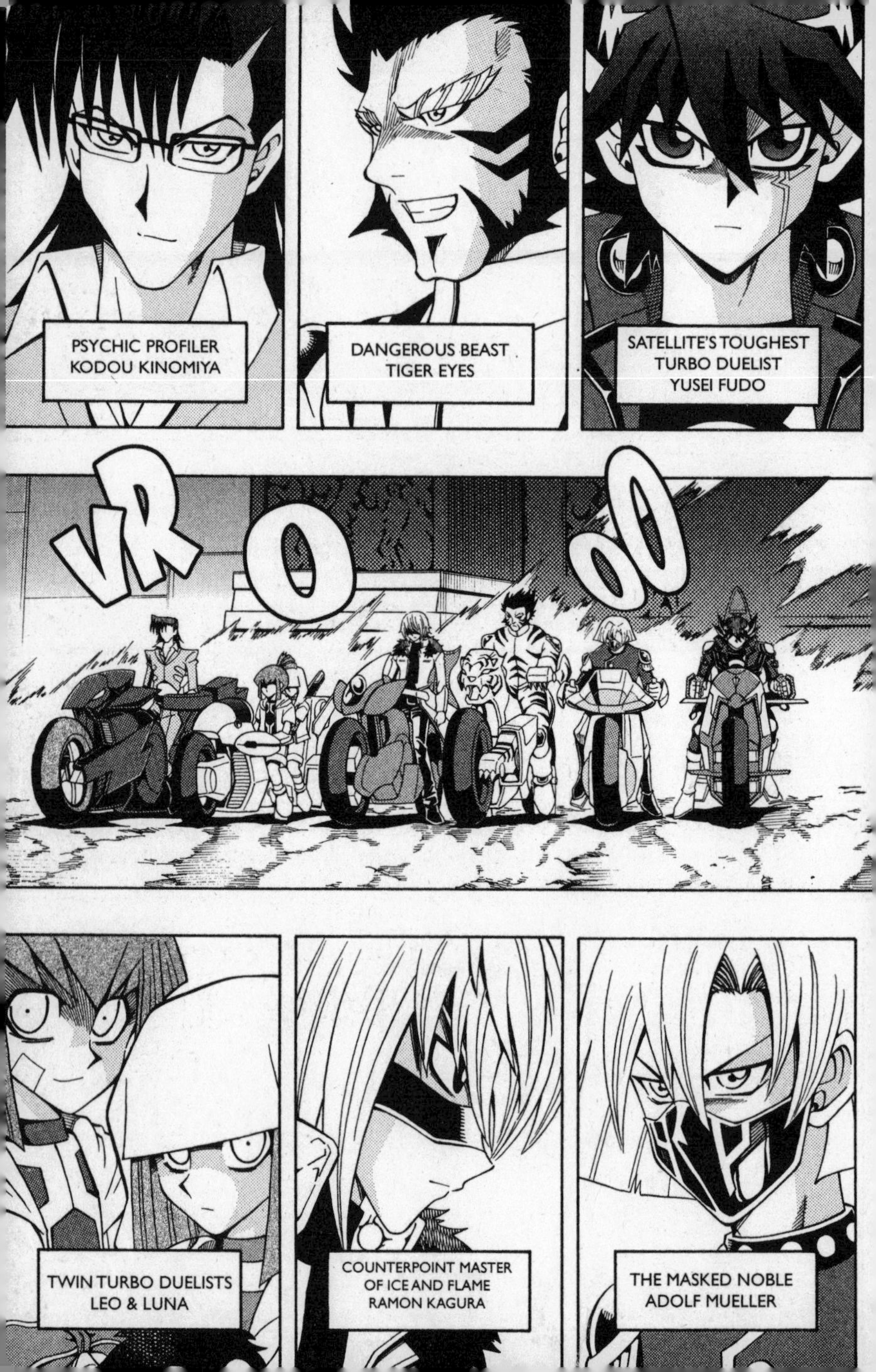
SATELLITE'S TOUGHEST TURBO DUELIST YUSEI FUDO
DANGEROUS BEAST TIGER EYES
PSYCHIC PROFILER KODOU KINOMIYA
VROOO
THE MASKED NOBLE ADOLF MUELLER
COUNTERPOINT MASTER OF ICE AND FLAME RAMON KAGURA
TWIN TURBO DUELISTS LEO & LUNA

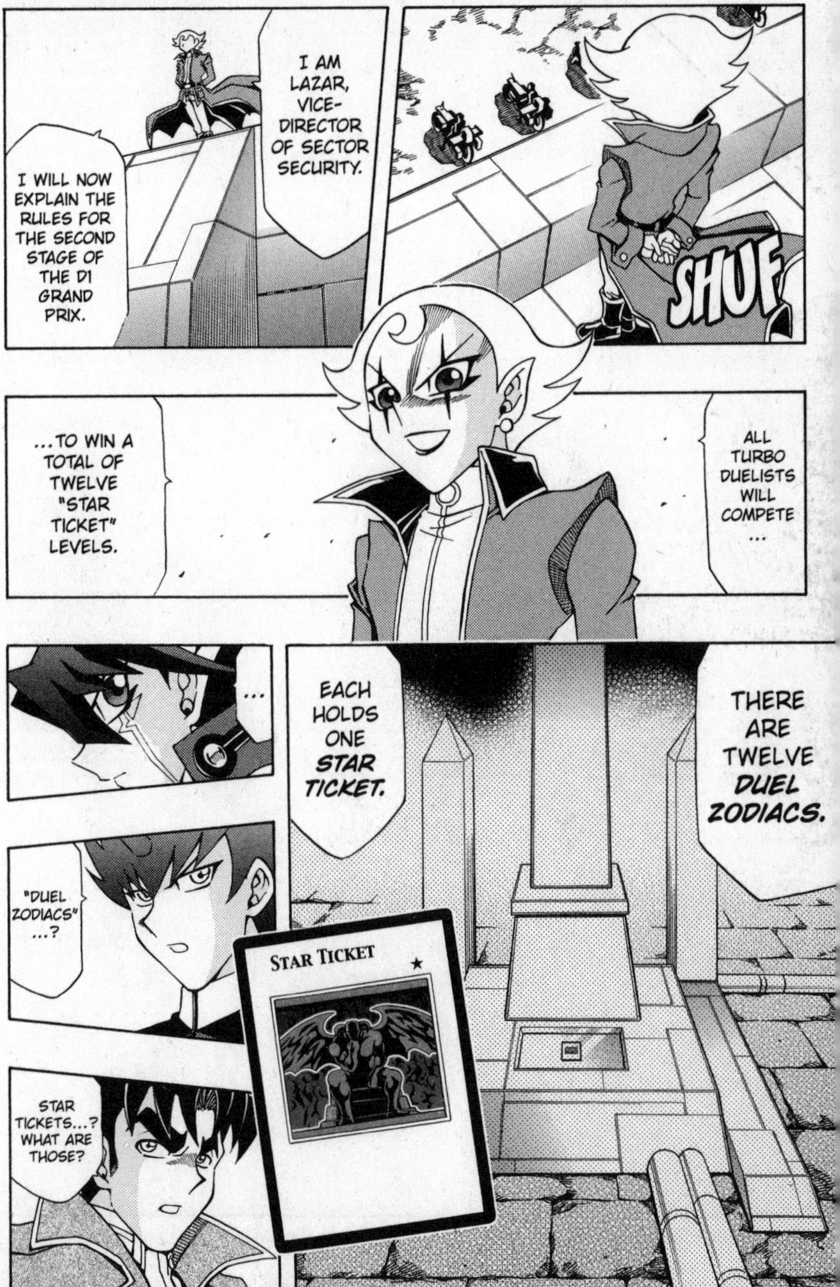
SHUF
I AM LAZAR, VICE-DIRECTOR OF SECTOR SECURITY.
I WILL NOW EXPLAIN THE RULES FOR THE SECOND STAGE OF THE D1 GRAND PRIX.
ALL TURBO DUELISTS WILL COMPETE ...
...TO WIN A TOTAL OF TWELVE "STAR TICKET" LEVELS.
THERE ARE TWELVE *DUEL ZODIACS.*
EACH HOLDS ONE *STAR TICKET.*
STAR TICKET
...
"DUEL ZODIACS" ...?
STAR TICKETS...? WHAT ARE THOSE?

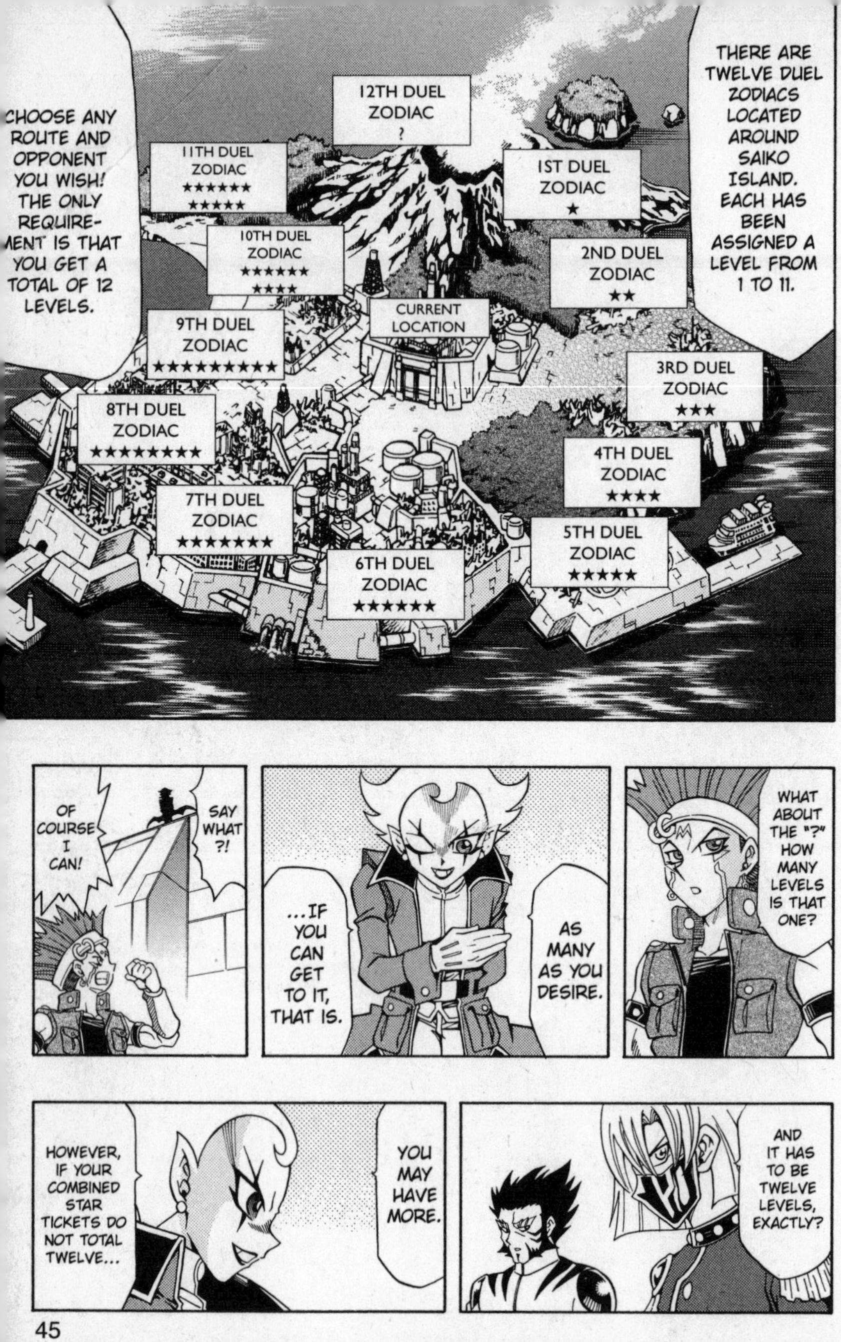
THERE ARE TWELVE DUEL ZODIACS LOCATED AROUND SAIKO ISLAND. EACH HAS BEEN ASSIGNED A LEVEL FROM 1 TO 11.
12TH DUEL ZODIAC ?
1ST DUEL ZODIAC ★
2ND DUEL ZODIAC ★★
3RD DUEL ZODIAC ★★★
4TH DUEL ZODIAC ★★★★
5TH DUEL ZODIAC ★★★★★
6TH DUEL ZODIAC ★★★★★★
7TH DUEL ZODIAC ★★★★★★★
8TH DUEL ZODIAC ★★★★★★★★
9TH DUEL ZODIAC ★★★★★★★★★
10TH DUEL ZODIAC ★★★★★★ ★★★★
11TH DUEL ZODIAC ★★★★★★ ★★★★★
CURRENT LOCATION
CHOOSE ANY ROUTE AND OPPONENT YOU WISH! THE ONLY REQUIRE-MENT IS THAT YOU GET A TOTAL OF 12 LEVELS.
WHAT ABOUT THE "?" HOW MANY LEVELS IS THAT ONE?
AS MANY AS YOU DESIRE.
...IF YOU CAN GET TO IT, THAT IS.
SAY WHAT?!
OF COURSE I CAN!
AND IT HAS TO BE TWELVE LEVELS, EXACTLY?
YOU MAY HAVE MORE.
HOWEVER, IF YOUR COMBINED STAR TICKETS DO NOT TOTAL TWELVE...

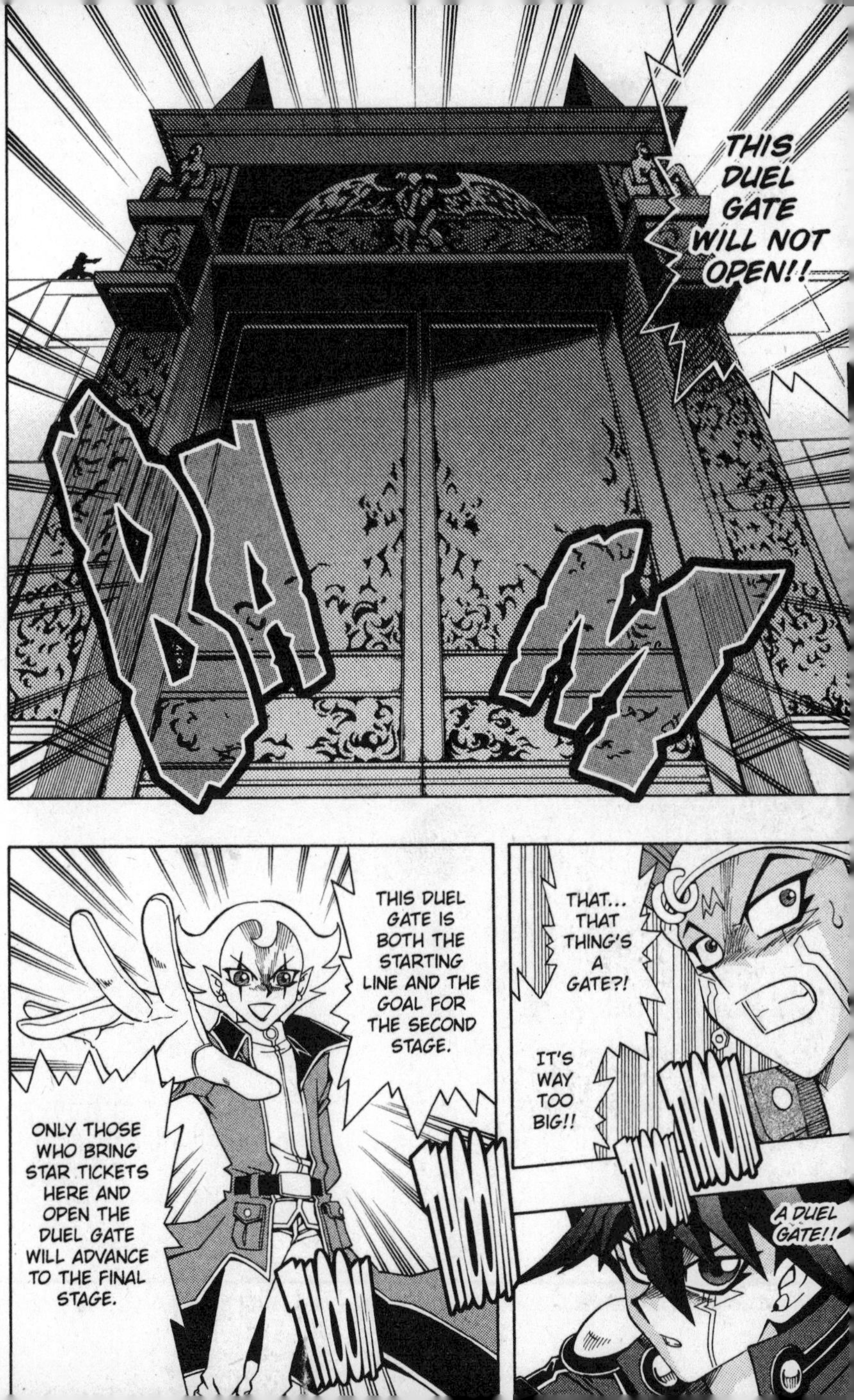
BAM
THIS DUEL GATE WILL NOT OPEN!!
THAT... THAT THING'S A GATE?!
IT'S WAY TOO BIG!!
THOOM THOOM
A DUEL GATE!!
THIS DUEL GATE IS BOTH THE STARTING LINE AND THE GOAL FOR THE SECOND STAGE.
ONLY THOSE WHO BRING STAR TICKETS HERE AND OPEN THE DUEL GATE WILL ADVANCE TO THE FINAL STAGE.
THOOM THOOM

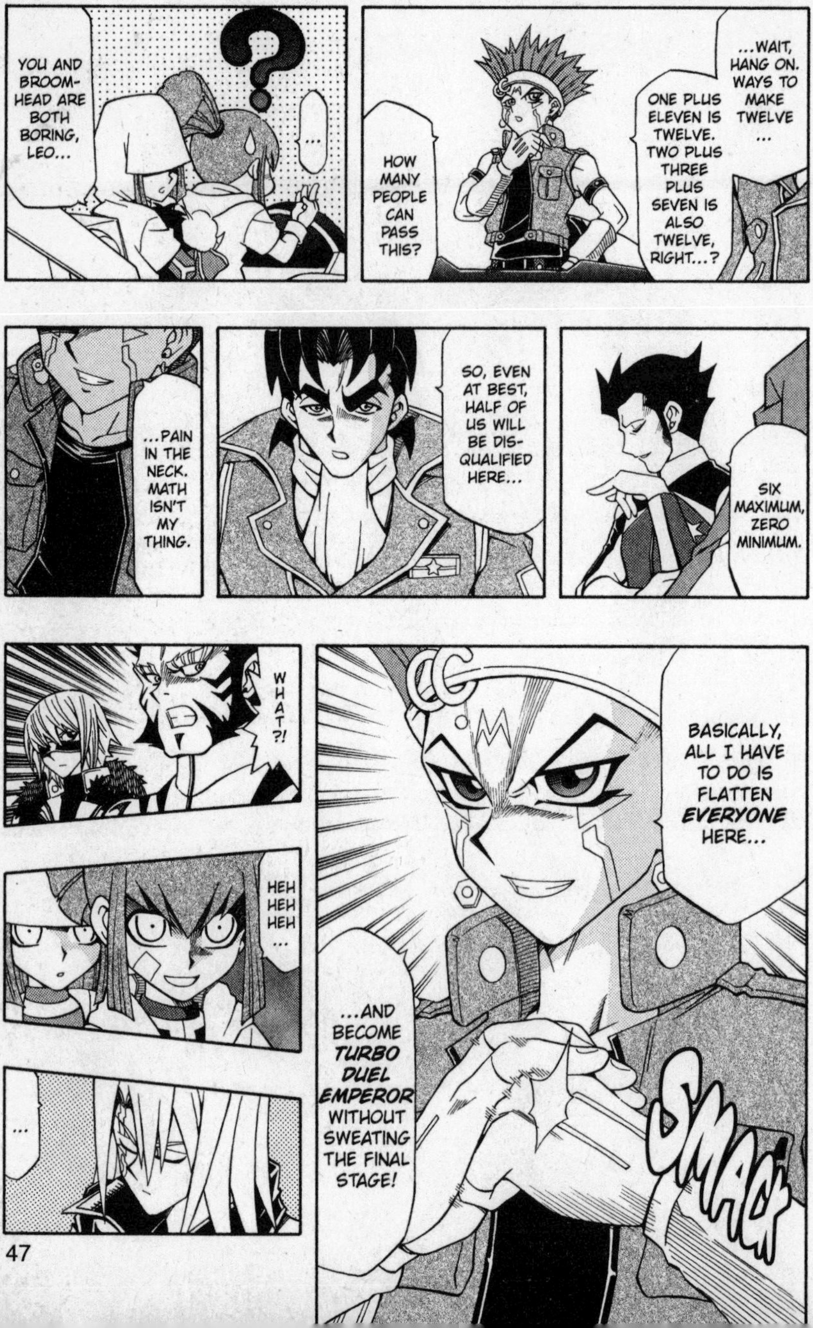
...WAIT, HANG ON. WAYS TO MAKE TWELVE...
ONE PLUS ELEVEN IS TWELVE. TWO PLUS THREE PLUS SEVEN IS ALSO TWELVE, RIGHT...?
HOW MANY PEOPLE CAN PASS THIS?
YOU AND BROOMHEAD ARE BOTH BORING, LEO...
...
SIX MAXIMUM, ZERO MINIMUM.
SO, EVEN AT BEST, HALF OF US WILL BE DISQUALIFIED HERE...
...PAIN IN THE NECK. MATH ISN'T MY THING.
BASICALLY, ALL I HAVE TO DO IS FLATTEN ***EVERYONE*** HERE...
...AND BECOME ***TURBO DUEL EMPEROR*** WITHOUT SWEATING THE FINAL STAGE!
SMACK
WHAT?!
HEH HEH HEH...
...

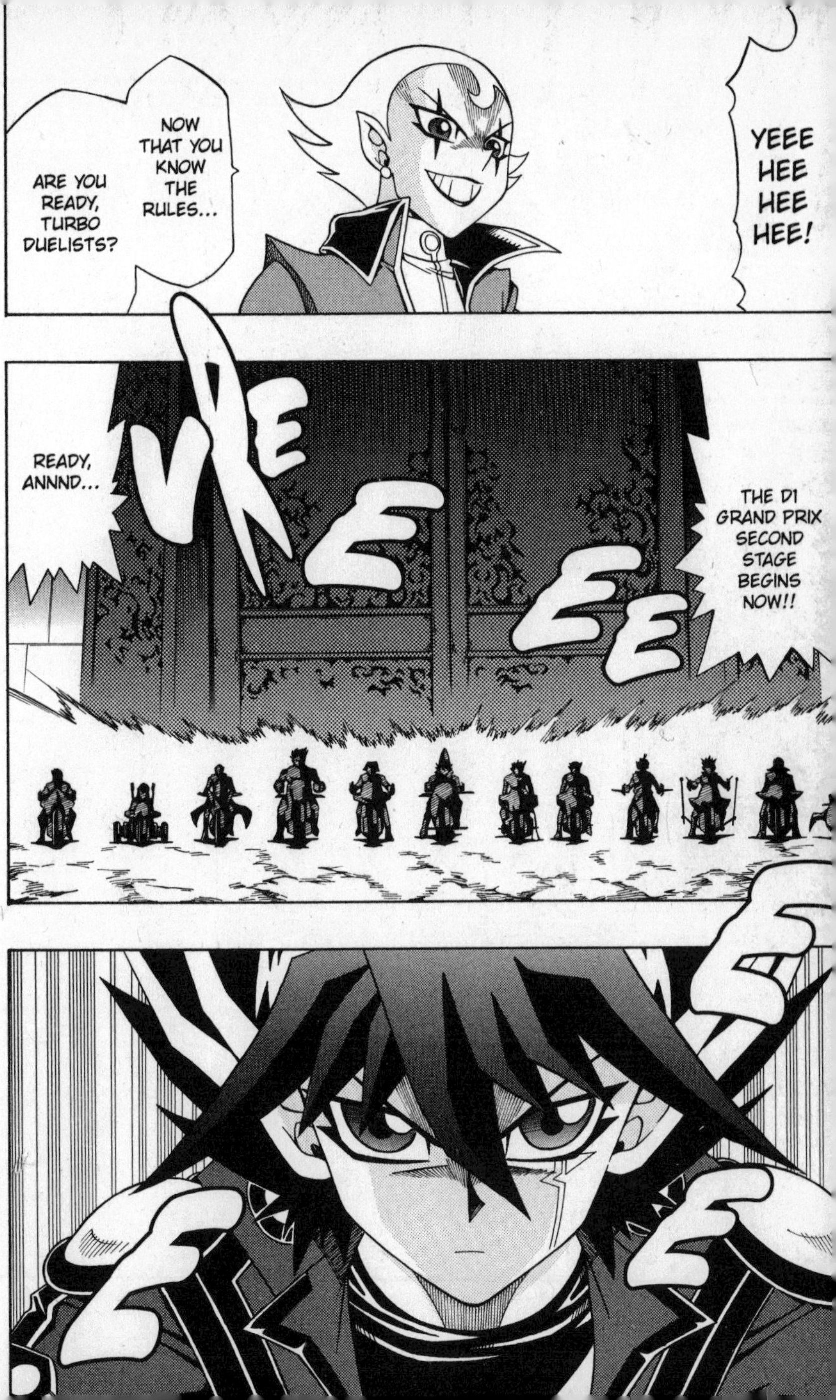
YEEE HEE HEE HEE!
NOW THAT YOU KNOW THE RULES...
ARE YOU READY, TURBO DUELISTS?
READY, ANNND...
VREEEE
THE D1 GRAND PRIX SECOND STAGE BEGINS NOW!!
EEEE

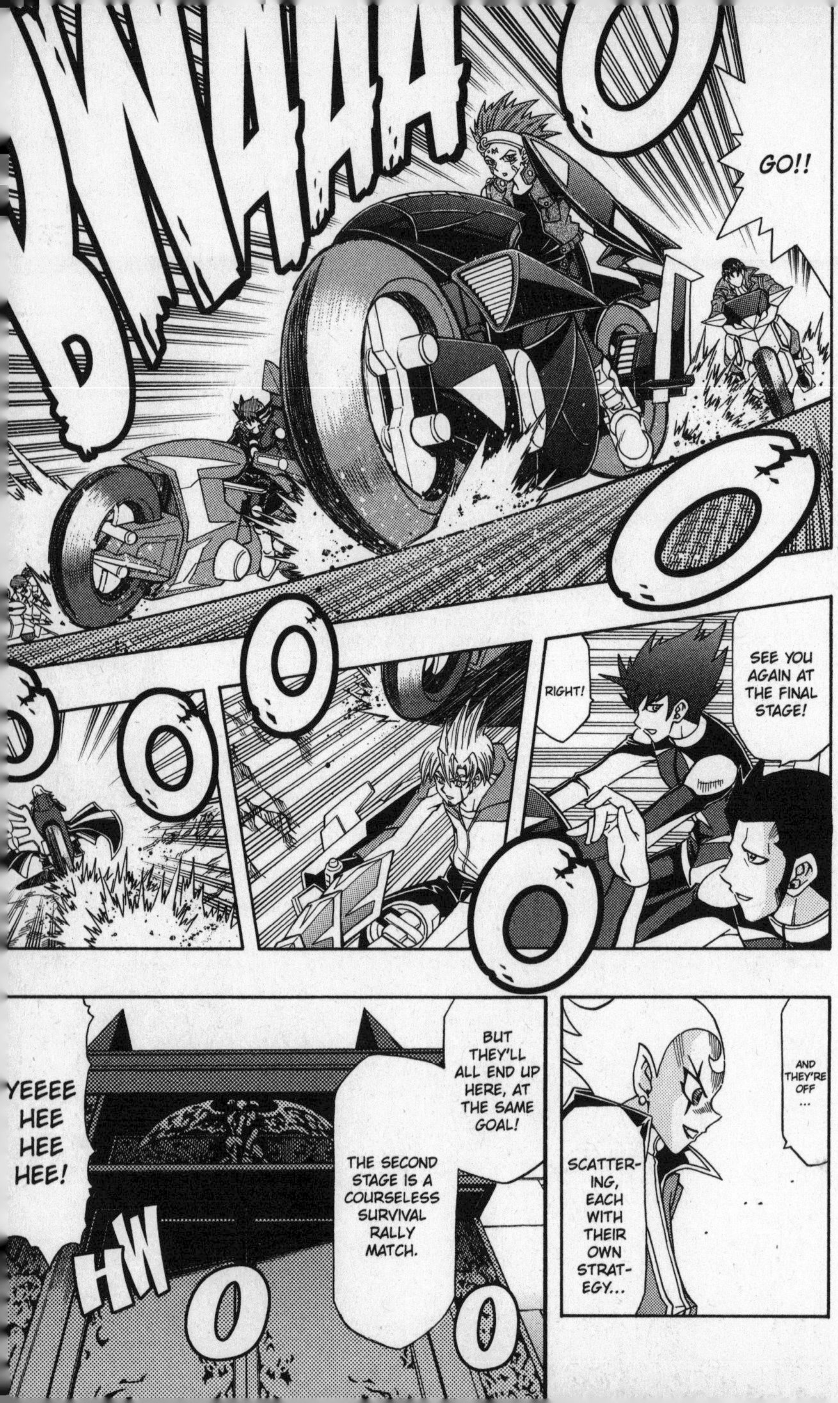
GO!!
SEE YOU AGAIN AT THE FINAL STAGE!
RIGHT!
AND THEY'RE OFF ...
SCATTER-ING, EACH WITH THEIR OWN STRAT-EGY...
BUT THEY'LL ALL END UP HERE, AT THE SAME GOAL!
THE SECOND STAGE IS A COURSELESS SURVIVAL RALLY MATCH.
YEEEE HEE HEE HEE!
HWOO

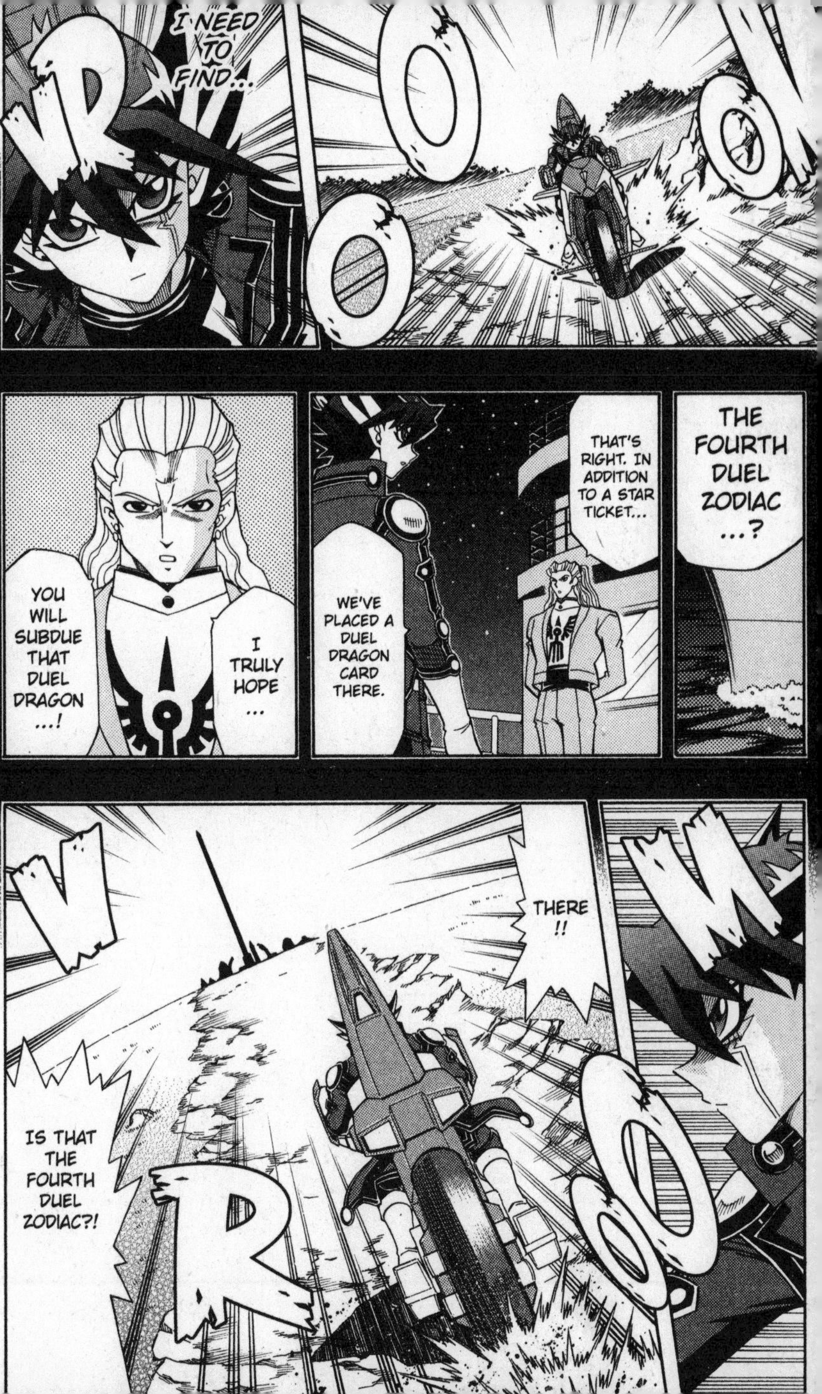
VROOOO
I NEED TO FIND...
THE FOURTH DUEL ZODIAC ...?
THAT'S RIGHT. IN ADDITION TO A STAR TICKET...
WE'VE PLACED A DUEL DRAGON CARD THERE.
I TRULY HOPE ...
YOU WILL SUBDUE THAT DUEL DRAGON ...!
VROOOM
THERE !!
IS THAT THE FOURTH DUEL ZODIAC?!

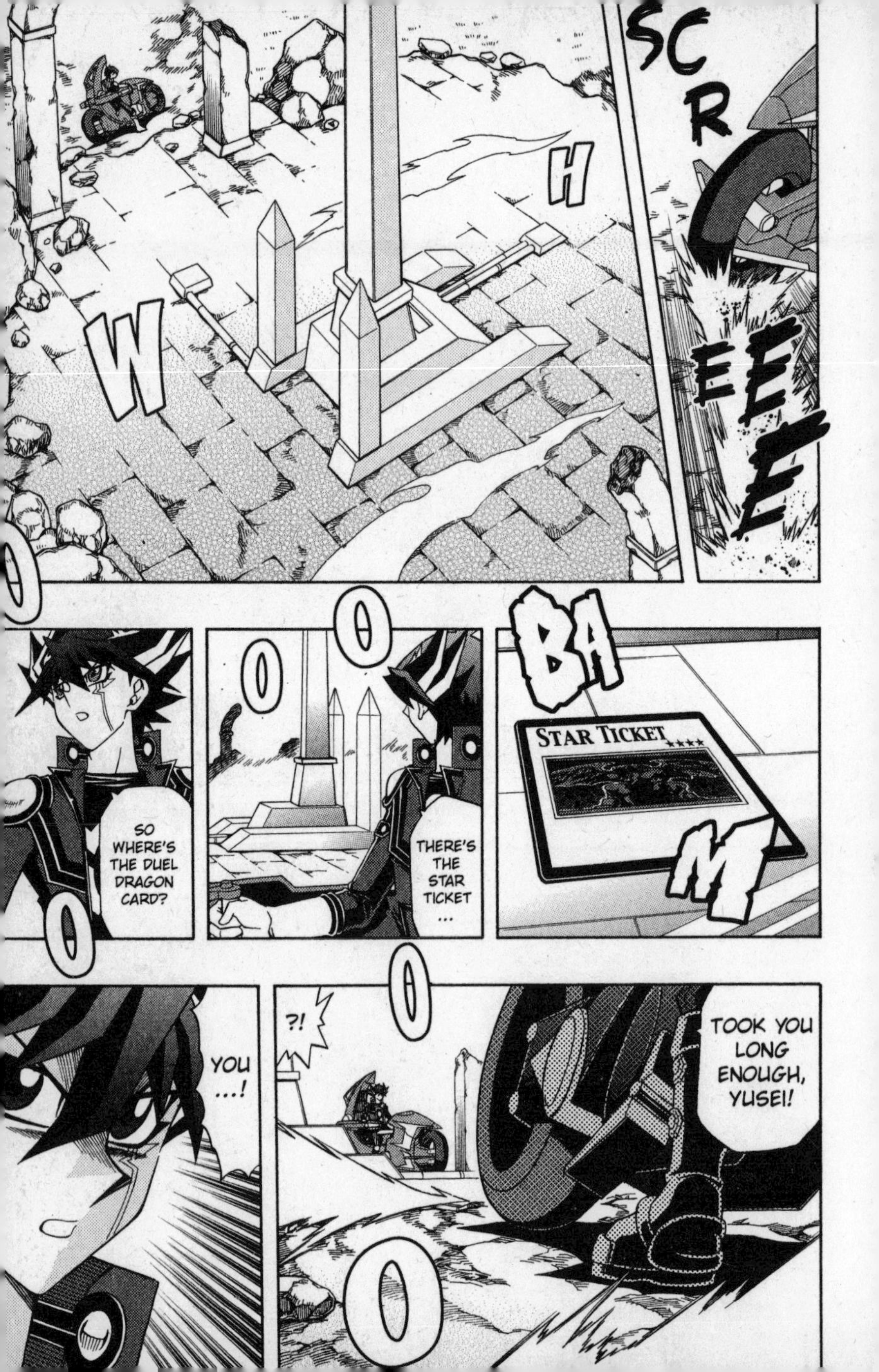

SCREEEE
WHOOOOOO
BAM
STAR TICKET
THERE'S THE STAR TICKET ...
SO WHERE'S THE DUEL DRAGON CARD?
?!
TOOK YOU LONG ENOUGH, YUSEI!
YOU ...!

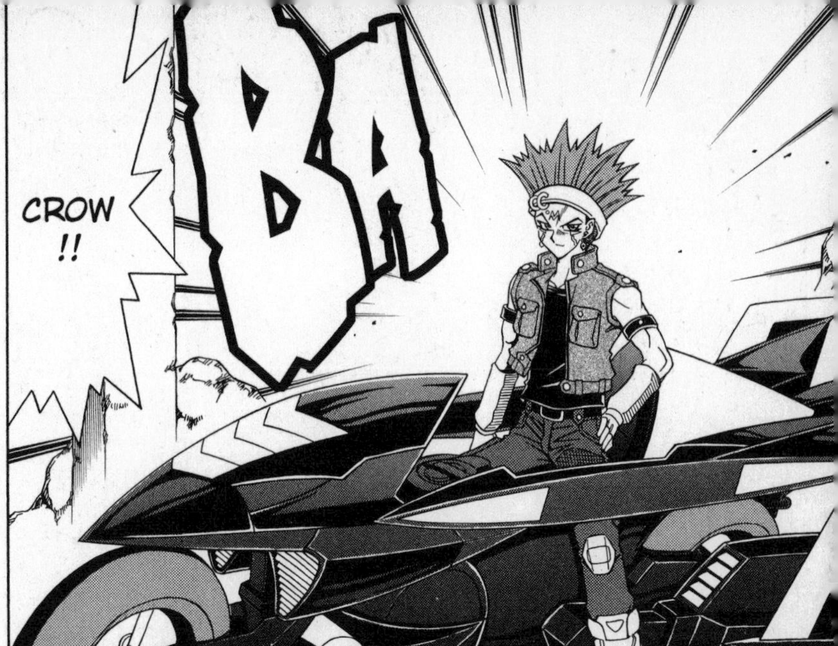
BAM
CROW !!
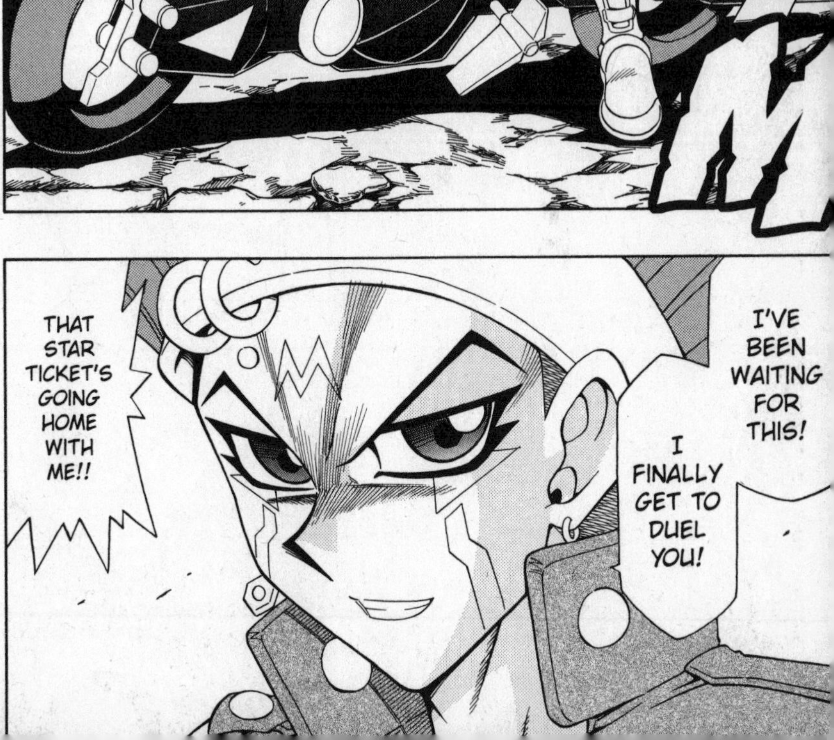
I'VE BEEN WAITING FOR THIS!
I FINALLY GET TO DUEL YOU!
THAT STAR TICKET'S GOING HOME WITH ME!!

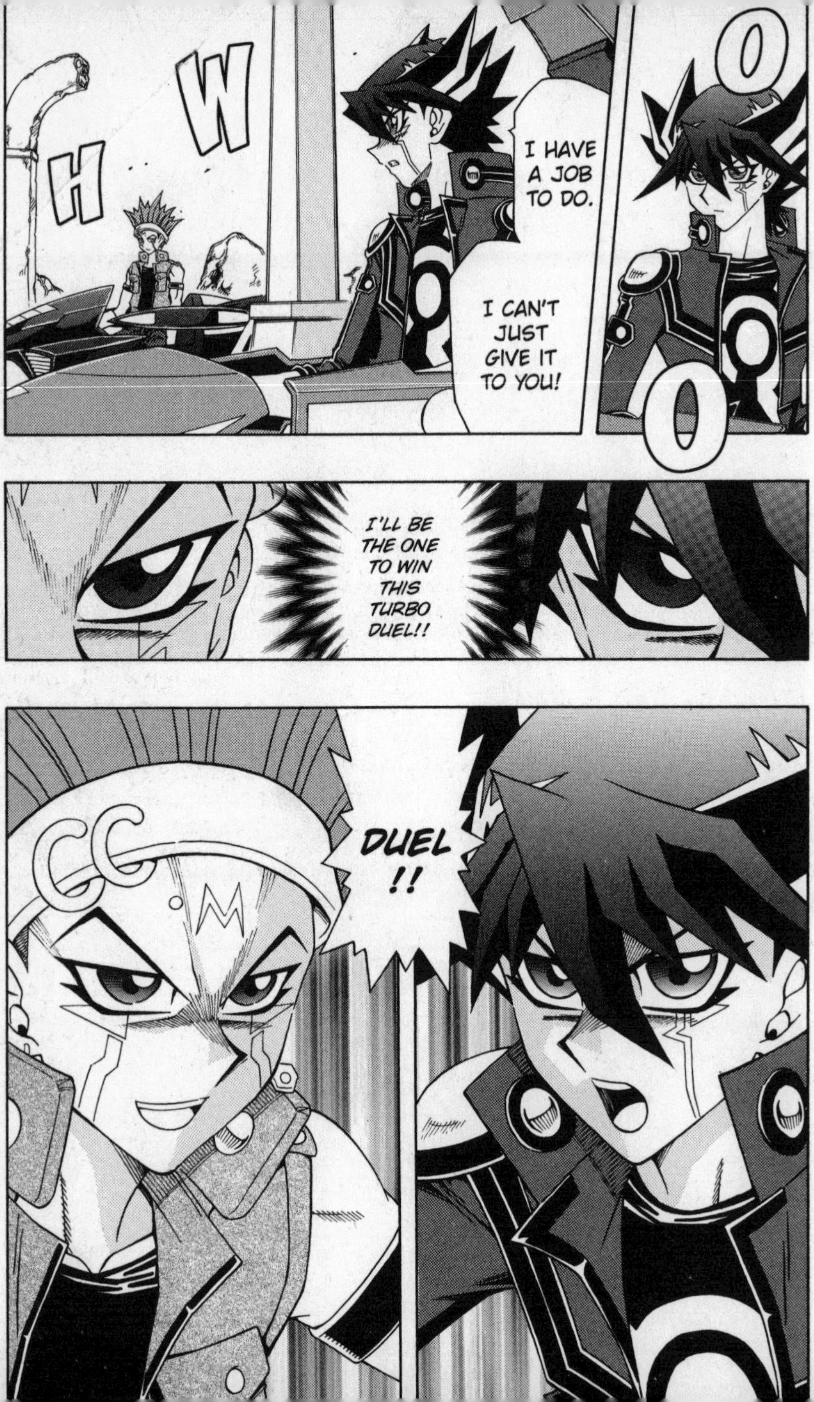
O
O
I HAVE A JOB TO DO.
I CAN'T JUST GIVE IT TO YOU!
W
H
I'LL BE THE ONE TO WIN THIS TURBO DUEL!!
DUEL!!

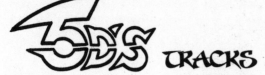

5D's TRACKS

THE 26TH

BY SATOMASA

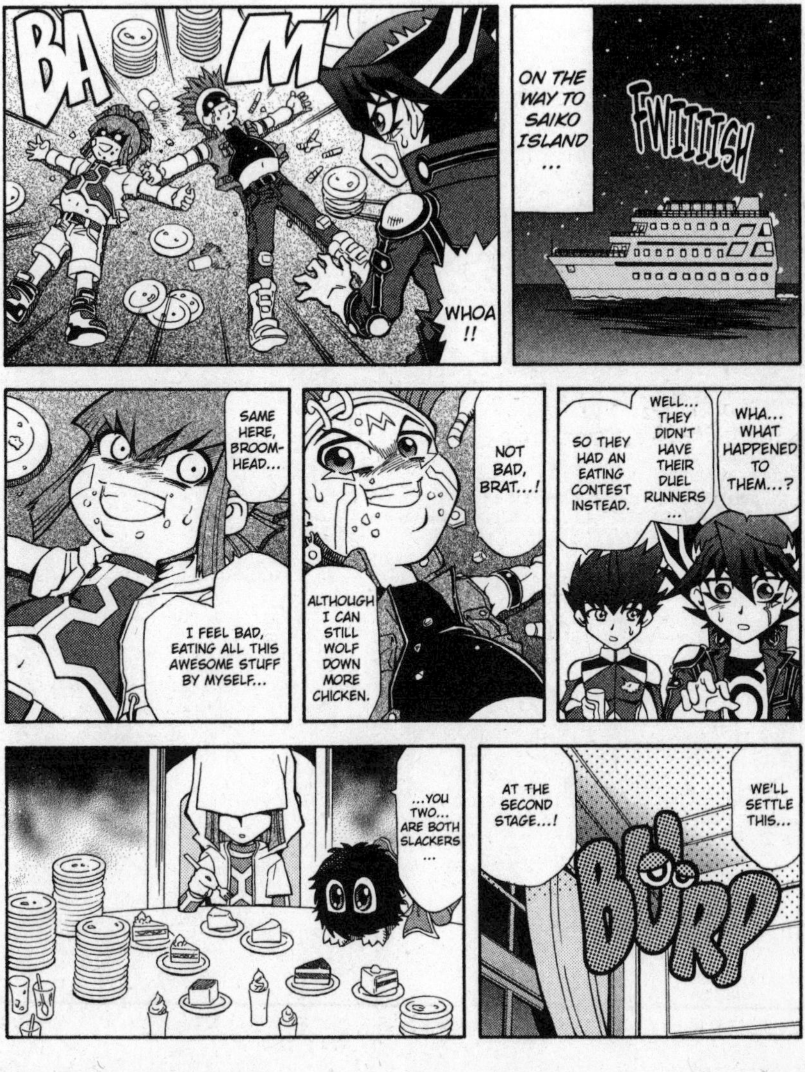

ON THE WAY TO SAIKO ISLAND ...
FWIIIIISH
BAM
WHOA !!
WHA... WHAT HAPPENED TO THEM...?
WELL... THEY DIDN'T HAVE THEIR DUEL RUNNERS ...
SO THEY HAD AN EATING CONTEST INSTEAD.
NOT BAD, BRAT...!
ALTHOUGH I CAN STILL WOLF DOWN MORE CHICKEN.
SAME HERE, BROOM-HEAD...
I FEEL BAD, EATING ALL THIS AWESOME STUFF BY MYSELF...
WE'LL SETTLE THIS...
AT THE SECOND STAGE...!
BURP
...YOU TWO... ARE BOTH SLACKERS ...

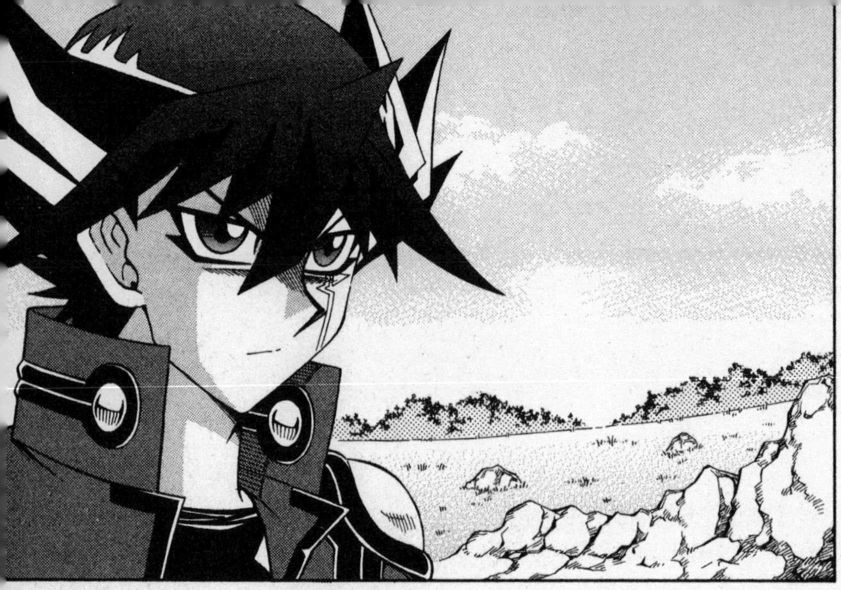

RIDE-27

SYNCHRO VS. SYNCHRO!!

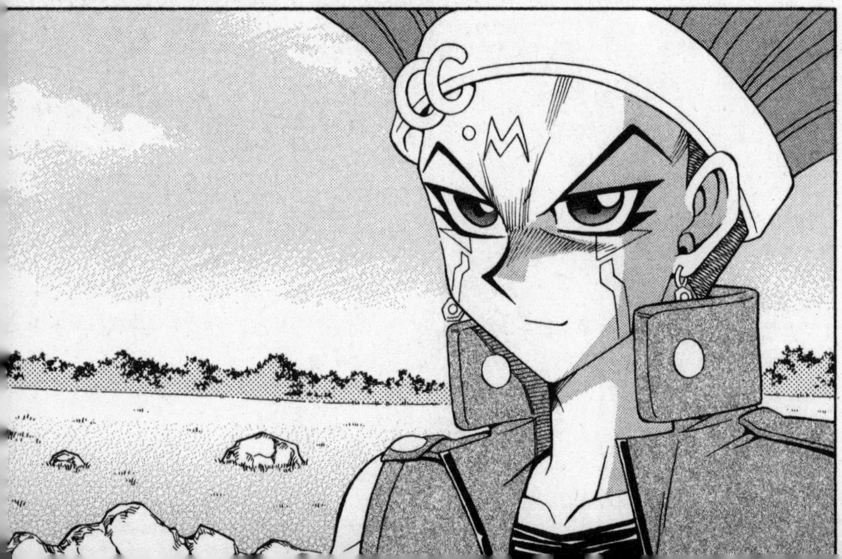

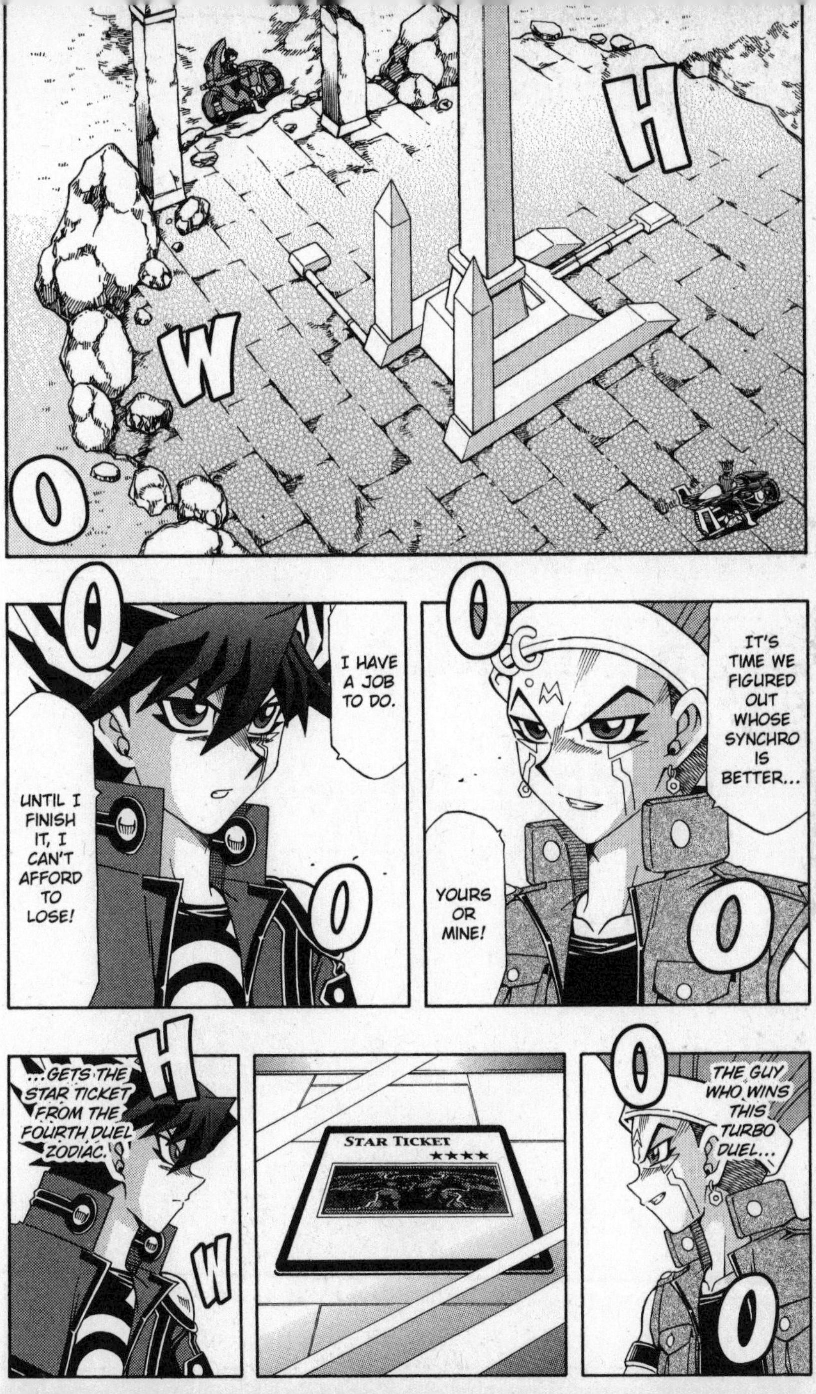
H
W
O
O
IT'S TIME WE FIGURED OUT WHOSE SYNCHRO IS BETTER...
YOURS OR MINE!
O
O
I HAVE A JOB TO DO.
UNTIL I FINISH IT, I CAN'T AFFORD TO LOSE!
O
O
THE GUY WHO WINS THIS TURBO DUEL...
O
STAR TICKET
★★★★
H
...GETS THE STAR TICKET FROM THE FOURTH DUEL ZODIAC.
W

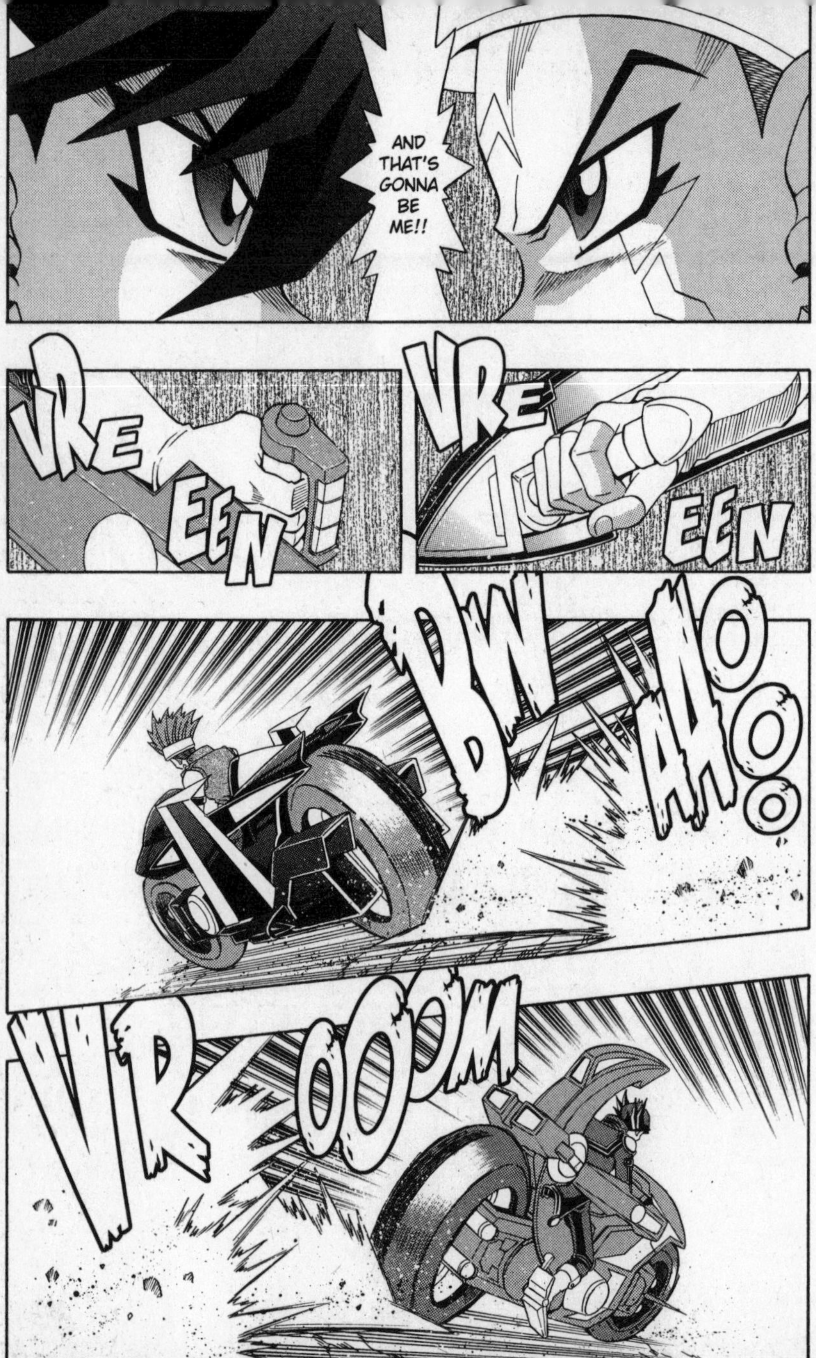
AND THAT'S GONNA BE ME!!
VREEEN
VREEEN
BWAHOOO
VROOOM

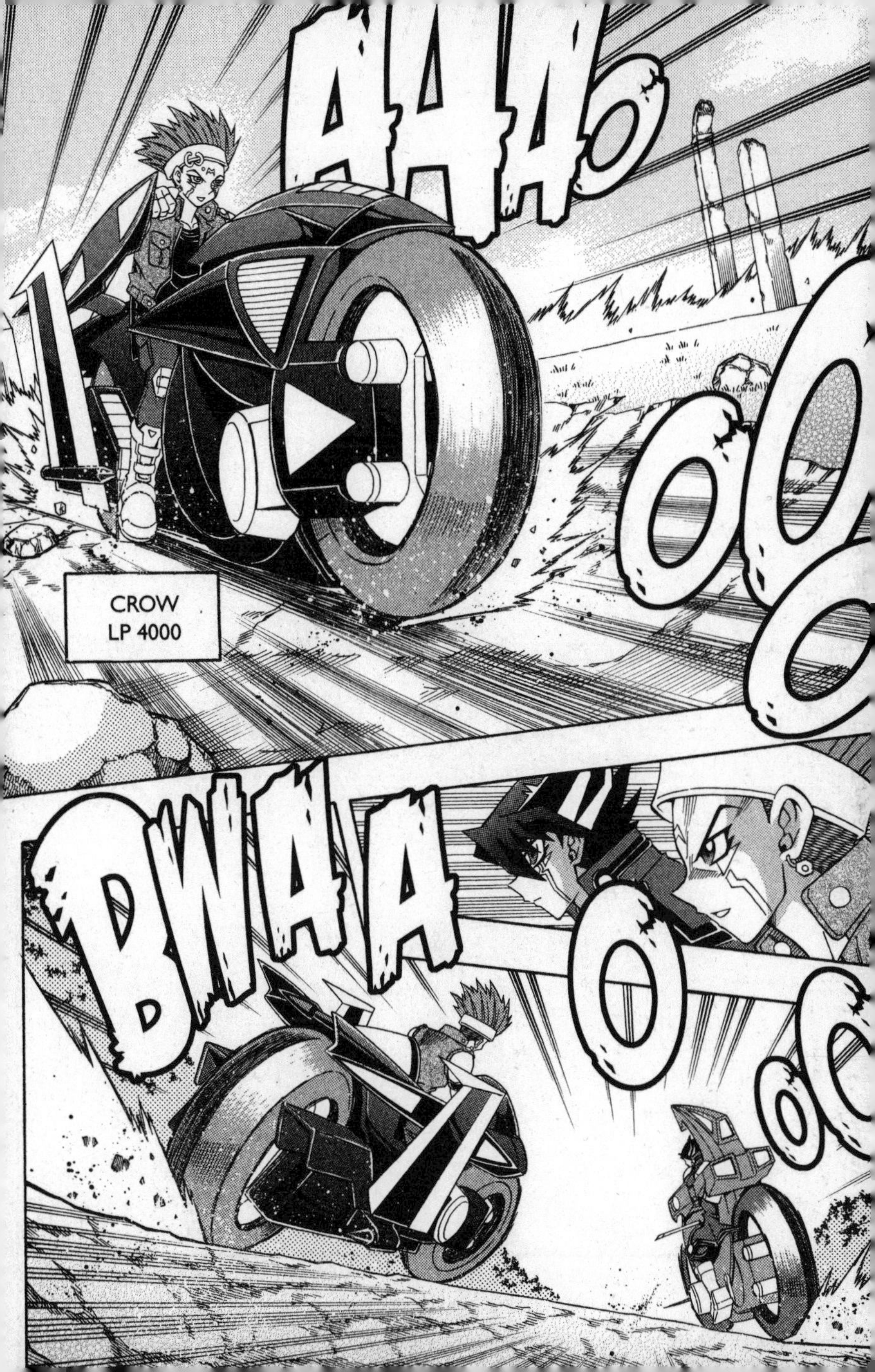
AAAOOOO
CROW
LP 4000
BWAAOOOO

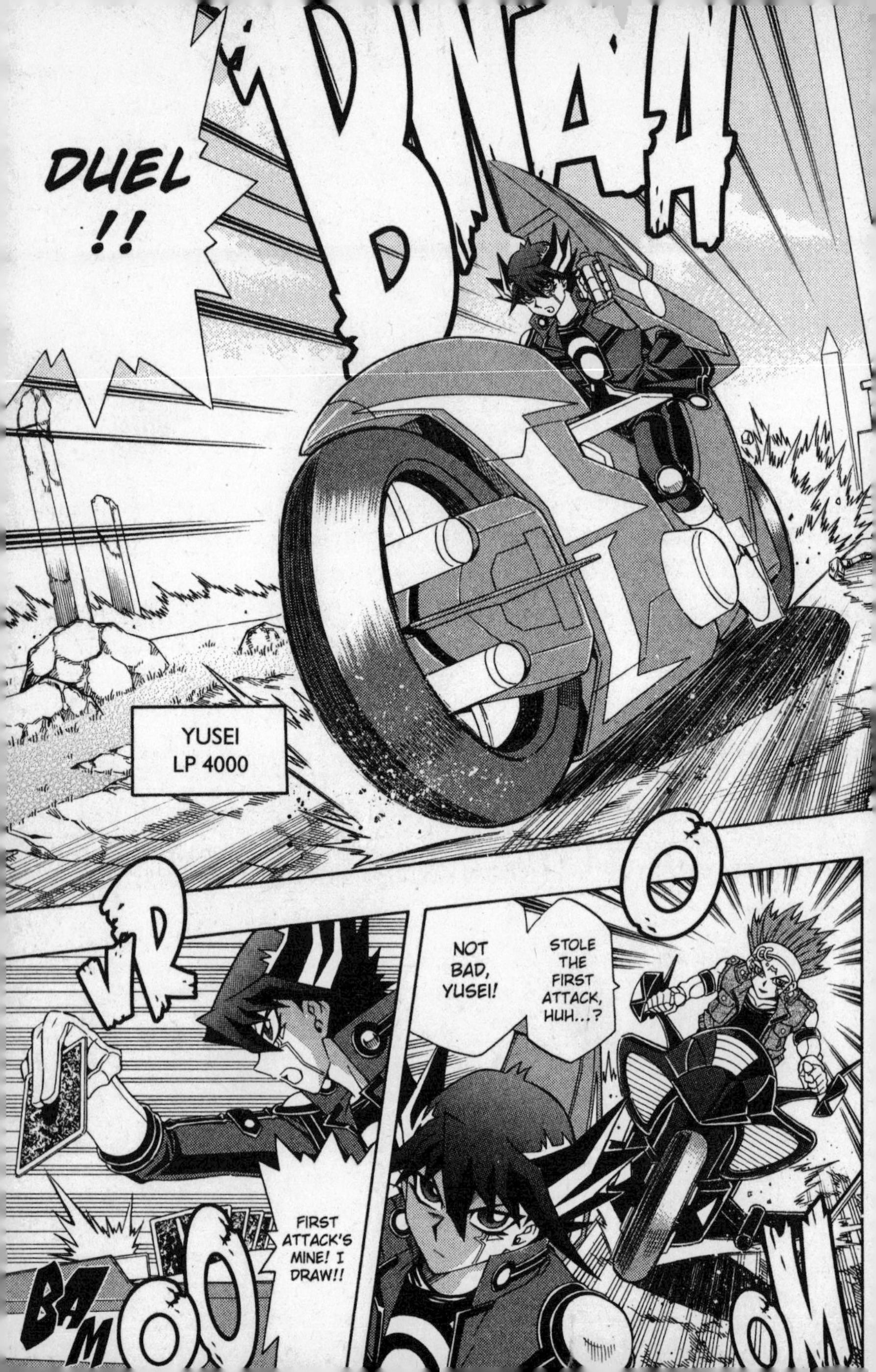
DUEL !!
YUSEI
LP 4000
STOLE THE FIRST ATTACK, HUH...?
NOT BAD, YUSEI!
FIRST ATTACK'S MINE! I DRAW!!
BAM

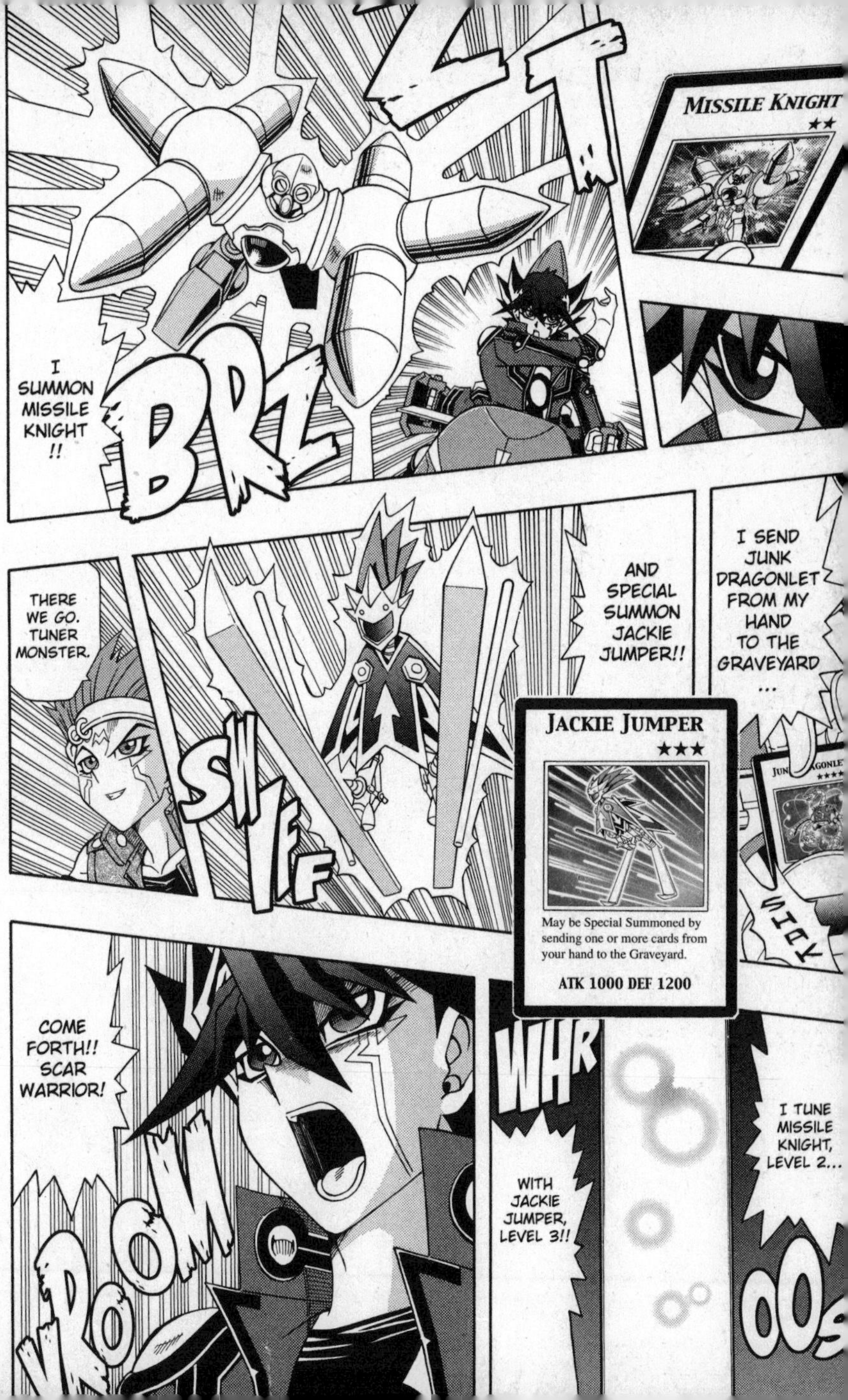
MISSILE KNIGHT
★★
I SUMMON MISSILE KNIGHT!!
BRZ
I SEND JUNK DRAGONLET FROM MY HAND TO THE GRAVEYARD...
AND SPECIAL SUMMON JACKIE JUMPER!!
JACKIE JUMPER
★★★
May be Special Summoned by sending one or more cards from your hand to the Graveyard.
ATK 1000 DEF 1200
THERE WE GO. TUNER MONSTER.
SWIFF
I TUNE MISSILE KNIGHT, LEVEL 2...
WITH JACKIE JUMPER, LEVEL 3!!
WHR
COME FORTH!! SCAR WARRIOR!
VROOM

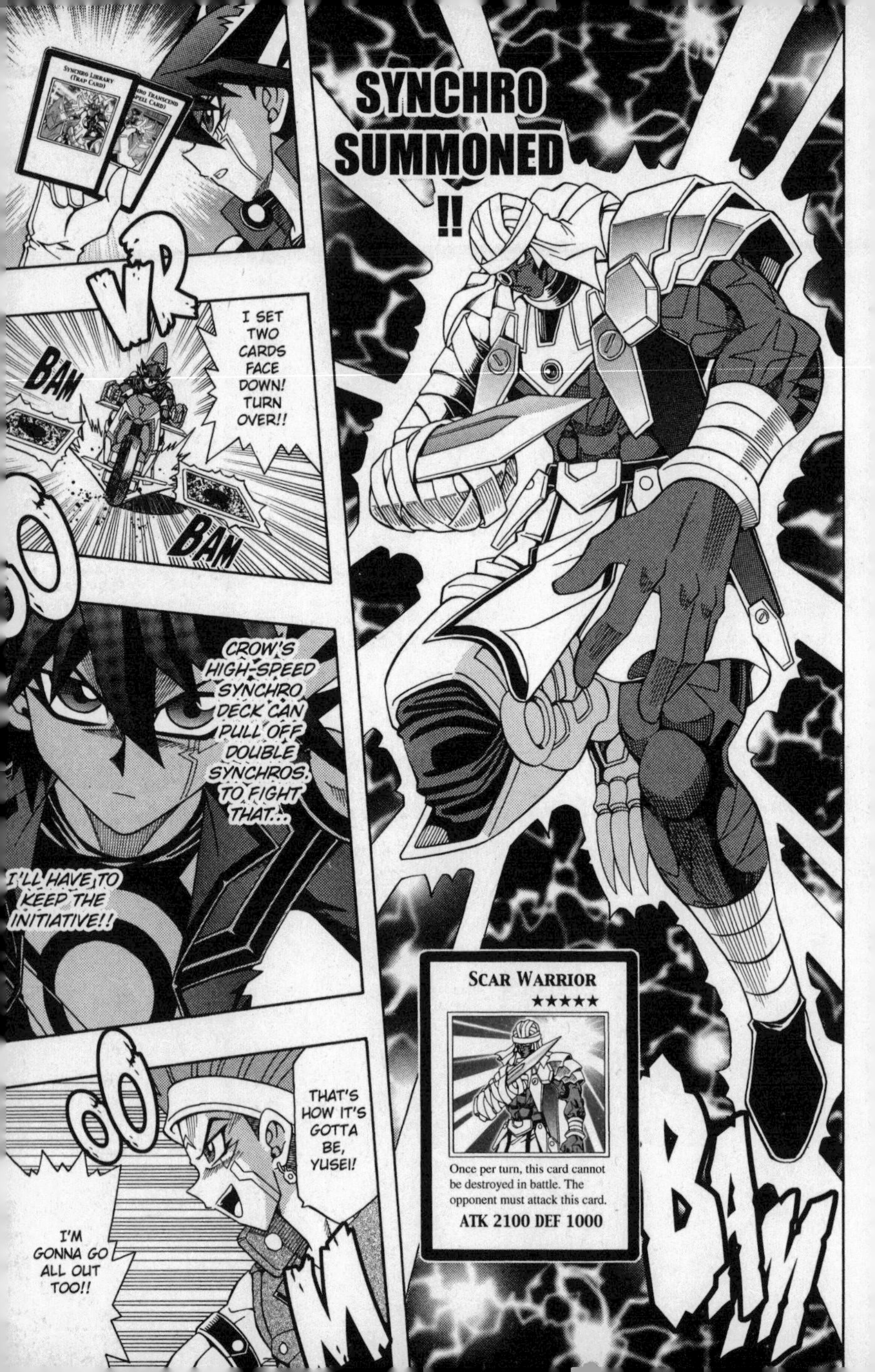
SYNCHRO SUMMONED!!
SCAR WARRIOR
★★★★★
Once per turn, this card cannot be destroyed in battle. The opponent must attack this card.
ATK 2100 DEF 1000
BAM
SYNCHRO LIBRARY (TRAP CARD)
VR
BAM
I SET TWO CARDS FACE DOWN! TURN OVER!!
BAM
OO
CROW'S HIGH-SPEED SYNCHRO DECK CAN PULL OFF DOUBLE SYNCHROS. TO FIGHT THAT...
I'LL HAVE TO KEEP THE INITIATIVE!!
OOO
THAT'S HOW IT'S GOTTA BE, YUSEI!
I'M GONNA GO ALL OUT TOO!!
M

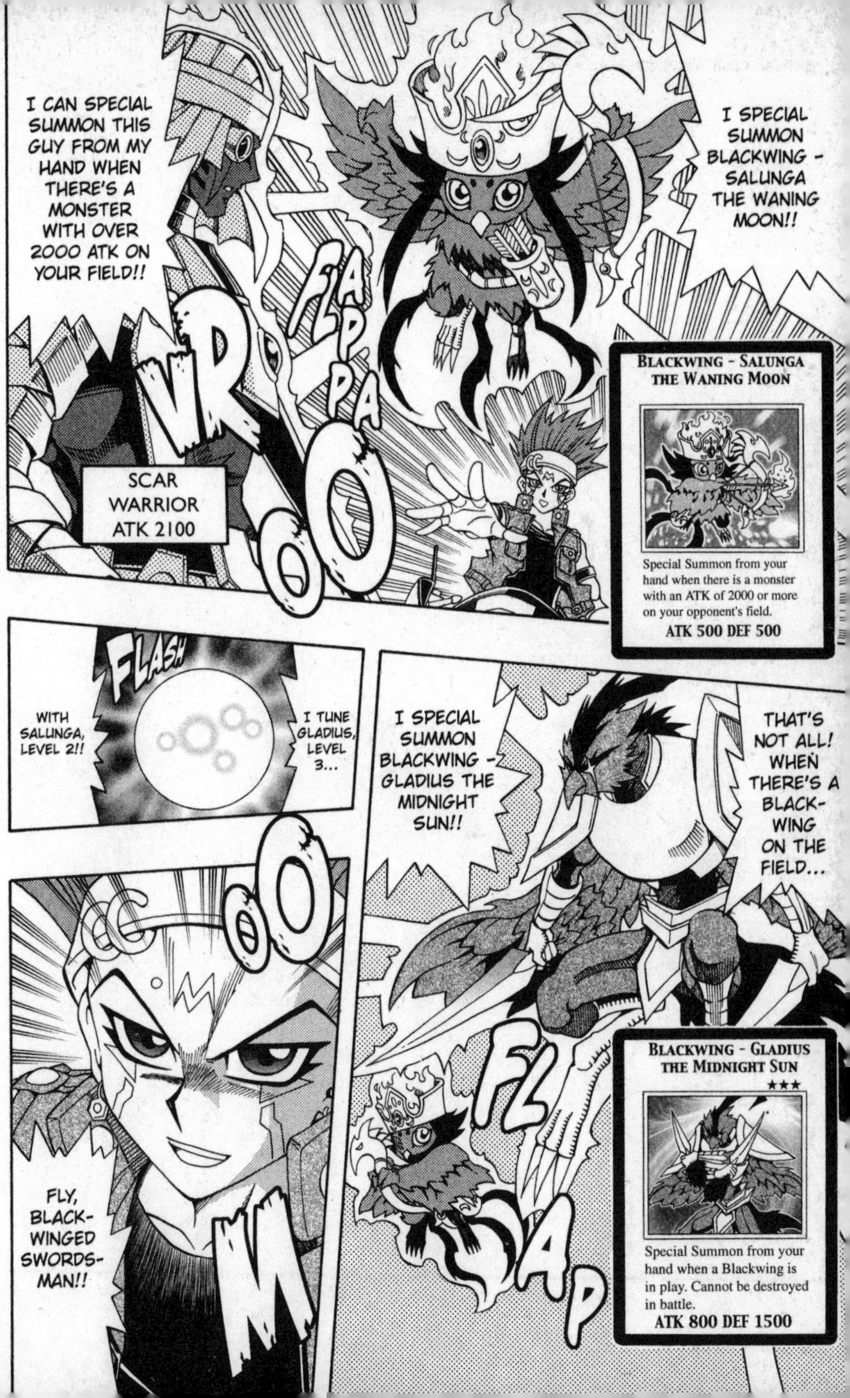
I SPECIAL SUMMON BLACKWING - SALUNGA THE WANING MOON!!
I CAN SPECIAL SUMMON THIS GUY FROM MY HAND WHEN THERE'S A MONSTER WITH OVER 2000 ATK ON YOUR FIELD!!
FLAPPA
VROOO
BLACKWING - SALUNGA THE WANING MOON
Special Summon from your hand when there is a monster with an ATK of 2000 or more on your opponent's field.
ATK 500 DEF 500
SCAR WARRIOR ATK 2100
THAT'S NOT ALL! WHEN THERE'S A BLACKWING ON THE FIELD...
I SPECIAL SUMMON BLACKWING - GLADIUS THE MIDNIGHT SUN!!
FLAP
BLACKWING - GLADIUS THE MIDNIGHT SUN
★★★
Special Summon from your hand when a Blackwing is in play. Cannot be destroyed in battle.
ATK 800 DEF 1500
FLASH
I TUNE GLADIUS, LEVEL 3...
WITH SALUNGA, LEVEL 2!!
VROOOM
FLY, BLACK-WINGED SWORDS-MAN!!

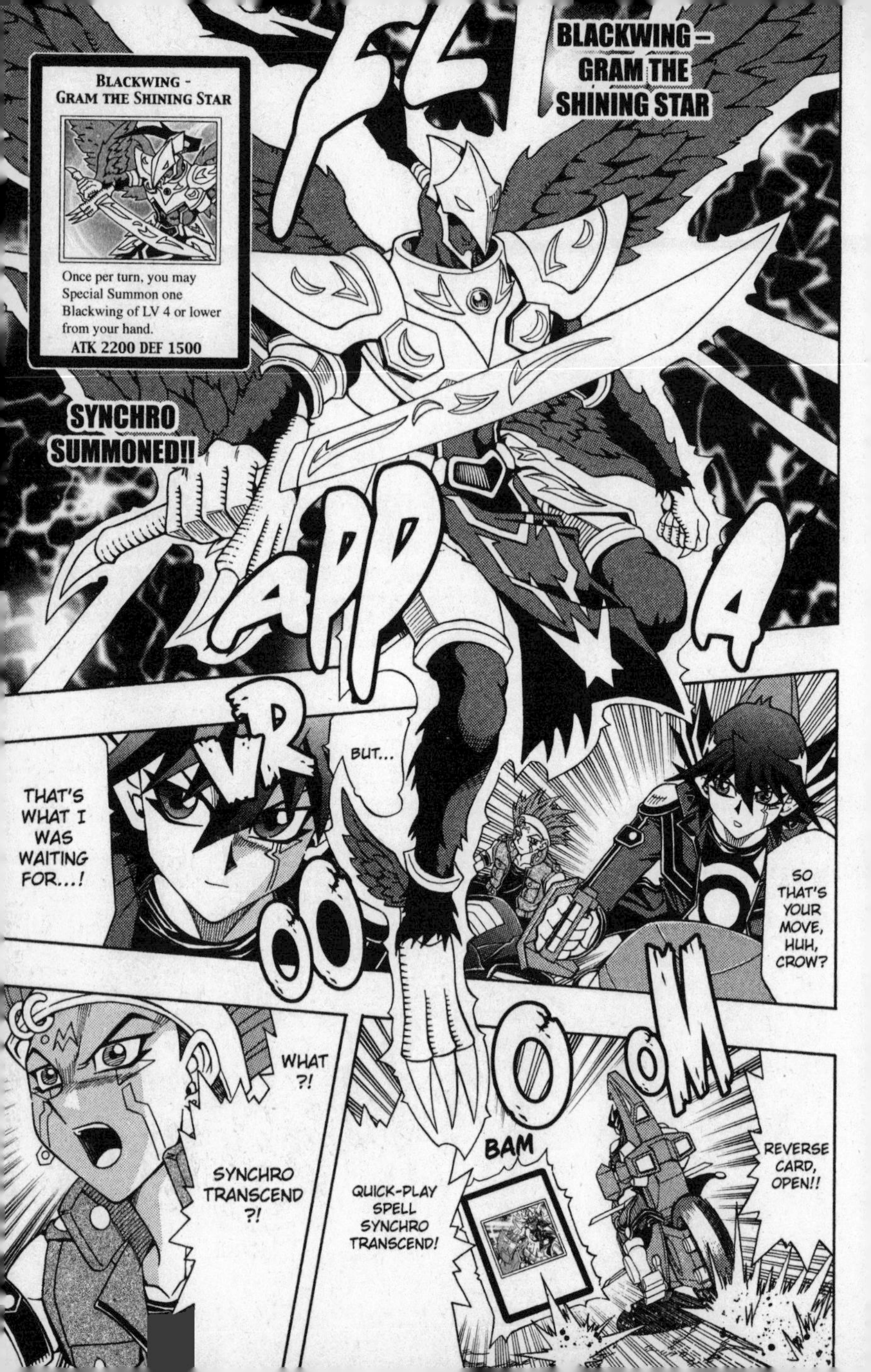
BLACKWING – GRAM THE SHINING STAR
BLACKWING - GRAM THE SHINING STAR
Once per turn, you may Special Summon one Blackwing of LV 4 or lower from your hand.
ATK 2200 DEF 1500
SYNCHRO SUMMONED!!
ZAPPA
SO THAT'S YOUR MOVE, HUH, CROW?
BUT...
THAT'S WHAT I WAS WAITING FOR...!
VROOOOM
REVERSE CARD, OPEN!!
BAM
QUICK-PLAY SPELL SYNCHRO TRANSCEND!
WHAT ?!
SYNCHRO TRANSCEND ?!

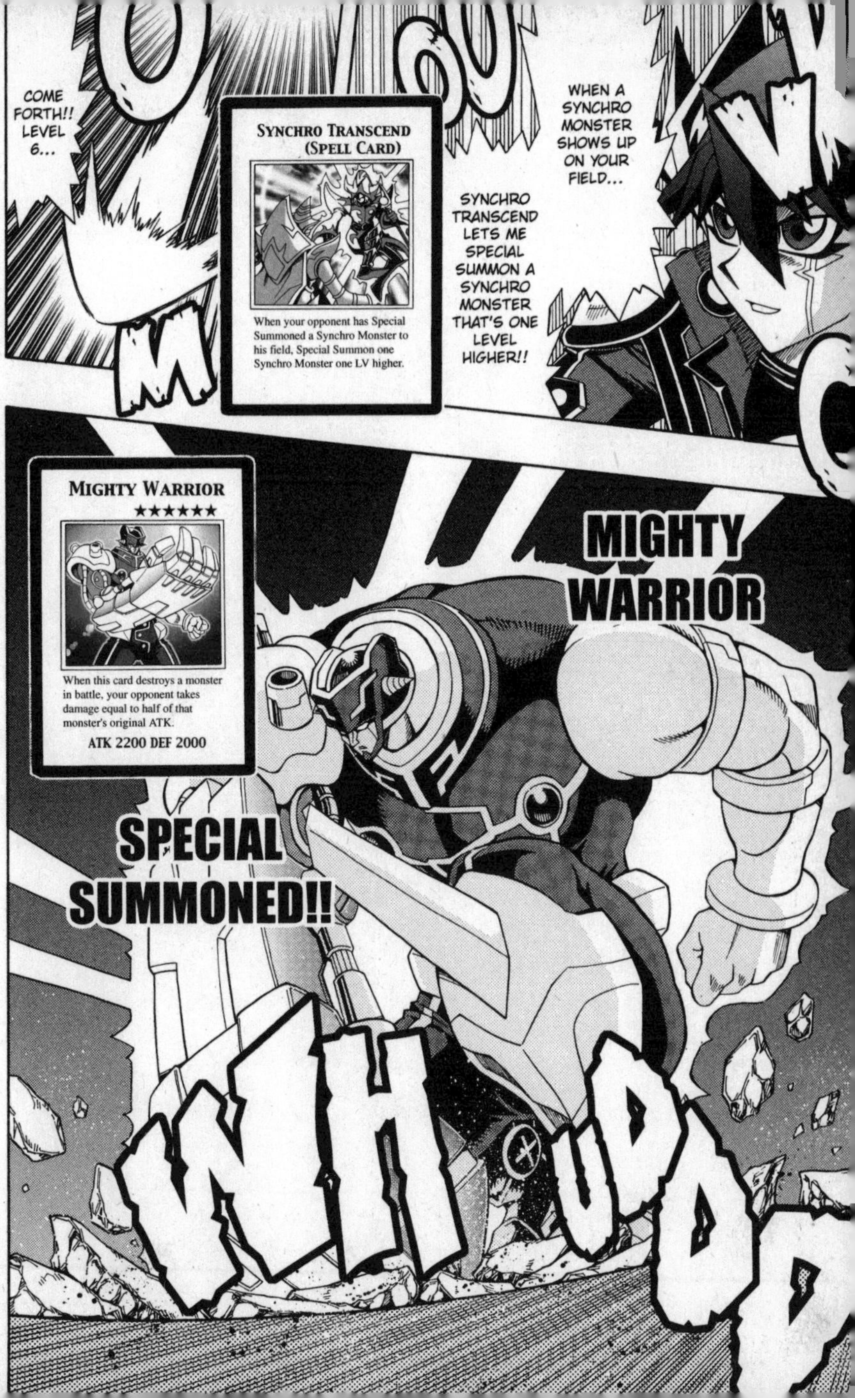
WHEN A SYNCHRO MONSTER SHOWS UP ON YOUR FIELD...
SYNCHRO TRANSCEND LETS ME SPECIAL SUMMON A SYNCHRO MONSTER THAT'S ONE LEVEL HIGHER!!
SYNCHRO TRANSCEND
(SPELL CARD)
When your opponent has Special Summoned a Synchro Monster to his field, Special Summon one Synchro Monster one LV higher.
COME FORTH!! LEVEL 6...
MIGHTY WARRIOR
MIGHTY WARRIOR
★★★★★★
When this card destroys a monster in battle, your opponent takes damage equal to half of that monster's original ATK.
ATK 2200 DEF 2000
SPECIAL SUMMONED!!

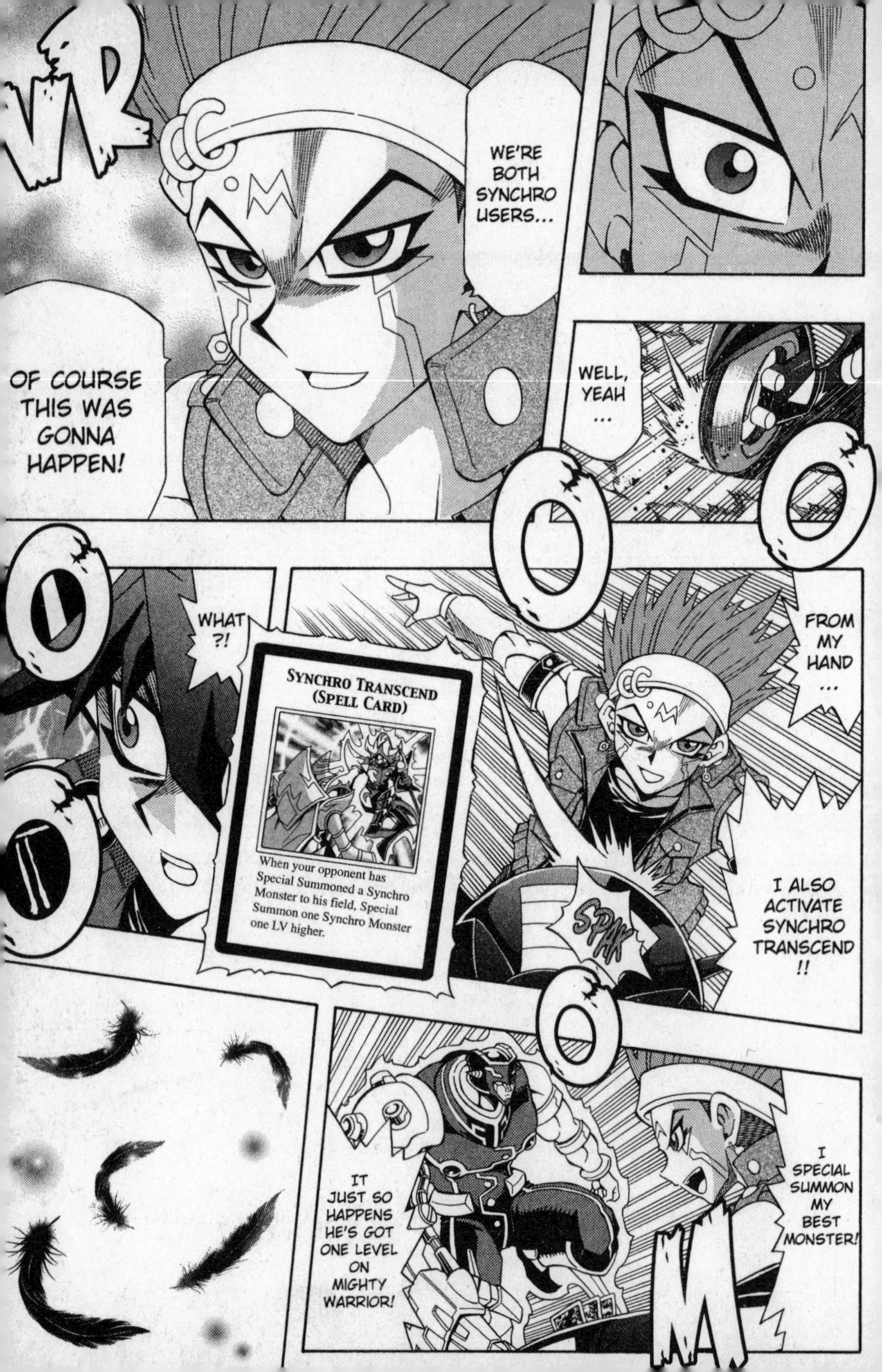
WELL, YEAH ...
WE'RE BOTH SYNCHRO USERS...
OF COURSE THIS WAS GONNA HAPPEN!
FROM MY HAND ...
I ALSO ACTIVATE SYNCHRO TRANSCEND !!
SPAK
SYNCHRO TRANSCEND (SPELL CARD)
When your opponent has Special Summoned a Synchro Monster to his field, Special Summon one Synchro Monster one LV higher.
WHAT ?!
I SPECIAL SUMMON MY BEST MONSTER!
IT JUST SO HAPPENS HE'S GOT ONE LEVEL ON MIGHTY WARRIOR!

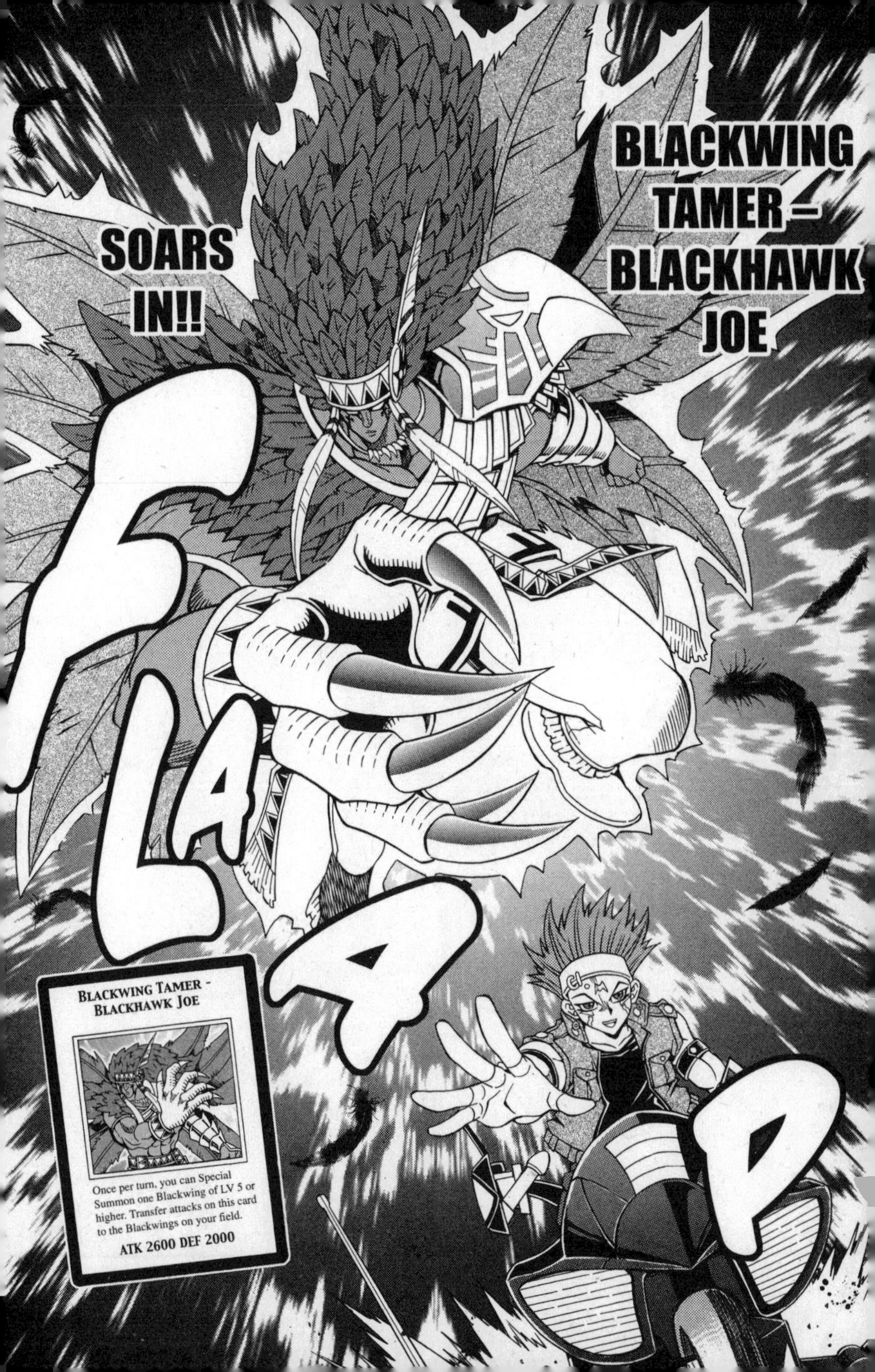
BLACKWING TAMER – BLACKHAWK JOE
SOARS IN!!
FLAAAP
BLACKWING TAMER - BLACKHAWK JOE
Once per turn, you can Special Summon one Blackwing of LV 5 or higher. Transfer attacks on this card to the Blackwings on your field.
ATK 2600 DEF 2000

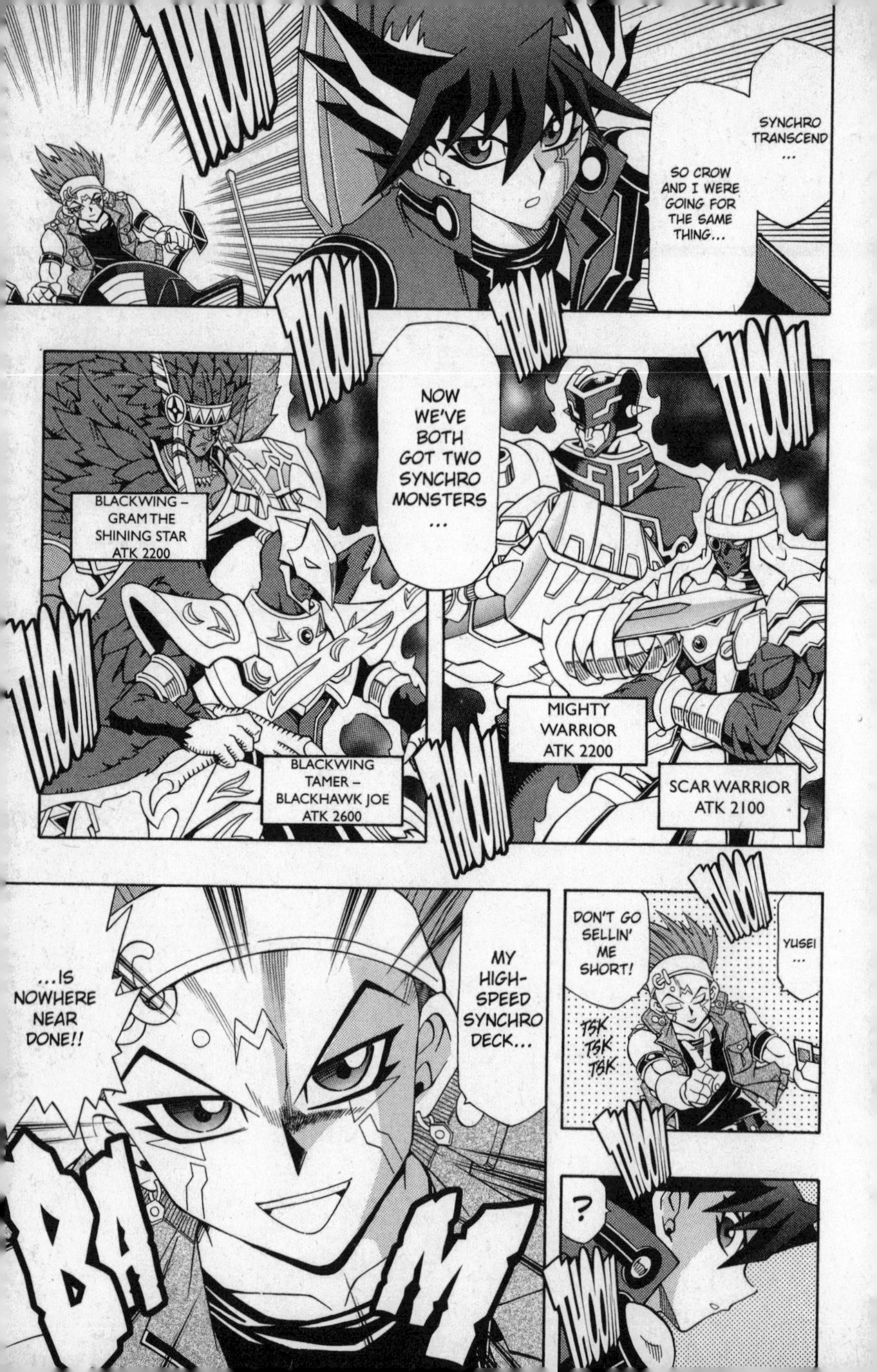
THOOM
SYNCHRO TRANSCEND ...
SO CROW AND I WERE GOING FOR THE SAME THING...
THOOM
THOOM
THOOM
NOW WE'VE BOTH GOT TWO SYNCHRO MONSTERS ...
MIGHTY WARRIOR ATK 2200
SCAR WARRIOR ATK 2100
BLACKWING – GRAM THE SHINING STAR ATK 2200
BLACKWING TAMER – BLACKHAWK JOE ATK 2600
THOOM
THOOM
THOOM
YUSEI ...
DON'T GO SELLIN' ME SHORT!
TSK TSK TSK
THOOM
?
THOOM
MY HIGH-SPEED SYNCHRO DECK...
...IS NOWHERE NEAR DONE!!
BAM

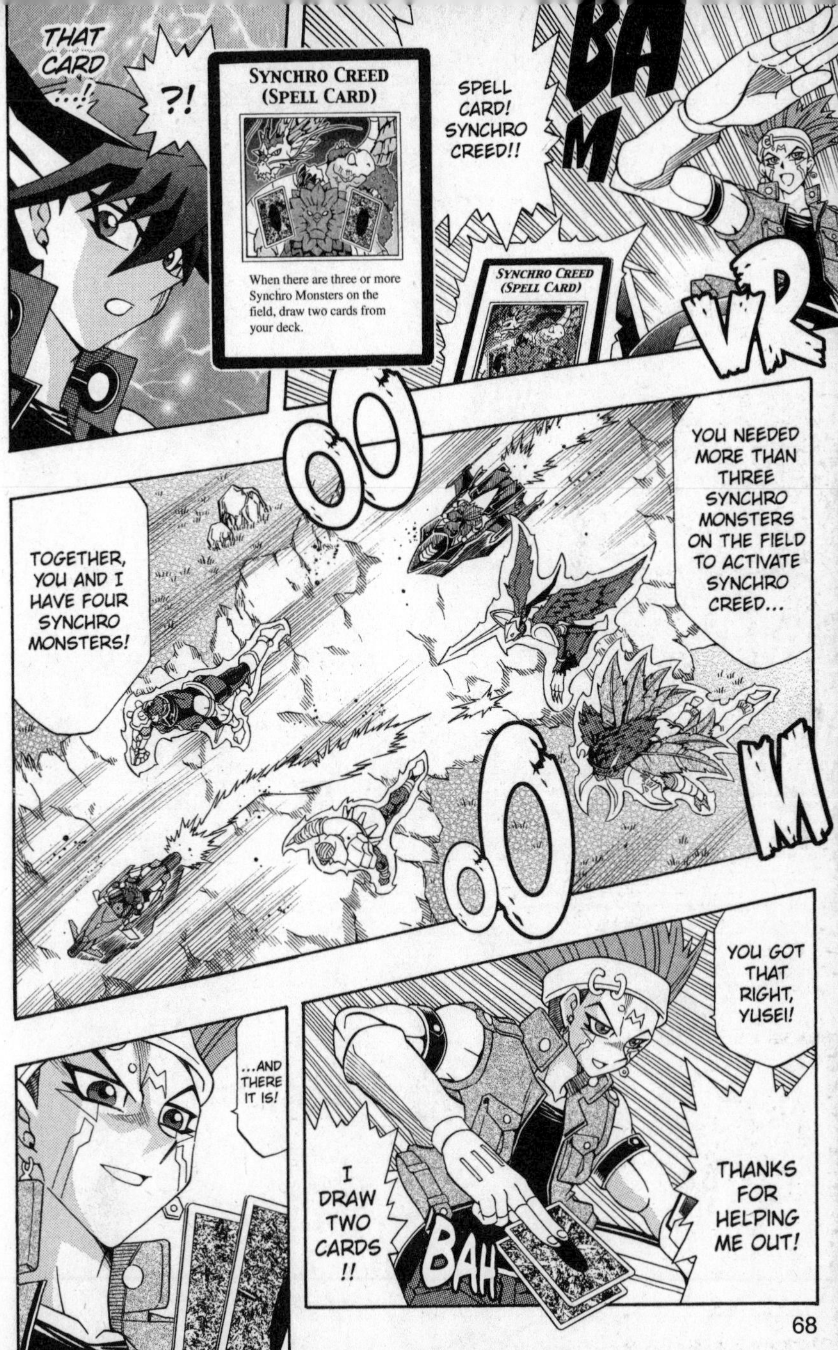
BAM
SPELL CARD! SYNCHRO CREED!!
VR
SYNCHRO CREED (SPELL CARD)
SYNCHRO CREED (SPELL CARD)
When there are three or more Synchro Monsters on the field, draw two cards from your deck.
?!
THAT CARD...!
OO
YOU NEEDED MORE THAN THREE SYNCHRO MONSTERS ON THE FIELD TO ACTIVATE SYNCHRO CREED...
TOGETHER, YOU AND I HAVE FOUR SYNCHRO MONSTERS!
O
M
YOU GOT THAT RIGHT, YUSEI!
THANKS FOR HELPING ME OUT!
I DRAW TWO CARDS!!
BAH
...AND THERE IT IS!

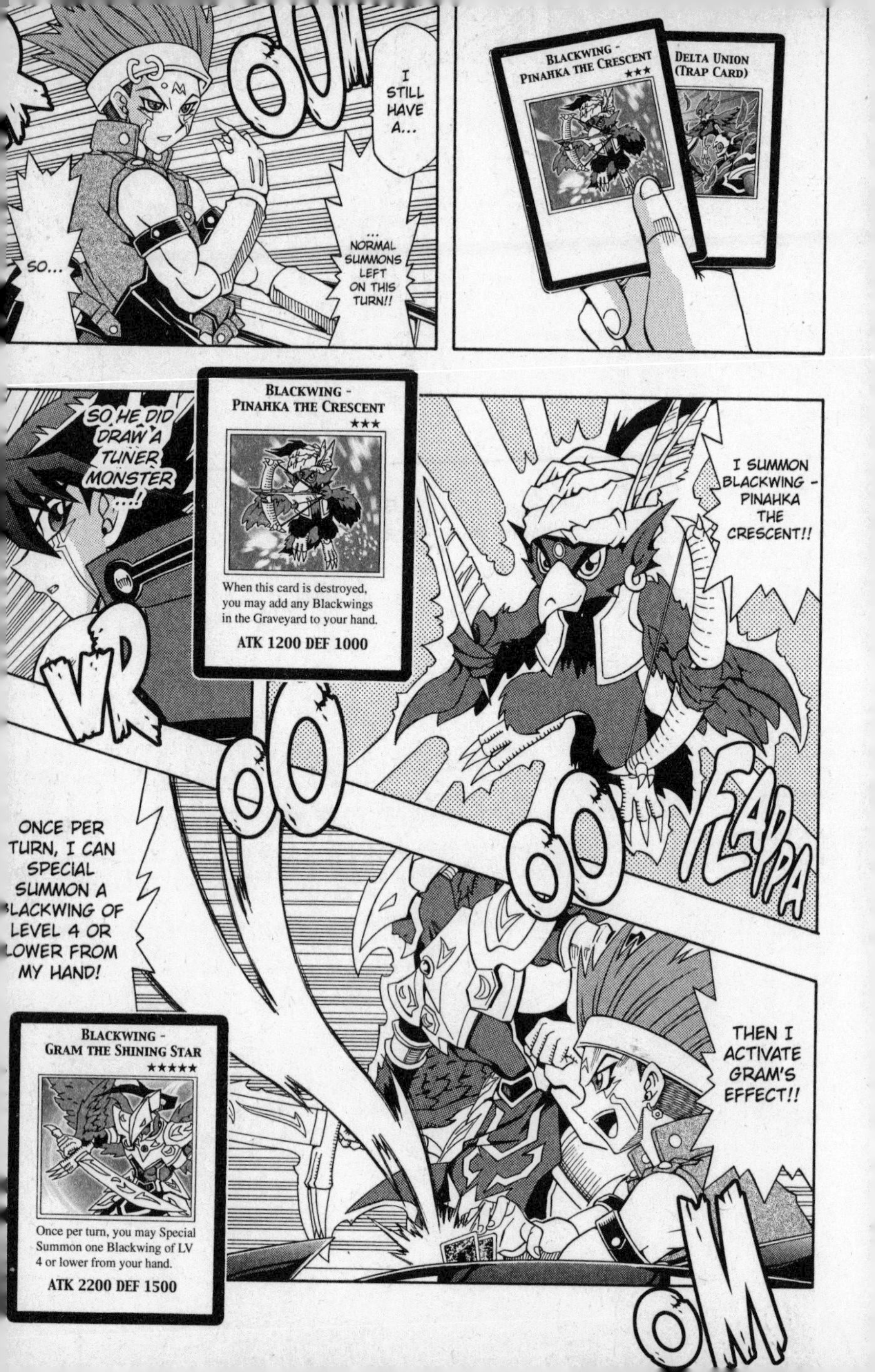
BLACKWING - PINAHKA THE CRESCENT ★★★
DELTA UNION (TRAP CARD)
I STILL HAVE A...
...NORMAL SUMMONS LEFT ON THIS TURN!!
SO...
I SUMMON BLACKWING - PINAHKA THE CRESCENT!!
FLAPPA
BLACKWING - PINAHKA THE CRESCENT
★★★
When this card is destroyed, you may add any Blackwings in the Graveyard to your hand.
ATK 1200 DEF 1000
SO HE DID DRAW A TUNER MONSTER...!
THEN I ACTIVATE GRAM'S EFFECT!!
ONCE PER TURN, I CAN SPECIAL SUMMON A LACKWING OF LEVEL 4 OR LOWER FROM MY HAND!
BLACKWING - GRAM THE SHINING STAR
★★★★★
Once per turn, you may Special Summon one Blackwing of LV 4 or lower from your hand.
ATK 2200 DEF 1500

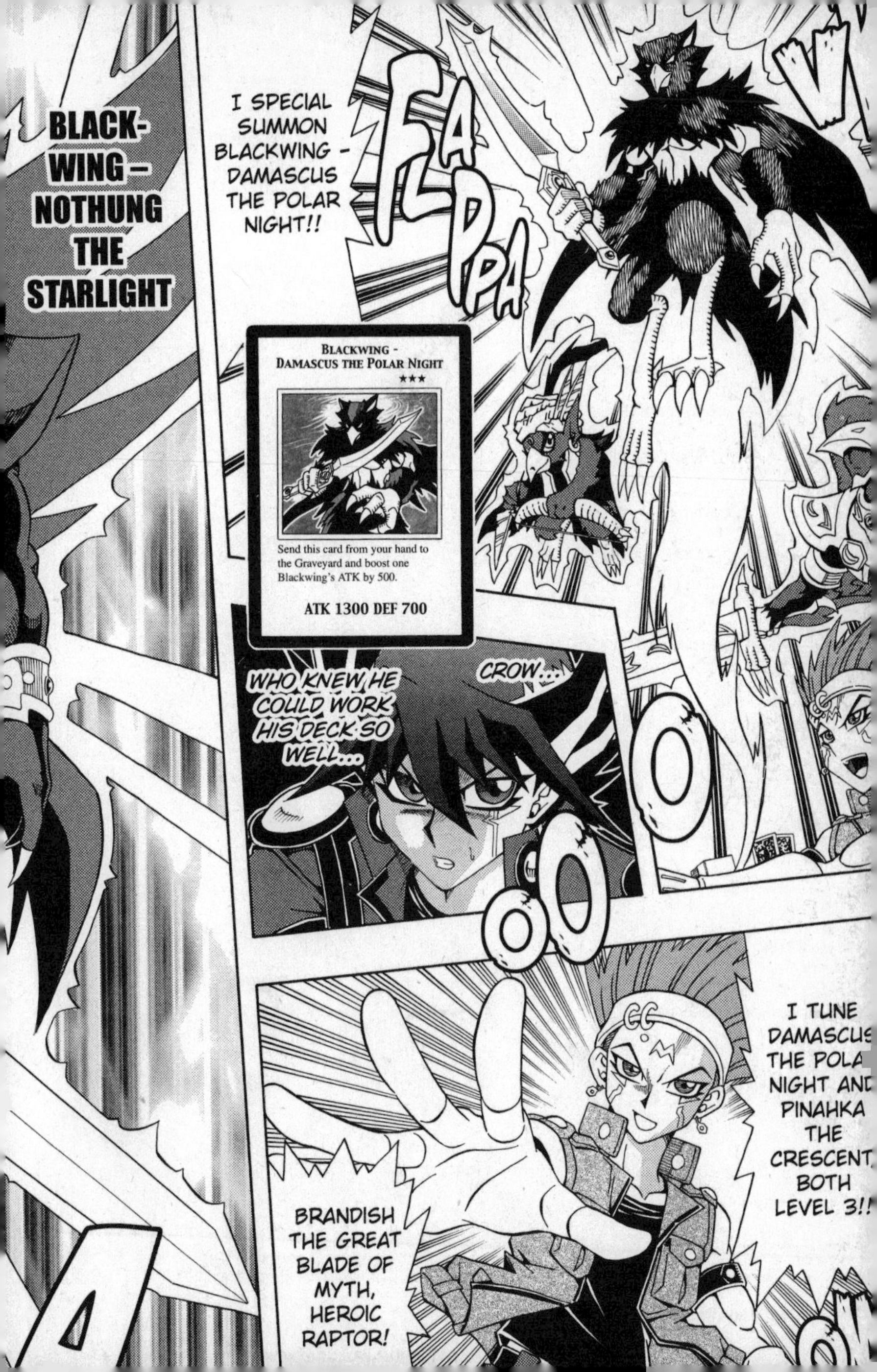
FLAPPA
I SPECIAL SUMMON BLACKWING – DAMASCUS THE POLAR NIGHT!!
BLACKWING - DAMASCUS THE POLAR NIGHT
★★★
Send this card from your hand to the Graveyard and boost one Blackwing's ATK by 500.
ATK 1300 DEF 700
CROW...
WHO KNEW HE COULD WORK HIS DECK SO WELL...
I TUNE DAMASCUS THE POLAR NIGHT AND PINAHKA THE CRESCENT, BOTH LEVEL 3!!
BRANDISH THE GREAT BLADE OF MYTH, HEROIC RAPTOR!
BLACK-WING – NOTHUNG THE STARLIGHT

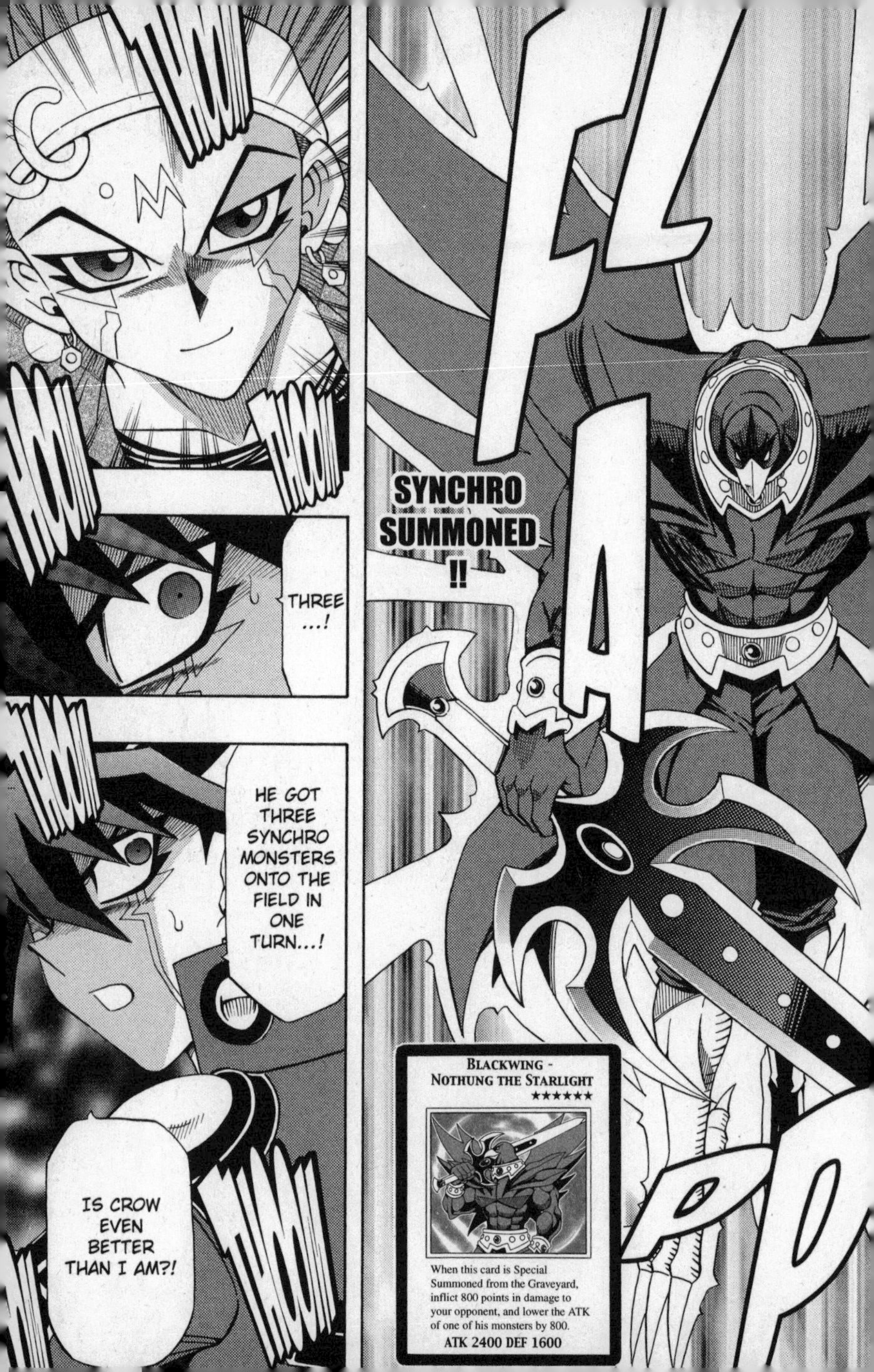
SYNCHRO SUMMONED !!
BLACKWING - NOTHUNG THE STARLIGHT
★★★★★★
When this card is Special Summoned from the Graveyard, inflict 800 points in damage to your opponent, and lower the ATK of one of his monsters by 800.
ATK 2400 DEF 1600
THREE ...!
HE GOT THREE SYNCHRO MONSTERS ONTO THE FIELD IN ONE TURN...!
IS CROW EVEN BETTER THAN I AM?!

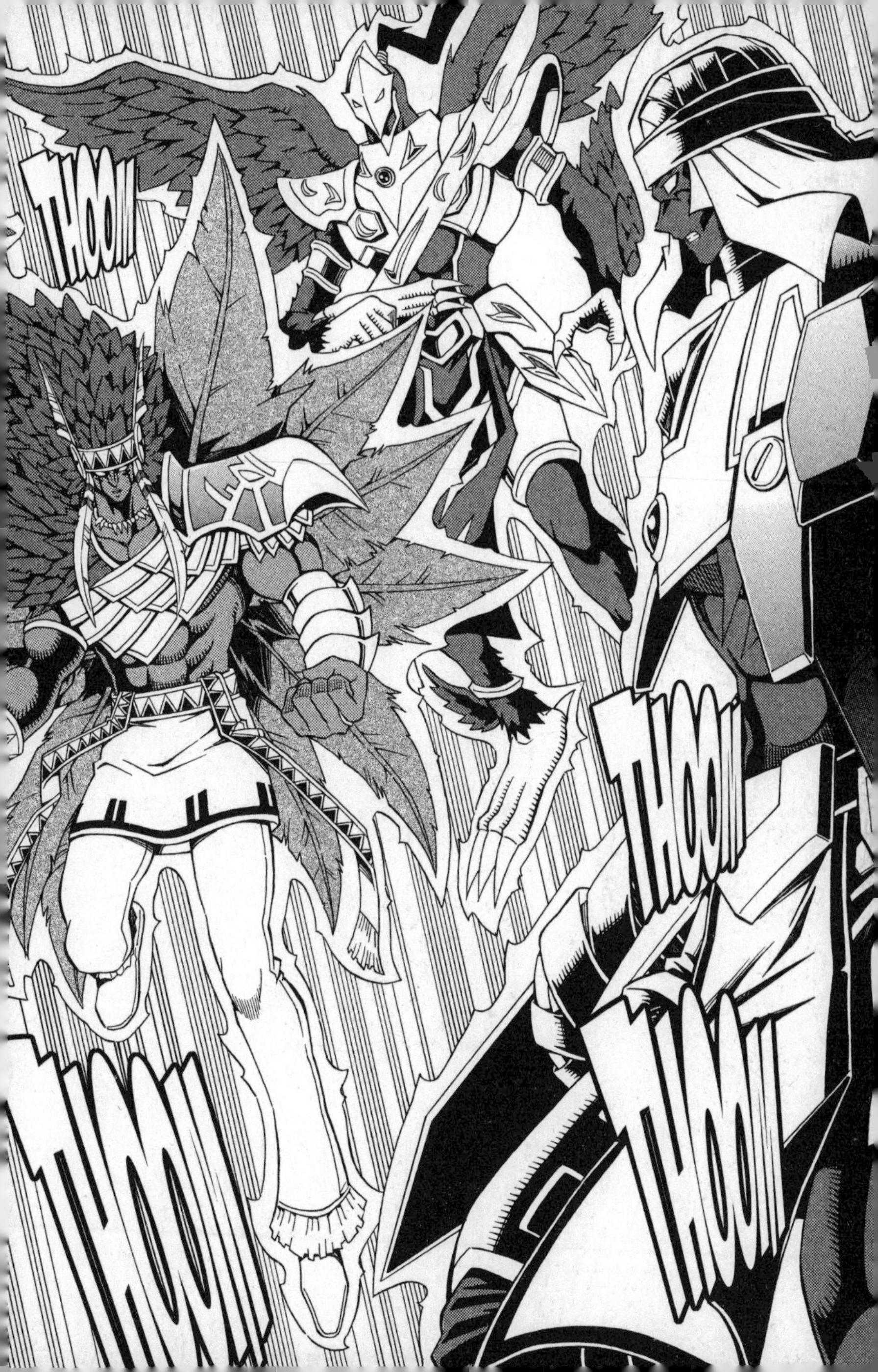
THOOM
THOOM
THOOM
THOOM

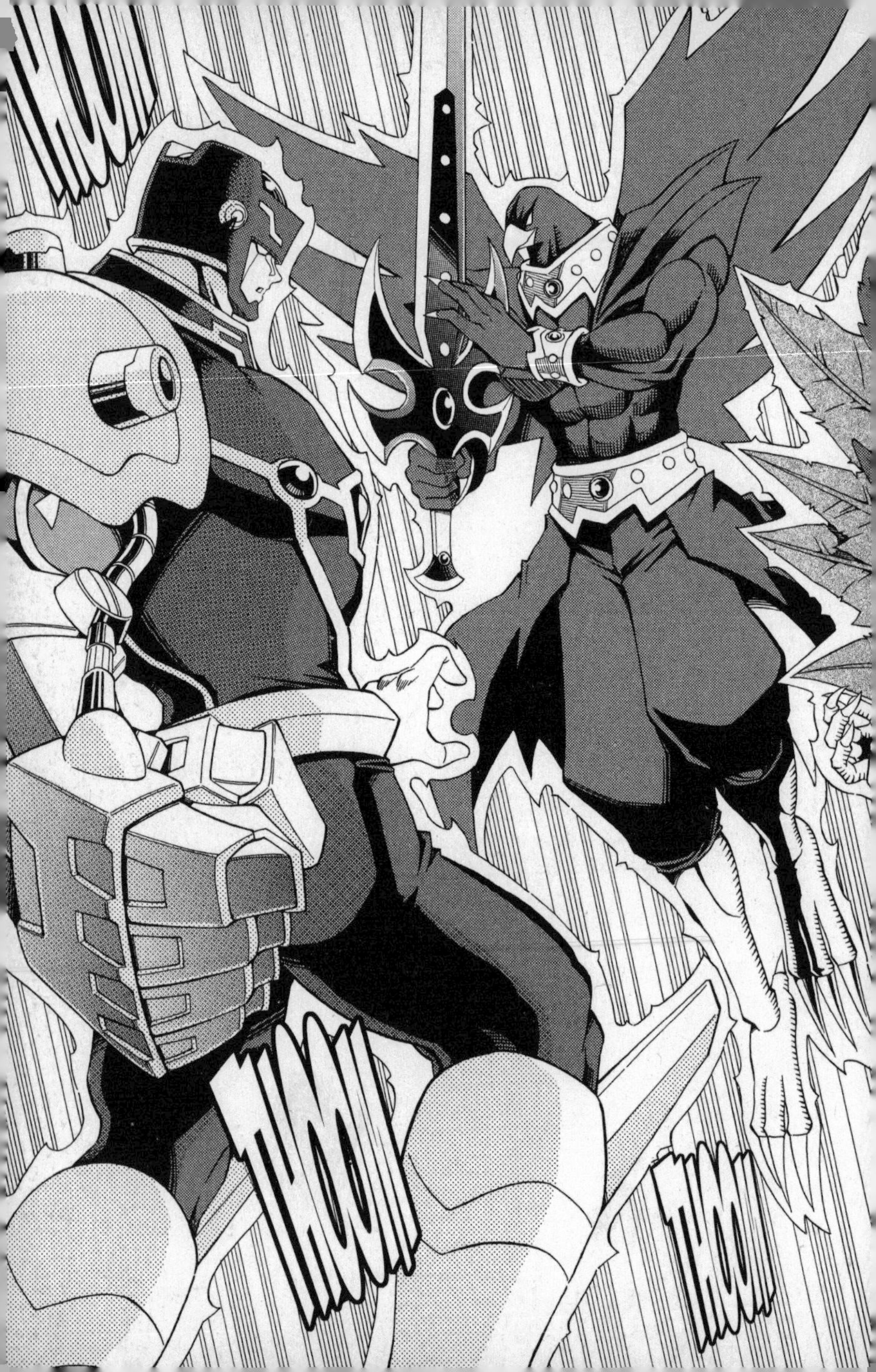
THOOM
THOOM
THOOM

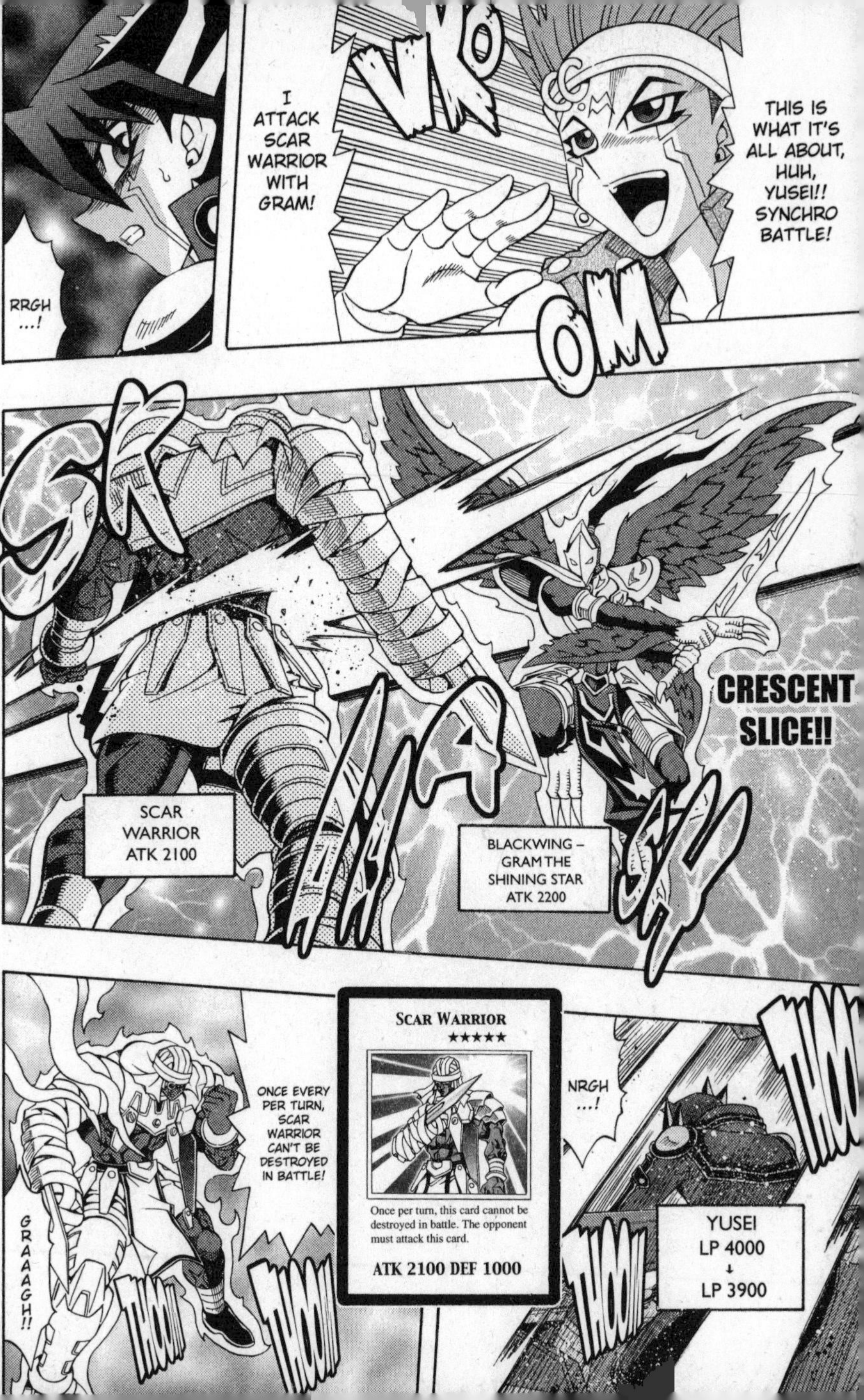
THIS IS WHAT IT'S ALL ABOUT, HUH, YUSEI!! SYNCHRO BATTLE!
I ATTACK SCAR WARRIOR WITH GRAM!
RRGH ...!
CRESCENT SLICE!!
BLACKWING – GRAM THE SHINING STAR ATK 2200
SCAR WARRIOR ATK 2100
NRGH ...!
YUSEI LP 4000 ↓ LP 3900
SCAR WARRIOR
★★★★★
Once per turn, this card cannot be destroyed in battle. The opponent must attack this card.
ATK 2100 DEF 1000
ONCE EVERY PER TURN, SCAR WARRIOR CAN'T BE DESTROYED IN BATTLE!
GRAAAAGH!!

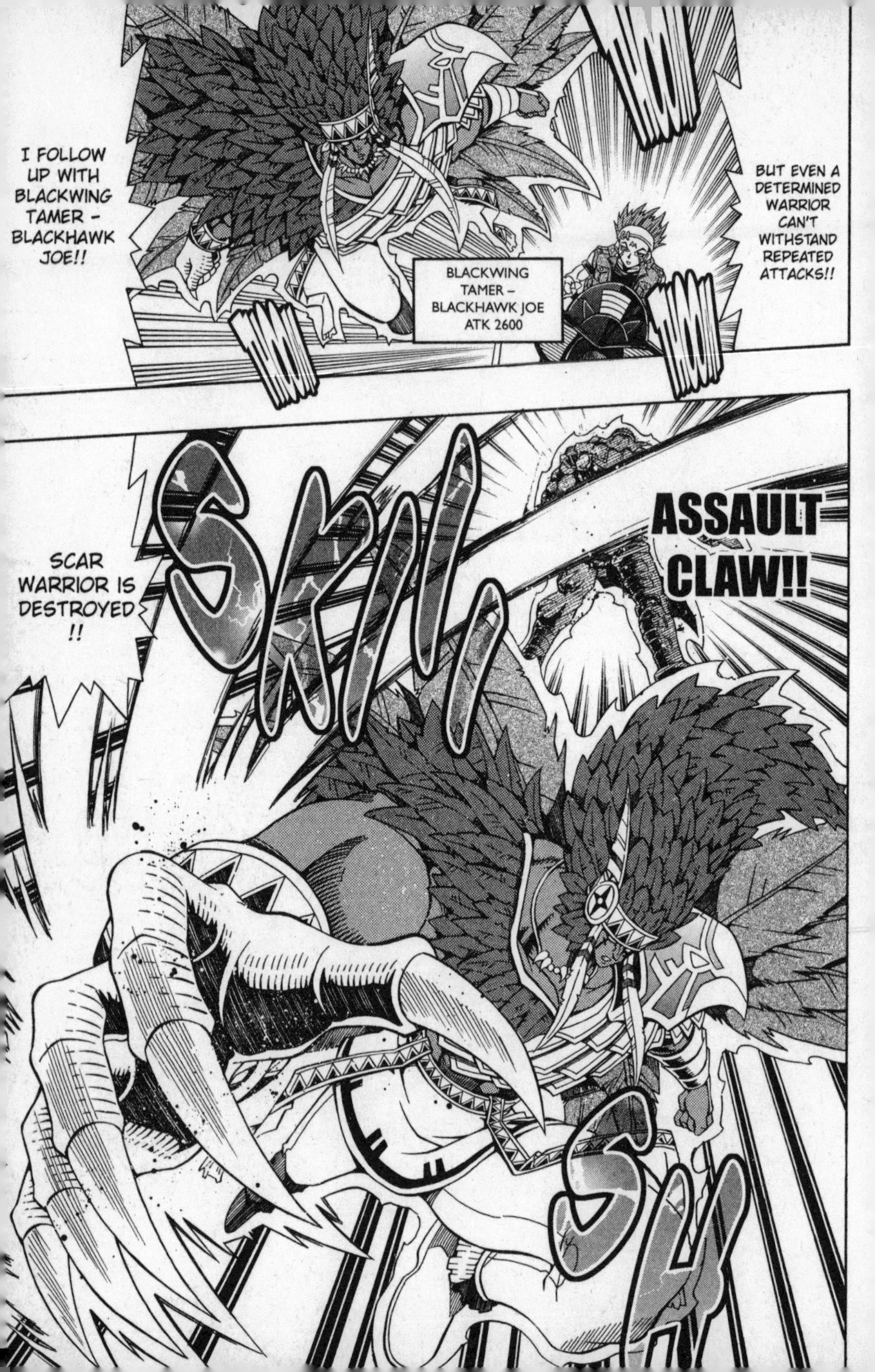
BUT EVEN A DETERMINED WARRIOR CAN'T WITHSTAND REPEATED ATTACKS!!
BLACKWING TAMER – BLACKHAWK JOE ATK 2600
I FOLLOW UP WITH BLACKWING TAMER – BLACKHAWK JOE!!
ASSAULT CLAW!!
SCAR WARRIOR IS DESTROYED !!

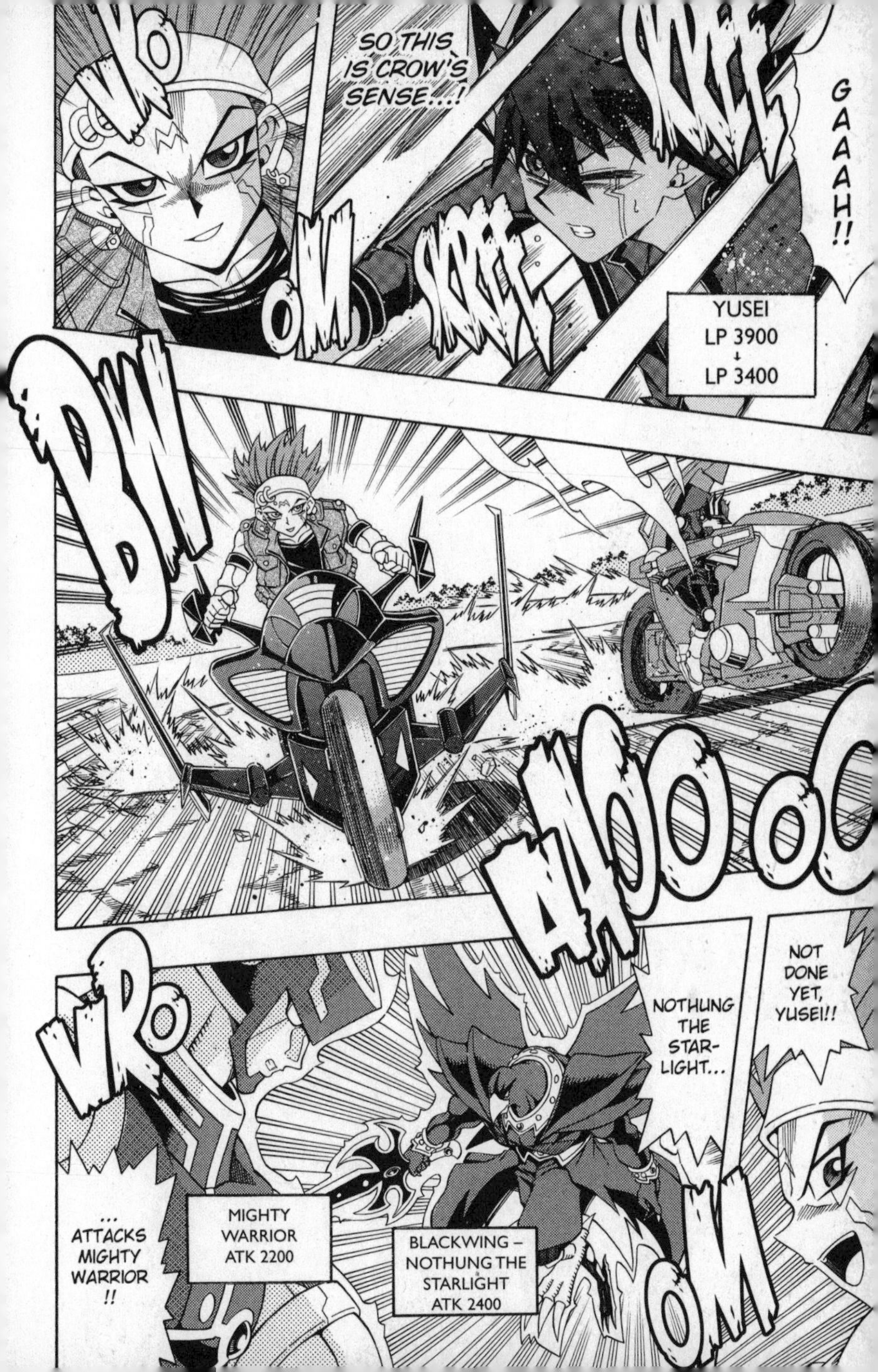
GAAAAH!!
YUSEI
LP 3900
↓
LP 3400
SO THIS IS CROW'S SENSE...!
NOT DONE YET, YUSEI!!
NOTHUNG THE STAR-LIGHT...
BLACKWING – NOTHUNG THE STARLIGHT ATK 2400
MIGHTY WARRIOR ATK 2200
...ATTACKS MIGHTY WARRIOR!!

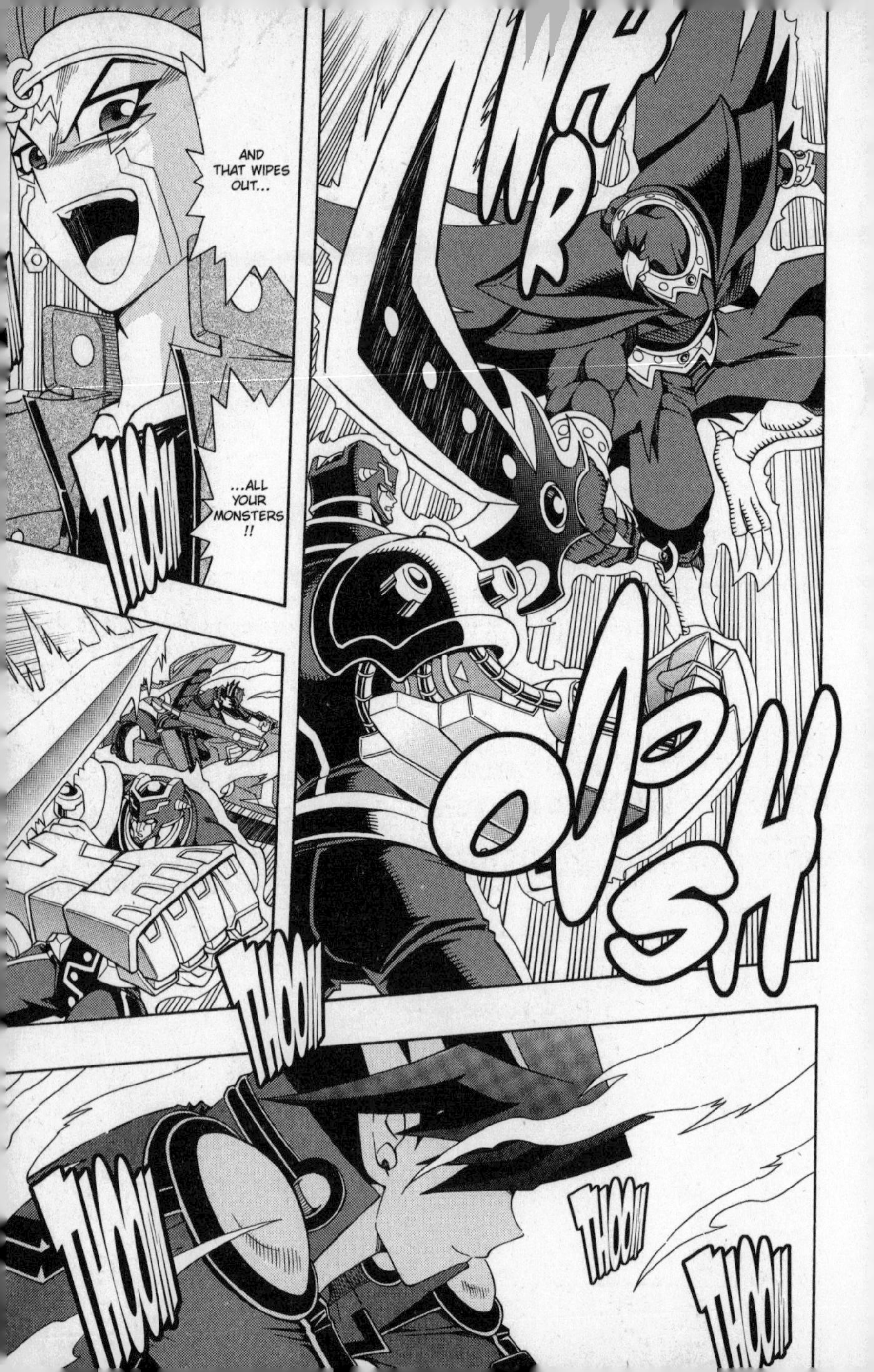
AND THAT WIPES OUT...
THOOM
...ALL YOUR MONSTERS!!
THOOM
THOOM
THOOM
THOOM

5D's TRACKS

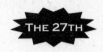

THE 27TH

BY SATOMASA

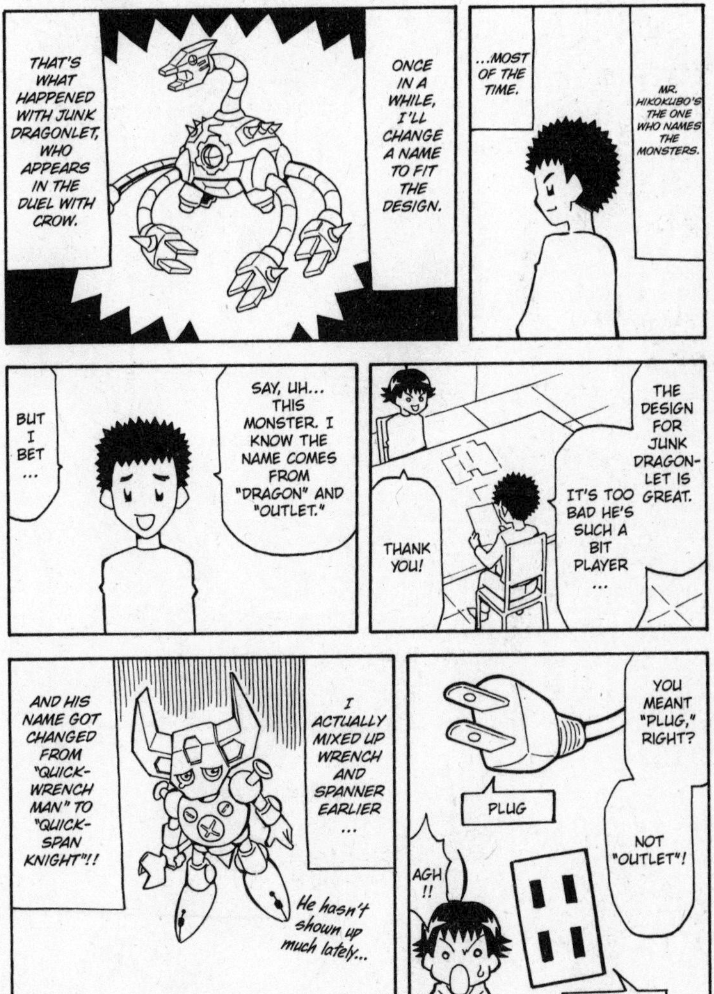
MR. HIKOKUBO'S THE ONE WHO NAMES THE MONSTERS.
...MOST OF THE TIME.
ONCE IN A WHILE, I'LL CHANGE A NAME TO FIT THE DESIGN.
THAT'S WHAT HAPPENED WITH JUNK DRAGONLET, WHO APPEARS IN THE DUEL WITH CROW.
THE DESIGN FOR JUNK DRAGON-LET IS GREAT.
IT'S TOO BAD HE'S SUCH A BIT PLAYER...
THANK YOU!
SAY, UH... THIS MONSTER. I KNOW THE NAME COMES FROM "DRAGON" AND "OUTLET."
BUT I BET...
YOU MEANT "PLUG," RIGHT?
PLUG
NOT "OUTLET"!
AGH!!
OUTLET
I ACTUALLY MIXED UP WRENCH AND SPANNER EARLIER...
AND HIS NAME GOT CHANGED FROM "QUICK-WRENCH MAN" TO "QUICK-SPAN KNIGHT"!!
He hasn't shown up much lately...

RIDE-28 RESONANCE...!!

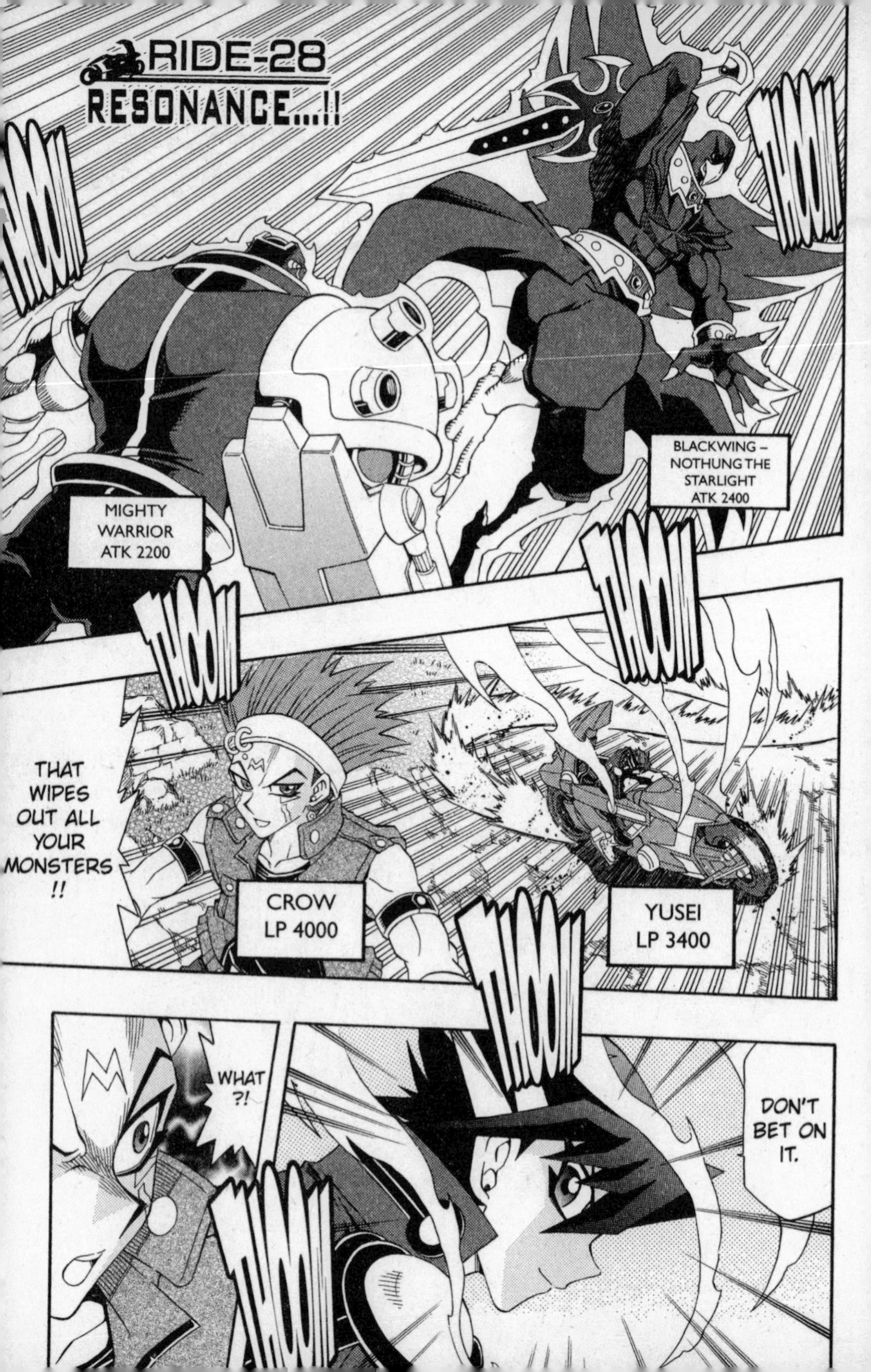
THOOM
BLACKWING – NOTHUNG THE STARLIGHT ATK 2400
THOOM
MIGHTY WARRIOR ATK 2200
THOOM
THOOM
YUSEI LP 3400
CROW LP 4000
THAT WIPES OUT ALL YOUR MONSTERS !!
THOOM
DON'T BET ON IT.
THOOM
WHAT ?!

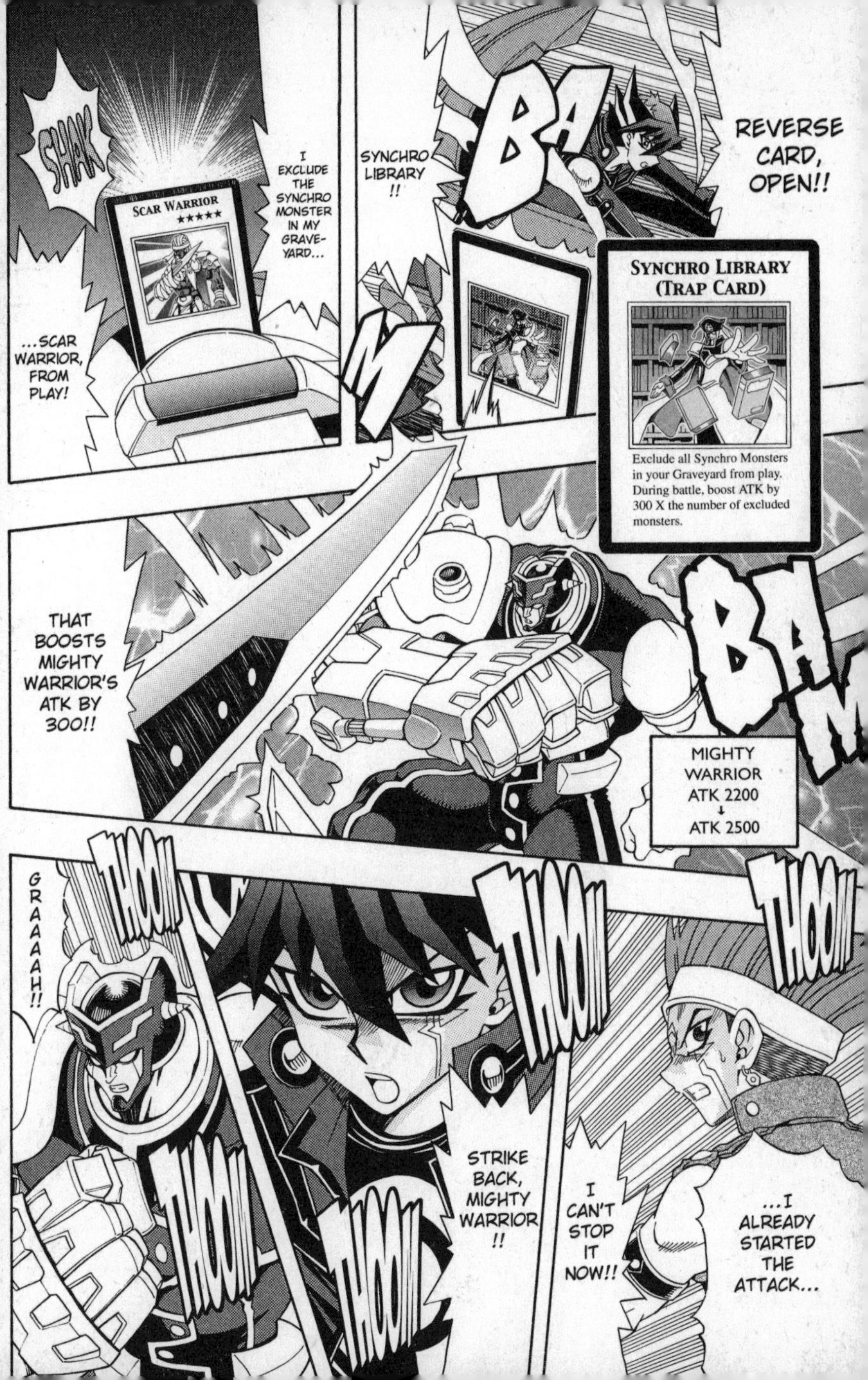
REVERSE CARD, OPEN!!
BAM
SYNCHRO LIBRARY !!
SYNCHRO LIBRARY
(TRAP CARD)
Exclude all Synchro Monsters in your Graveyard from play. During battle, boost ATK by 300 X the number of excluded monsters.
I EXCLUDE THE SYNCHRO MONSTER IN MY GRAVEYARD...
SHAK
SCAR WARRIOR
★★★★★
...SCAR WARRIOR, FROM PLAY!
BAM
MIGHTY WARRIOR ATK 2200 ↓ ATK 2500
THAT BOOSTS MIGHTY WARRIOR'S ATK BY 300!!
THOOM
...I ALREADY STARTED THE ATTACK...
I CAN'T STOP IT NOW!!
THOOM
STRIKE BACK, MIGHTY WARRIOR !!
THOOM
THOOM
THOOM
GRAAAAAH!!

RIDE-28 RESONANCE...!!

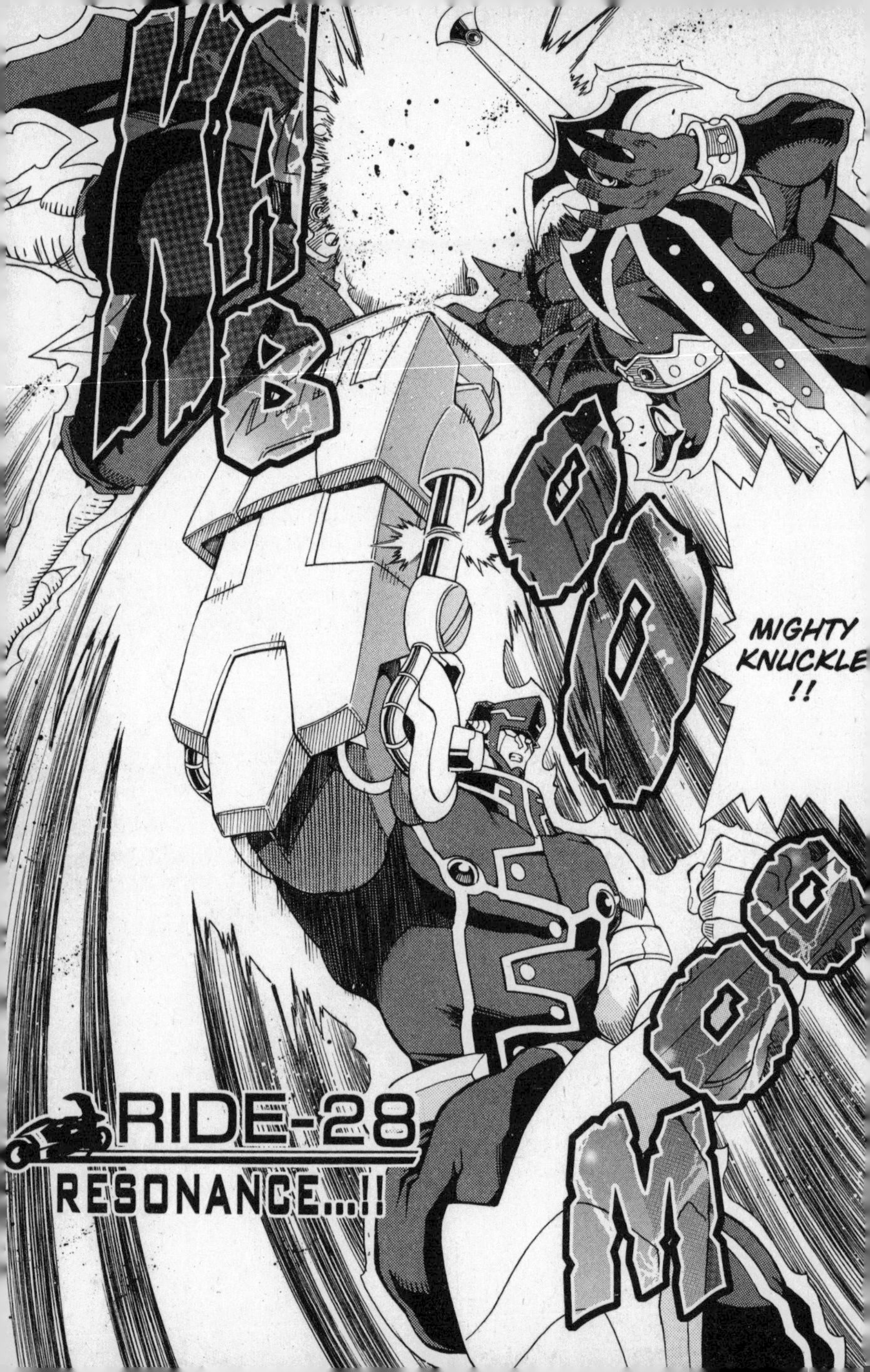
MIGHTY KNUCKLE !!
KABOOOOM

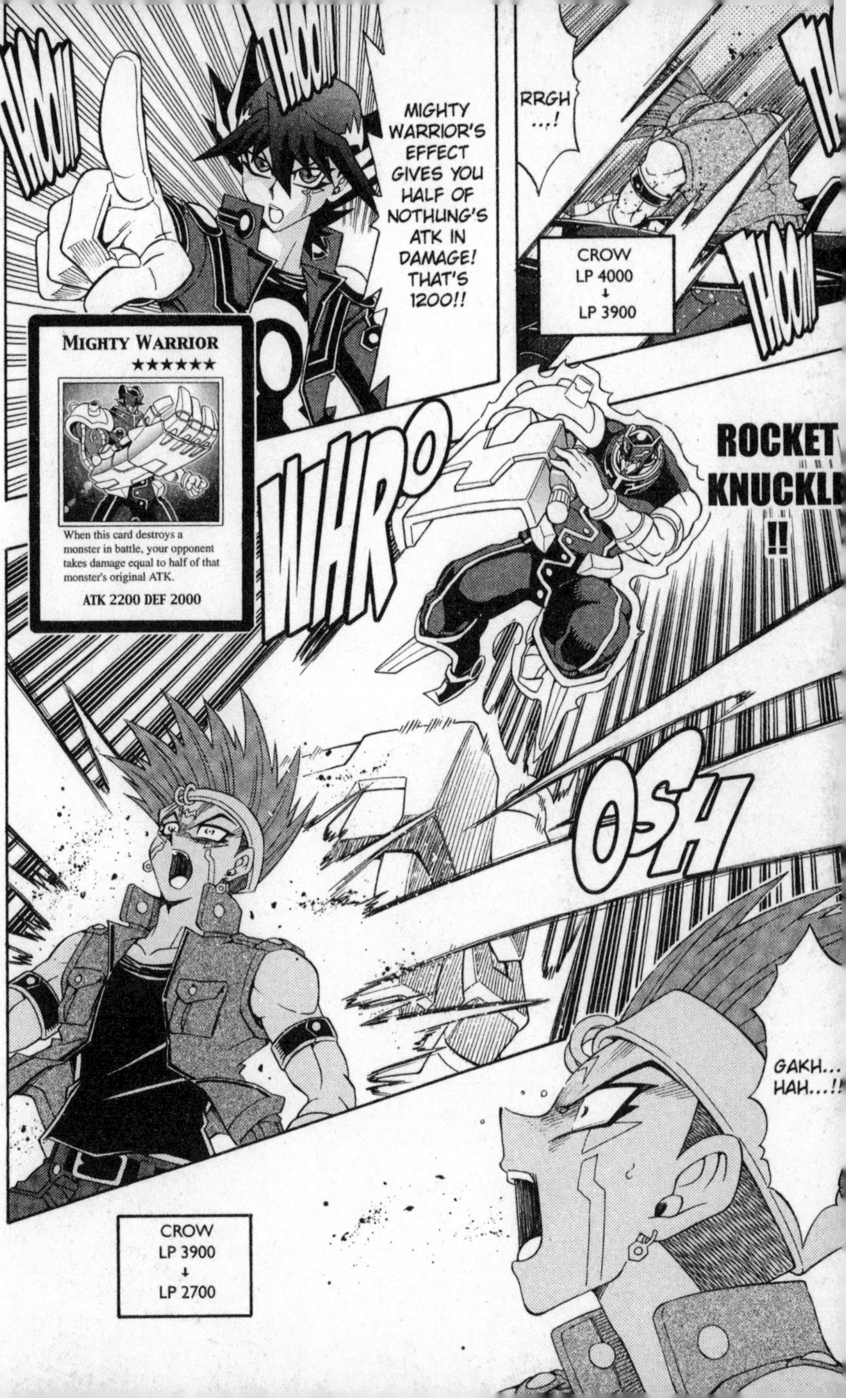
RRGH ...!
THOOM
CROW
LP 4000
↓
LP 3900
THOOM
THOOM
THOOM
MIGHTY WARRIOR'S EFFECT GIVES YOU HALF OF NOTHUNG'S ATK IN DAMAGE! THAT'S 1200!!
Mighty Warrior
★★★★★★
When this card destroys a monster in battle, your opponent takes damage equal to half of that monster's original ATK.
ATK 2200 DEF 2000
ROCKET KNUCKLE!!
WHRO
OSH
GAKH... HAH...!!
CROW
LP 3900
↓
LP 2700

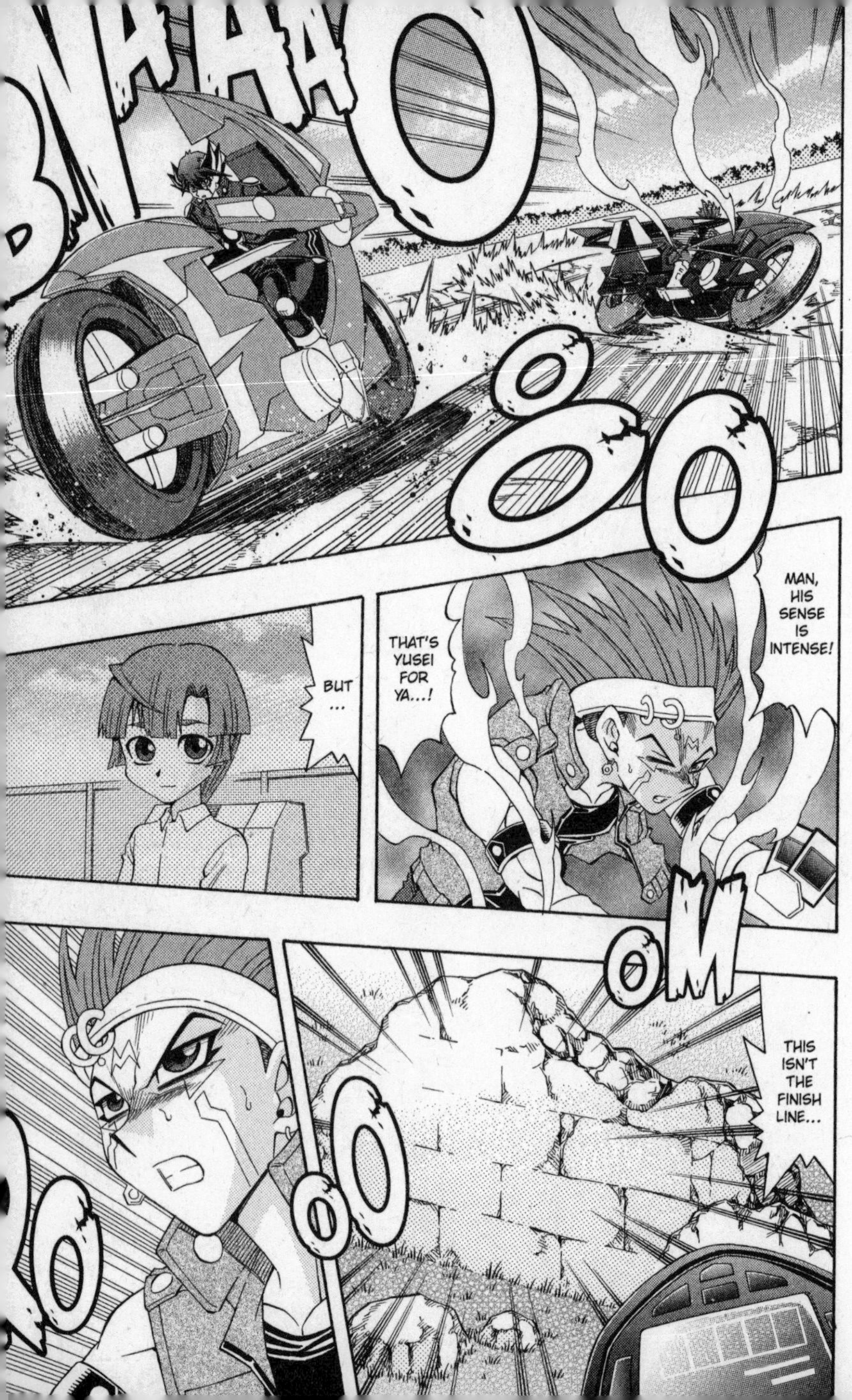
MAN, HIS SENSE IS INTENSE!
THAT'S YUSEI FOR YA...!
BUT ...
THIS ISN'T THE FINISH LINE...

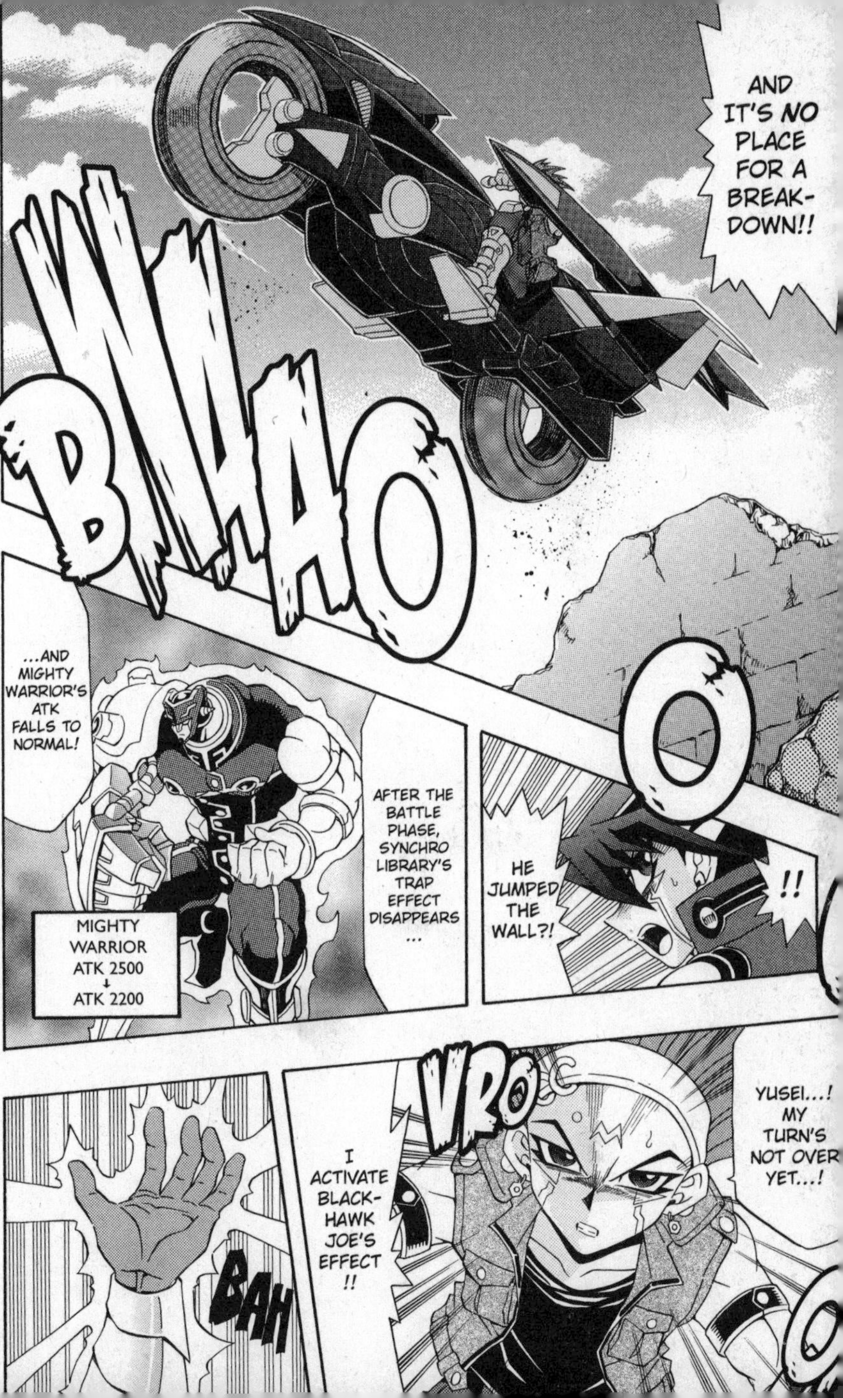
AND IT'S NO PLACE FOR A BREAK-DOWN!!
BWHAOO
!!
HE JUMPED THE WALL?!
AFTER THE BATTLE PHASE, SYNCHRO LIBRARY'S TRAP EFFECT DISAPPEARS...
...AND MIGHTY WARRIOR'S ATK FALLS TO NORMAL!
MIGHTY WARRIOR ATK 2500 ↓ ATK 2200
YUSEI...! MY TURN'S NOT OVER YET...!
VRO
I ACTIVATE BLACK-HAWK JOE'S EFFECT!!
BAH

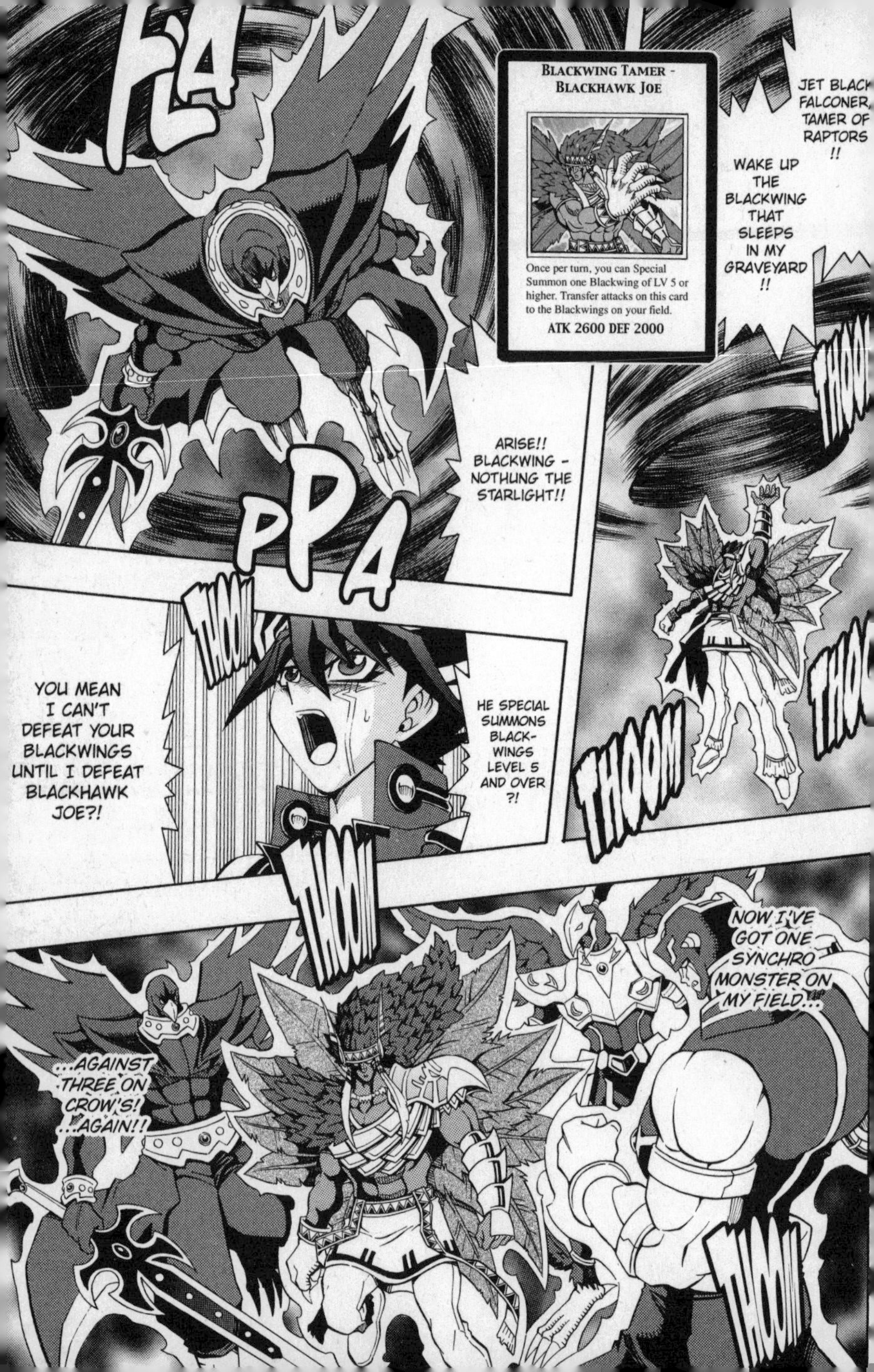
BLACKWING TAMER - BLACKHAWK JOE
Once per turn, you can Special Summon one Blackwing of LV 5 or higher. Transfer attacks on this card to the Blackwings on your field.
ATK 2600 DEF 2000
JET BLACK FALCONER, TAMER OF RAPTORS!!
WAKE UP THE BLACKWING THAT SLEEPS IN MY GRAVEYARD!!
FLA
ARISE!! BLACKWING - NOTHUNG THE STARLIGHT!!
PPA
THOOM
THOOM
THOOM
HE SPECIAL SUMMONS BLACKWINGS LEVEL 5 AND OVER?!
YOU MEAN I CAN'T DEFEAT YOUR BLACKWINGS UNTIL I DEFEAT BLACKHAWK JOE?!
THOOM
THOOM
NOW I'VE GOT ONE SYNCHRO MONSTER ON MY FIELD...
...AGAINST THREE ON CROW'S! ...AGAIN!!
THOOM

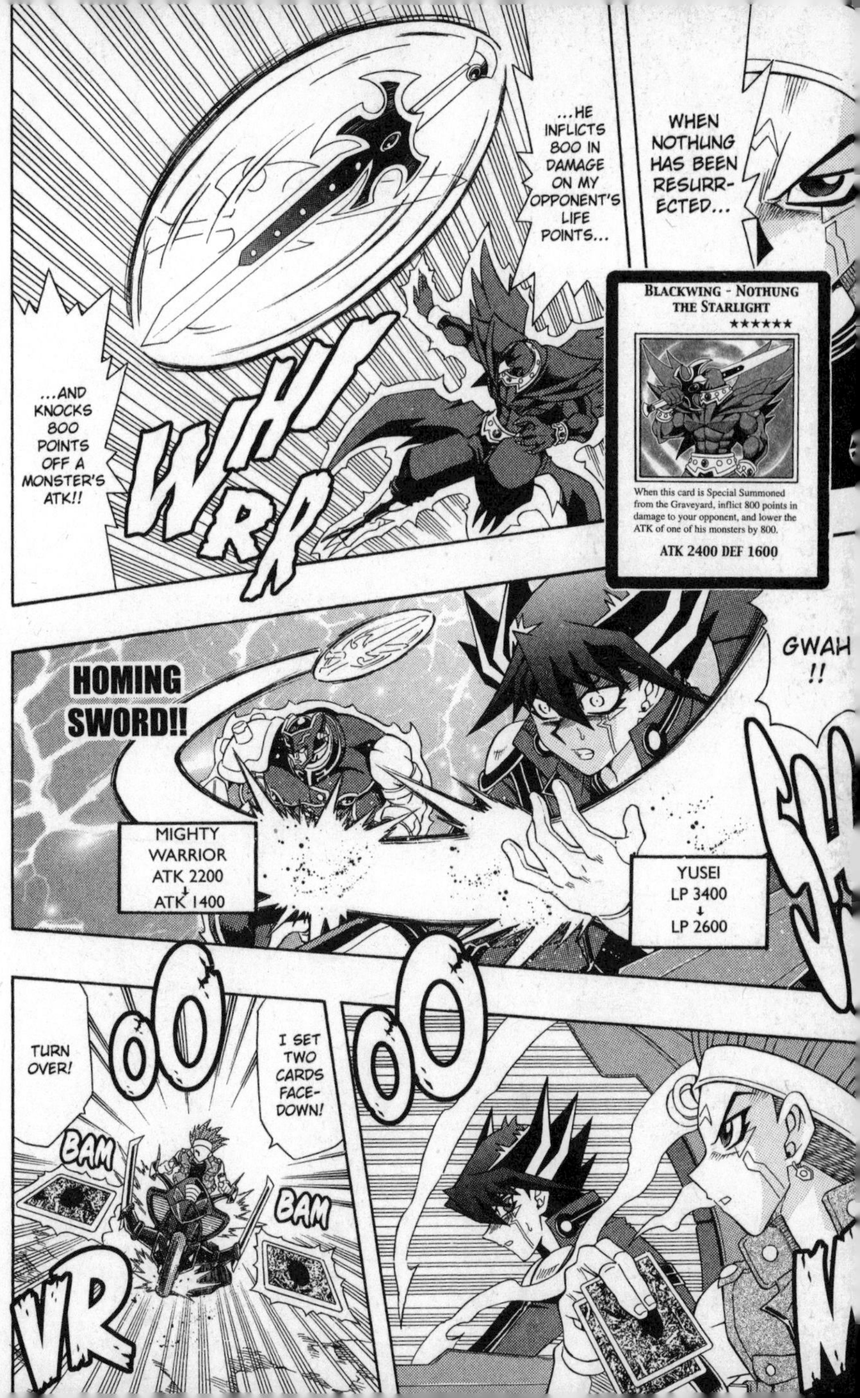
WHEN NOTHUNG HAS BEEN RESURR-ECTED...
...HE INFLICTS 800 IN DAMAGE ON MY OPPONENT'S LIFE POINTS...
BLACKWING - NOTHUNG THE STARLIGHT
★★★★★★
When this card is Special Summoned from the Graveyard, inflict 800 points in damage to your opponent, and lower the ATK of one of his monsters by 800.
ATK 2400 DEF 1600
...AND KNOCKS 800 POINTS OFF A MONSTER'S ATK!!
WHI WRR
GWAH!!
HOMING SWORD!!
YUSEI LP 3400 ↓ LP 2600
MIGHTY WARRIOR ATK 2200 ↓ ATK 1400
I SET TWO CARDS FACE-DOWN!
TURN OVER!
BAM
BAM
VR

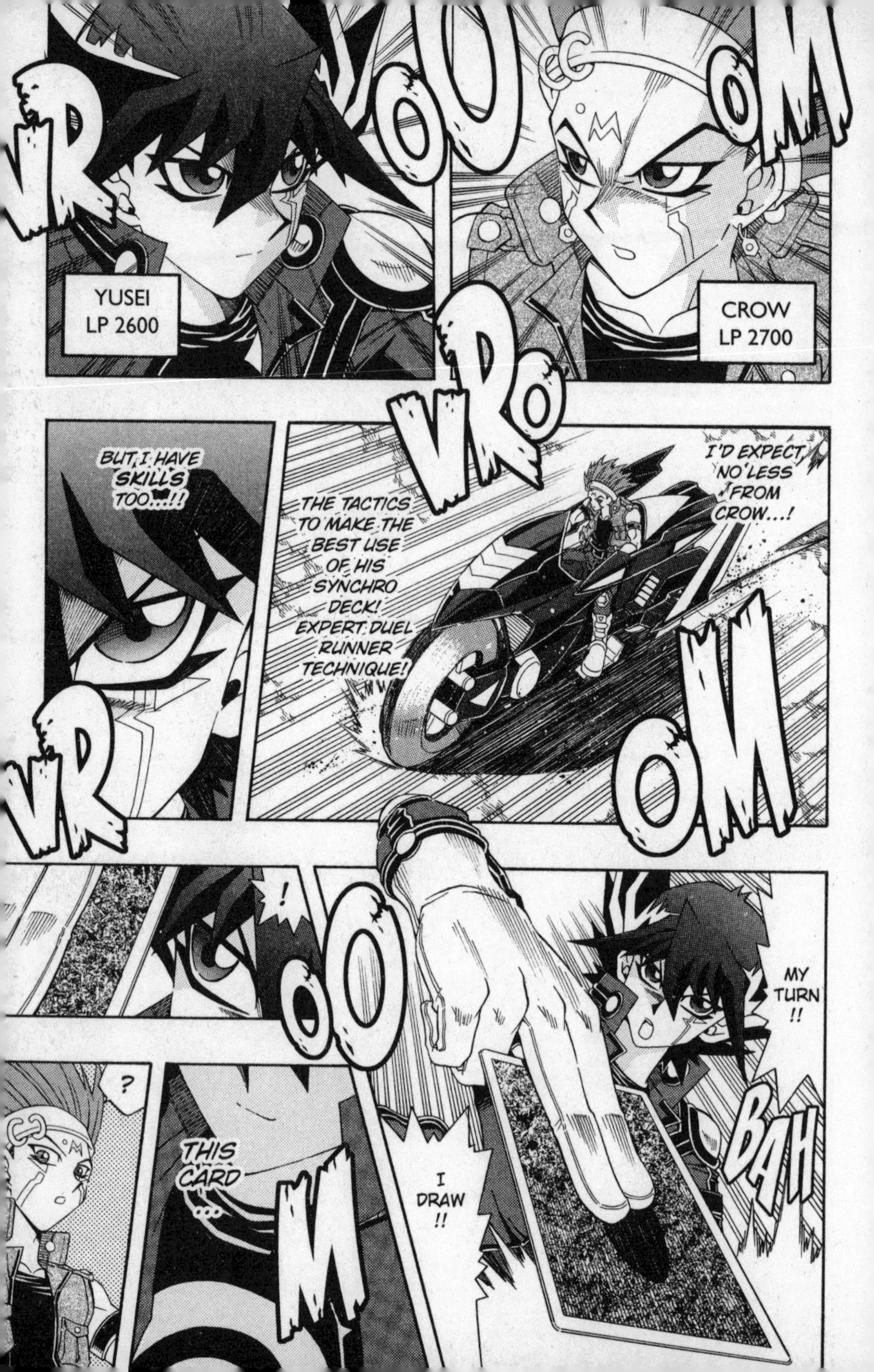
CROW
LP 2700
YUSEI
LP 2600
I'D EXPECT NO LESS FROM CROW...!
THE TACTICS TO MAKE THE BEST USE OF HIS SYNCHRO DECK! EXPERT DUEL RUNNER TECHNIQUE!
BUT I HAVE SKILLS TOO...!!
MY TURN!!
!
BAH
I DRAW!!
THIS CARD...
?

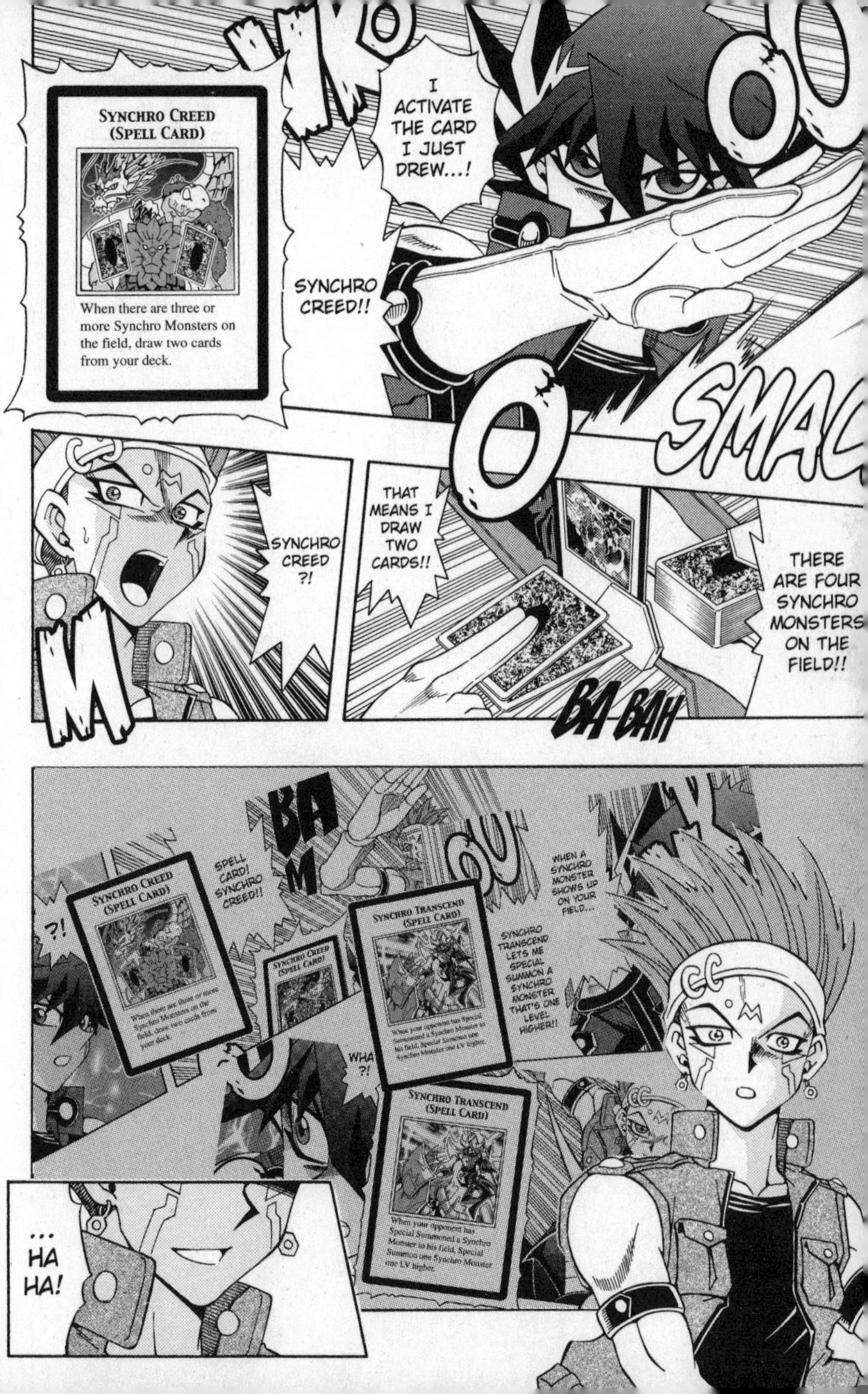
I ACTIVATE THE CARD I JUST DREW...!
SYNCHRO CREED!!
SYNCHRO CREED (SPELL CARD)
When there are three or more Synchro Monsters on the field, draw two cards from your deck.
SMAC
THERE ARE FOUR SYNCHRO MONSTERS ON THE FIELD!!
THAT MEANS I DRAW TWO CARDS!!
BA BAH
SYNCHRO CREED ?!
M
WHEN A SYNCHRO MONSTER SHOWS UP ON YOUR FIELD...
SYNCHRO TRANSCEND LETS ME SPECIAL SUMMON A SYNCHRO MONSTER THAT'S ONE LEVEL HIGHER!!
BAM
SPELL CARD! SYNCHRO CREED!!
SYNCHRO CREED (SPELL CARD)
SYNCHRO TRANSCEND (SPELL CARD)
?!
WHA ?!
SYNCHRO TRANSCEND (SPELL CARD)
When your opponent has Special Summoned a Synchro Monster to his field, Special Summon one Synchro Monster one LV higher.
...HA HA!

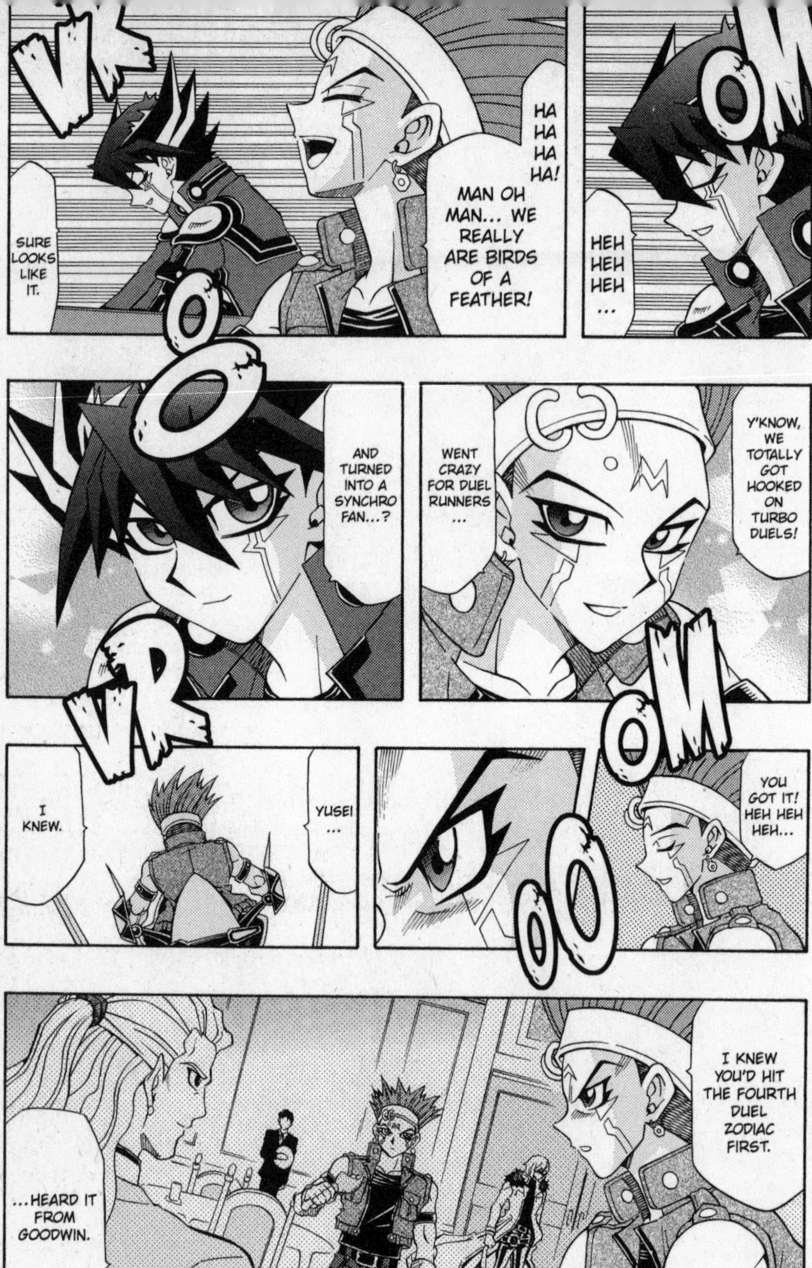
HEH HEH HEH ...
OOM
HA HA HA HA!
MAN OH MAN... WE REALLY ARE BIRDS OF A FEATHER!
VR
SURE LOOKS LIKE IT.
O
Y'KNOW, WE TOTALLY GOT HOOKED ON TURBO DUELS!
WENT CRAZY FOR DUEL RUNNERS ...
AND TURNED INTO A SYNCHRO FAN...?
O
OOM
VR
YOU GOT IT! HEH HEH HEH...
OO
YUSEI ...
I KNEW.
I KNEW YOU'D HIT THE FOURTH DUEL ZODIAC FIRST.
...HEARD IT FROM GOODWIN.

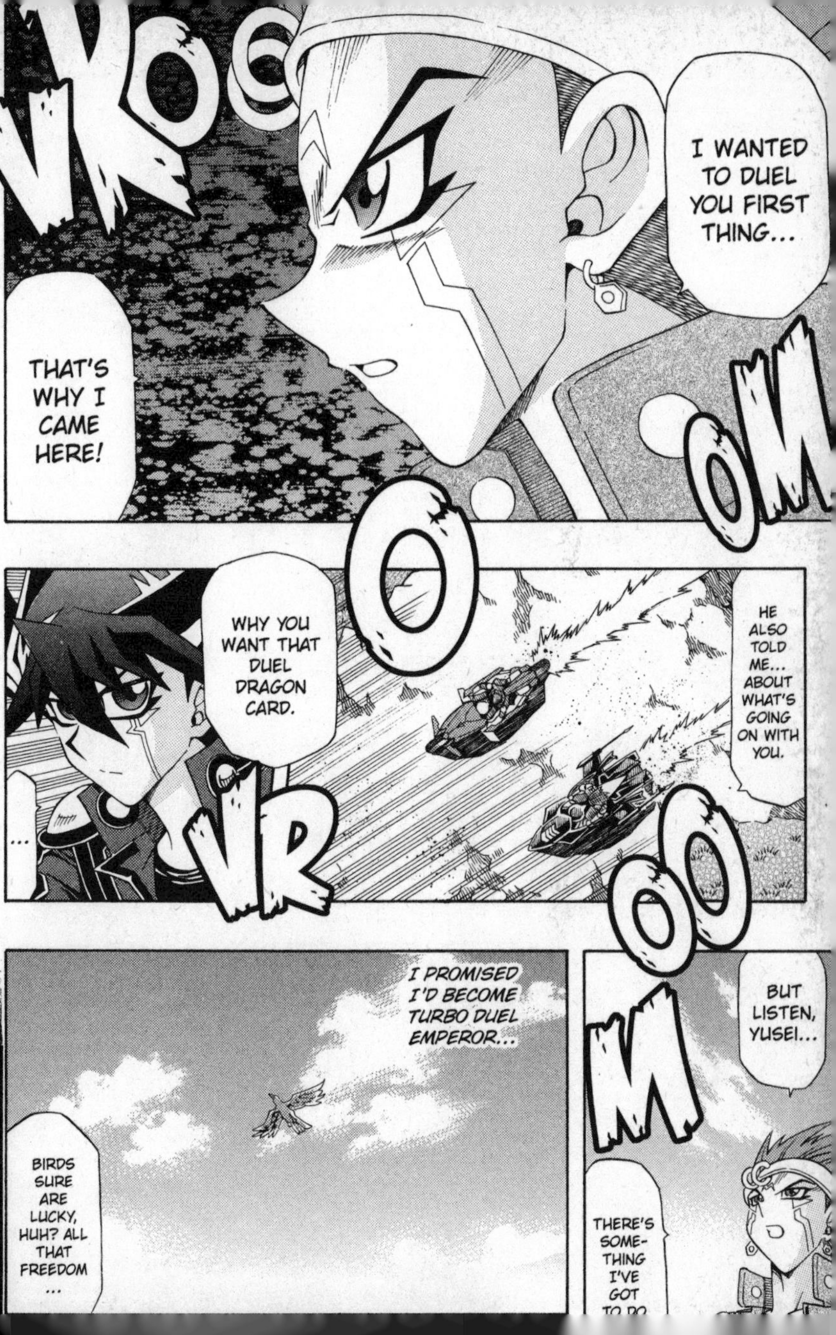
VROOOOM
I WANTED TO DUEL YOU FIRST THING...
THAT'S WHY I CAME HERE!
HE ALSO TOLD ME... ABOUT WHAT'S GOING ON WITH YOU.
WHY YOU WANT THAT DUEL DRAGON CARD.
...
VROOOOM
BUT LISTEN, YUSEI...
THERE'S SOME-THING I'VE GOT TO DO
I PROMISED I'D BECOME TURBO DUEL EMPEROR...
BIRDS SURE ARE LUCKY, HUH? ALL THAT FREEDOM...

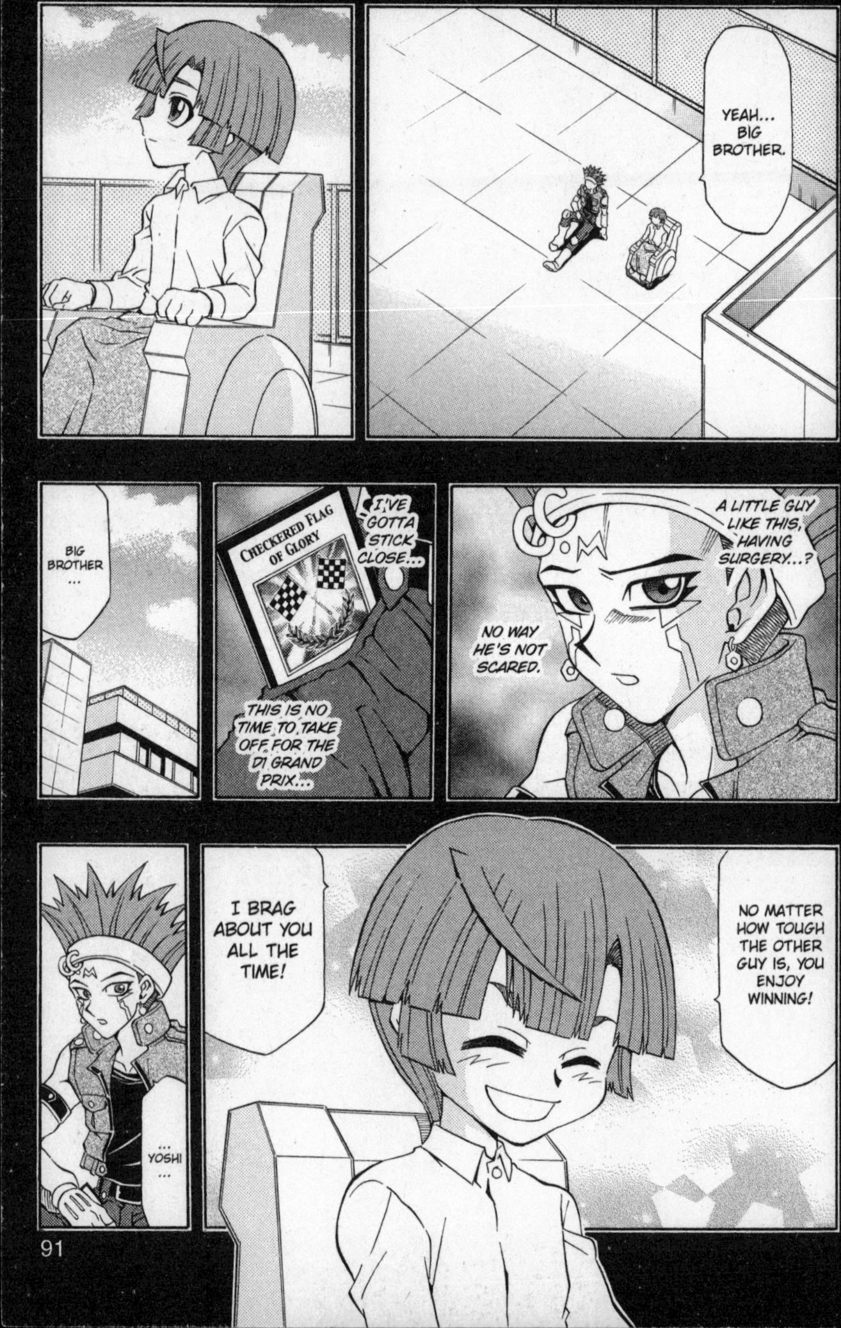
YEAH... BIG BROTHER.
A LITTLE GUY LIKE THIS, HAVING SURGERY...?
NO WAY HE'S NOT SCARED.
I'VE GOTTA STICK CLOSE...
CHECKERED FLAG OF GLORY
THIS IS NO TIME TO TAKE OFF FOR THE D1 GRAND PRIX...
BIG BROTHER ...
NO MATTER HOW TOUGH THE OTHER GUY IS, YOU ENJOY WINNING!
I BRAG ABOUT YOU ALL THE TIME!
... YOSHI ...

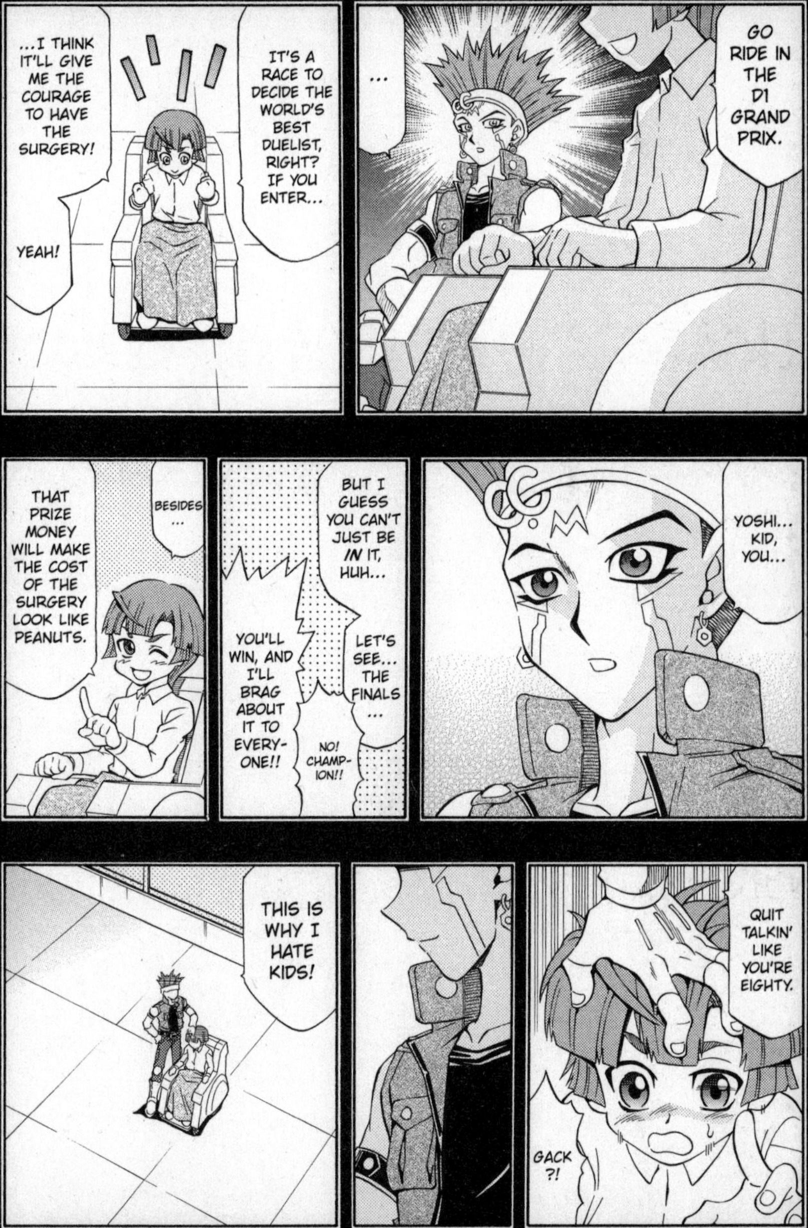
GO RIDE IN THE D1 GRAND PRIX.
...
IT'S A RACE TO DECIDE THE WORLD'S BEST DUELIST, RIGHT? IF YOU ENTER...
...I THINK IT'LL GIVE ME THE COURAGE TO HAVE THE SURGERY!
YEAH!
YOSHI... KID, YOU...
BUT I GUESS YOU CAN'T JUST BE *IN* IT, HUH...
LET'S SEE... THE FINALS...
NO! CHAMPION!!
YOU'LL WIN, AND I'LL BRAG ABOUT IT TO EVERYONE!!
BESIDES...
THAT PRIZE MONEY WILL MAKE THE COST OF THE SURGERY LOOK LIKE PEANUTS.
QUIT TALKIN' LIKE YOU'RE EIGHTY.
GACK?!
THIS IS WHY I HATE KIDS!

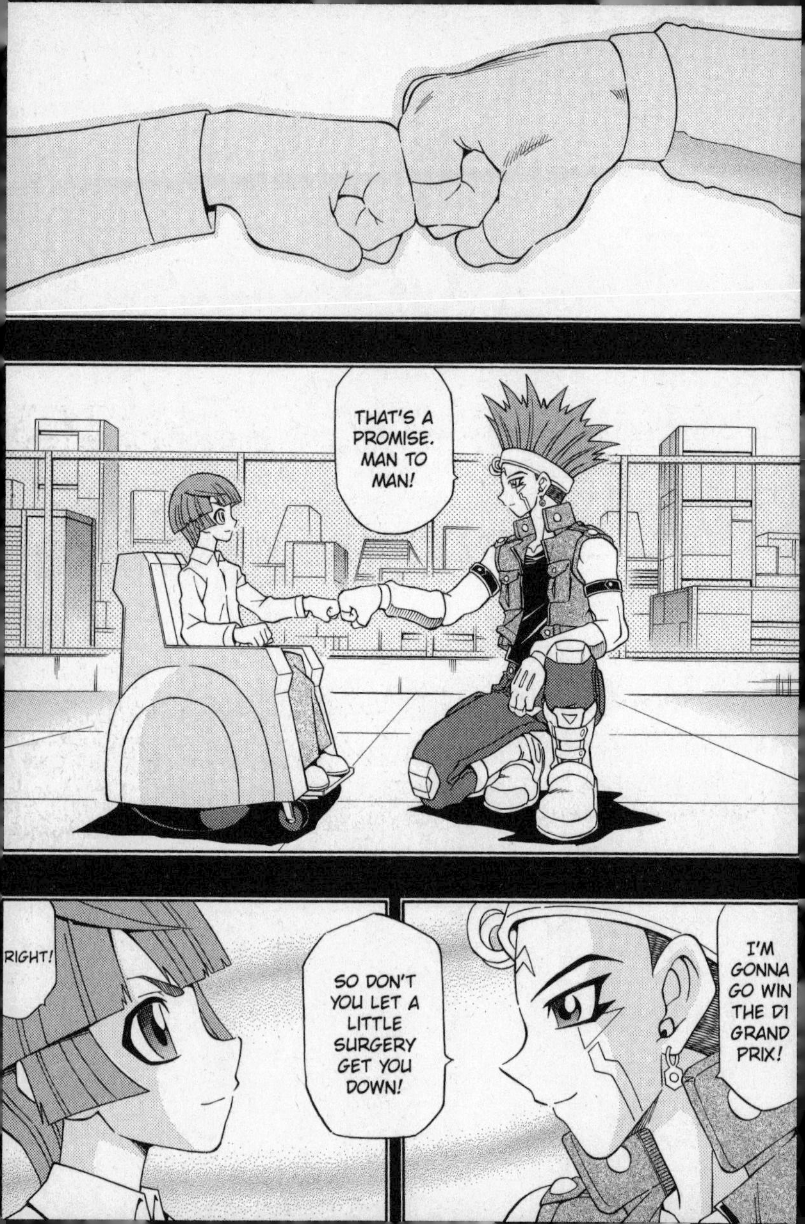
THAT'S A PROMISE. MAN TO MAN!
I'M GONNA GO WIN THE D1 GRAND PRIX!
SO DON'T YOU LET A LITTLE SURGERY GET YOU DOWN!
RIGHT!

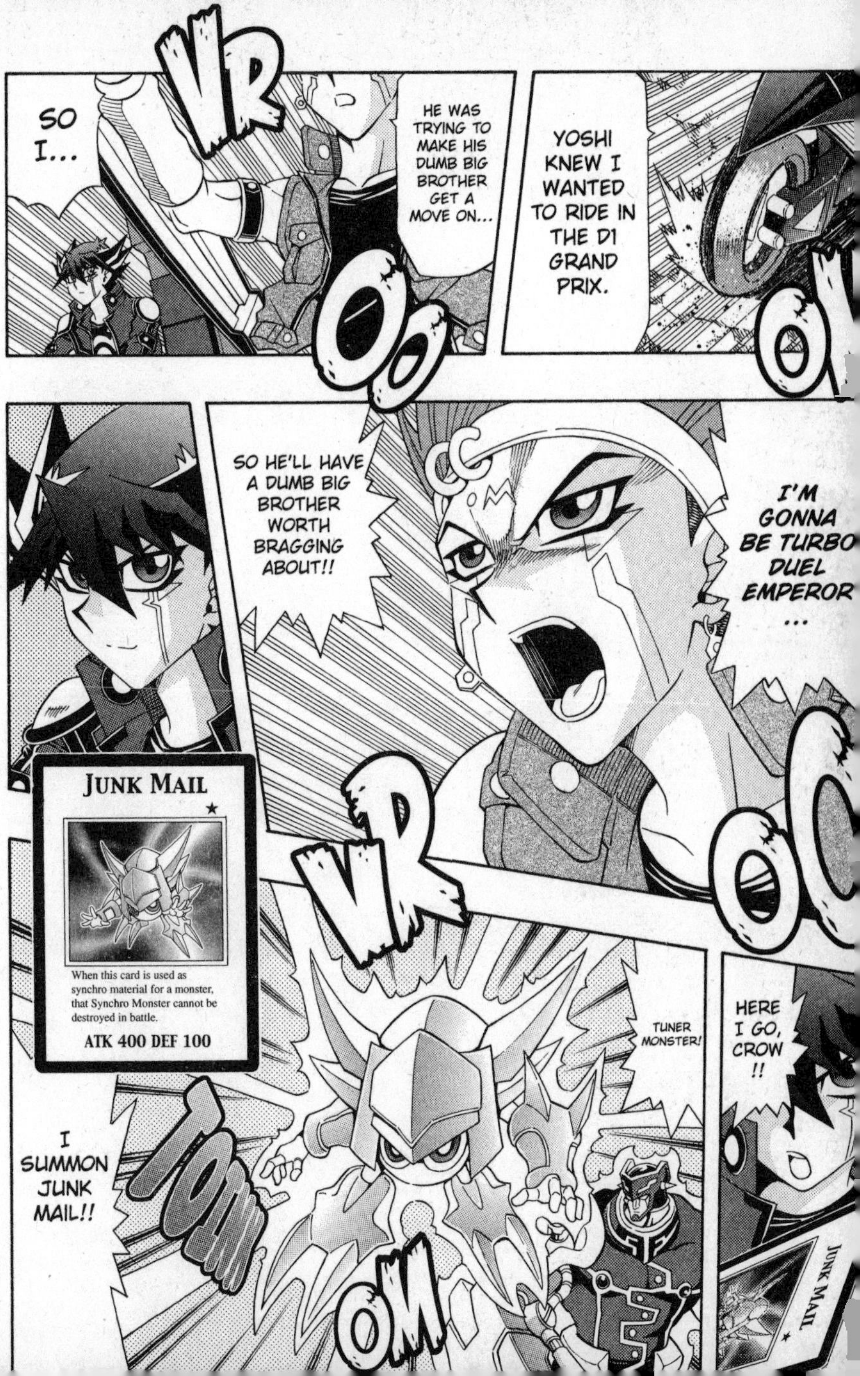
YOSHI KNEW I WANTED TO RIDE IN THE D1 GRAND PRIX.
HE WAS TRYING TO MAKE HIS DUMB BIG BROTHER GET A MOVE ON...
SO I...
VR
OOO
I'M GONNA BE TURBO DUEL EMPEROR...
SO HE'LL HAVE A DUMB BIG BROTHER WORTH BRAGGING ABOUT!!
VR
OOO
HERE I GO, CROW!!
JUNK MAIL
JUNK MAIL
When this card is used as synchro material for a monster, that Synchro Monster cannot be destroyed in battle.
ATK 400 DEF 100
TUNER MONSTER!
I SUMMON JUNK MAIL!!

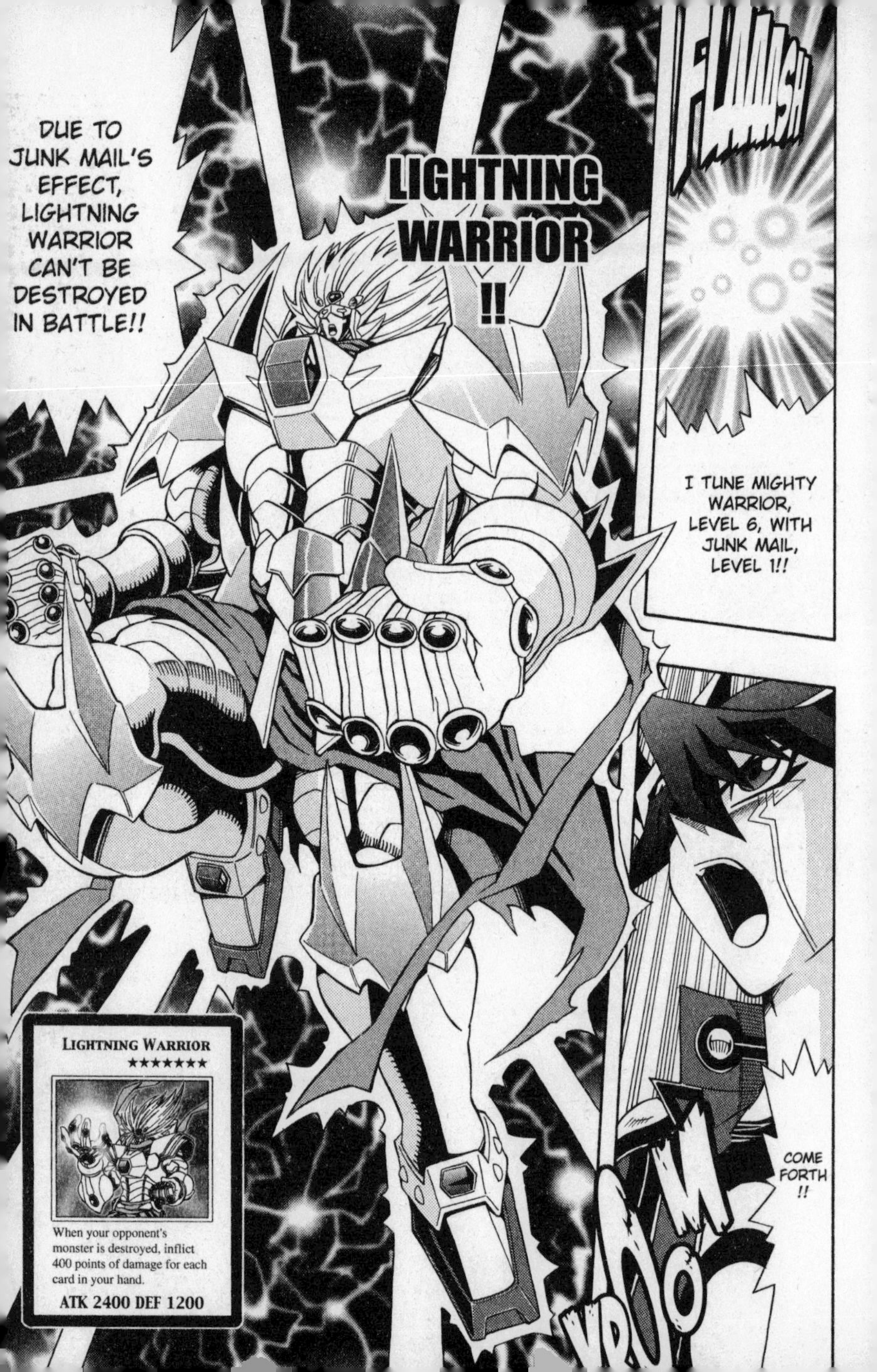
FLAAASH
I TUNE MIGHTY WARRIOR, LEVEL 6, WITH JUNK MAIL, LEVEL 1!!
COME FORTH !!
VROOOM
LIGHTNING WARRIOR !!
DUE TO JUNK MAIL'S EFFECT, LIGHTNING WARRIOR CAN'T BE DESTROYED IN BATTLE!!
LIGHTNING WARRIOR
★★★★★★★
When your opponent's monster is destroyed, inflict 400 points of damage for each card in your hand.
ATK 2400 DEF 1200

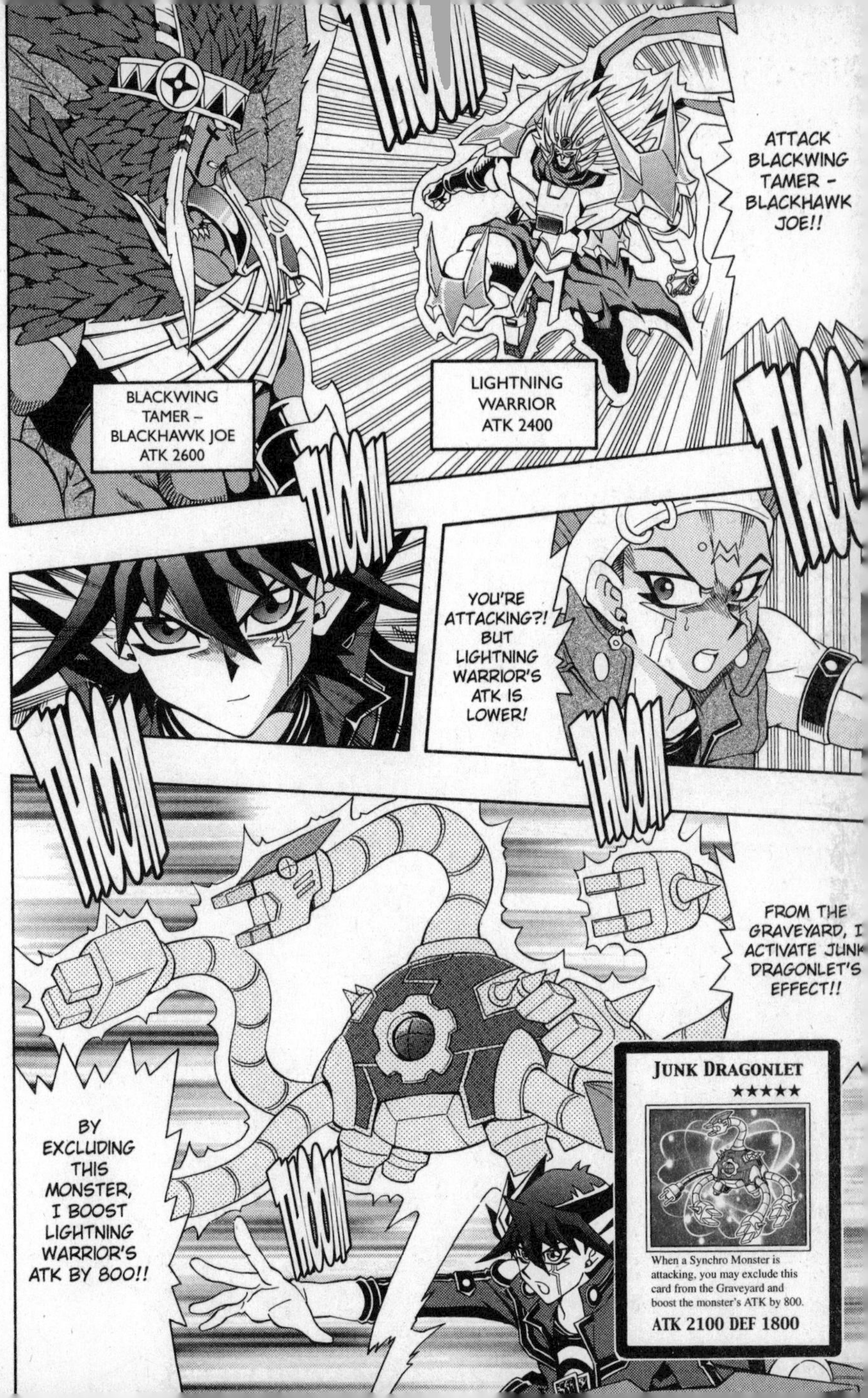
THOOM
ATTACK BLACKWING TAMER – BLACKHAWK JOE!!
LIGHTNING WARRIOR ATK 2400
BLACKWING TAMER – BLACKHAWK JOE ATK 2600
THOOM
THOOM
YOU'RE ATTACKING?! BUT LIGHTNING WARRIOR'S ATK IS LOWER!
THOOM
THOOM
FROM THE GRAVEYARD, I ACTIVATE JUNK DRAGONLET'S EFFECT!!
JUNK DRAGONLET
★★★★★
When a Synchro Monster is attacking, you may exclude this card from the Graveyard and boost the monster's ATK by 800.
ATK 2100 DEF 1800
THOOM
BY EXCLUDING THIS MONSTER, I BOOST LIGHTNING WARRIOR'S ATK BY 800!!

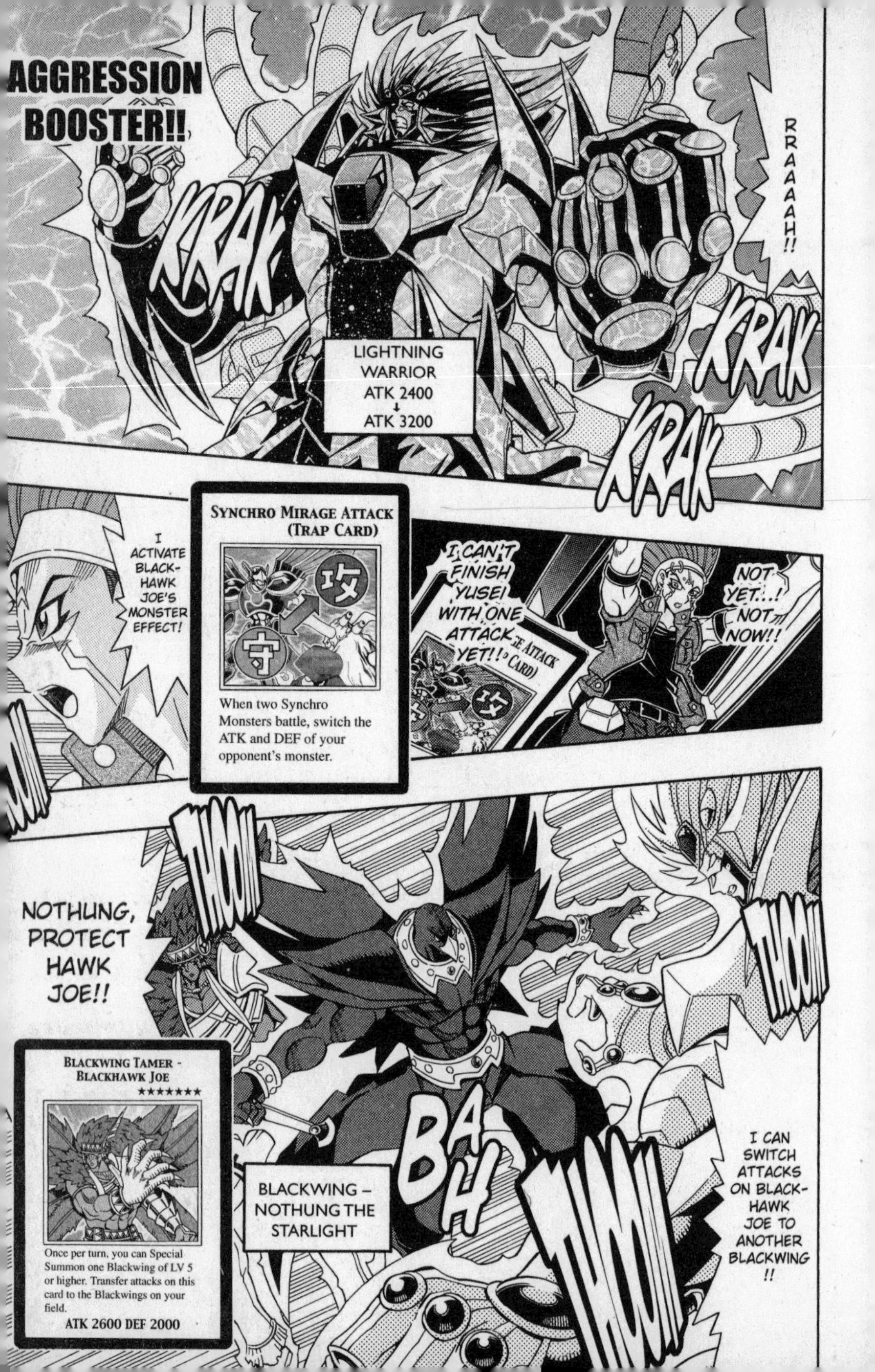
RRAAAAAH!!
AGGRESSION BOOSTER!!
KRAK
KRAK
KRAK
LIGHTNING WARRIOR
ATK 2400
↓
ATK 3200
NOT YET...! NOT NOW!!
I CAN'T FINISH YUSEI WITH ONE ATTACK YET!!
SYNCHRO MIRAGE ATTACK (TRAP CARD)
When two Synchro Monsters battle, switch the ATK and DEF of your opponent's monster.
I ACTIVATE BLACK-HAWK JOE'S MONSTER EFFECT!
THOOM
I CAN SWITCH ATTACKS ON BLACK-HAWK JOE TO ANOTHER BLACKWING!!
THOOM
BAH
BLACKWING – NOTHUNG THE STARLIGHT
NOTHUNG, PROTECT HAWK JOE!!
BLACKWING TAMER - BLACKHAWK JOE
★★★★★★★
Once per turn, you can Special Summon one Blackwing of LV 5 or higher. Transfer attacks on this card to the Blackwings on your field.
ATK 2600 DEF 2000
THOOM

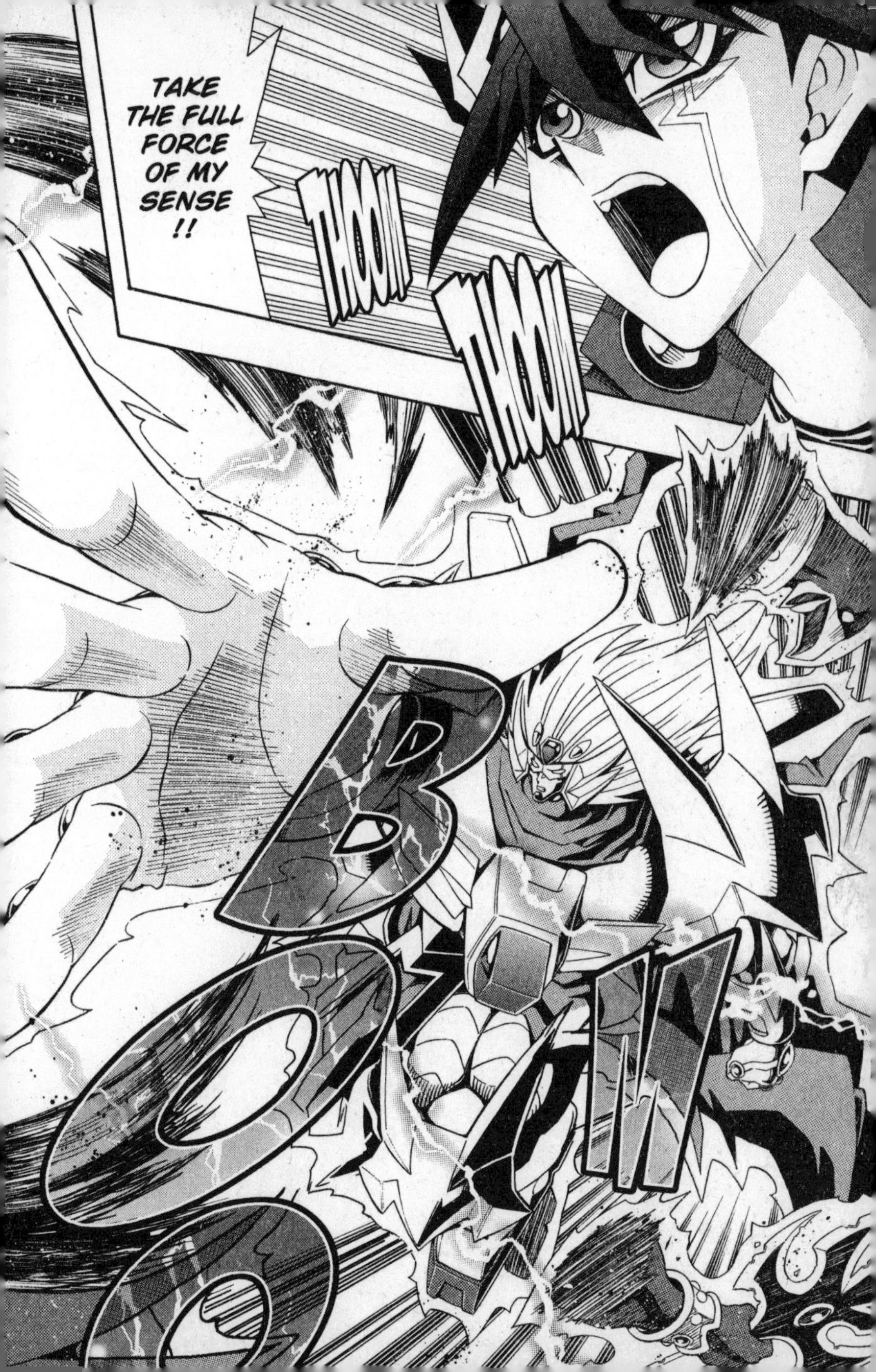
TAKE THE FULL FORCE OF MY SENSE !!
THOOM
THOOM
BOOM

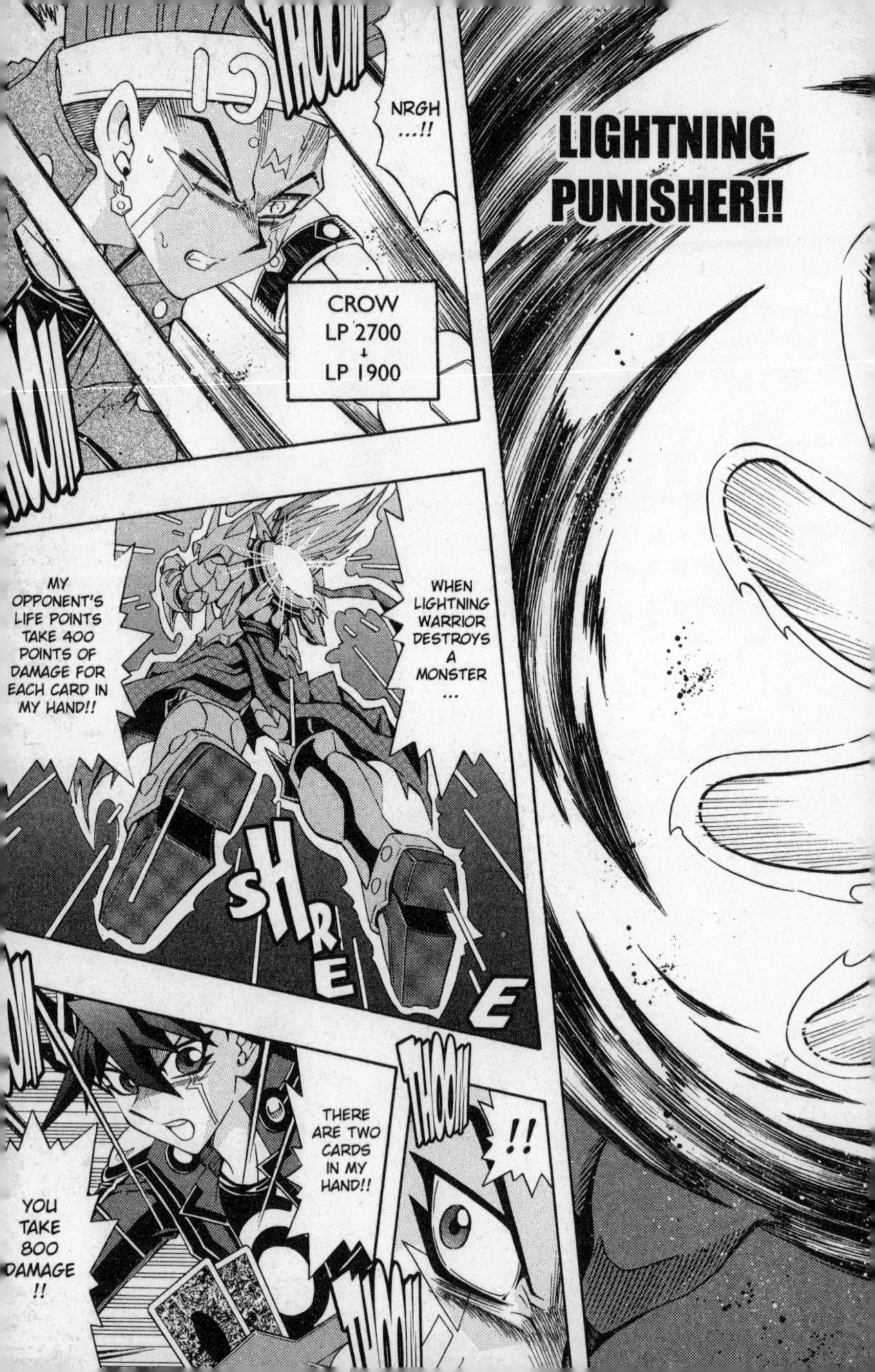
LIGHTNING PUNISHER!!
THOOM
NRGH ...!!
CROW
LP 2700
↓
LP 1900
WHEN LIGHTNING WARRIOR DESTROYS A MONSTER ...
MY OPPONENT'S LIFE POINTS TAKE 400 POINTS OF DAMAGE FOR EACH CARD IN MY HAND!!
SHREEE
THOOM
!!
THERE ARE TWO CARDS IN MY HAND!!
YOU TAKE 800 DAMAGE !!

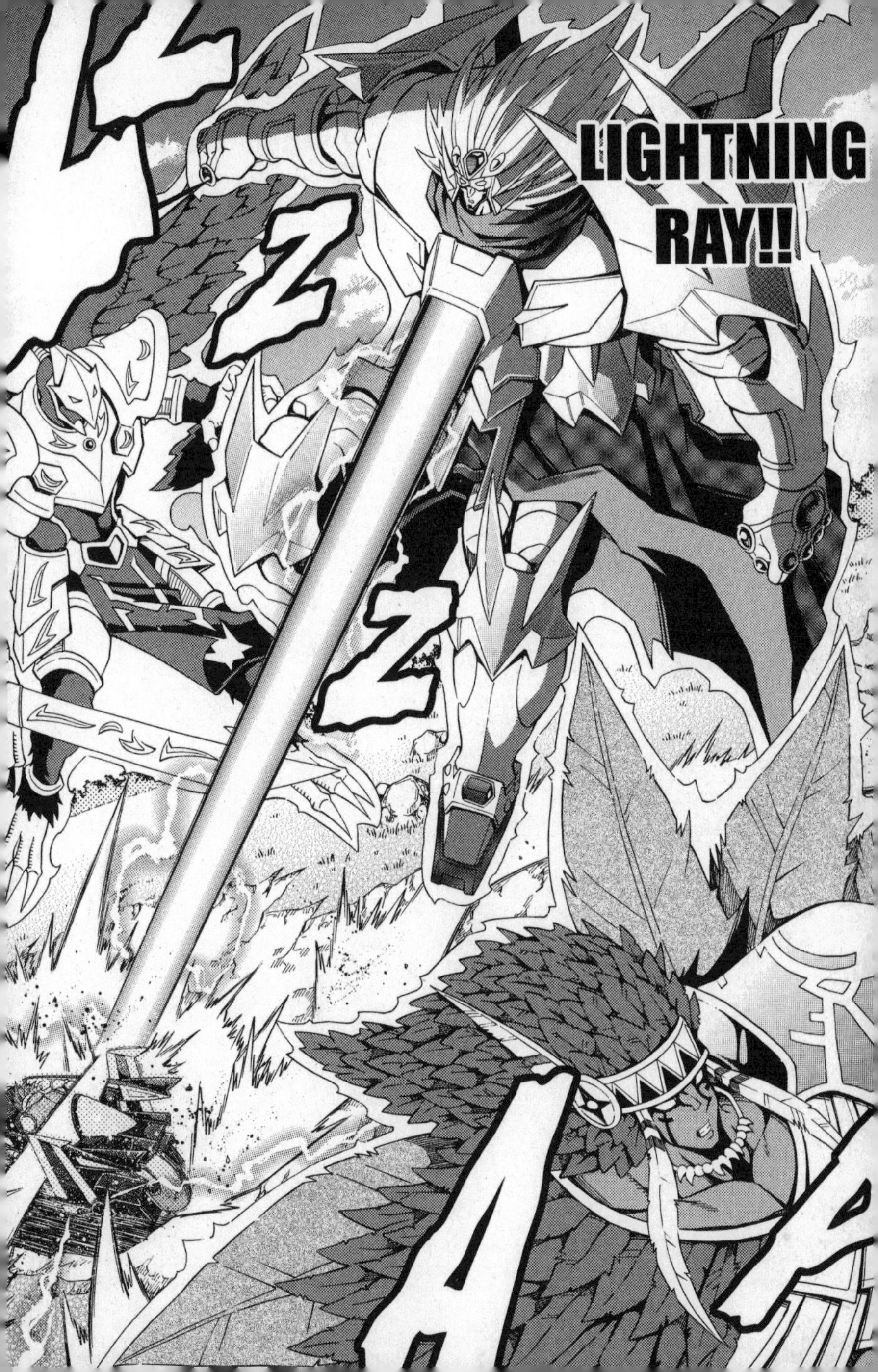
LIGHTNING RAY!!

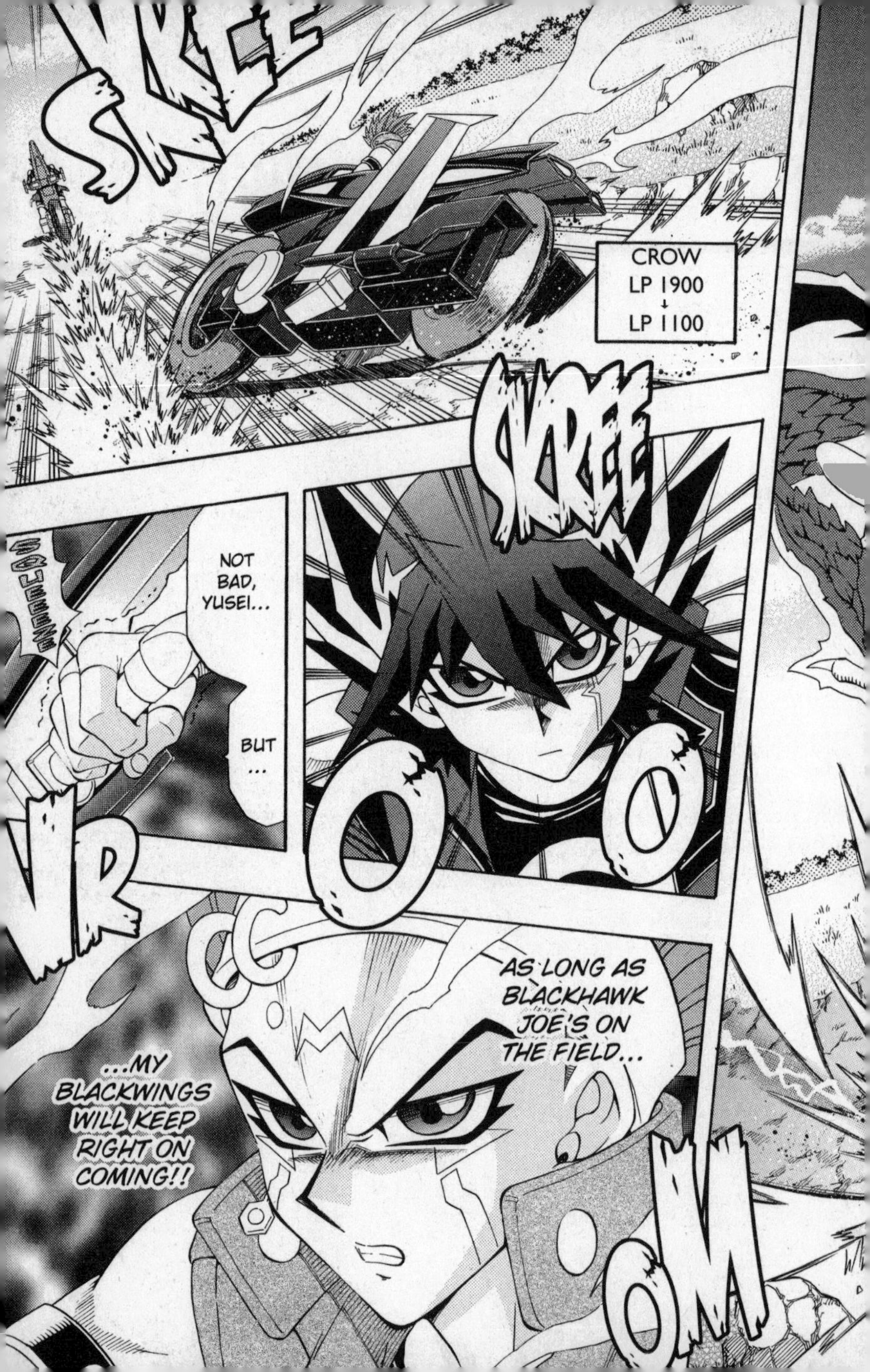
CROW
LP 1900
↓
LP 1100
SKREE
NOT BAD, YUSEI...
BUT ...
AS LONG AS BLACKHAWK JOE'S ON THE FIELD...
...MY BLACKWINGS WILL KEEP RIGHT ON COMING!!

RIDE-29
SUPER-FAST SHOWDOWN!!

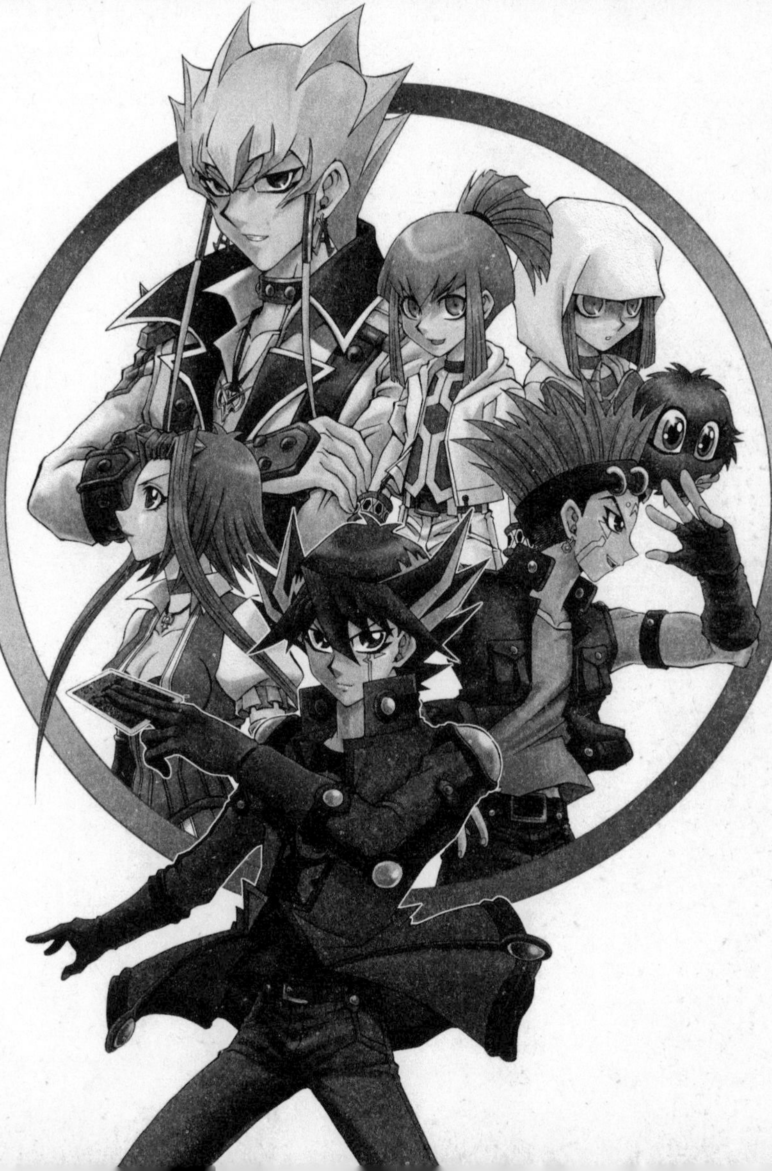

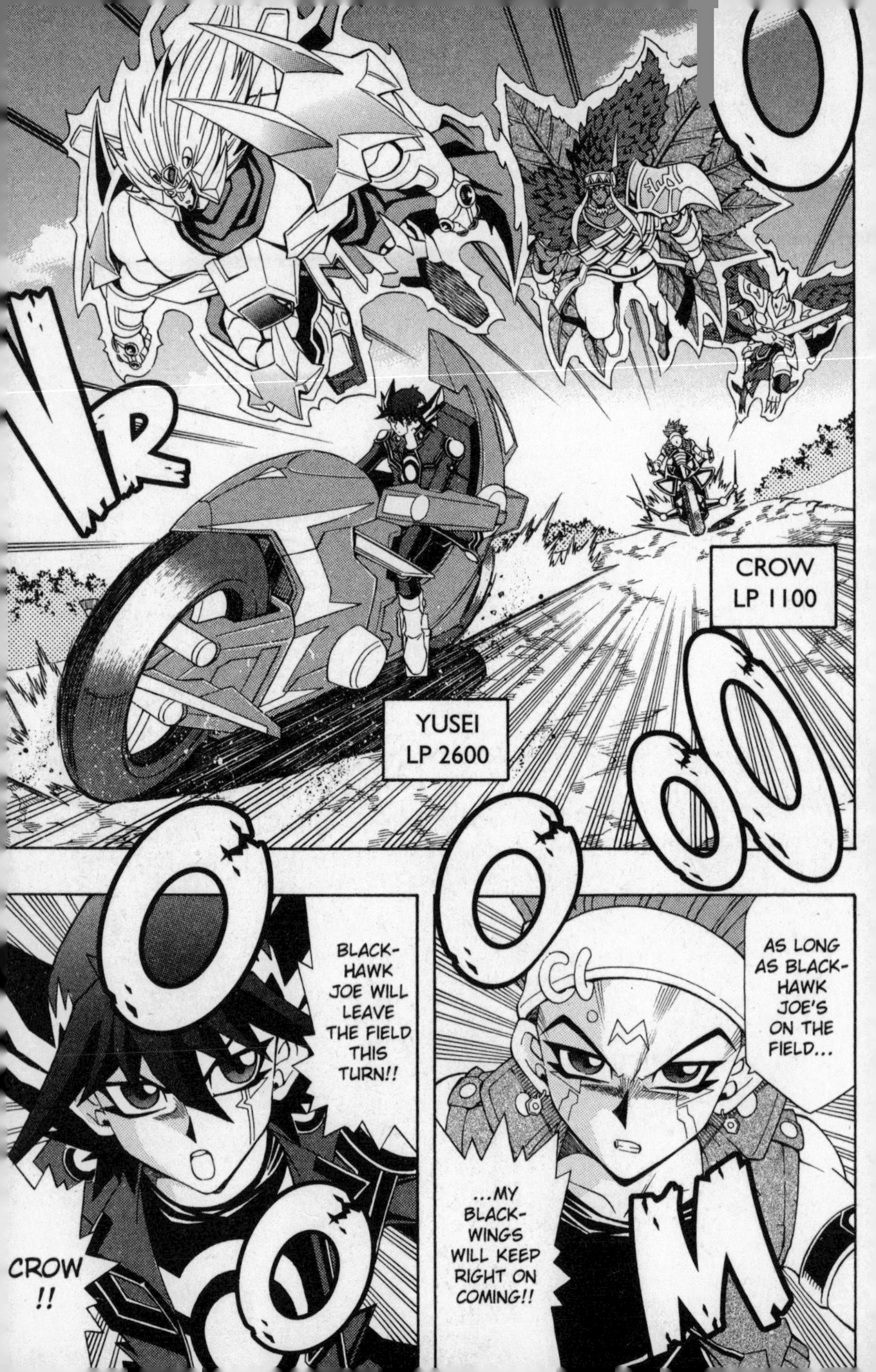
CROW
LP 1100
YUSEI
LP 2600
AS LONG AS BLACK-HAWK JOE'S ON THE FIELD...
...MY BLACK-WINGS WILL KEEP RIGHT ON COMING!!
BLACK-HAWK JOE WILL LEAVE THE FIELD THIS TURN!!
CROW!!

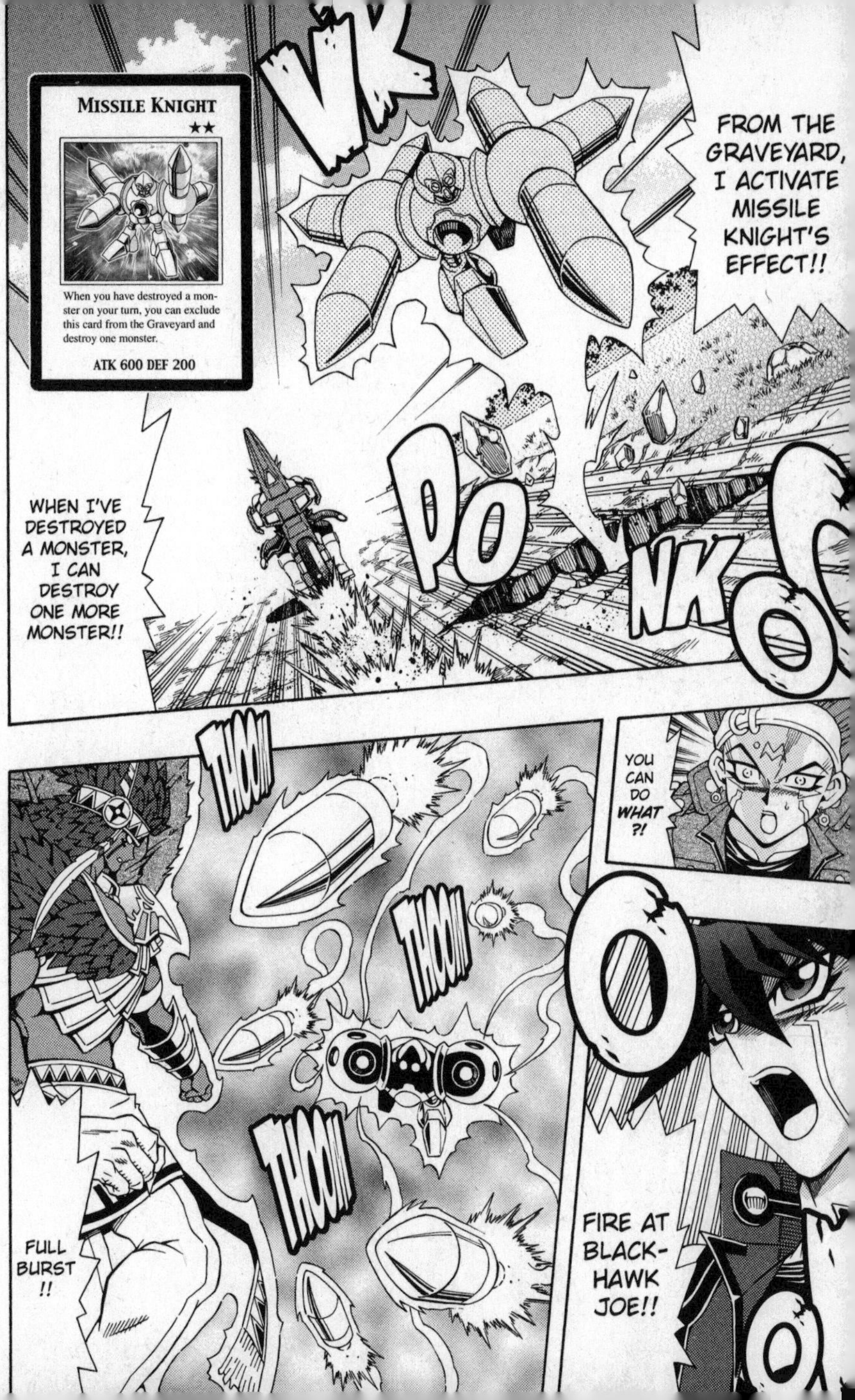
FROM THE GRAVEYARD, I ACTIVATE MISSILE KNIGHT'S EFFECT!!
VK
MISSILE KNIGHT
★★
When you have destroyed a monster on your turn, you can exclude this card from the Graveyard and destroy one monster.
ATK 600 DEF 200
PO
NK
WHEN I'VE DESTROYED A MONSTER, I CAN DESTROY ONE MORE MONSTER!!
YOU CAN DO WHAT?!
FIRE AT BLACK-HAWK JOE!!
THOOM
THOOM
THOOM
FULL BURST!!

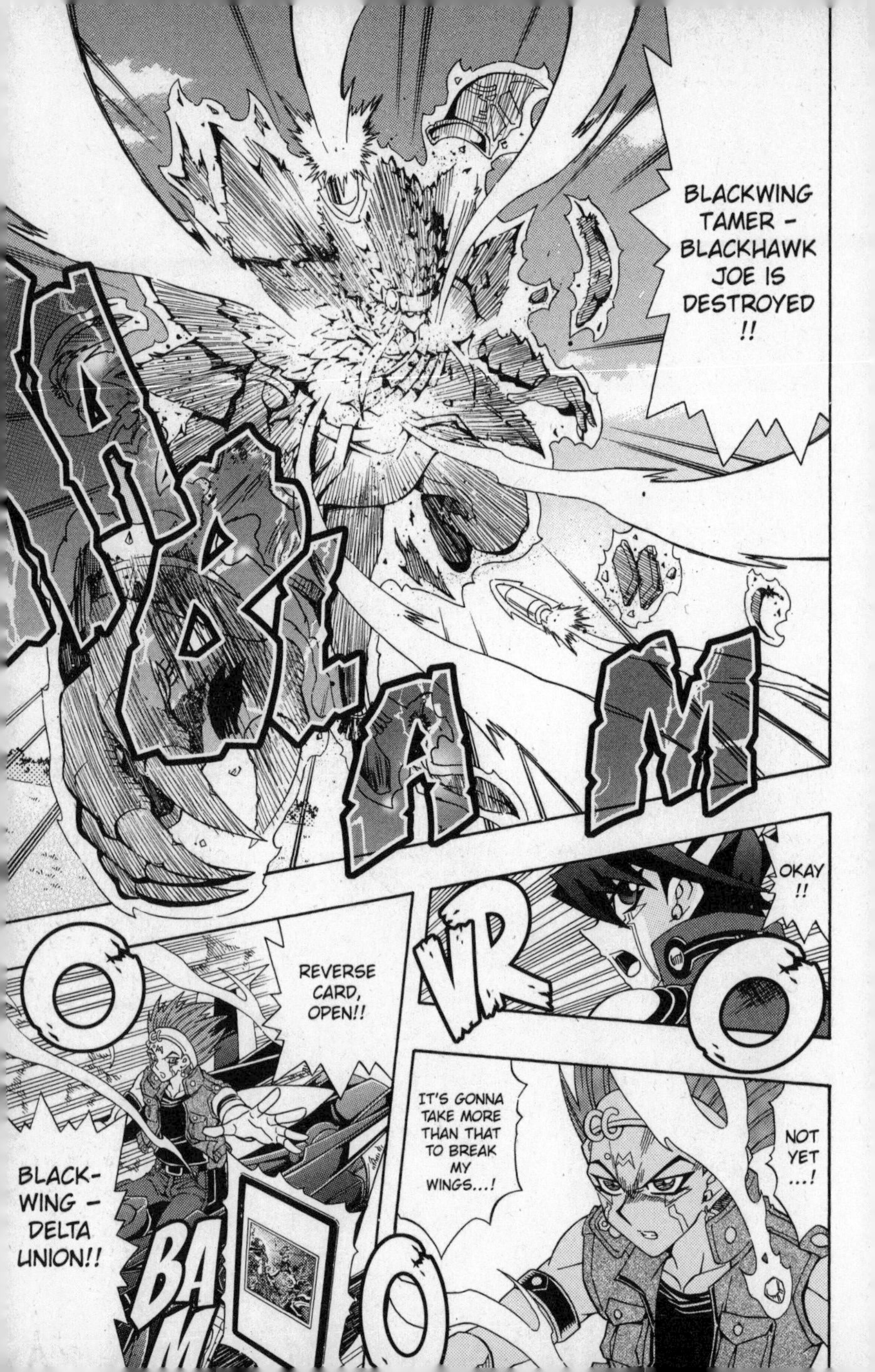
BLACKWING TAMER - BLACKHAWK JOE IS DESTROYED!!
BLAM
OKAY!!
NOT YET...!
IT'S GONNA TAKE MORE THAN THAT TO BREAK MY WINGS...!
REVERSE CARD, OPEN!!
BLACK-WING - DELTA UNION!!
BAM

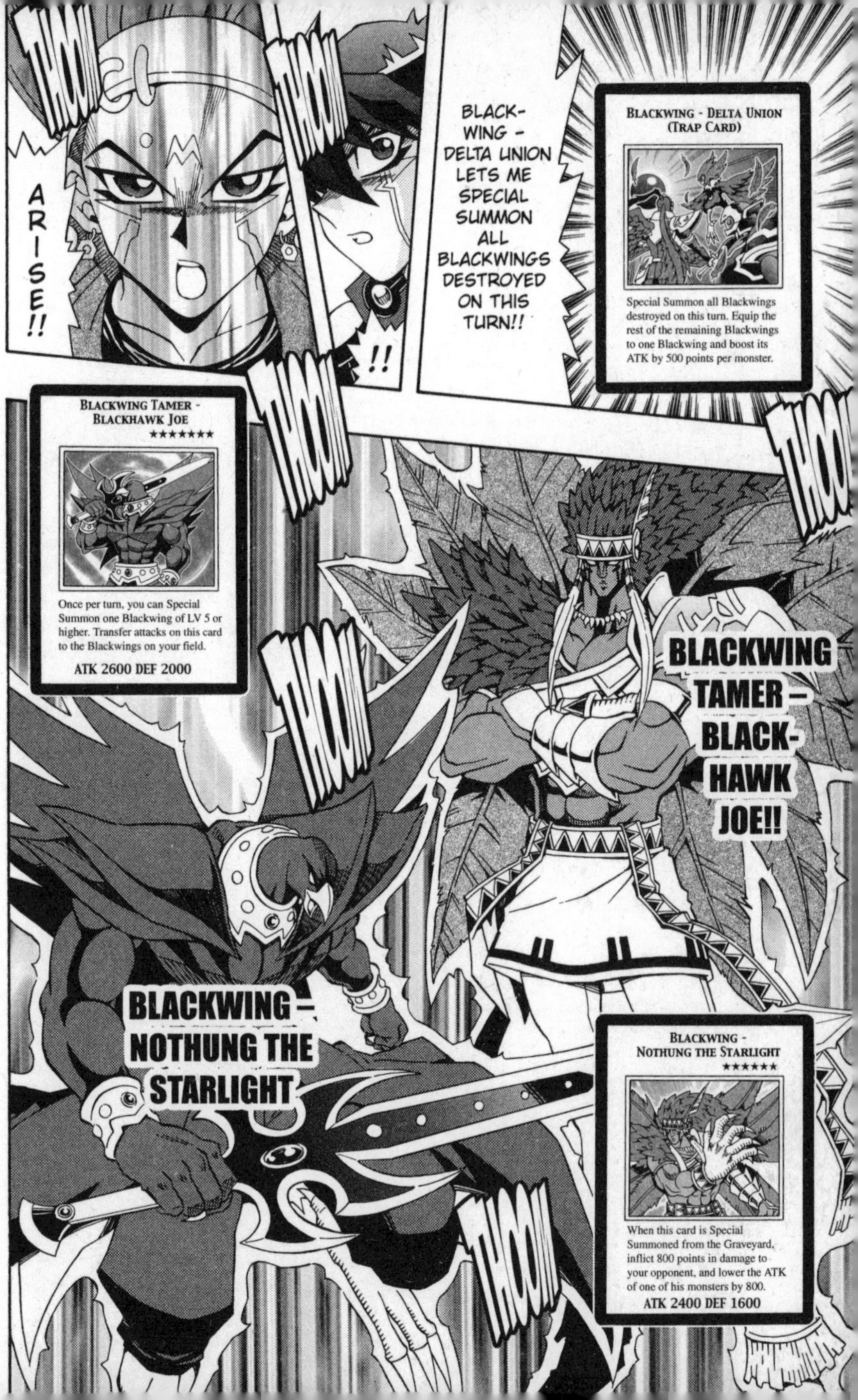

BLACKWING - DELTA UNION
(TRAP CARD)
Special Summon all Blackwings destroyed on this turn. Equip the rest of the remaining Blackwings to one Blackwing and boost its ATK by 500 points per monster.
BLACKWING - DELTA UNION LETS ME SPECIAL SUMMON ALL BLACKWINGS DESTROYED ON THIS TURN!!
THOOM
!!
THOOM
ARISE!!
THOOM
THOOM
THOOM
BLACKWING TAMER – BLACKHAWK JOE!!
BLACKWING TAMER - BLACKHAWK JOE
★★★★★★★
Once per turn, you can Special Summon one Blackwing of LV 5 or higher. Transfer attacks on this card to the Blackwings on your field.
ATK 2600 DEF 2000
THOOM
BLACKWING – NOTHUNG THE STARLIGHT
BLACKWING - NOTHUNG THE STARLIGHT
★★★★★★
When this card is Special Summoned from the Graveyard, inflict 800 points in damage to your opponent, and lower the ATK of one of his monsters by 800.
ATK 2400 DEF 1600
THOOM

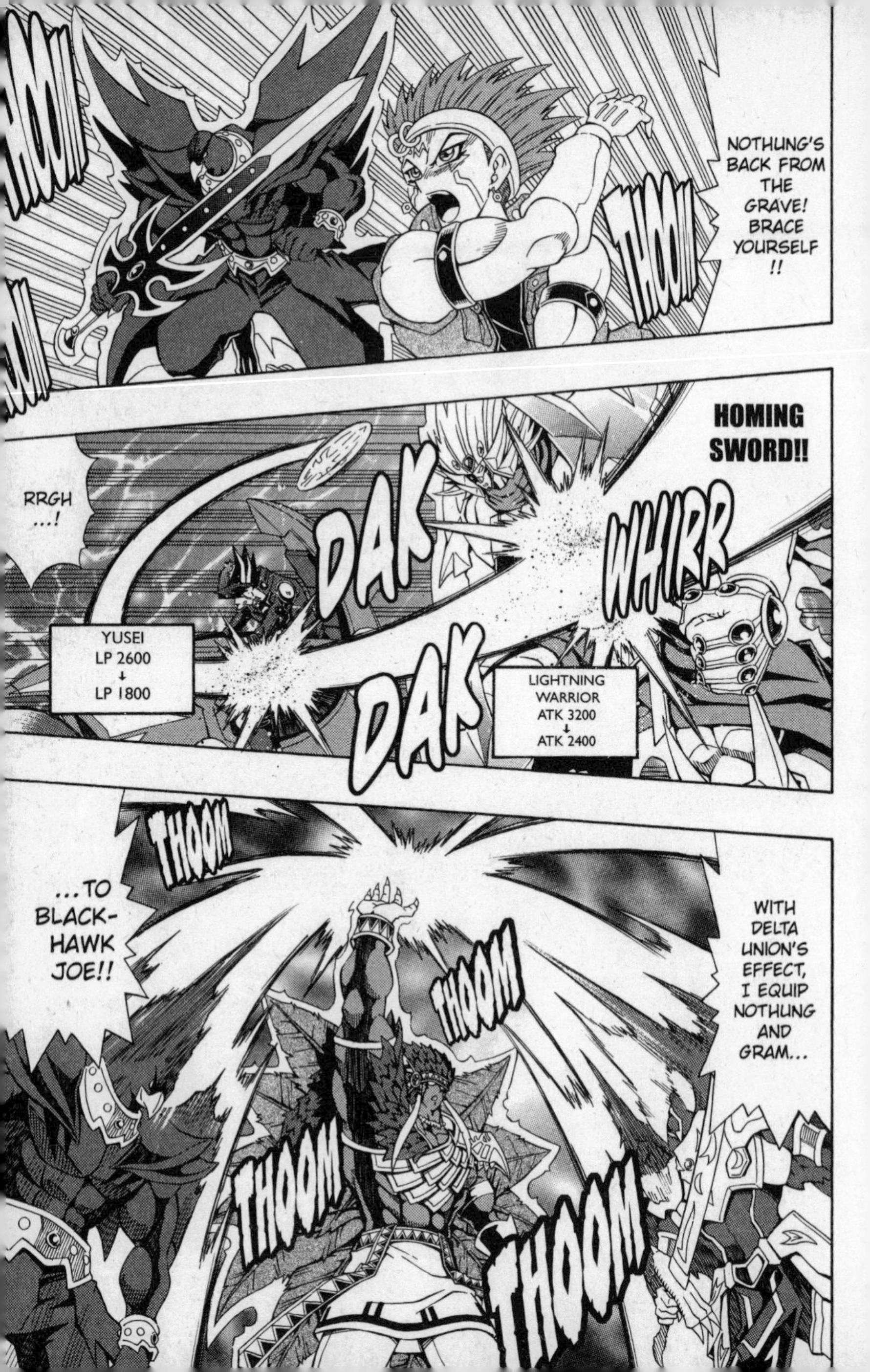
NOTHUNG'S BACK FROM THE GRAVE! BRACE YOURSELF!!
THOOM
HOMING SWORD!!
WHIRR
DAK
DAK
LIGHTNING WARRIOR ATK 3200 ↓ ATK 2400
YUSEI LP 2600 ↓ LP 1800
RRGH ...!
WITH DELTA UNION'S EFFECT, I EQUIP NOTHUNG AND GRAM...
THOOM
THOOM
...TO BLACK-HAWK JOE!!
THOOM
THOOM

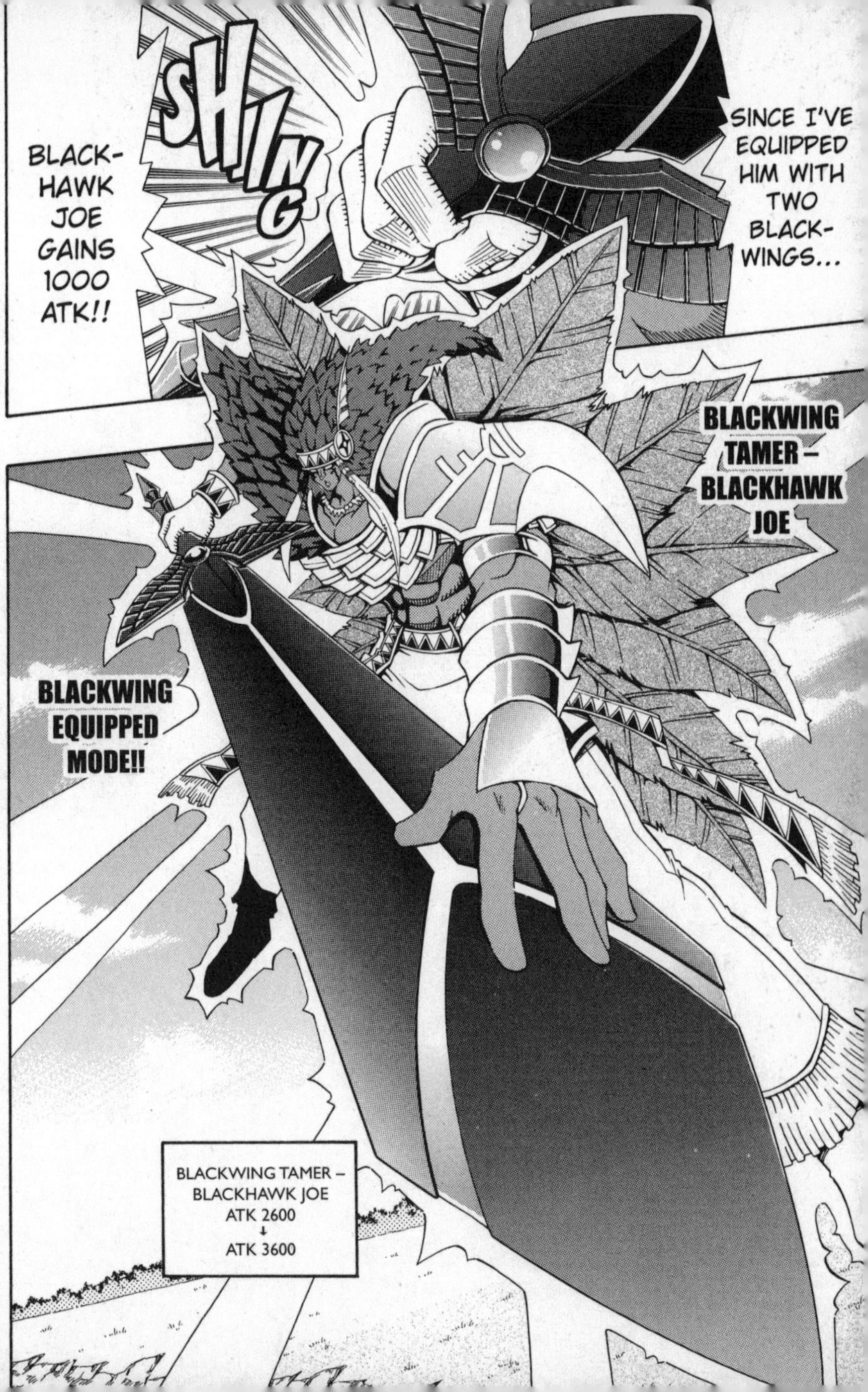
SINCE I'VE EQUIPPED HIM WITH TWO BLACK-WINGS...
SHING
BLACK-HAWK JOE GAINS 1000 ATK!!
BLACKWING TAMER – BLACKHAWK JOE
BLACKWING EQUIPPED MODE!!
BLACKWING TAMER – BLACKHAWK JOE ATK 2600 ↓ ATK 3600

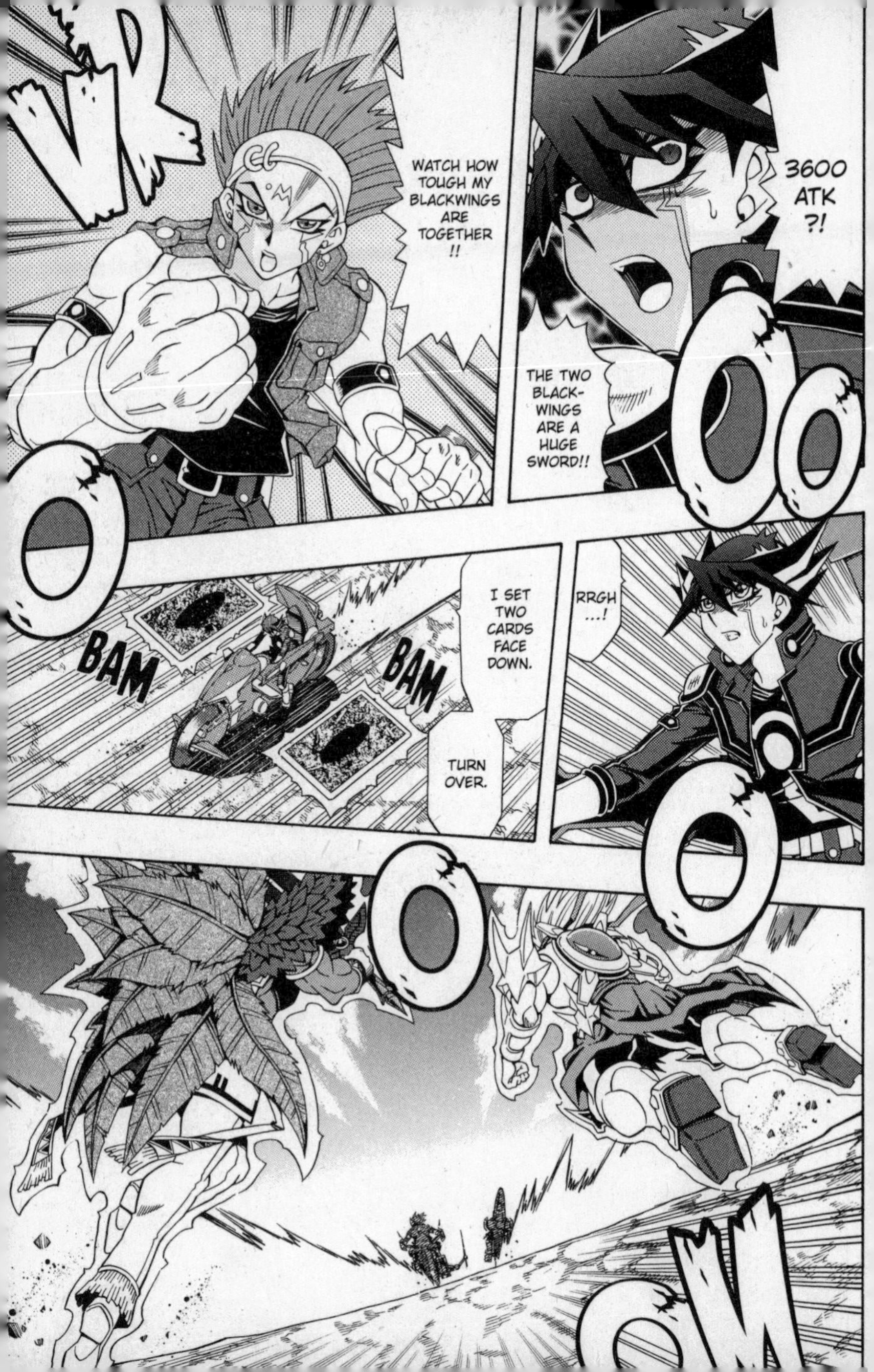
3600 ATK ?!
THE TWO BLACK-WINGS ARE A HUGE SWORD!!
WATCH HOW TOUGH MY BLACKWINGS ARE TOGETHER !!
RRGH ...!
I SET TWO CARDS FACE DOWN.
BAM
BAM
TURN OVER.

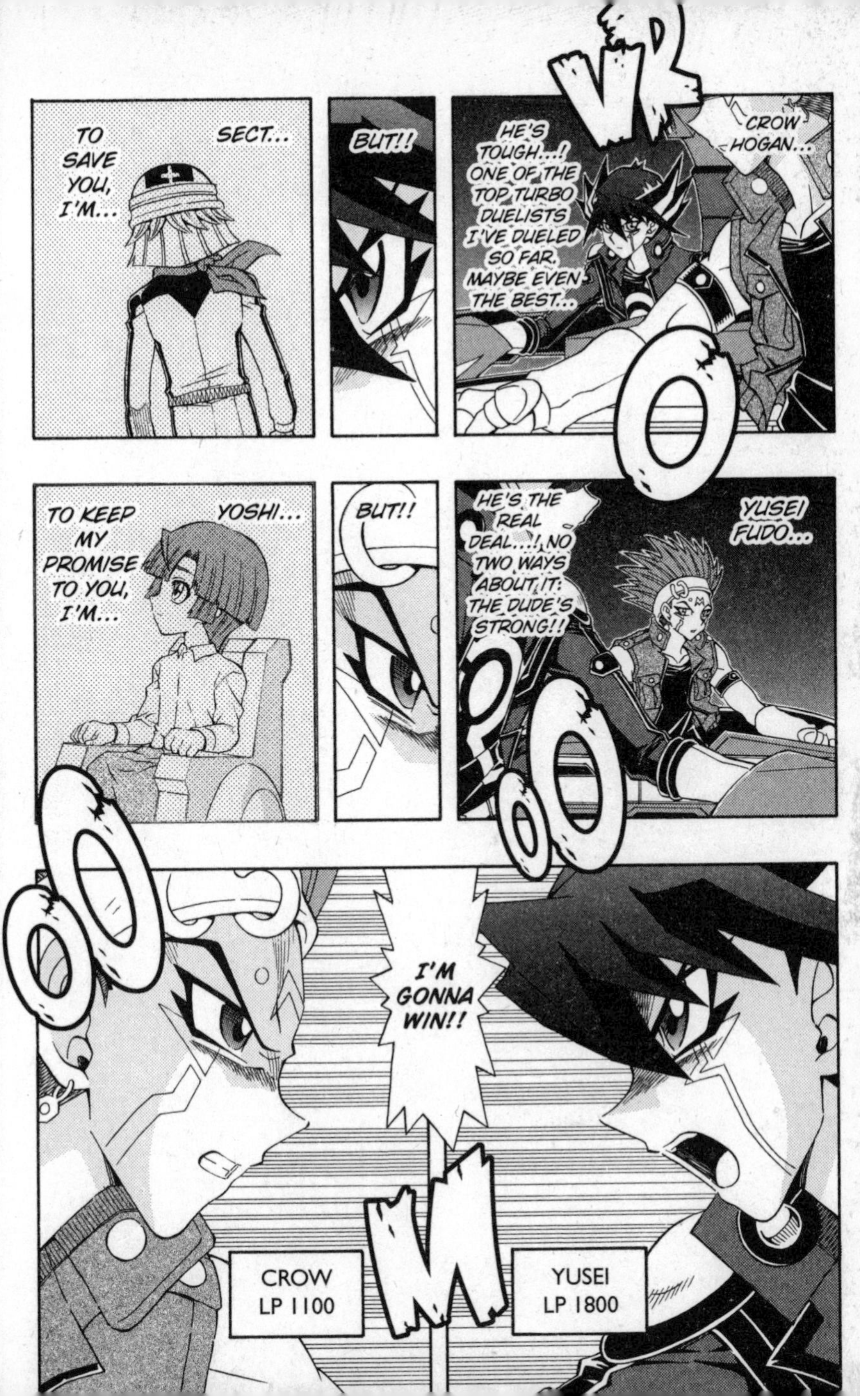
VR
CROW HOGAN...
HE'S TOUGH...! ONE OF THE TOP TURBO DUELISTS I'VE DUELED SO FAR. MAYBE EVEN THE BEST...
BUT!!
SECT...
TO SAVE YOU, I'M...
YUSEI FUDO...
HE'S THE REAL DEAL...! NO TWO WAYS ABOUT IT: THE DUDE'S STRONG!!
BUT!!
YOSHI...
TO KEEP MY PROMISE TO YOU, I'M...
I'M GONNA WIN!!
YUSEI LP 1800
M
CROW LP 1100

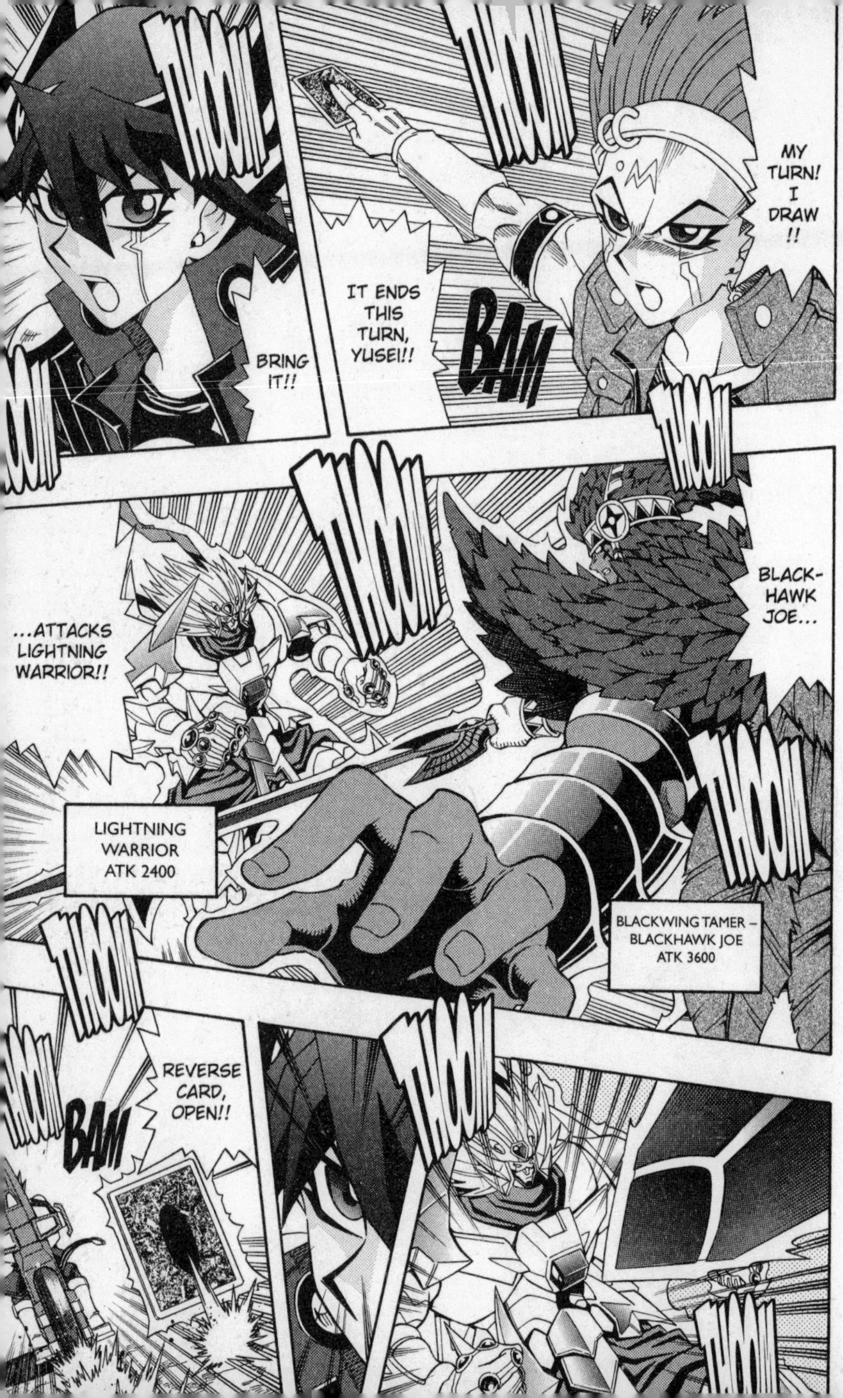
THOOM
MY TURN! I DRAW!!
IT ENDS THIS TURN, YUSEI!!
BAM
THOOM
THOOM
BRING IT!!
THOOM
THOOM
THOOM
BLACKHAWK JOE...
...ATTACKS LIGHTNING WARRIOR!!
BLACKWING TAMER – BLACKHAWK JOE ATK 3600
LIGHTNING WARRIOR ATK 2400
THOOM
THOOM
THOOM
THOOM
REVERSE CARD, OPEN!!
BAM
THOOM

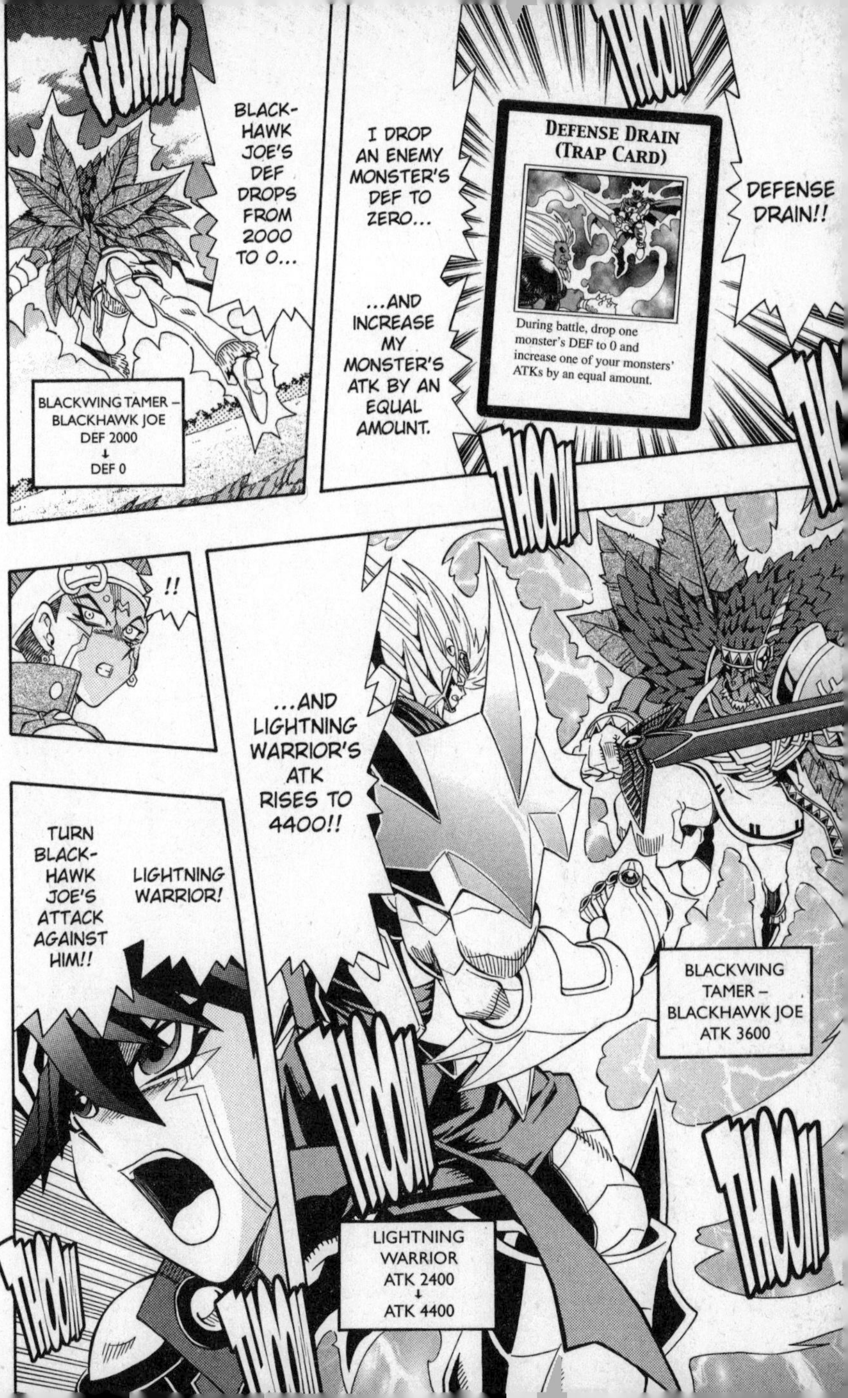
THOOM
DEFENSE DRAIN!!
DEFENSE DRAIN
(TRAP CARD)
During battle, drop one monster's DEF to 0 and increase one of your monsters' ATKs by an equal amount.
THOOM
THOOM
I DROP AN ENEMY MONSTER'S DEF TO ZERO...
...AND INCREASE MY MONSTER'S ATK BY AN EQUAL AMOUNT.
VUMM
BLACK-HAWK JOE'S DEF DROPS FROM 2000 TO 0...
BLACKWING TAMER – BLACKHAWK JOE DEF 2000 ↓ DEF 0
...AND LIGHTNING WARRIOR'S ATK RISES TO 4400!!
BLACKWING TAMER – BLACKHAWK JOE ATK 3600
THOOM
THOOM
LIGHTNING WARRIOR ATK 2400 ↓ ATK 4400
!!
LIGHTNING WARRIOR!
TURN BLACK-HAWK JOE'S ATTACK AGAINST HIM!!
THOOM
THOOM

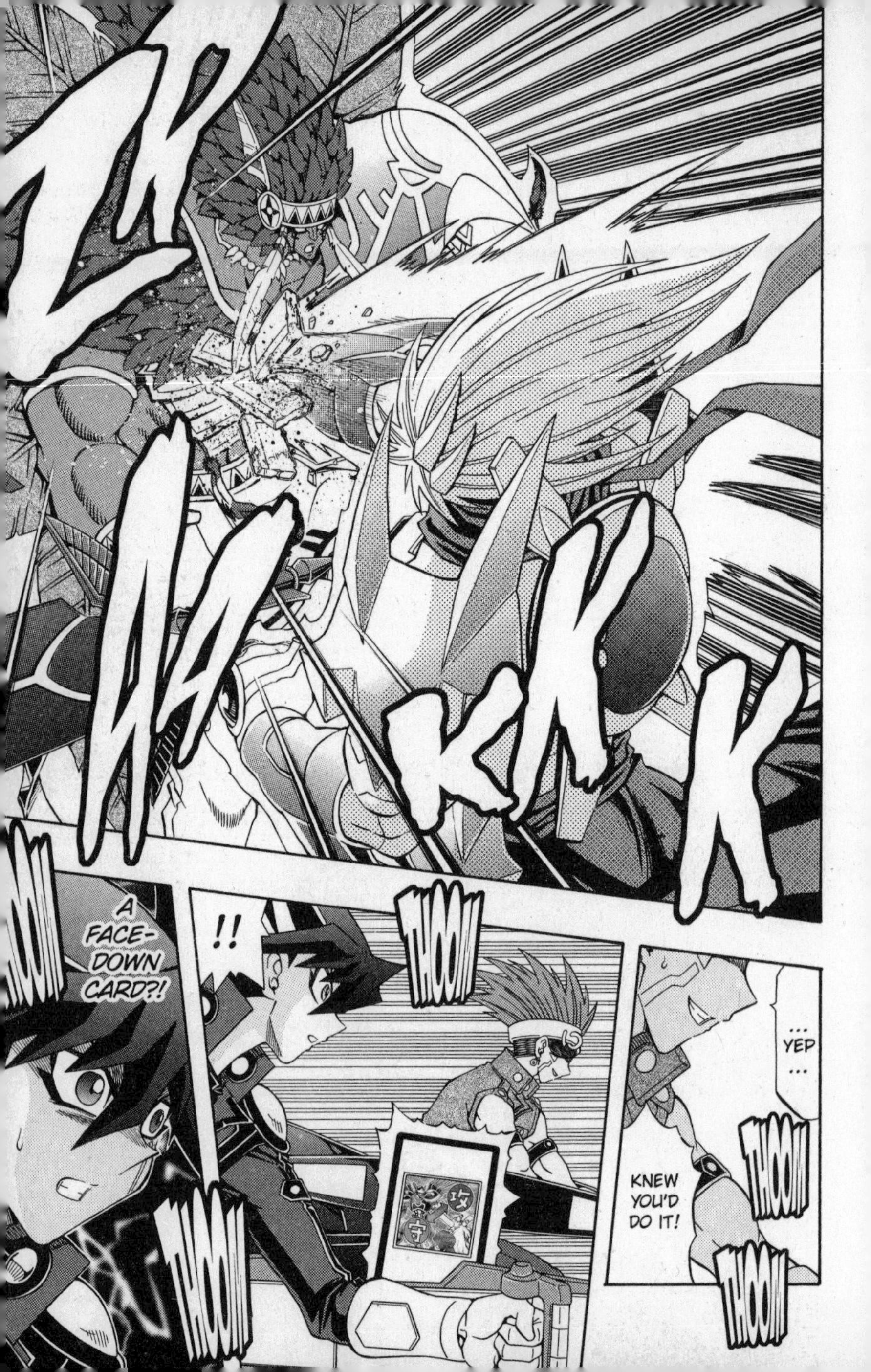
...YEP...
KNEW YOU'D DO IT!
THOOM
THOOM
!!
THOOM
A FACE-DOWN CARD?!
THOOM
THOOM

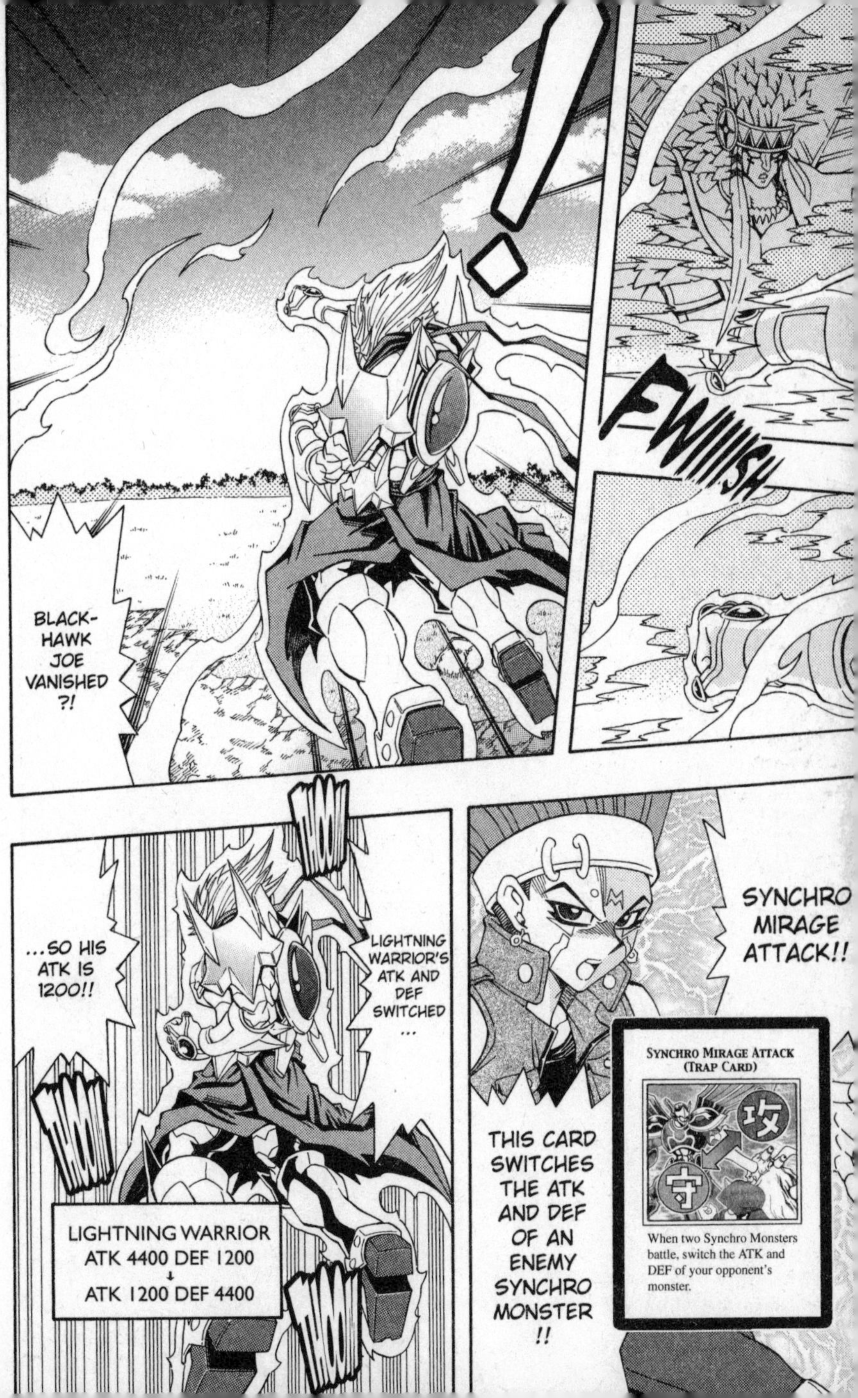
!
FWIIIISH
BLACK-HAWK JOE VANISHED?!
SYNCHRO MIRAGE ATTACK!!
SYNCHRO MIRAGE ATTACK
(TRAP CARD)
When two Synchro Monsters battle, switch the ATK and DEF of your opponent's monster.
THIS CARD SWITCHES THE ATK AND DEF OF AN ENEMY SYNCHRO MONSTER!!
THOOM
LIGHTNING WARRIOR'S ATK AND DEF SWITCHED...
...SO HIS ATK IS 1200!!
THOOM
THOOM
LIGHTNING WARRIOR
ATK 4400 DEF 1200
↓
ATK 1200 DEF 4400

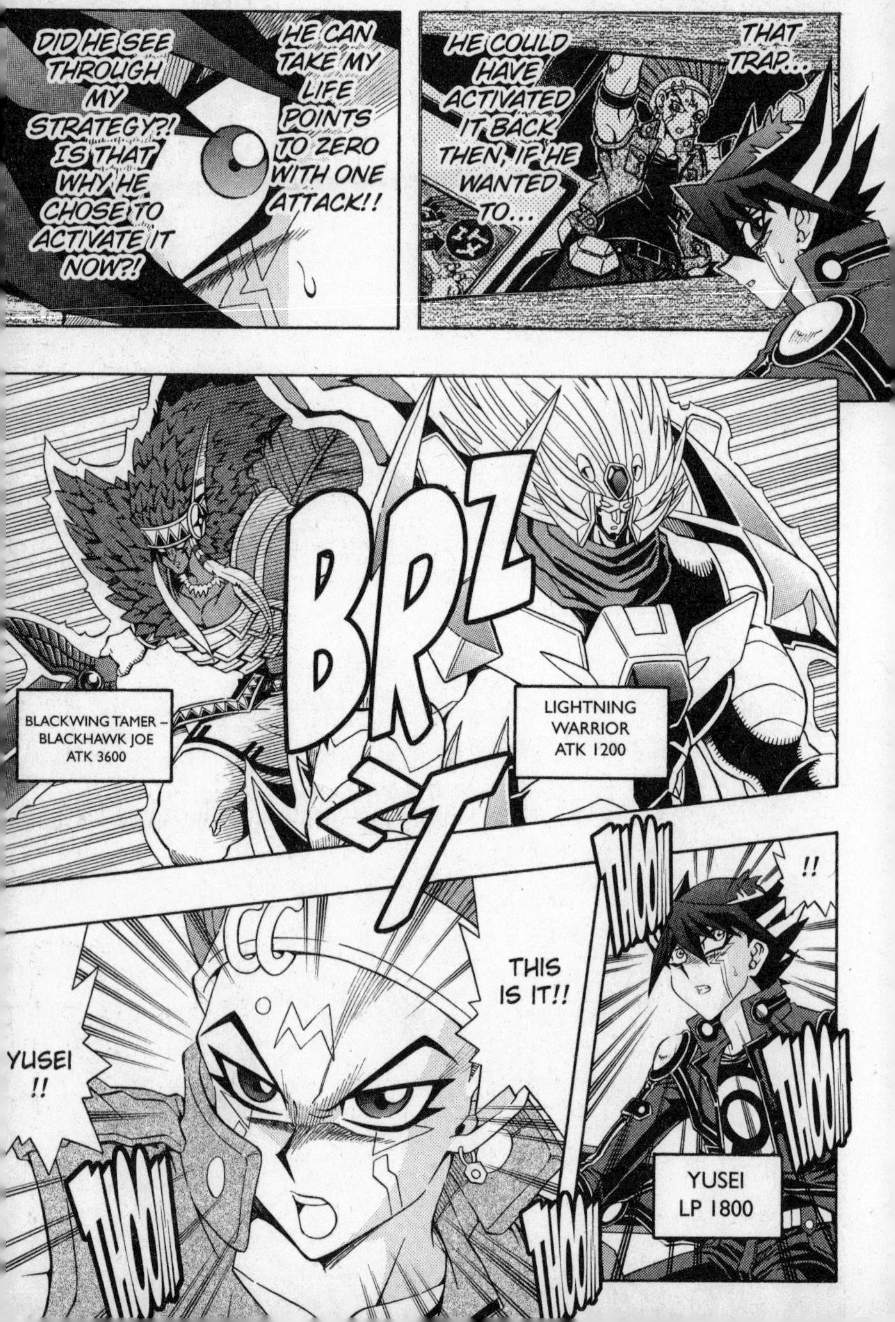

THAT TRAP...
HE COULD HAVE ACTIVATED IT BACK THEN, IF HE WANTED TO...
HE CAN TAKE MY LIFE POINTS TO ZERO WITH ONE ATTACK!!
DID HE SEE THROUGH MY STRATEGY?! IS THAT WHY HE CHOSE TO ACTIVATE IT NOW?!
LIGHTNING WARRIOR ATK 1200
BRZZT
BLACKWING TAMER – BLACKHAWK JOE ATK 3600
!!
THOOM
THIS IS IT!!
THOOM
YUSEI LP 1800
THOOM
YUSEI !!
THOOM

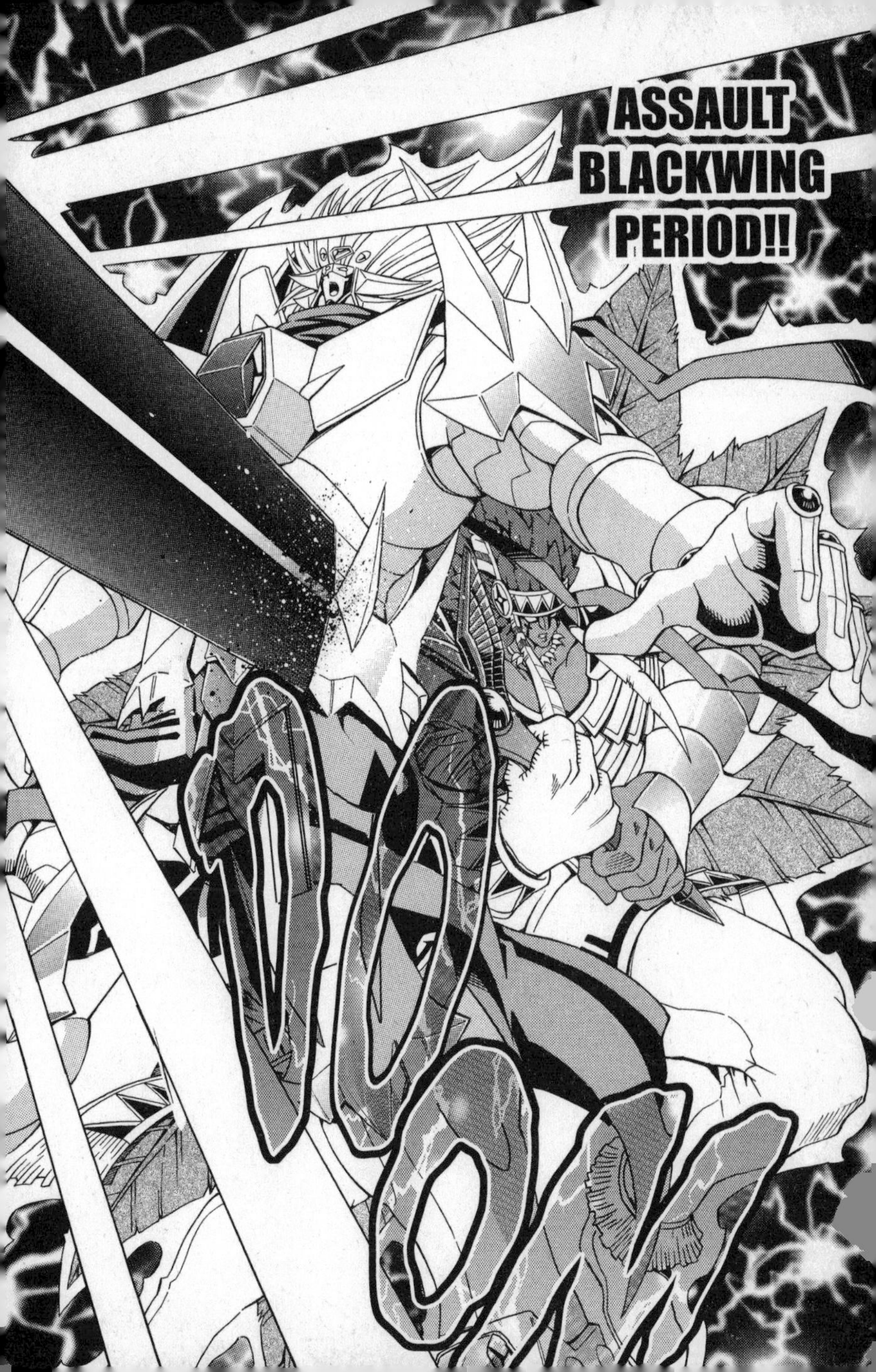
ASSAULT BLACKWING PERIOD!!

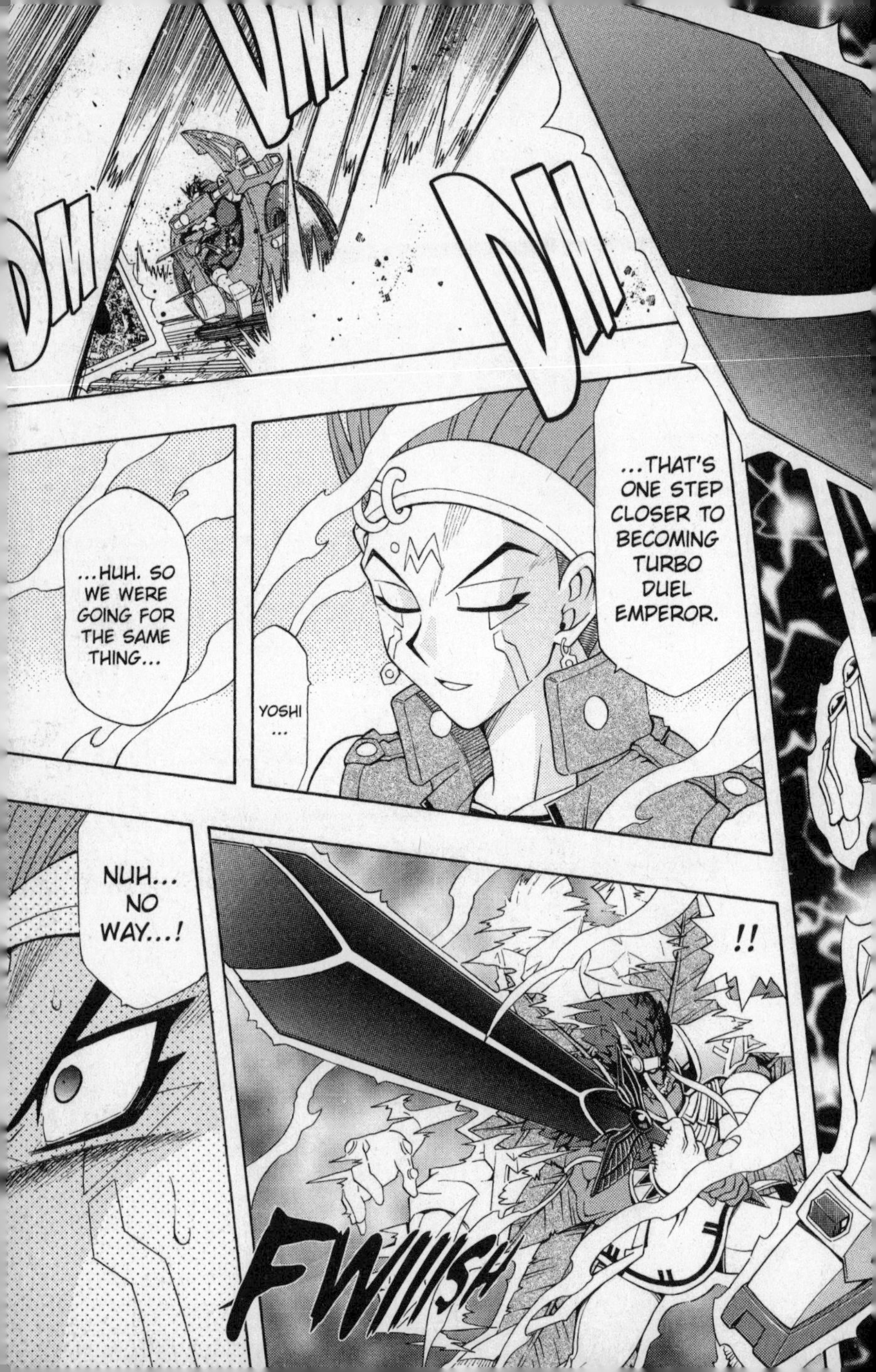
DM
DM
...THAT'S ONE STEP CLOSER TO BECOMING TURBO DUEL EMPEROR.
YOSHI ...
...HUH. SO WE WERE GOING FOR THE SAME THING...
!!
FWIIISH
NUH... NO WAY...!

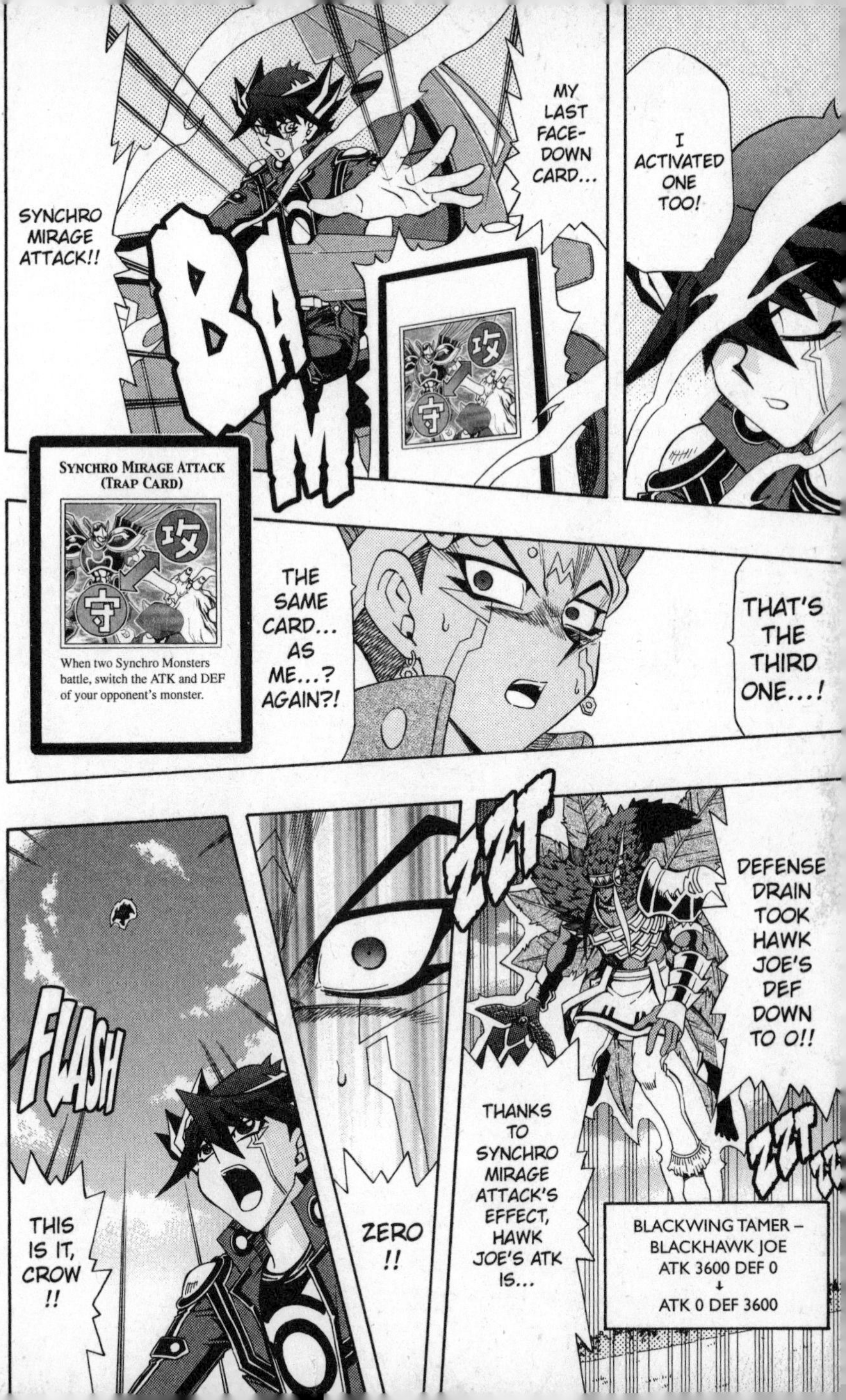
I ACTIVATED ONE TOO!
MY LAST FACE-DOWN CARD...
SYNCHRO MIRAGE ATTACK!!
BAM
THAT'S THE THIRD ONE...!
THE SAME CARD... AS ME...? AGAIN?!
SYNCHRO MIRAGE ATTACK (TRAP CARD)
When two Synchro Monsters battle, switch the ATK and DEF of your opponent's monster.
ZZZT
DEFENSE DRAIN TOOK HAWK JOE'S DEF DOWN TO 0!!
THANKS TO SYNCHRO MIRAGE ATTACK'S EFFECT, HAWK JOE'S ATK IS...
ZZZT
BLACKWING TAMER – BLACKHAWK JOE
ATK 3600 DEF 0
↓
ATK 0 DEF 3600
ZERO!!
FLASH
THIS IS IT, CROW!!

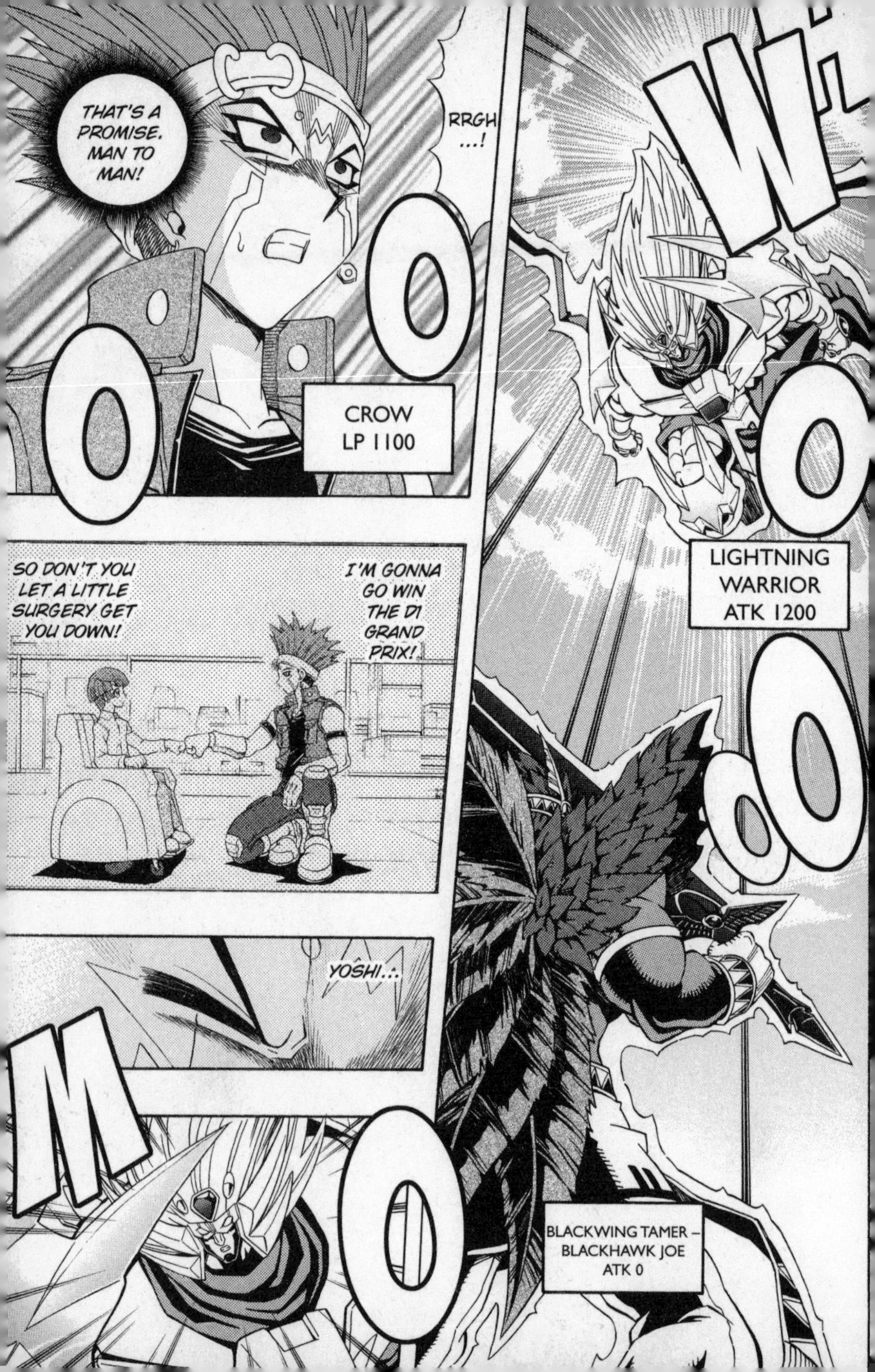
LIGHTNING WARRIOR ATK 1200
BLACKWING TAMER – BLACKHAWK JOE ATK 0
RRGH ...!
THAT'S A PROMISE, MAN TO MAN!
CROW LP 1100
I'M GONNA GO WIN THE D1 GRAND PRIX!
SO DON'T YOU LET A LITTLE SURGERY GET YOU DOWN!
YOSHI...

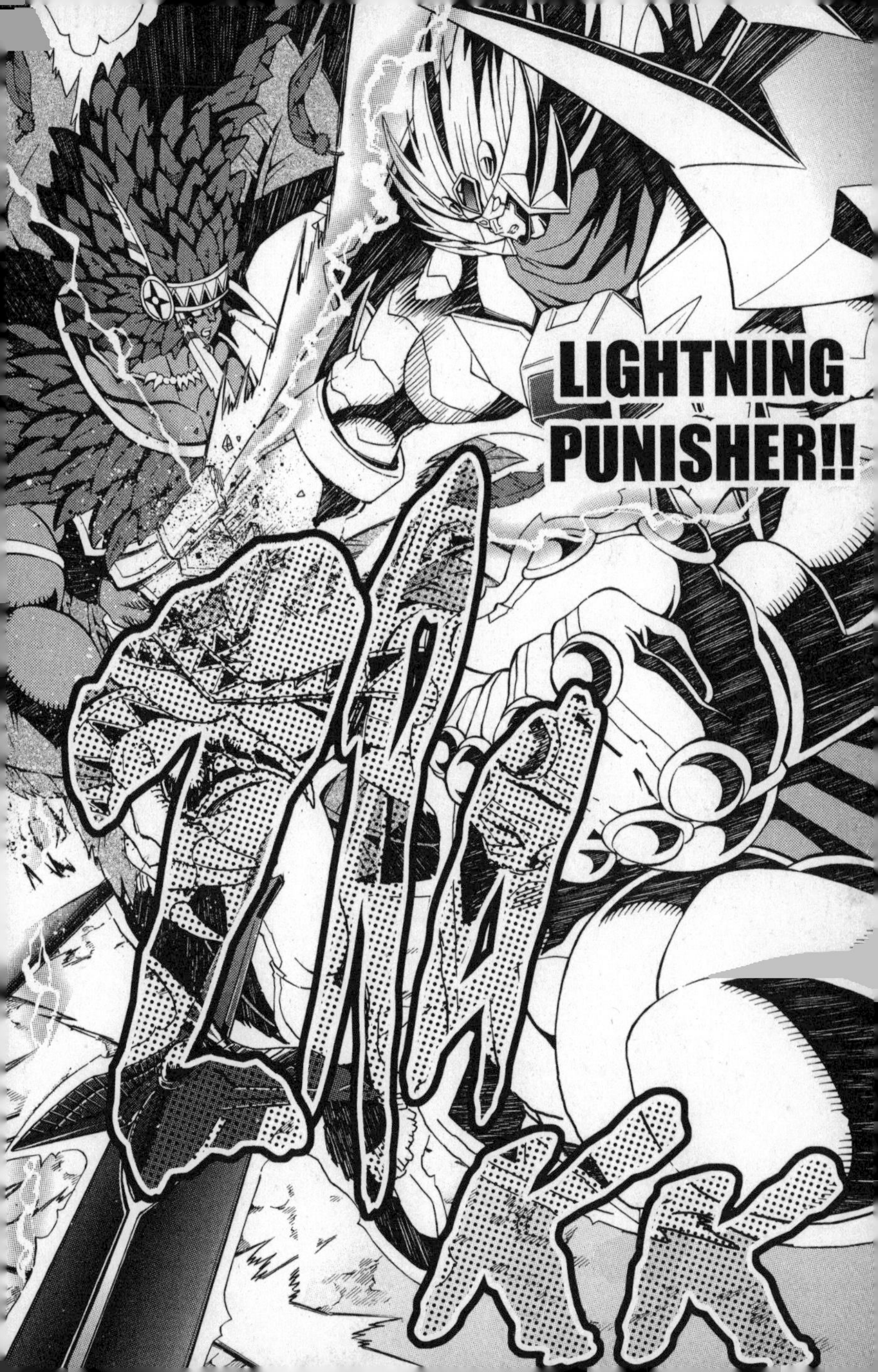
LIGHTNING
PUNISHER!!

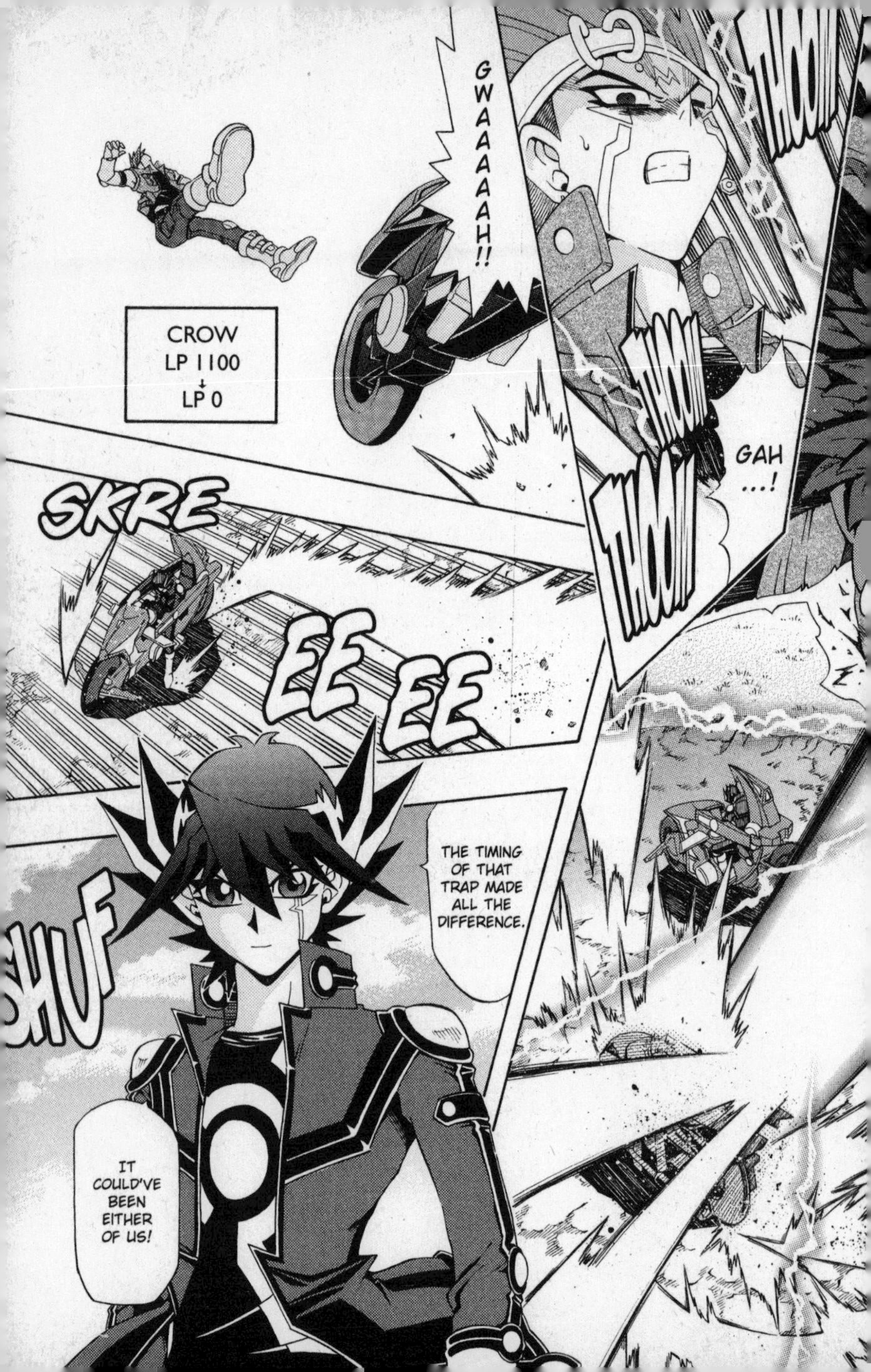
THOOM
THOOM
THOOM
GAH ...!
GWAAAAAAH!!
CROW LP 1100 → LP 0
SKRE
EE EE
THE TIMING OF THAT TRAP MADE ALL THE DIFFERENCE.
SHUF
IT COULD'VE BEEN EITHER OF US!

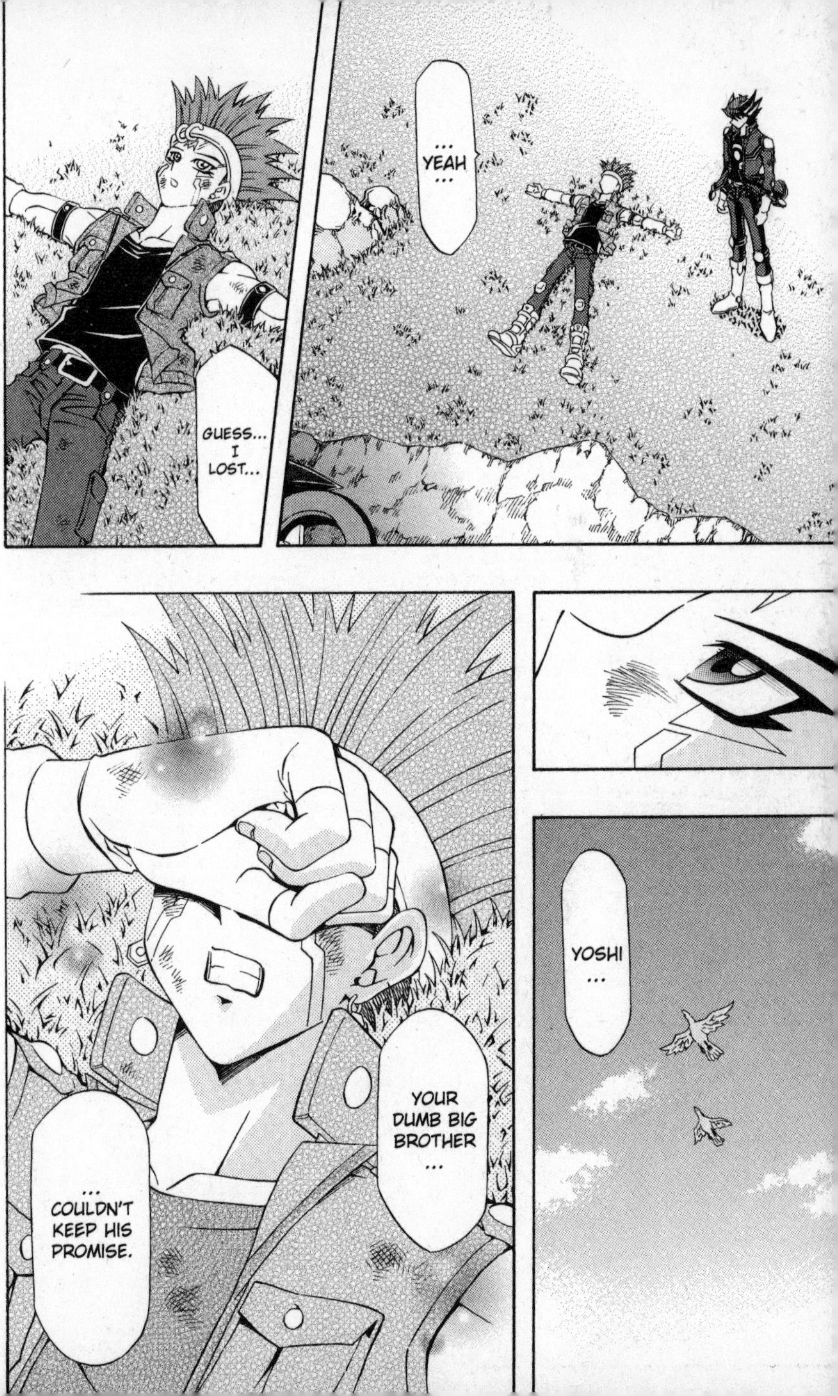
GUESS... I LOST...
... YEAH ...
YOUR DUMB BIG BROTHER ...
... COULDN'T KEEP HIS PROMISE.
YOSHI ...

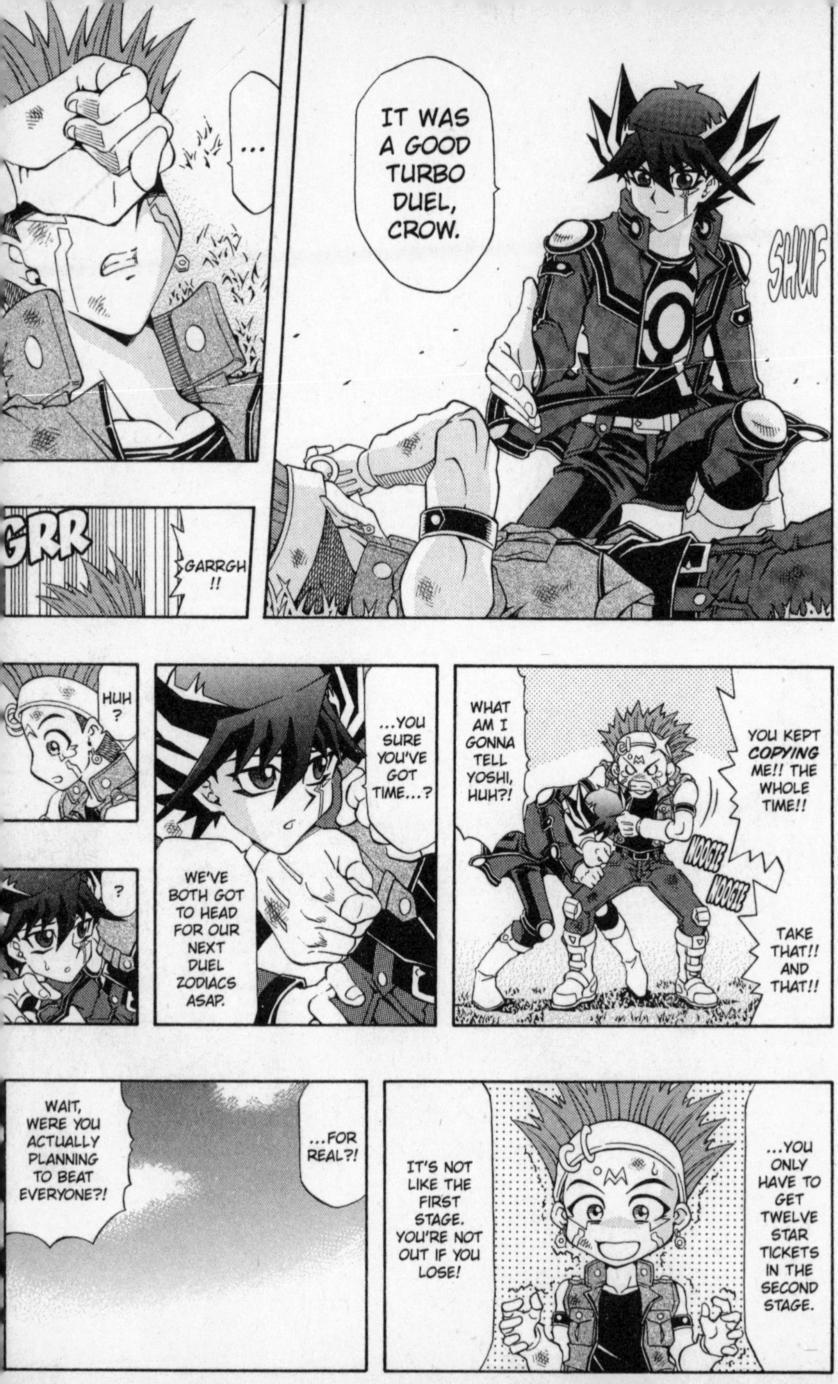
IT WAS A GOOD TURBO DUEL, CROW.
SHUF
...
GRR
GARRGH!!
WHAT AM I GONNA TELL YOSHI, HUH?!
YOU KEPT COPYING ME!! THE WHOLE TIME!!
NOOGIE
NOOGIE
TAKE THAT!! AND THAT!!
...YOU SURE YOU'VE GOT TIME...?
WE'VE BOTH GOT TO HEAD FOR OUR NEXT DUEL ZODIACS ASAP.
HUH?
?
...YOU ONLY HAVE TO GET TWELVE STAR TICKETS IN THE SECOND STAGE.
IT'S NOT LIKE THE FIRST STAGE. YOU'RE NOT OUT IF YOU LOSE!
...FOR REAL?!
WAIT, WERE YOU ACTUALLY PLANNING TO BEAT EVERYONE?!

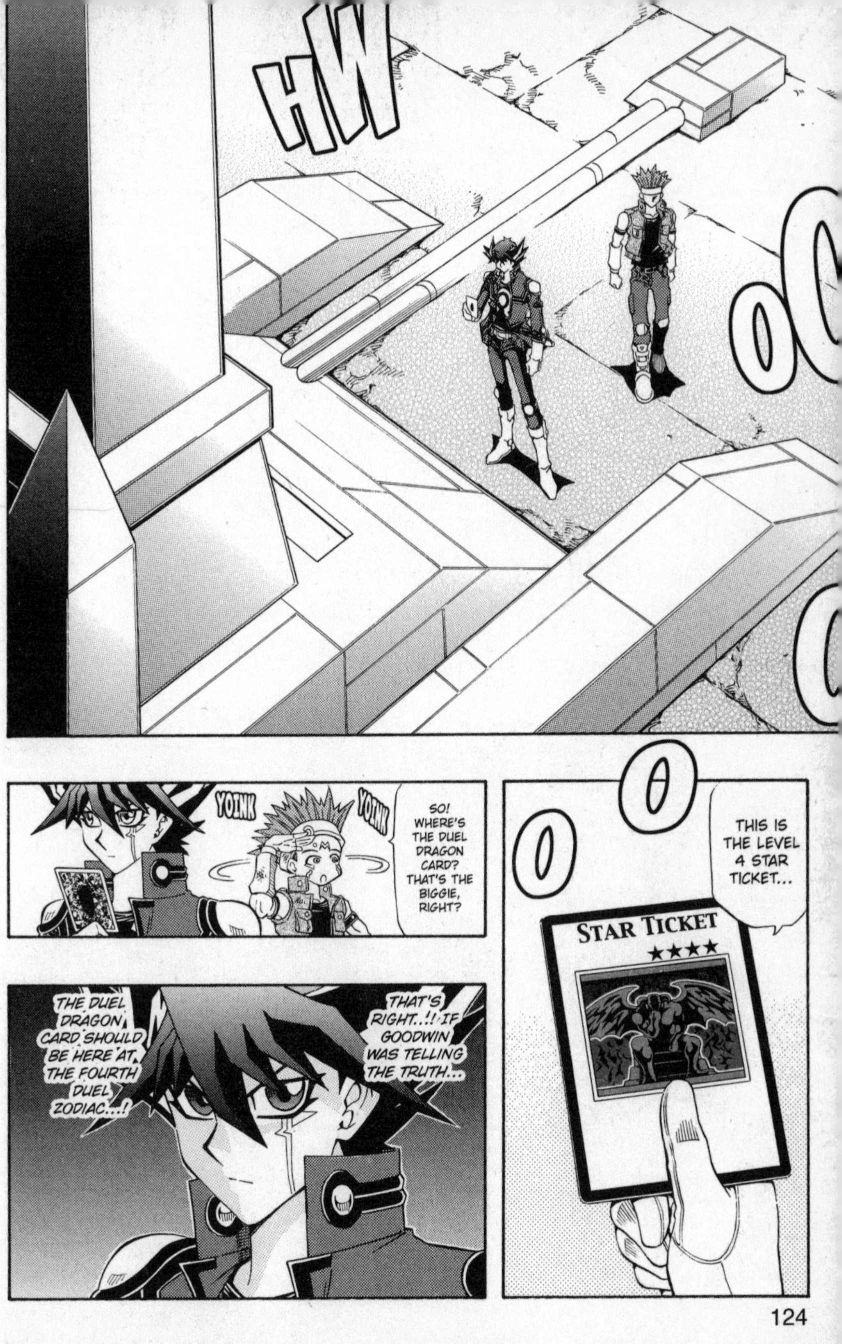
HW
THIS IS THE LEVEL 4 STAR TICKET...
STAR TICKET
YOINK
YOINK
SO! WHERE'S THE DUEL DRAGON CARD? THAT'S THE BIGGIE, RIGHT?
THAT'S RIGHT..!! IF GOODWIN WAS TELLING THE TRUTH...
THE DUEL DRAGON CARD SHOULD BE HERE AT THE FOURTH DUEL ZODIAC...!

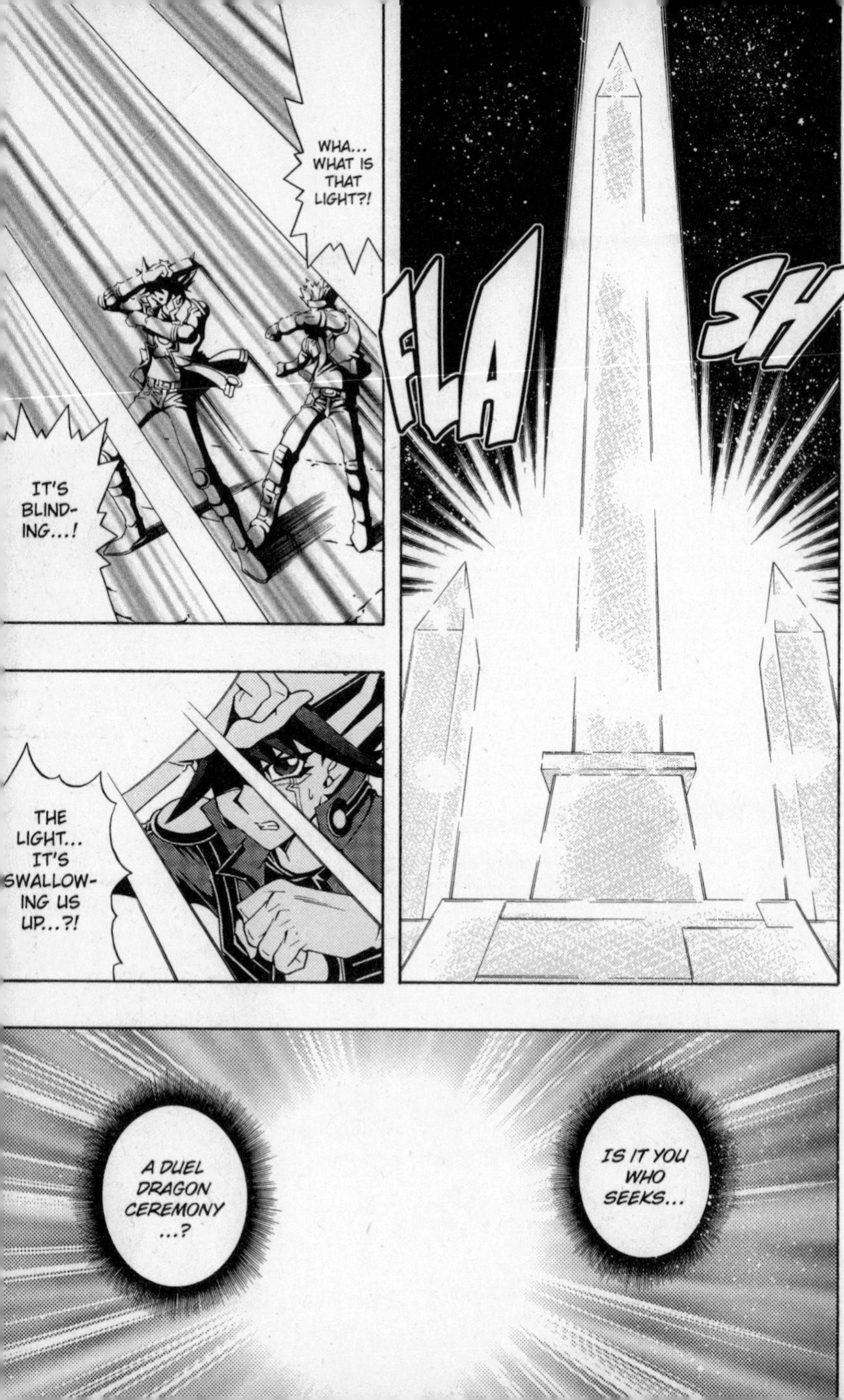
FLASH
WHA... WHAT IS THAT LIGHT?!
IT'S BLINDING...!
THE LIGHT... IT'S SWALLOWING US UP...?!
IS IT YOU WHO SEEKS...
A DUEL DRAGON CEREMONY...?

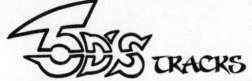

5D's TRACKS

THE 28TH

BY SATOMASA

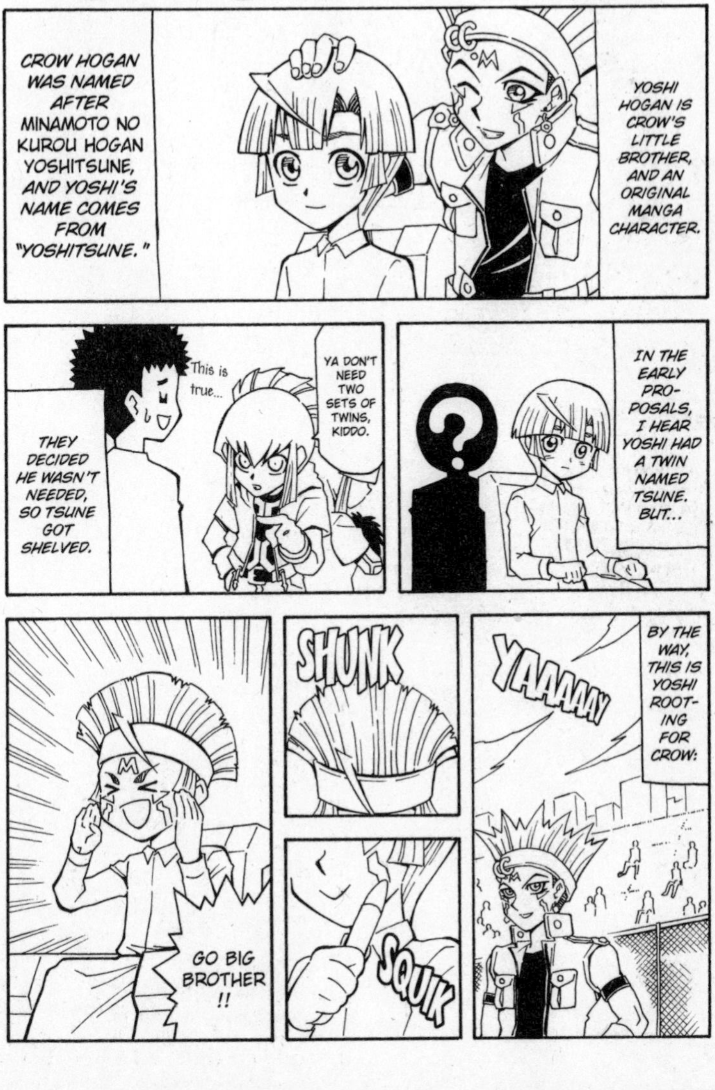
YOSHI HOGAN IS CROW'S LITTLE BROTHER, AND AN ORIGINAL MANGA CHARACTER.
CROW HOGAN WAS NAMED AFTER MINAMOTO NO KUROU HOGAN YOSHITSUNE, AND YOSHI'S NAME COMES FROM "YOSHITSUNE."
IN THE EARLY PROPOSALS, I HEAR YOSHI HAD A TWIN NAMED TSUNE. BUT...
YA DON'T NEED TWO SETS OF TWINS, KIDDO.
This is true...
THEY DECIDED HE WASN'T NEEDED, SO TSUNE GOT SHELVED.
BY THE WAY, THIS IS YOSHI ROOTING FOR CROW:
YAAAAAY
SHUNK
SQUIK
GO BIG BROTHER !!

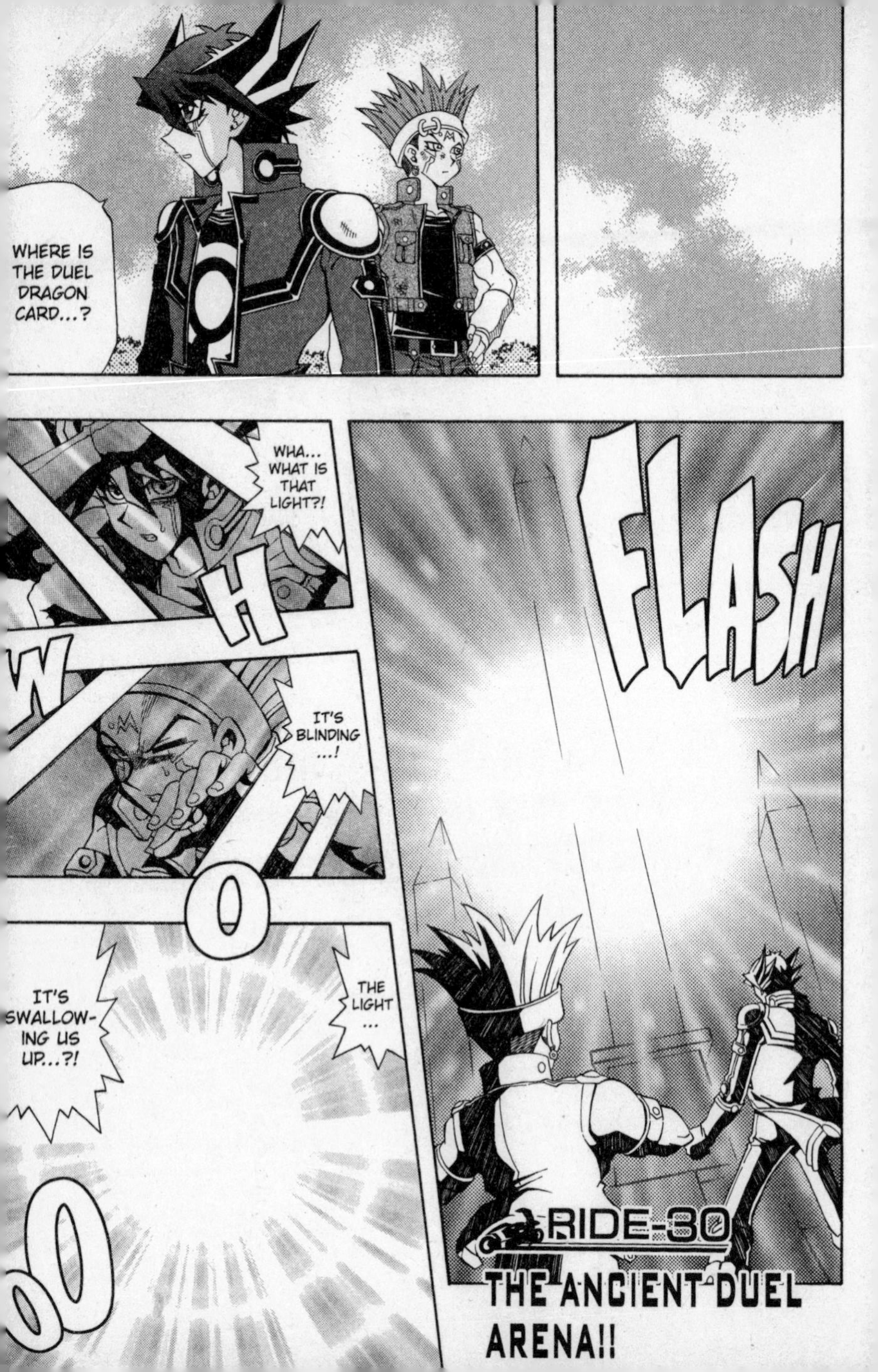
WHERE IS THE DUEL DRAGON CARD...?
FLASH
RIDE-30
THE ANCIENT DUEL ARENA!!
WHA... WHAT IS THAT LIGHT?!
WHOOO
IT'S BLINDING...!
THE LIGHT...
IT'S SWALLOWING US UP...?!

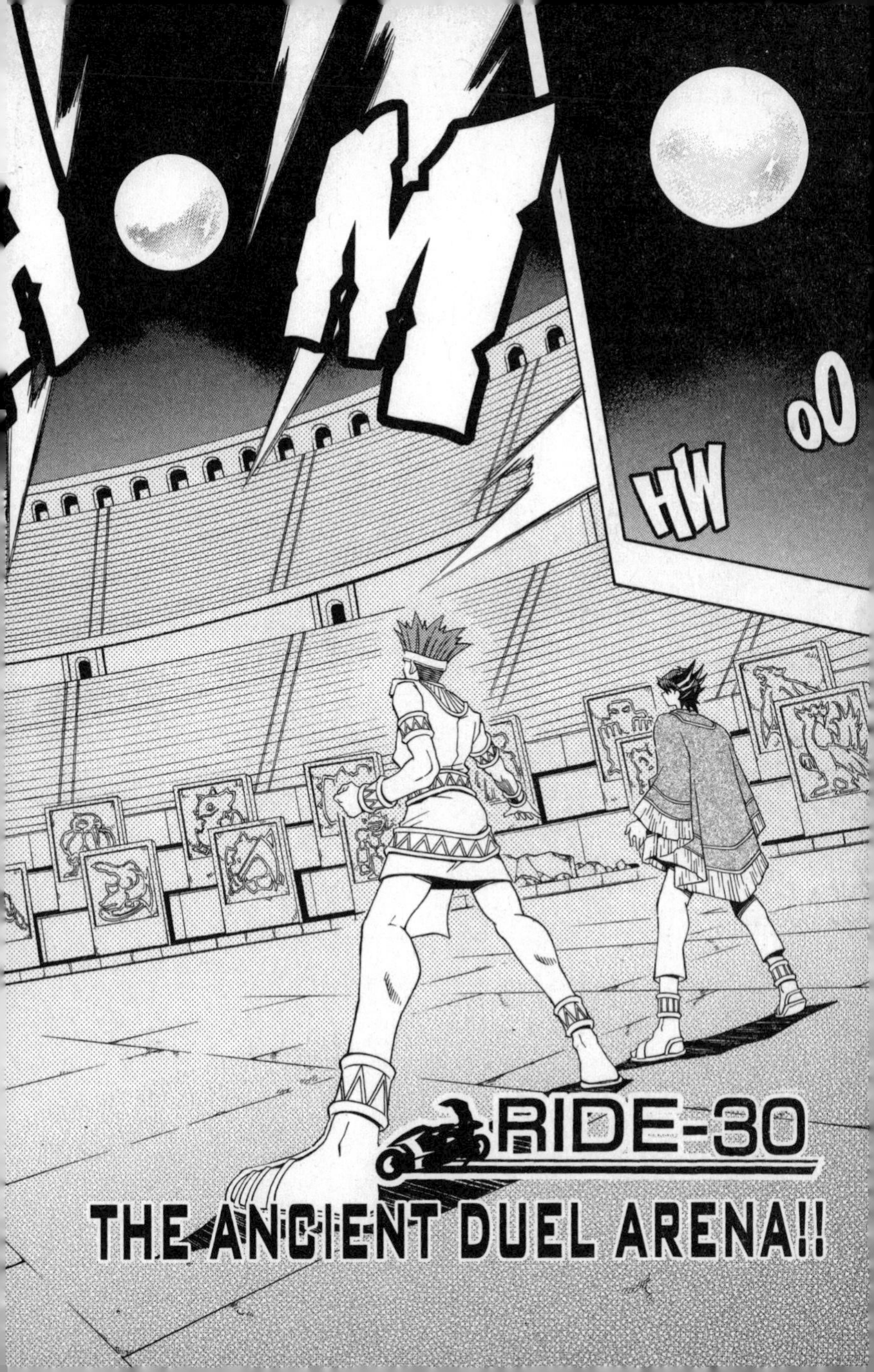
RIDE-30
THE ANCIENT DUEL ARENA!!

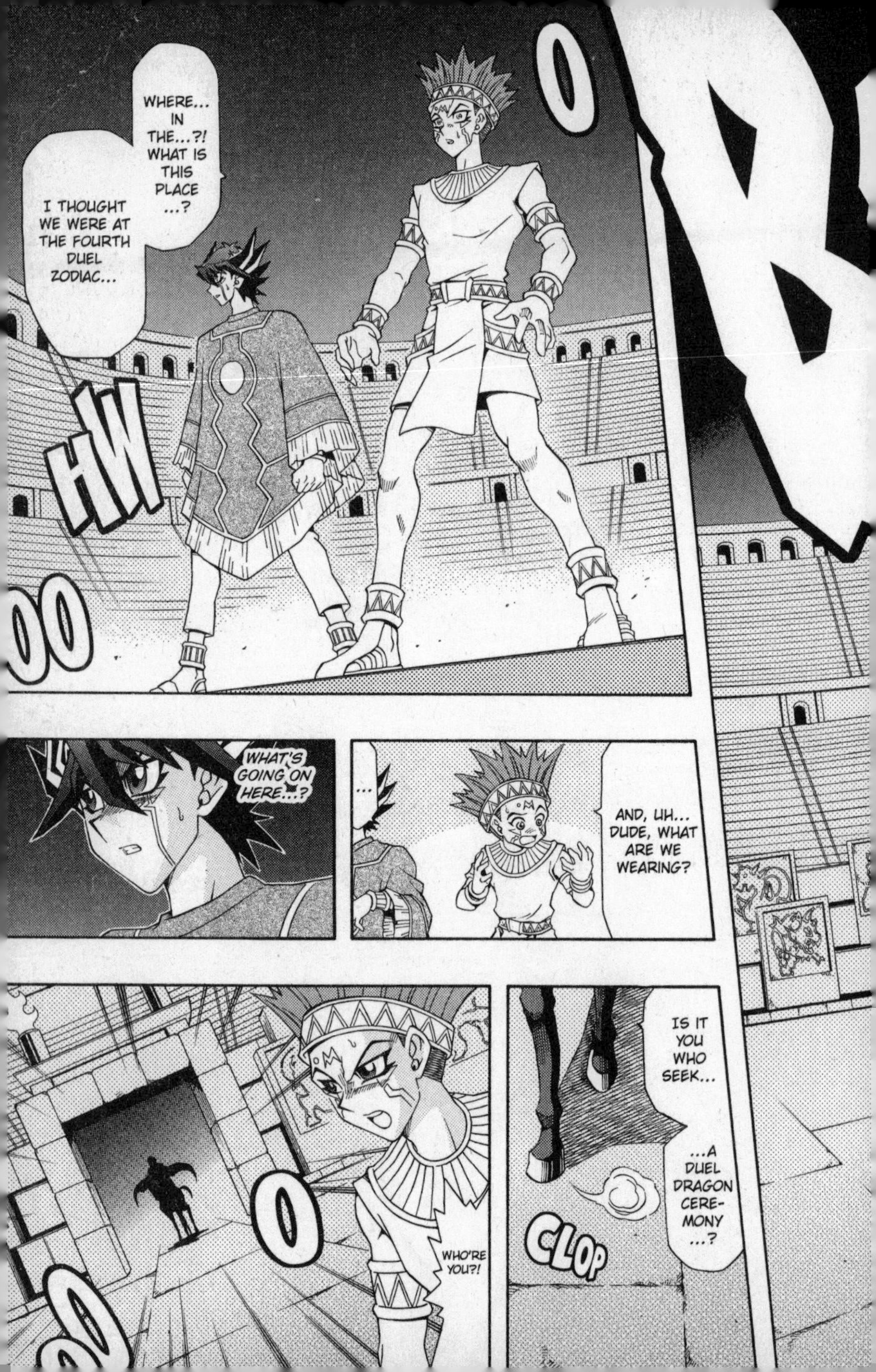
WHERE... IN THE...?! WHAT IS THIS PLACE ...?
I THOUGHT WE WERE AT THE FOURTH DUEL ZODIAC...
...
AND, UH... DUDE, WHAT ARE WE WEARING?
WHAT'S GOING ON HERE...?
IS IT YOU WHO SEEK...
...A DUEL DRAGON CERE-MONY ...?
CLOP
WHO'RE YOU?!

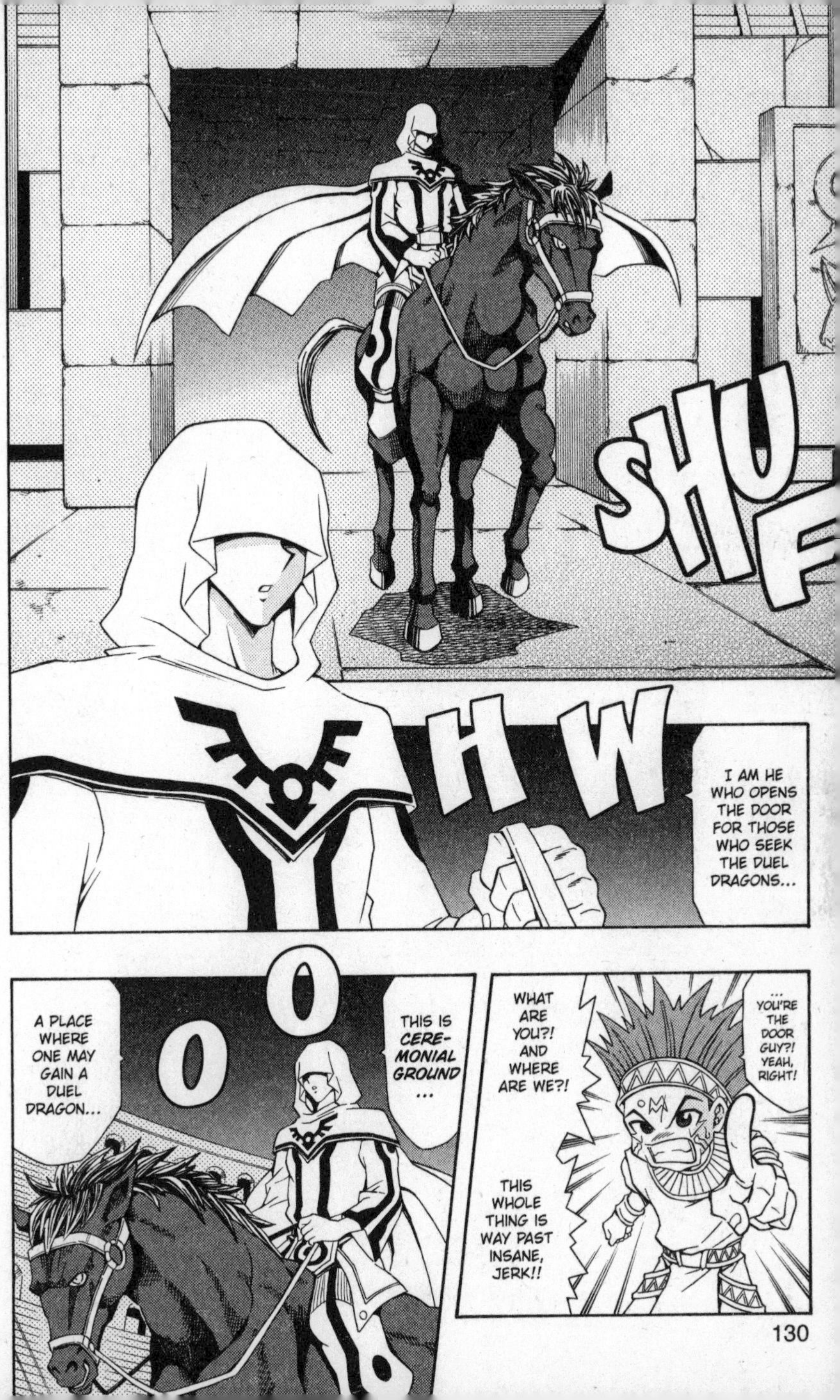
SHU
F
H W
O O
I AM HE WHO OPENS THE DOOR FOR THOSE WHO SEEK THE DUEL DRAGONS...
... YOU'RE THE DOOR GUY?! YEAH, RIGHT!
WHAT ARE YOU?! AND WHERE ARE WE?!
THIS WHOLE THING IS WAY PAST INSANE, JERK!!
THIS IS *CEREMONIAL GROUND* ...
A PLACE WHERE ONE MAY GAIN A DUEL DRAGON...

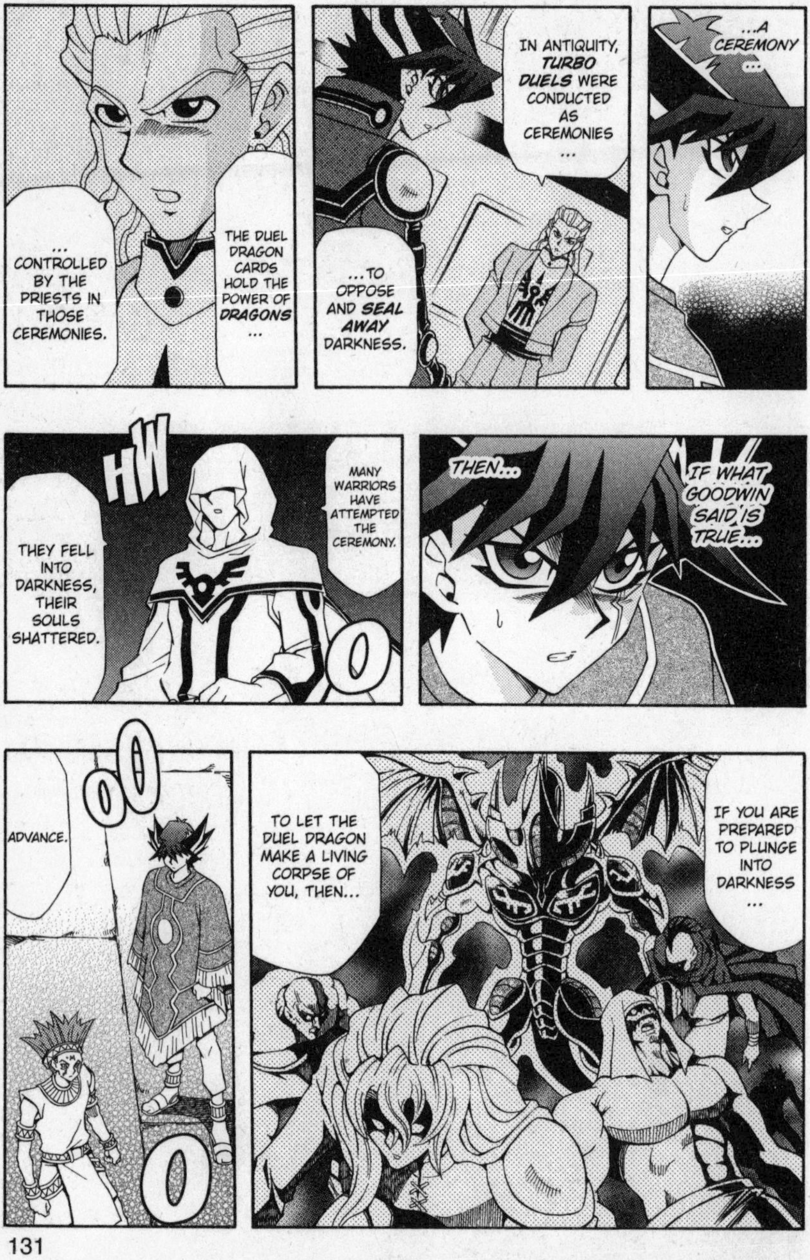

...A CEREMONY ...
IN ANTIQUITY, TURBO DUELS WERE CONDUCTED AS CEREMONIES ...
...TO OPPOSE AND SEAL AWAY DARKNESS.
THE DUEL DRAGON CARDS HOLD THE POWER OF DRAGONS ...
... CONTROLLED BY THE PRIESTS IN THOSE CEREMONIES.
IF WHAT GOODWIN SAID IS TRUE...
THEN...
MANY WARRIORS HAVE ATTEMPTED THE CEREMONY.
HW
O
THEY FELL INTO DARKNESS, THEIR SOULS SHATTERED.
IF YOU ARE PREPARED TO PLUNGE INTO DARKNESS ...
TO LET THE DUEL DRAGON MAKE A LIVING CORPSE OF YOU, THEN...
OO
O
ADVANCE.

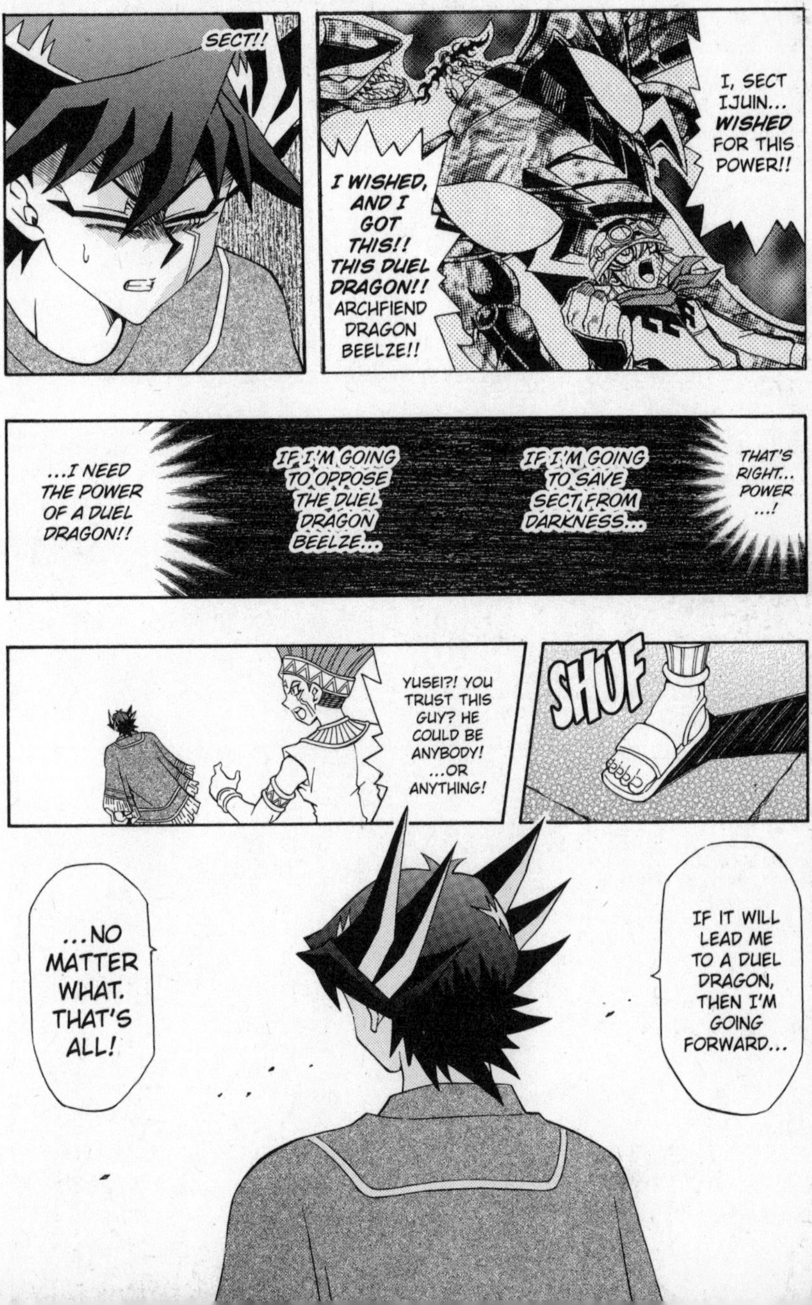
I, SECT IJUIN... WISHED FOR THIS POWER!!
I WISHED, AND I GOT THIS!! THIS DUEL DRAGON!! ARCHFIEND DRAGON BEELZE!!
SECT!!
THAT'S RIGHT... POWER ...!
IF I'M GOING TO SAVE SECT FROM DARKNESS...
IF I'M GOING TO OPPOSE THE DUEL DRAGON BEELZE...
...I NEED THE POWER OF A DUEL DRAGON!!
SHUF
YUSEI?! YOU TRUST THIS GUY? HE COULD BE ANYBODY! ...OR ANYTHING!
IF IT WILL LEAD ME TO A DUEL DRAGON, THEN I'M GOING FORWARD...
...NO MATTER WHAT. THAT'S ALL!

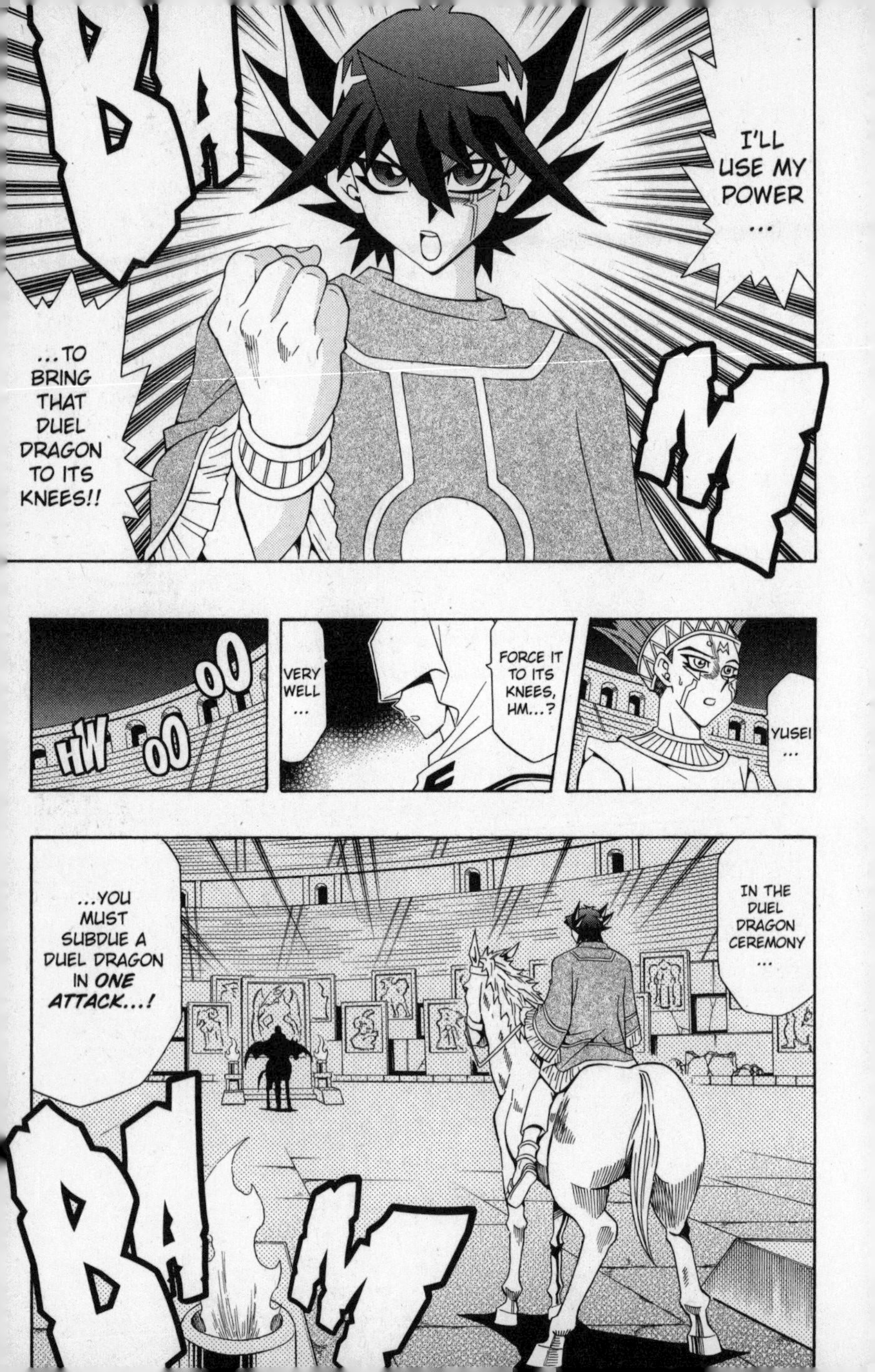
I'LL USE MY POWER ...
BAM
...TO BRING THAT DUEL DRAGON TO ITS KNEES!!
YUSEI ...
FORCE IT TO ITS KNEES, HM...?
VERY WELL ...
HWOOOO
IN THE DUEL DRAGON CEREMONY ...
...YOU MUST SUBDUE A DUEL DRAGON IN *ONE ATTACK*...!
BAM

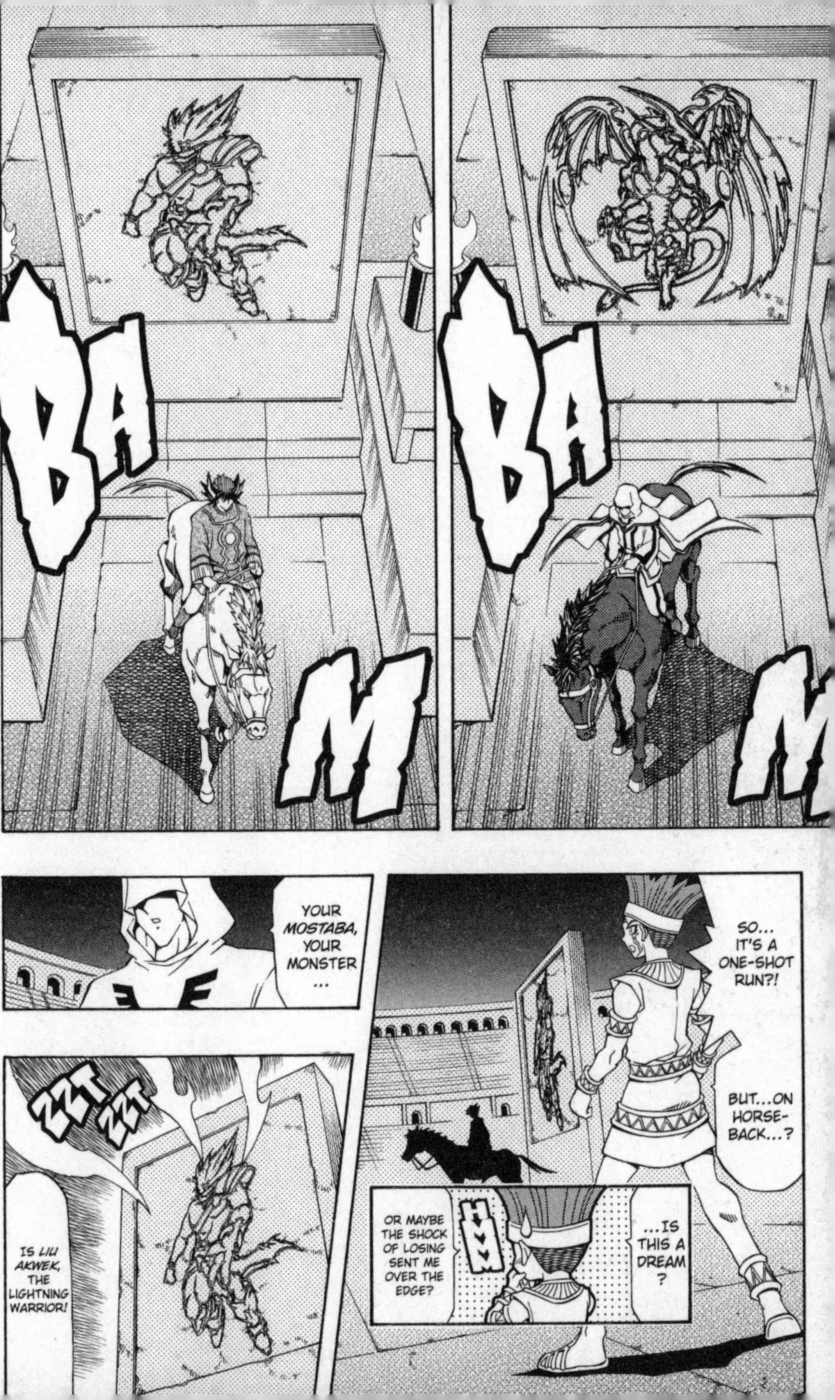
BA
M
BA
M
SO... IT'S A ONE-SHOT RUN?!
BUT...ON HORSE-BACK...?
...IS THIS A DREAM?
OR MAYBE THE SHOCK OF LOSING SENT ME OVER THE EDGE?
YOUR *MOSTABA,* YOUR MONSTER ...
ZZT ZZT
IS *LIU AKWEK,* THE LIGHTNING WARRIOR!

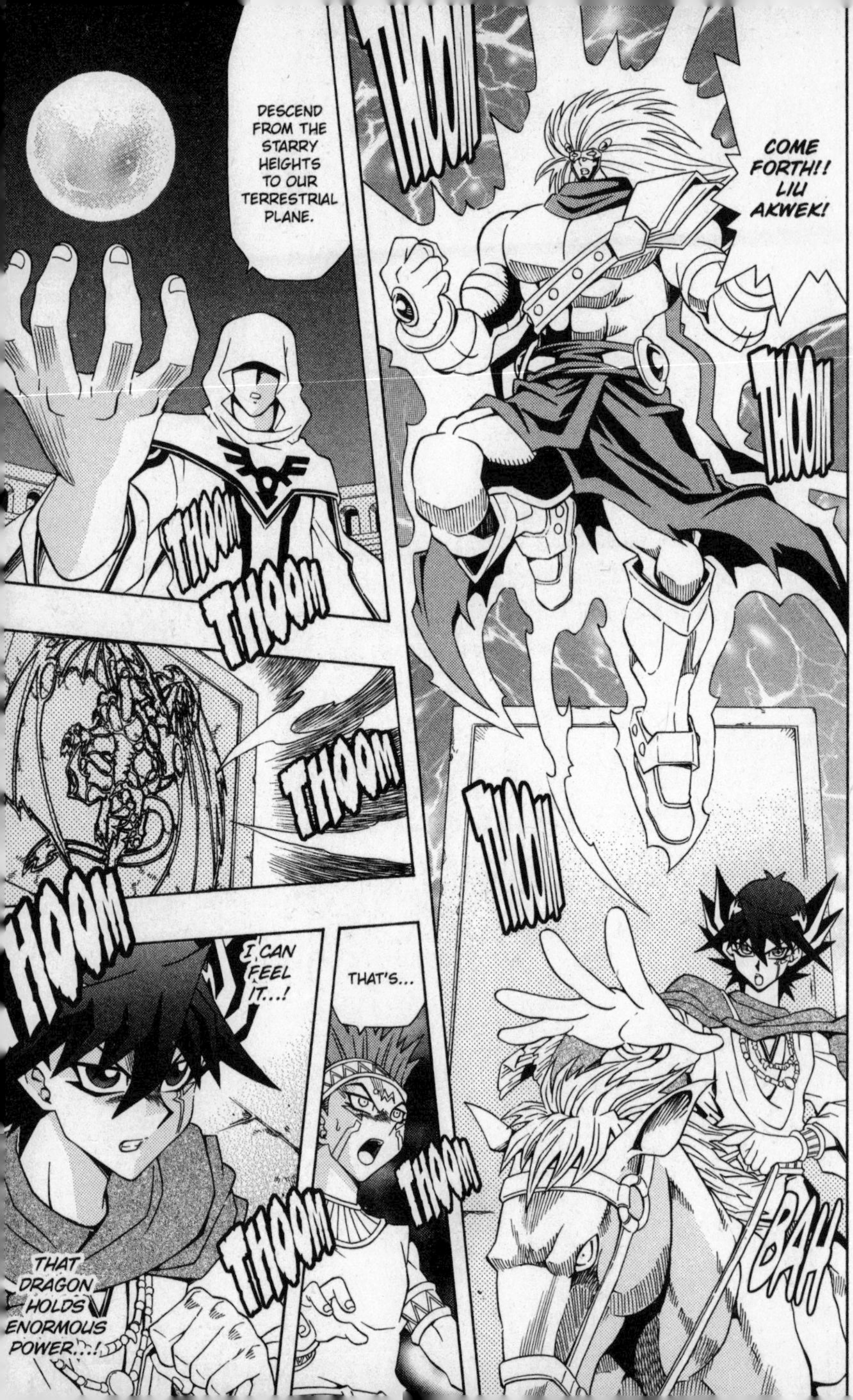
THOOM
COME FORTH!! LIU AKWEK!
THOOM
THOOM
BRAH
DESCEND FROM THE STARRY HEIGHTS TO OUR TERRESTRIAL PLANE.
THOOM
THOOM
THOOM
THOOM
THAT'S...
THOOM
THOOM
I CAN FEEL IT...!
THAT DRAGON HOLDS ENORMOUS POWER...!

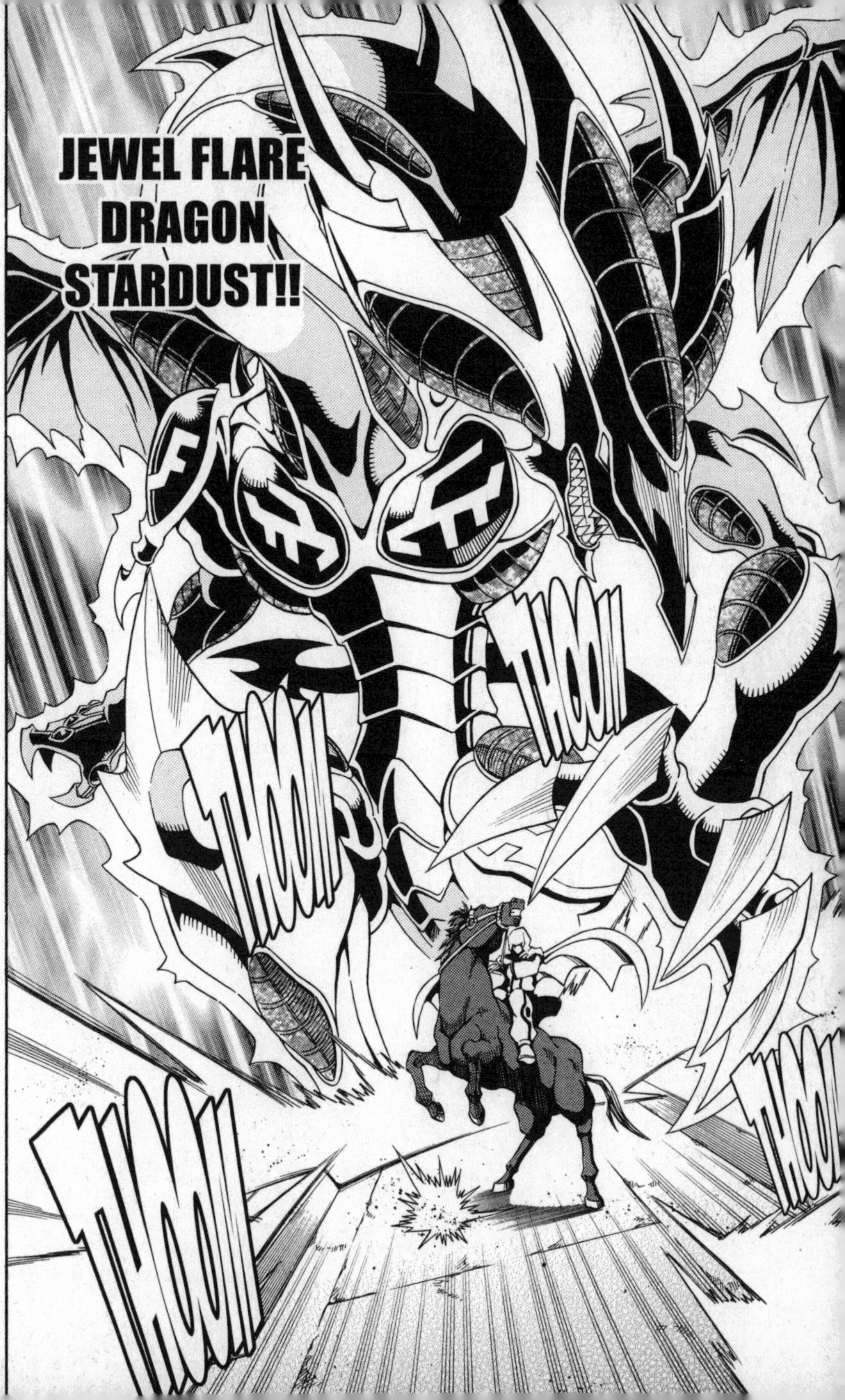
JEWEL FLARE DRAGON STARDUST!!
THOOM
THOOM
THOO
THOOM

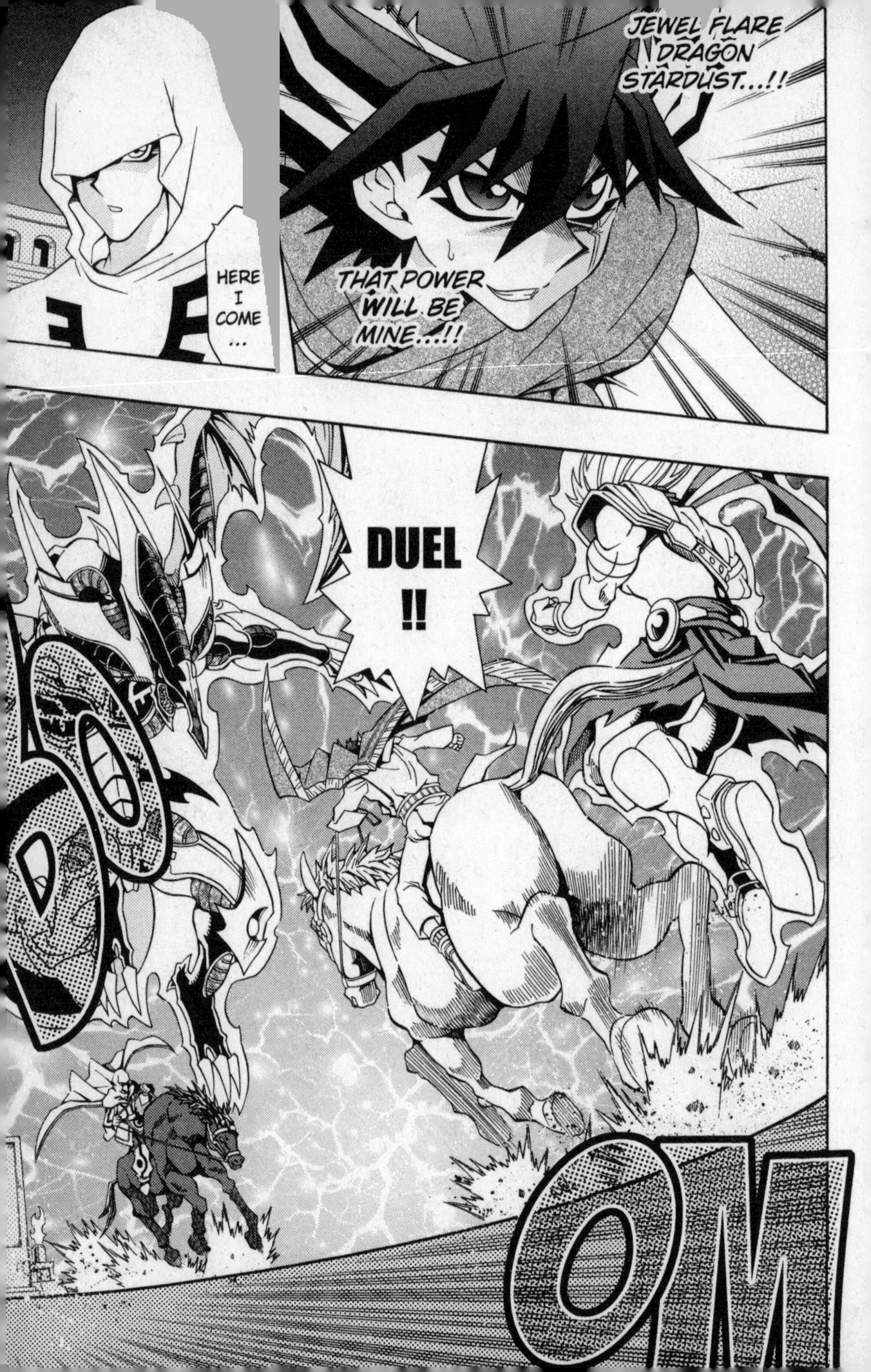
JEWEL FLARE DRAGON STARDUST...!!
THAT POWER WILL BE MINE...!!
HERE I COME ...
DUEL !!

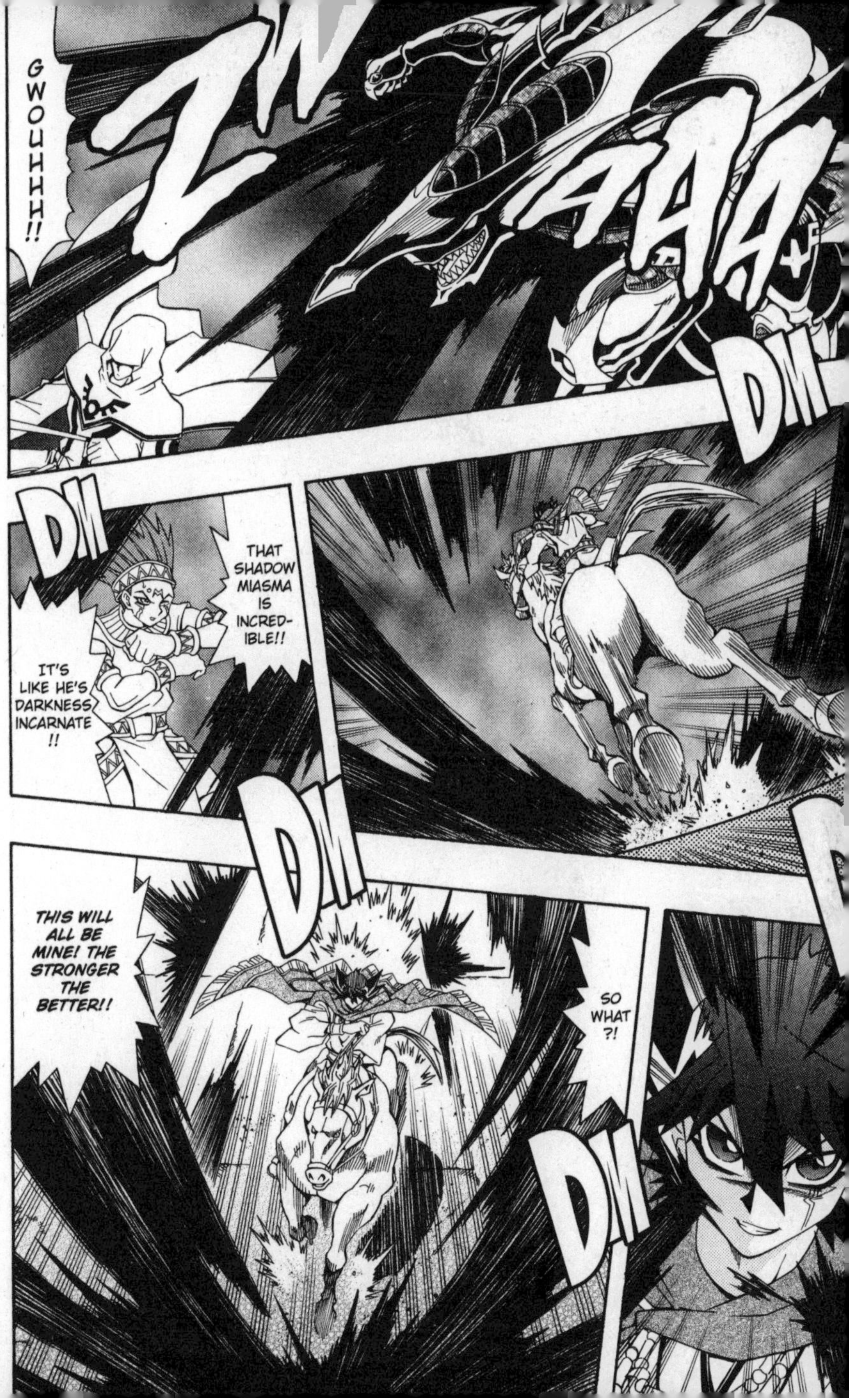
ZWAAA
GWOUHHHH!!
DM
DM
THAT SHADOW MIASMA IS INCREDIBLE!!
IT'S LIKE HE'S DARKNESS INCARNATE!!
DM
SO WHAT?!
DM
THIS WILL ALL BE MINE! THE STRONGER THE BETTER!!

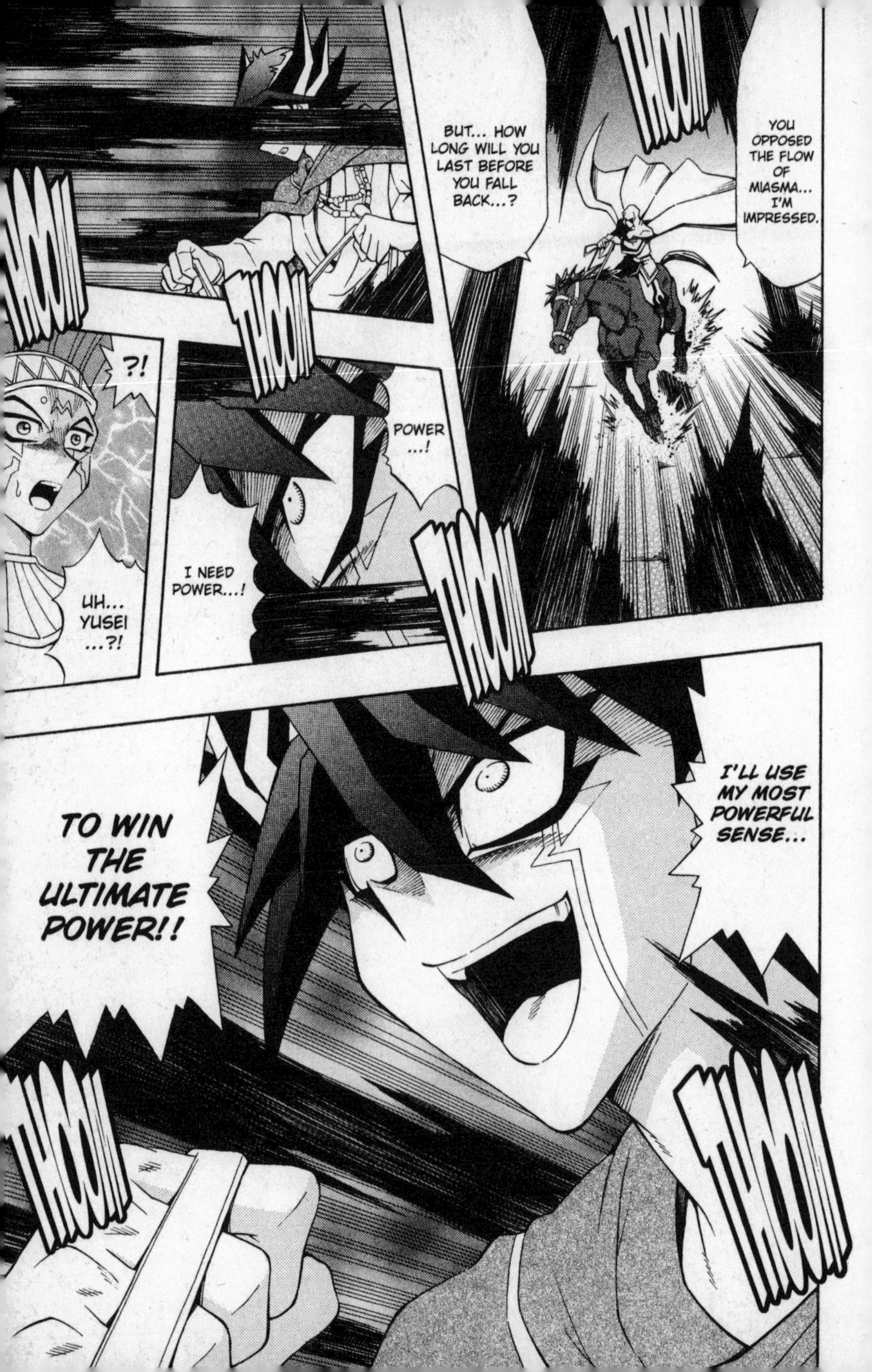
THOOM
YOU OPPOSED THE FLOW OF MIASMA... I'M IMPRESSED.
BUT... HOW LONG WILL YOU LAST BEFORE YOU FALL BACK...?
THOOM
THOOM
THOOM
POWER ...!
I NEED POWER...!
?!
UH... YUSEI ...?!
I'LL USE MY MOST POWERFUL SENSE...
TO WIN THE ULTIMATE POWER!!
THOOM
THOOM

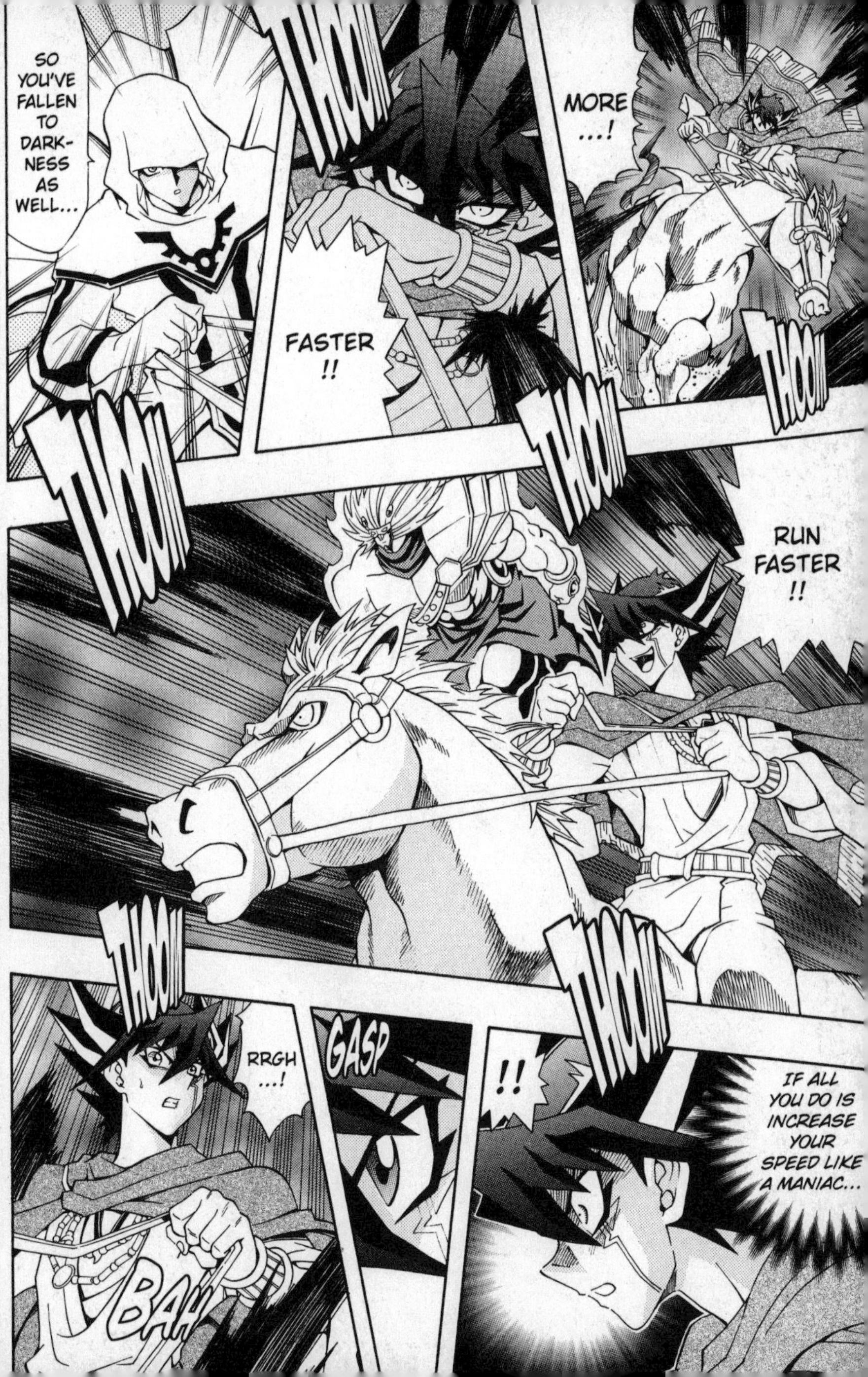
THOOM
MORE ...!
THOOM
THOOM
FASTER !!
THOOM
SO YOU'VE FALLEN TO DARKNESS AS WELL...
THOOM
RUN FASTER !!
THOOM
THOOM
IF ALL YOU DO IS INCREASE YOUR SPEED LIKE A MANIAC...
GASP
!!
RRGH ...!
BAH

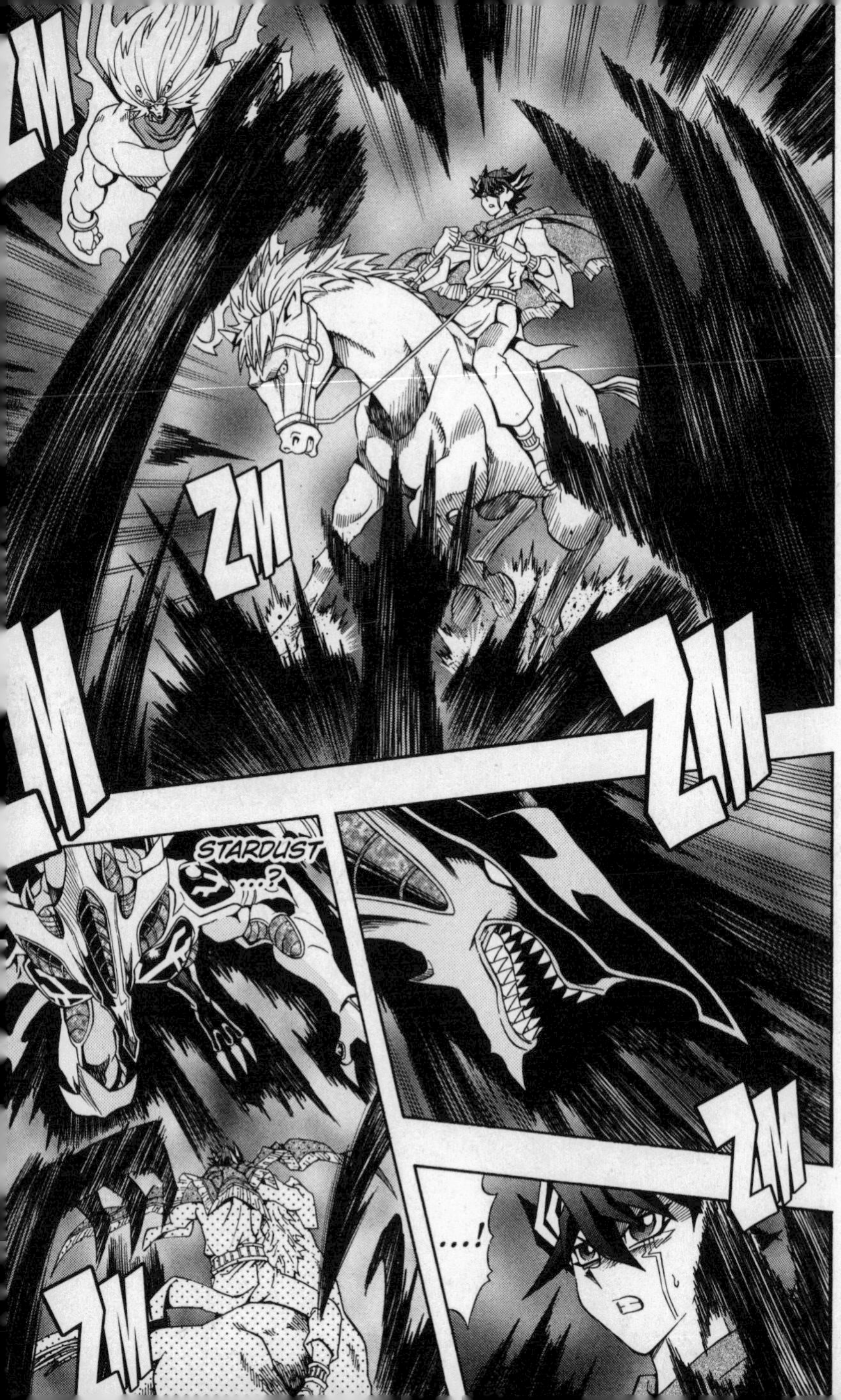
ZM
ZM
ZM
ZM
ZM
STARDUST ...?
ZM
...!
ZM

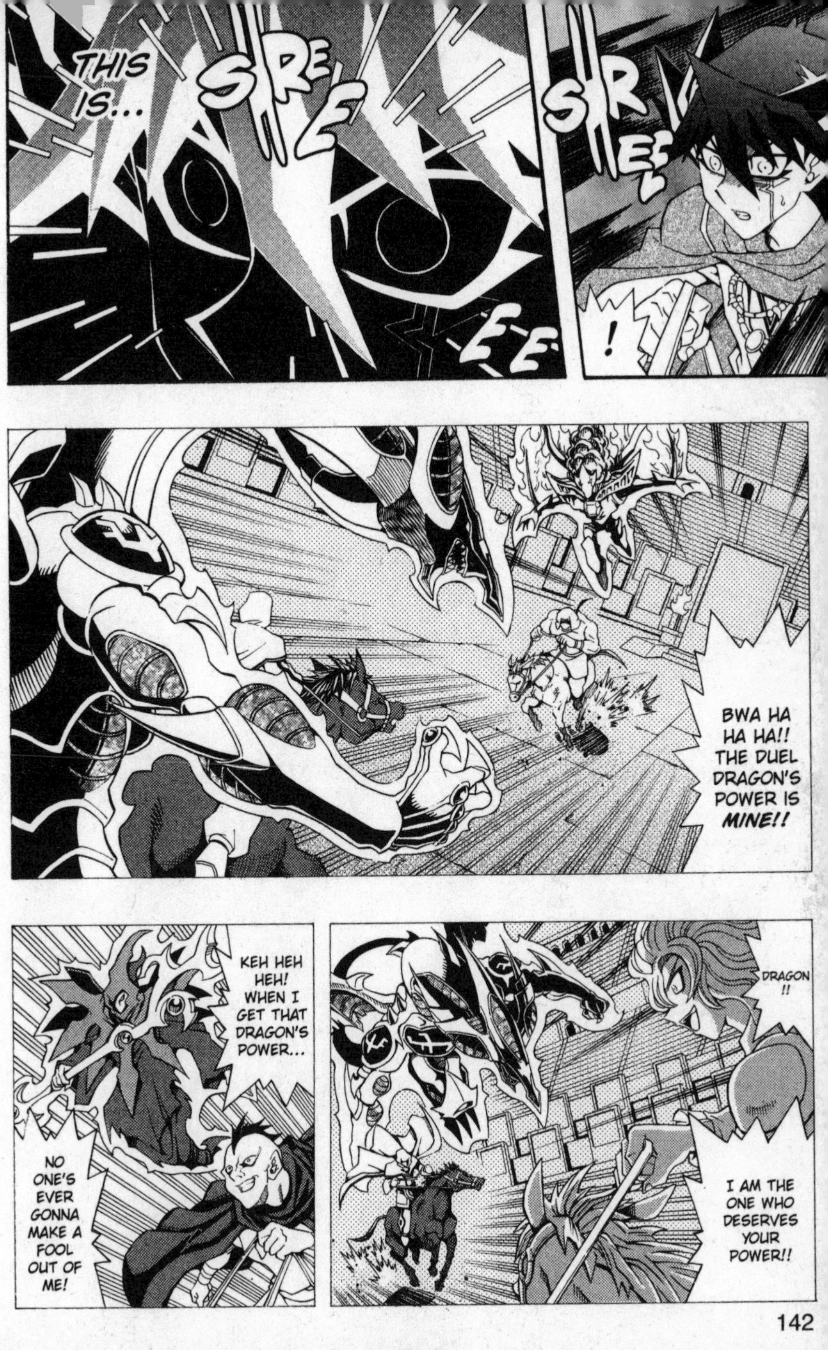
SRE
!
THIS IS...
SREE
EE
BWA HA HA HA!! THE DUEL DRAGON'S POWER IS *MINE!!*
DRAGON!!
I AM THE ONE WHO DESERVES YOUR POWER!!
KEH HEH HEH! WHEN I GET THAT DRAGON'S POWER...
NO ONE'S EVER GONNA MAKE A FOOL OUT OF ME!

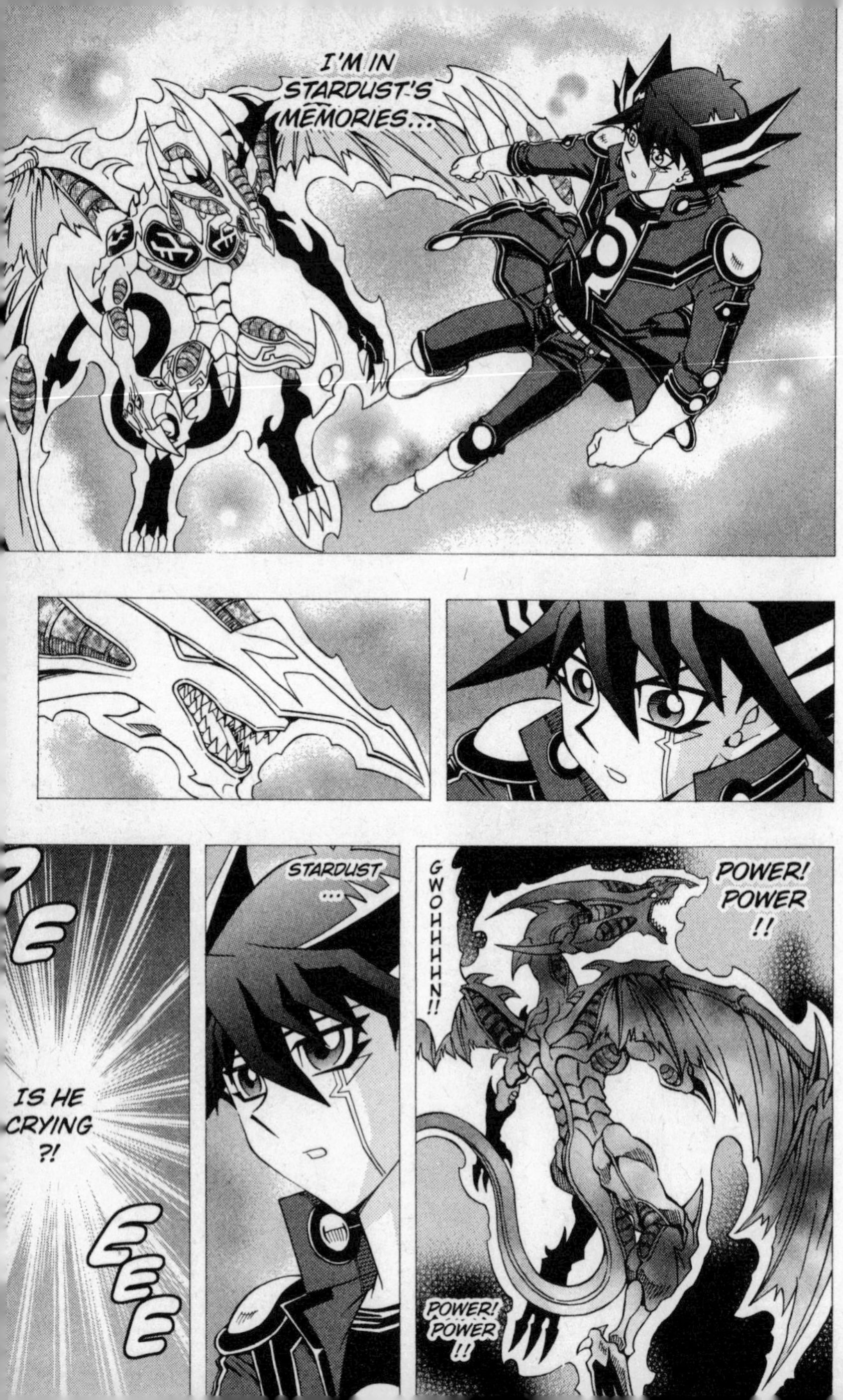
I'M IN STARDUST'S MEMORIES...
GWOHHHHN!!
POWER! POWER !!
POWER! POWER !!
STARDUST ...
IS HE CRYING ?!

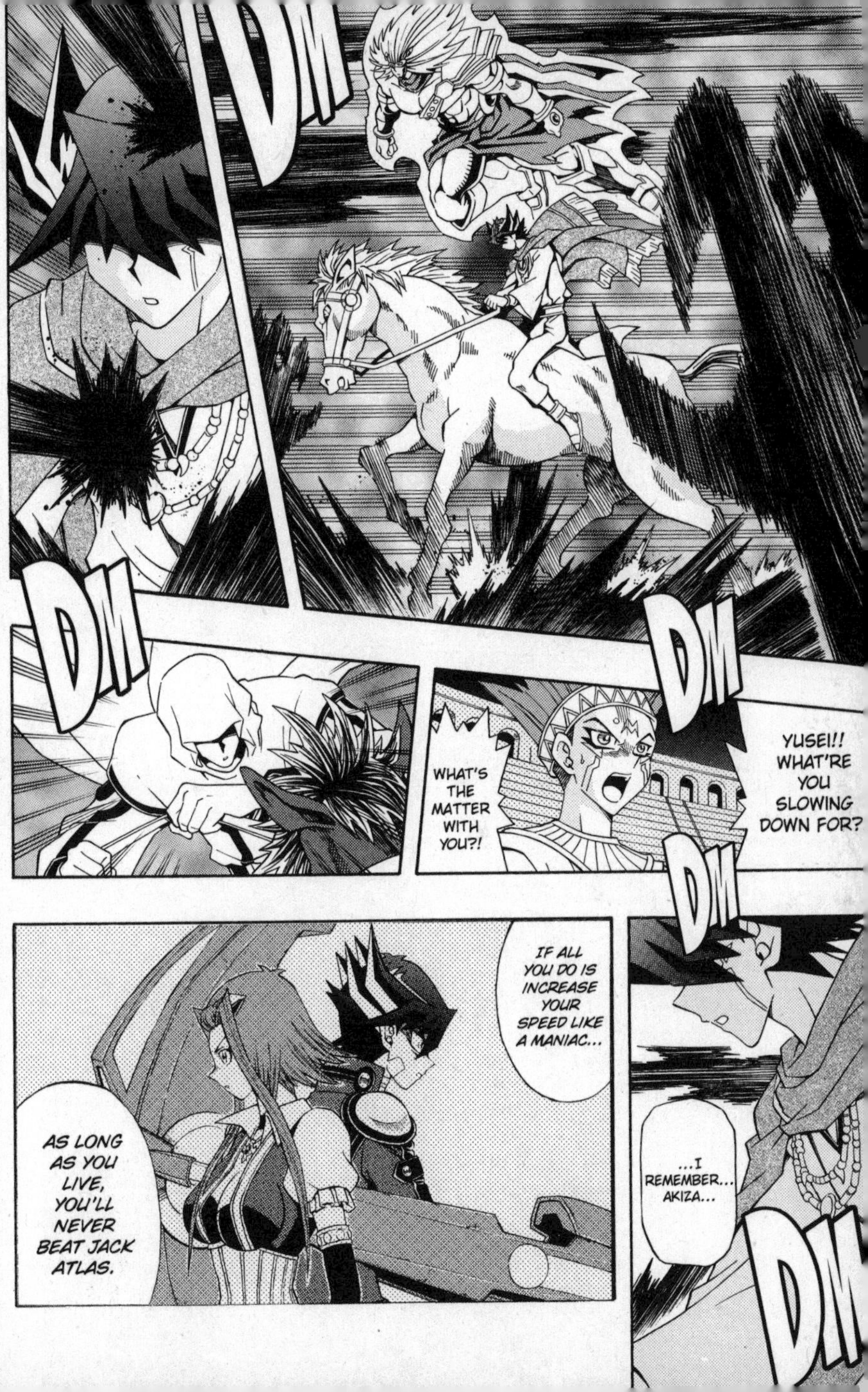
DM
DM
DM
DM
YUSEI!! WHAT'RE YOU SLOWING DOWN FOR?
WHAT'S THE MATTER WITH YOU?!
DM
...I REMEMBER... AKIZA...
DM
IF ALL YOU DO IS INCREASE YOUR SPEED LIKE A MANIAC...
AS LONG AS YOU LIVE, YOU'LL NEVER BEAT JACK ATLAS.

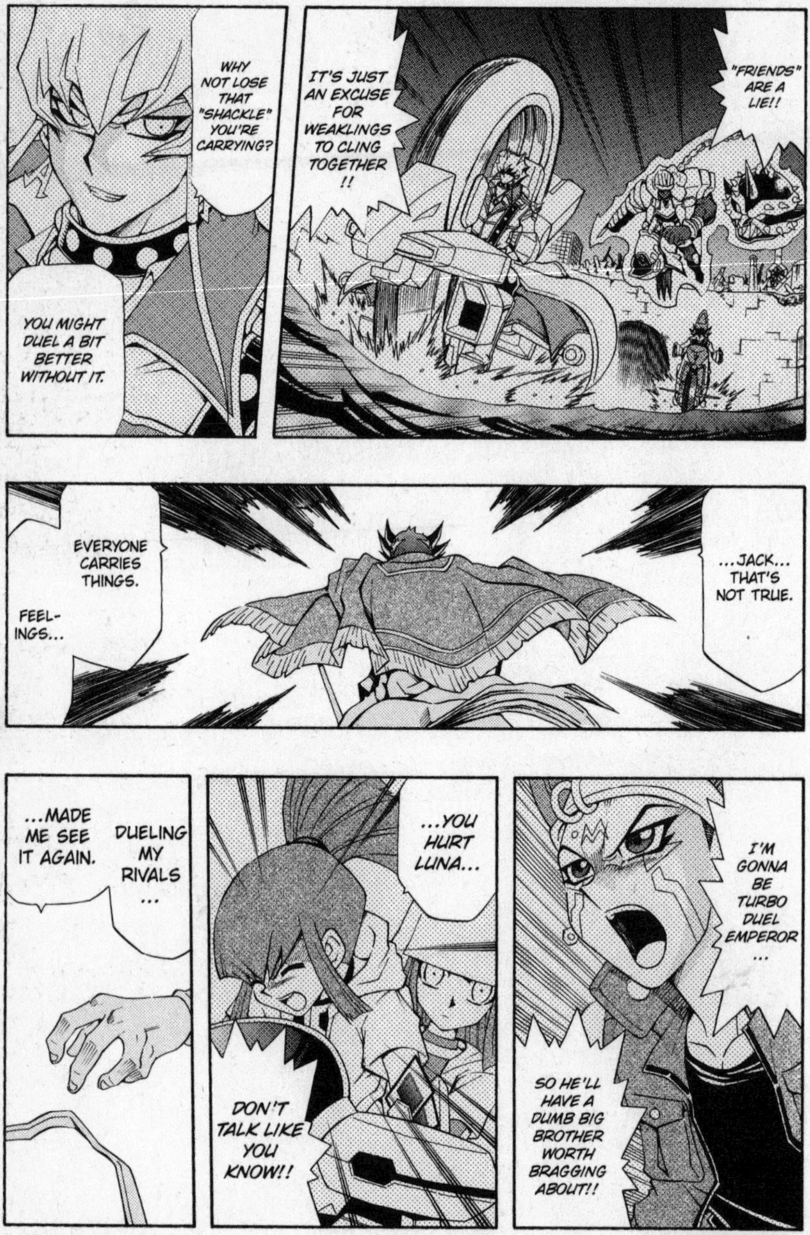
"FRIENDS" ARE A LIE!!
IT'S JUST AN EXCUSE FOR WEAKLINGS TO CLING TOGETHER!!
WHY NOT LOSE THAT "SHACKLE" YOU'RE CARRYING?
YOU MIGHT DUEL A BIT BETTER WITHOUT IT.
...JACK... THAT'S NOT TRUE.
EVERYONE CARRIES THINGS.
FEEL-INGS...
I'M GONNA BE TURBO DUEL EMPEROR...
SO HE'LL HAVE A DUMB BIG BROTHER WORTH BRAGGING ABOUT!!
...YOU HURT LUNA...
DON'T TALK LIKE YOU KNOW!!
DUELING MY RIVALS...
...MADE ME SEE IT AGAIN.

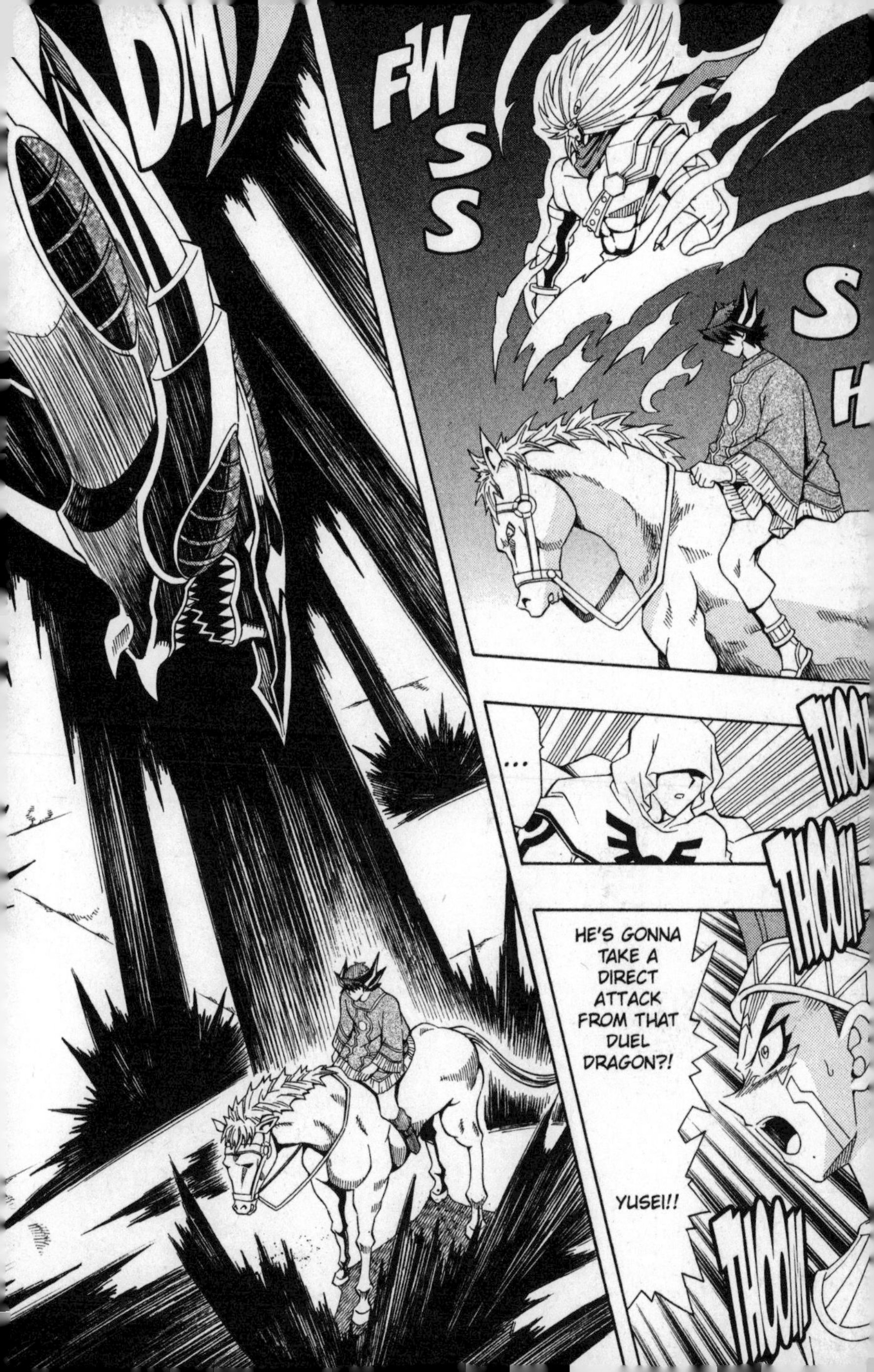

FWSS
SH
...
THOO
THOOM
HE'S GONNA TAKE A DIRECT ATTACK FROM THAT DUEL DRAGON?!
YUSEI!!
THOOM
DMM

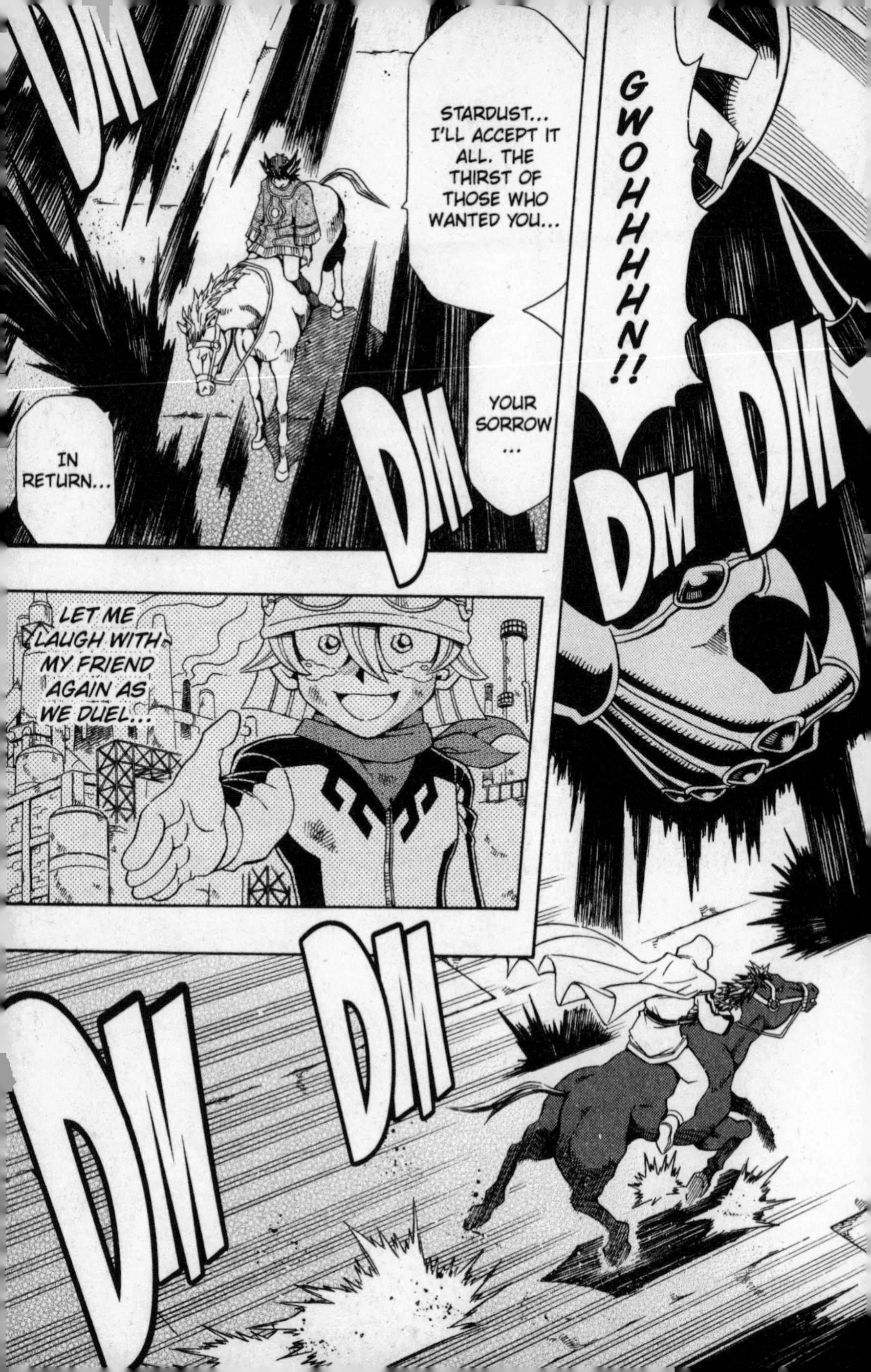
GWOHHHHHN!!
DM
DM
STARDUST... I'LL ACCEPT IT ALL. THE THIRST OF THOSE WHO WANTED YOU...
YOUR SORROW...
DM
IN RETURN...
LET ME LAUGH WITH MY FRIEND AGAIN AS WE DUEL...
DM
DM

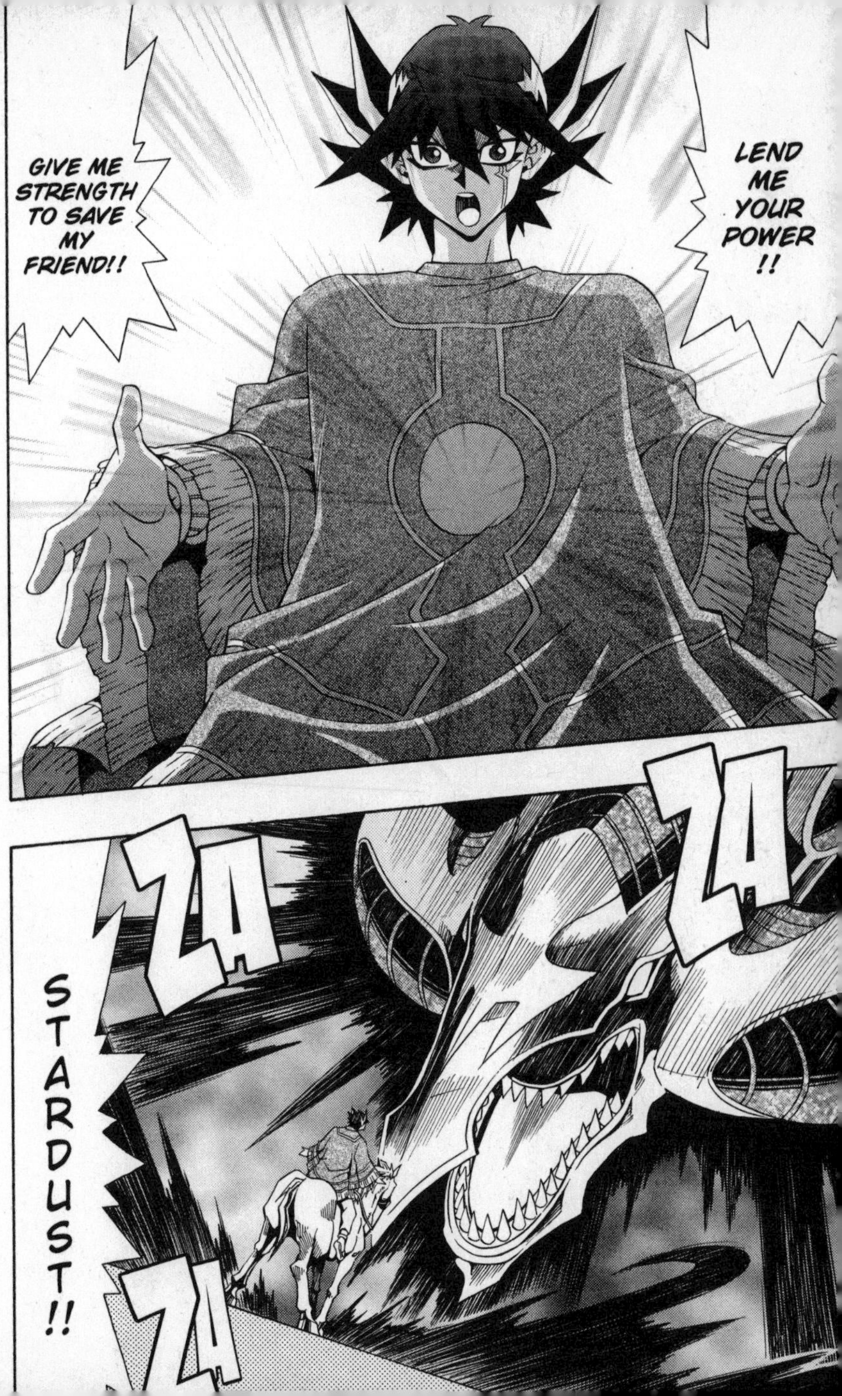
LEND ME YOUR POWER!!
GIVE ME STRENGTH TO SAVE MY FRIEND!!
ZA
ZA
STARDUST!!
ZA

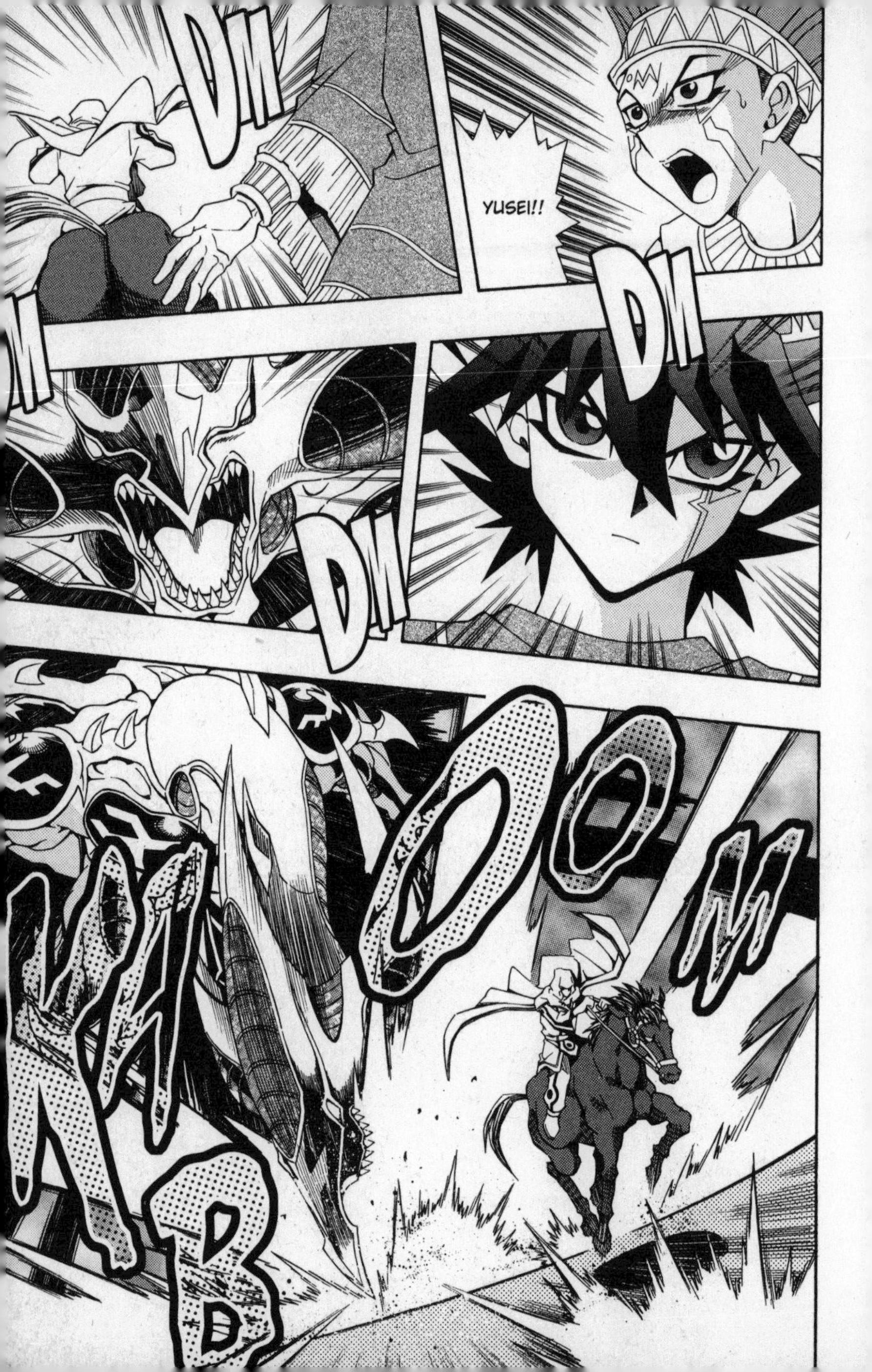
DM
YUSEI!!
DM
DM
DM
DM
DOOM

5D's TRACKS

THE 29TH

BY SATOMASA

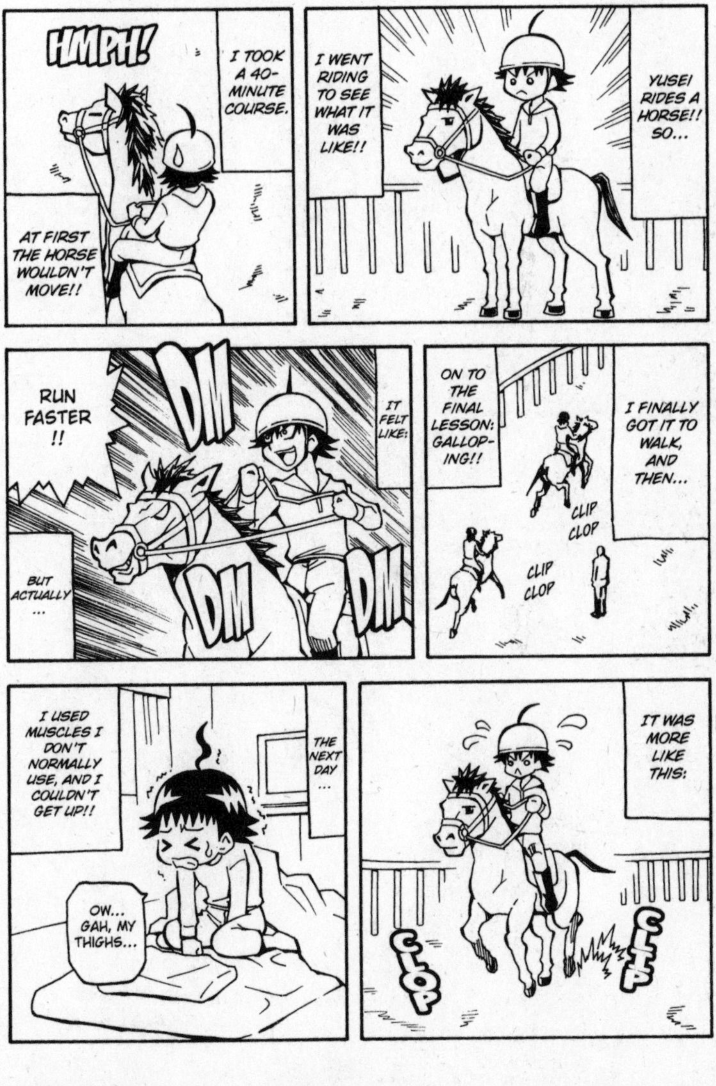

YUSEI RIDES A HORSE!! SO...
I WENT RIDING TO SEE WHAT IT WAS LIKE!!
I TOOK A 40-MINUTE COURSE.
HMPH!
AT FIRST THE HORSE WOULDN'T MOVE!!
I FINALLY GOT IT TO WALK, AND THEN...
ON TO THE FINAL LESSON: GALLOPING!!
CLIP CLOP
CLIP CLOP
IT FELT LIKE:
DM
RUN FASTER !!
DM
DM
BUT ACTUALLY ...
IT WAS MORE LIKE THIS:
CLIP
CLOP
THE NEXT DAY ...
I USED MUSCLES I DON'T NORMALLY USE, AND I COULDN'T GET UP!!
OW... GAH, MY THIGHS...

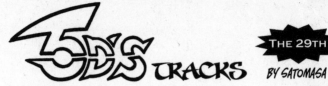

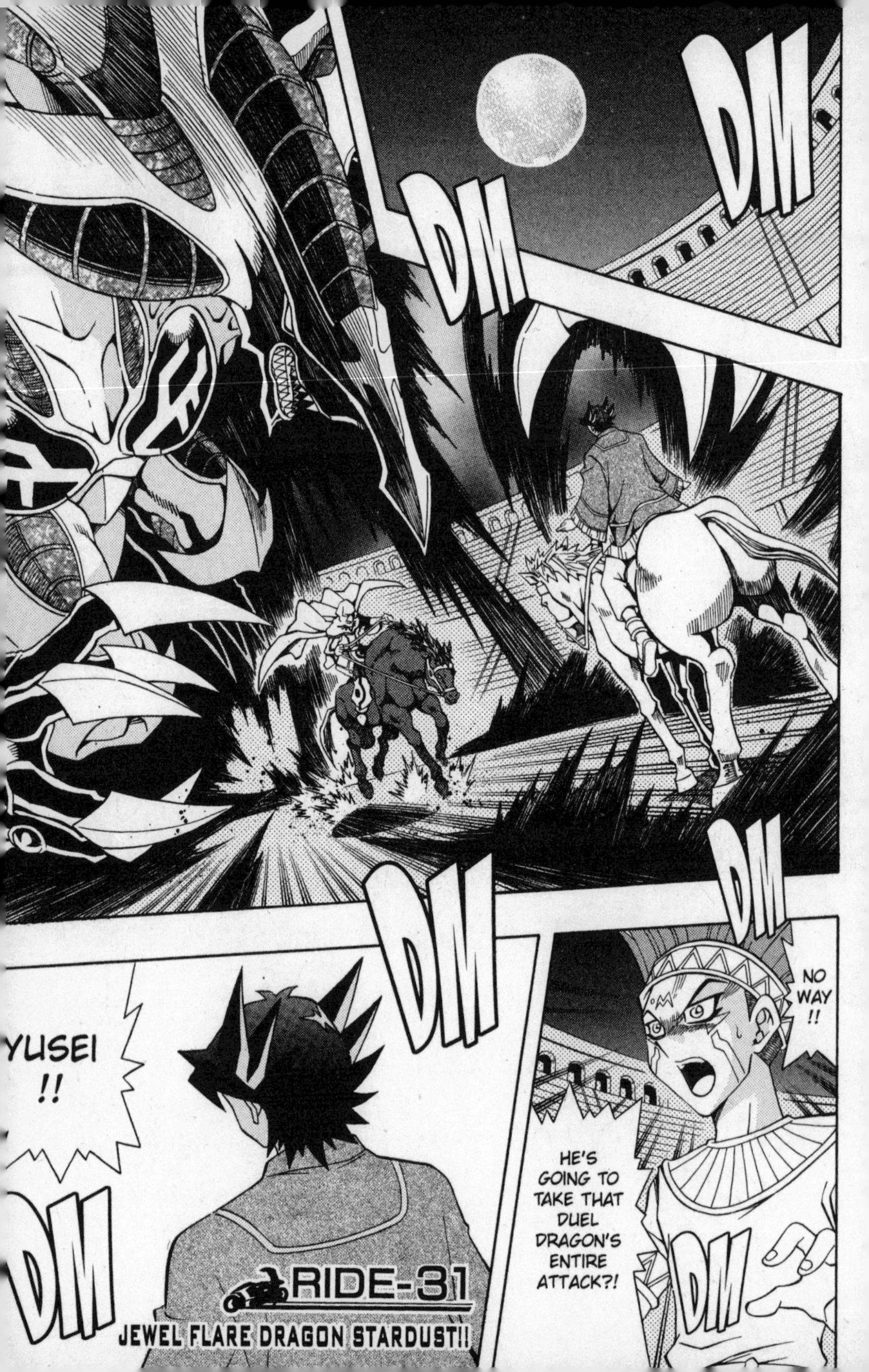
DM DM
DM DM
DM DM
NO WAY!!
HE'S GOING TO TAKE THAT DUEL DRAGON'S ENTIRE ATTACK?!
DM DM
DM DM
YUSEI!!
DM DM
RIDE-31
JEWEL FLARE DRAGON STARDUST!!

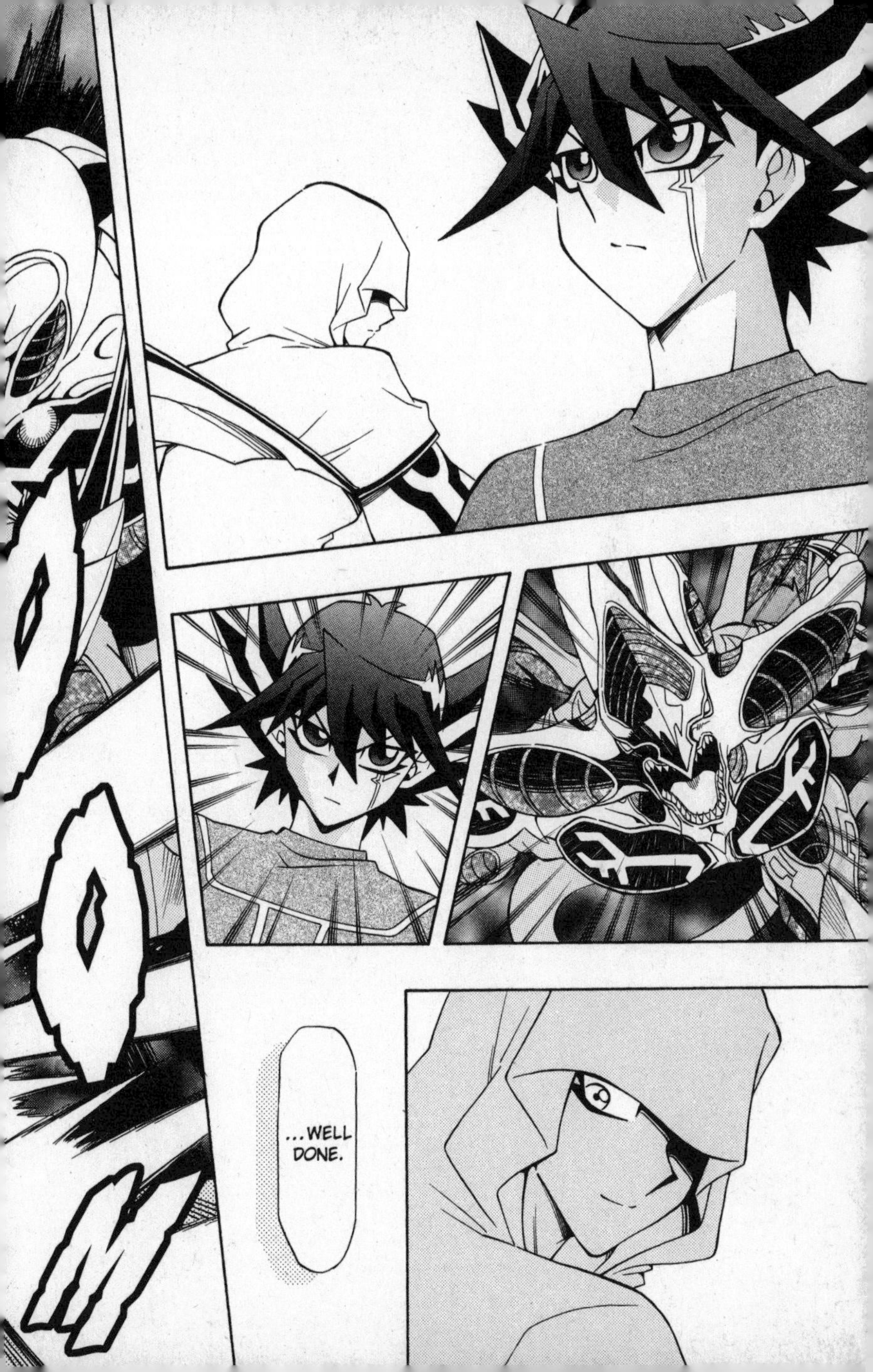
...WELL DONE.

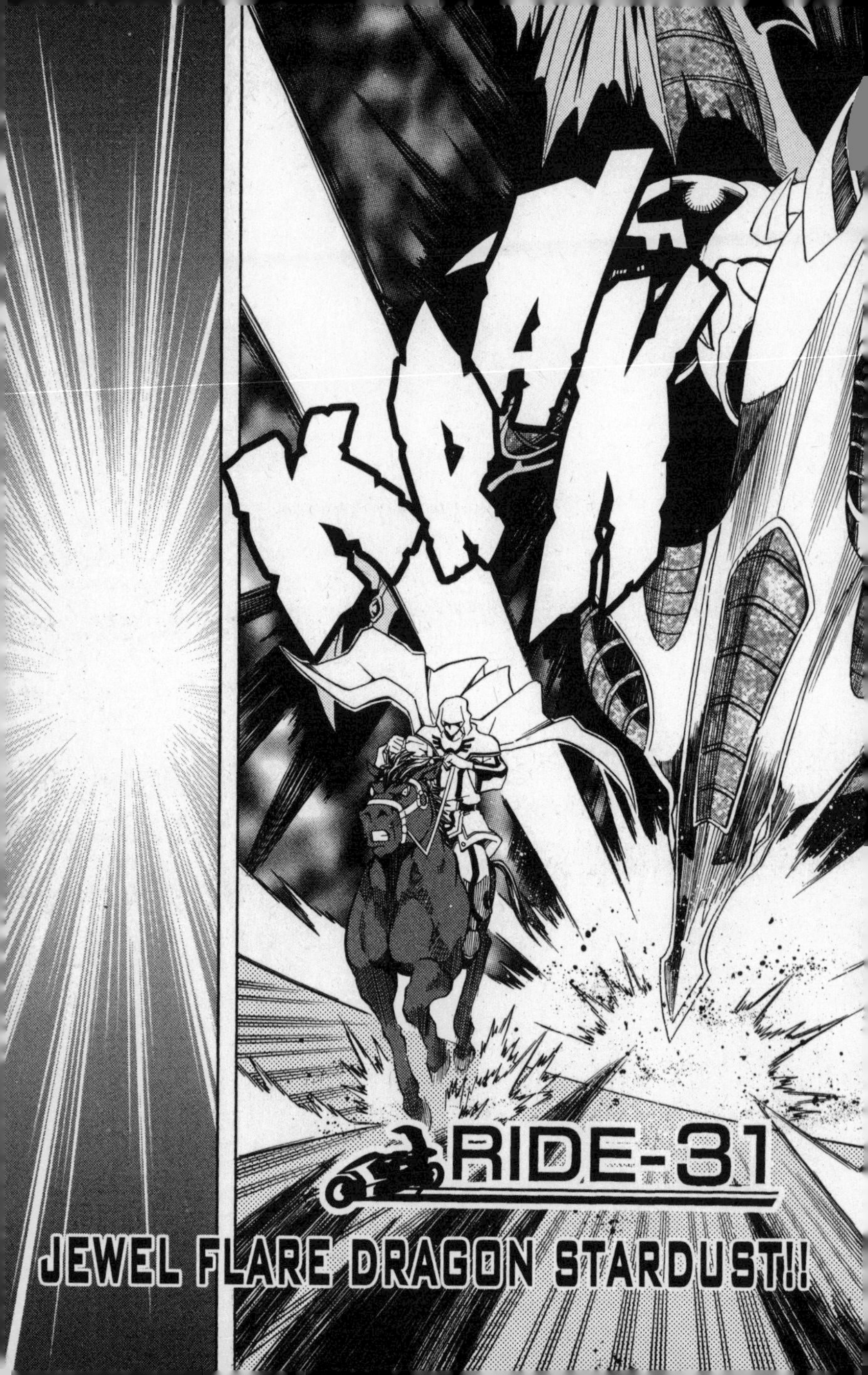
RIDE-31
JEWEL FLARE DRAGON STARDUST!!

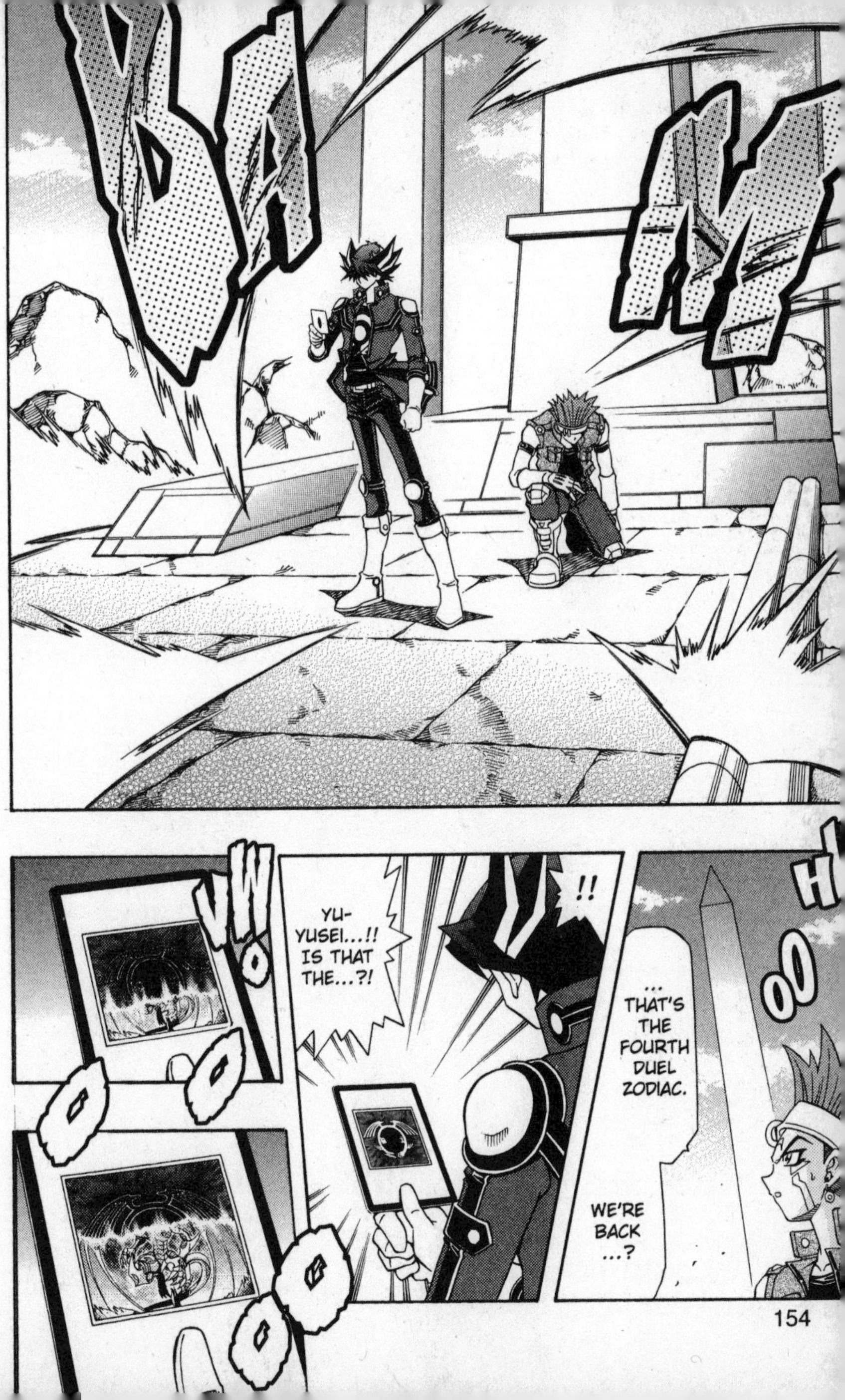
...
THAT'S THE FOURTH DUEL ZODIAC.
WE'RE BACK ...?
!!
YU- YUSEI...!! IS THAT THE...?!

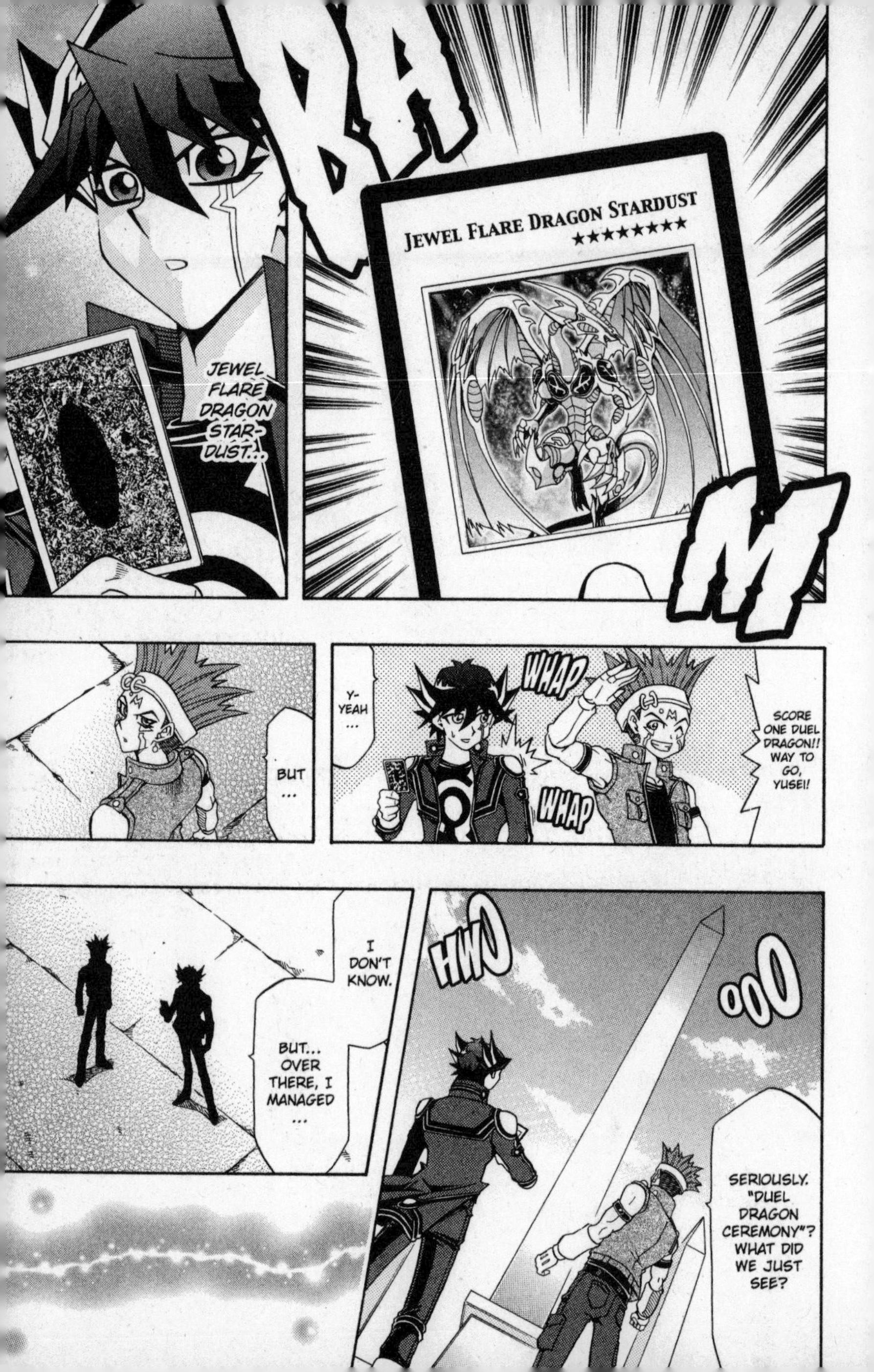
BAM
JEWEL FLARE DRAGON STARDUST
JEWEL FLARE DRAGON STARDUST...
SCORE ONE DUEL DRAGON!! WAY TO GO, YUSEI!
WHAP
WHAP
Y-YEAH...
BUT...
WHOOO
SERIOUSLY. "DUEL DRAGON CEREMONY"? WHAT DID WE JUST SEE?
I DON'T KNOW.
BUT... OVER THERE, I MANAGED...

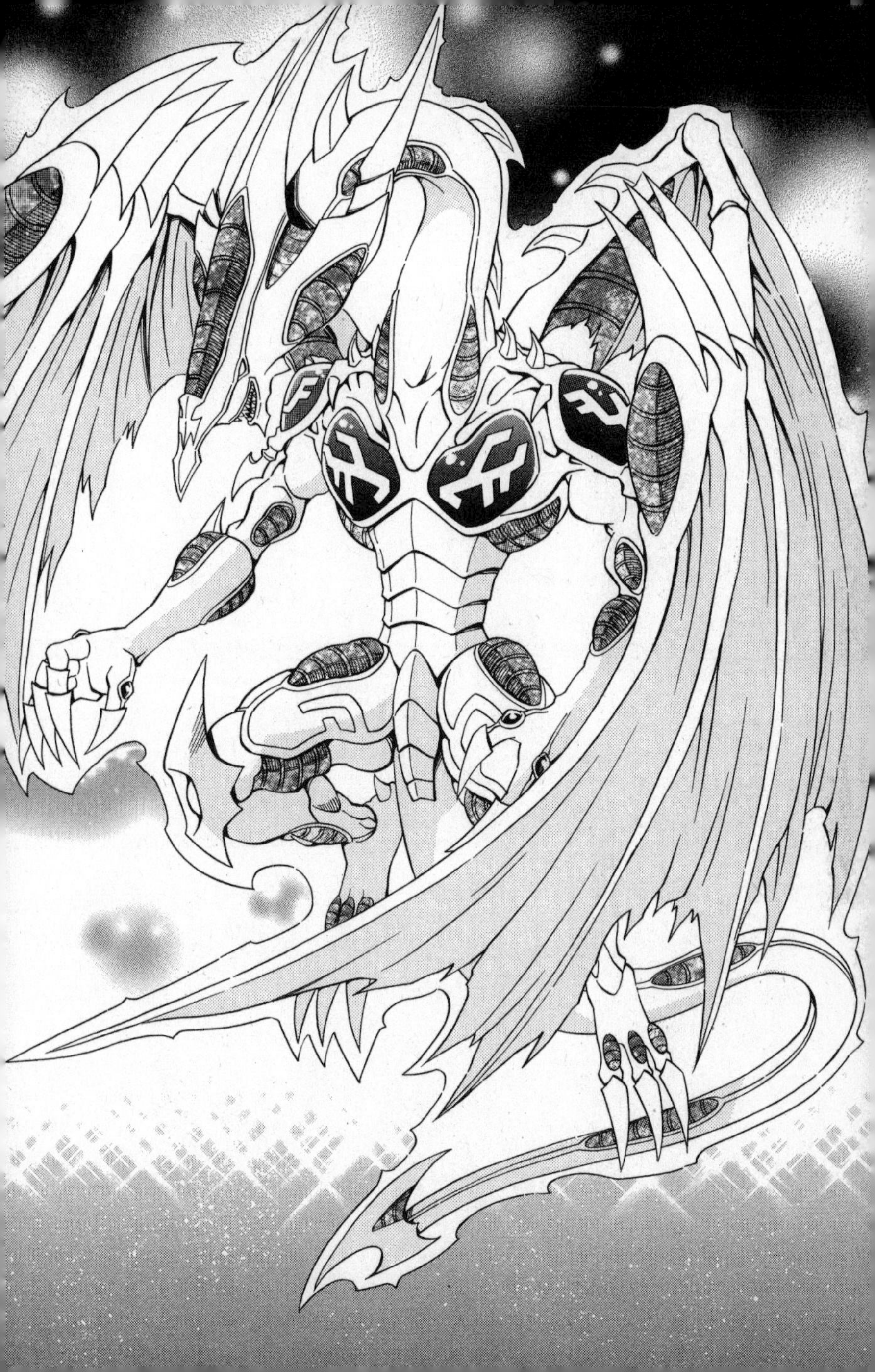

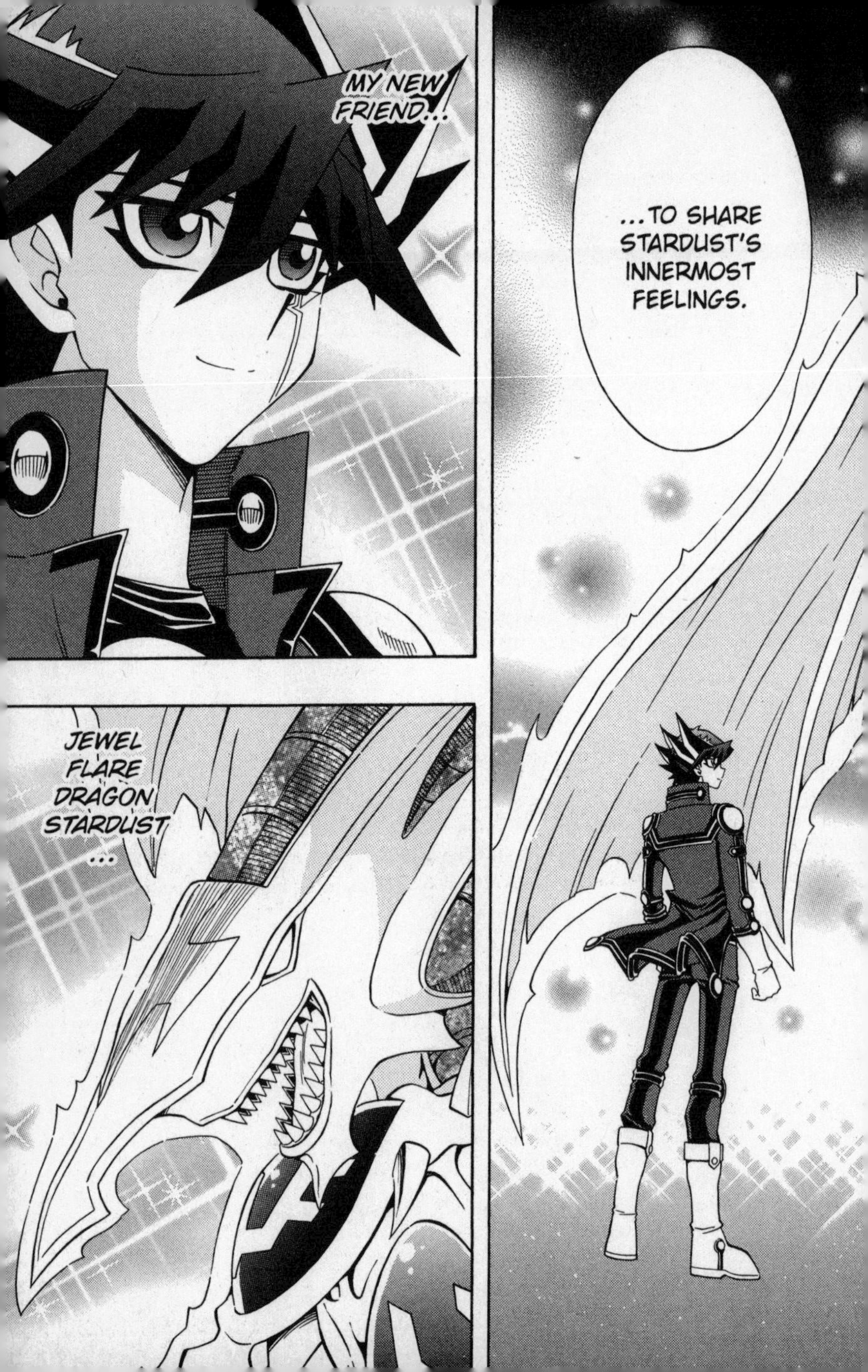
...TO SHARE STARDUST'S INNERMOST FEELINGS.
MY NEW FRIEND...
JEWEL FLARE DRAGON STARDUST ...

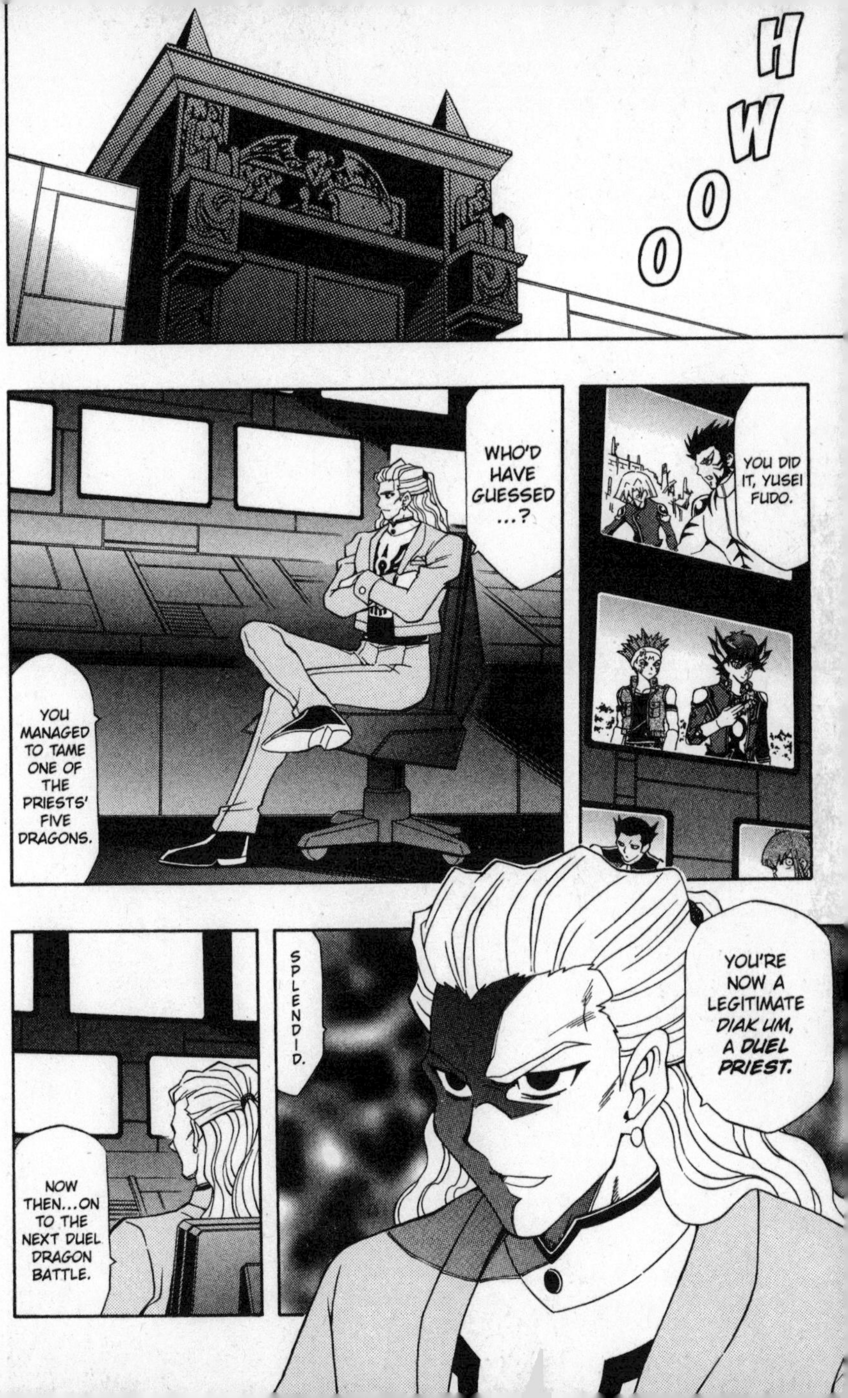
HWOOO
YOU DID IT, YUSEI FUDO.
WHO'D HAVE GUESSED...?
YOU MANAGED TO TAME ONE OF THE PRIESTS' FIVE DRAGONS.
YOU'RE NOW A LEGITIMATE *DIAK UM*, A ***DUEL PRIEST***.
SPLENDID.
NOW THEN...ON TO THE NEXT DUEL DRAGON BATTLE.

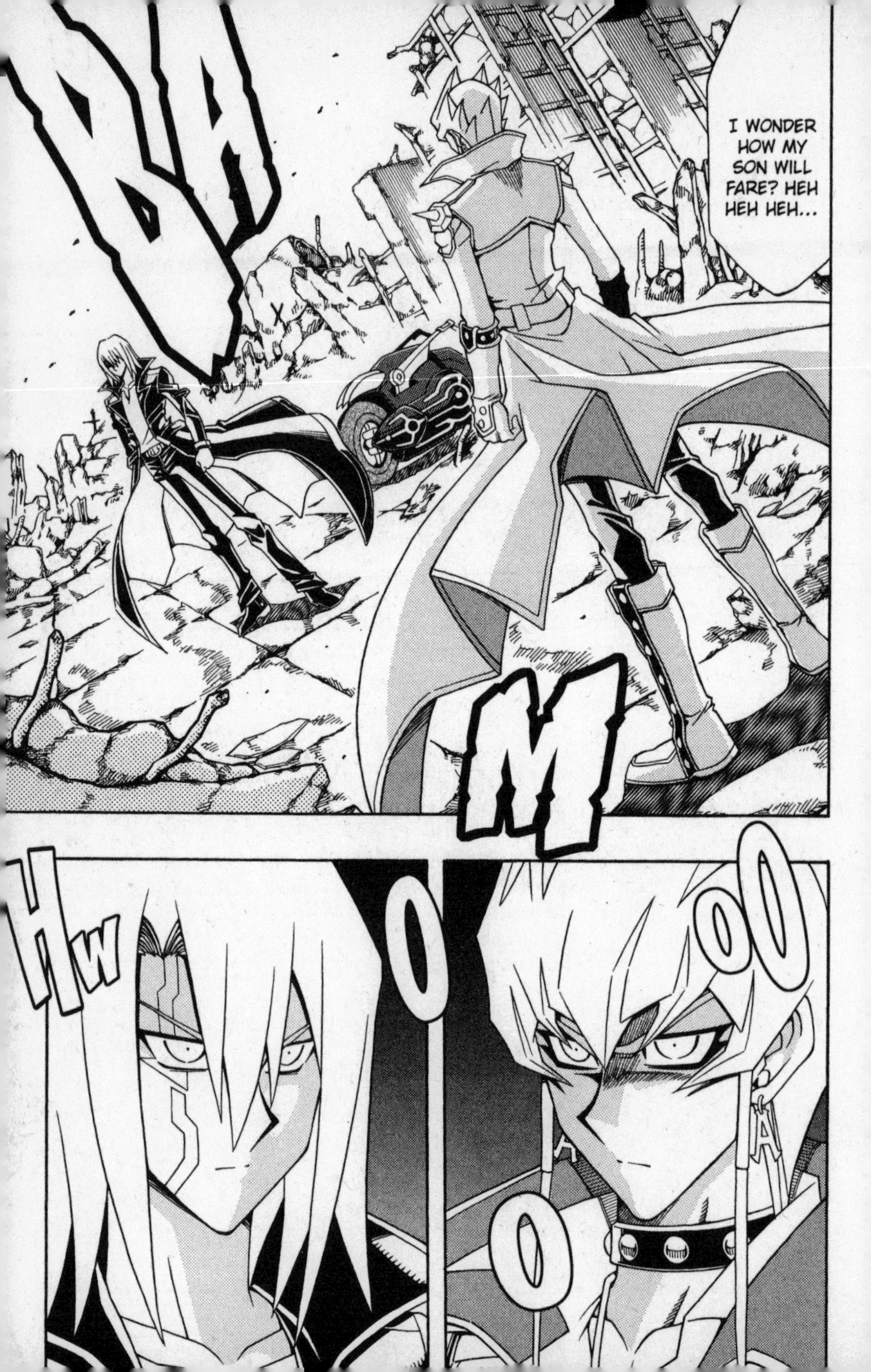
I WONDER HOW MY SON WILL FARE? HEH HEH HEH...

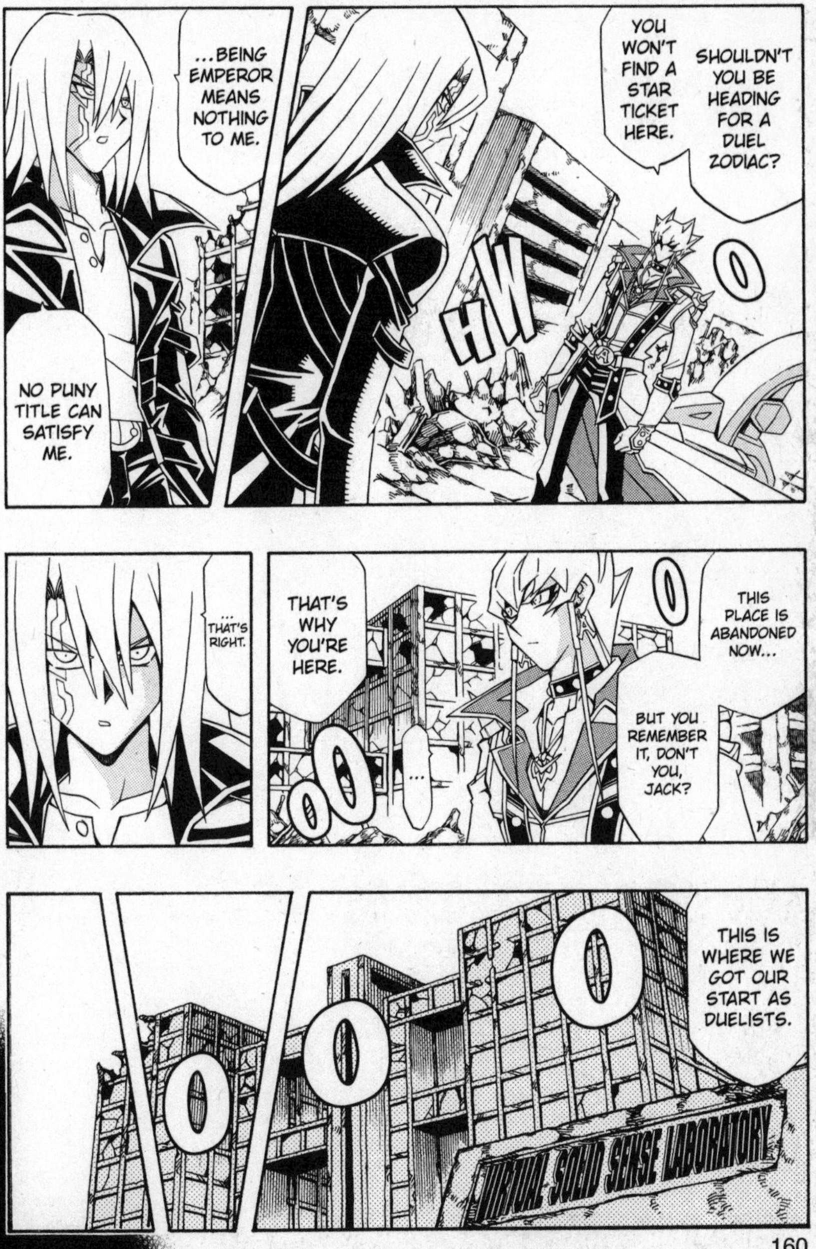
SHOULDN'T YOU BE HEADING FOR A DUEL ZODIAC?
YOU WON'T FIND A STAR TICKET HERE.
HWO
...BEING EMPEROR MEANS NOTHING TO ME.
NO PUNY TITLE CAN SATISFY ME.
THIS PLACE IS ABANDONED NOW...
BUT YOU REMEMBER IT, DON'T YOU, JACK?
THAT'S WHY YOU'RE HERE.
...
...THAT'S RIGHT.
THIS IS WHERE WE GOT OUR START AS DUELISTS.
VIRTUAL SOLID SENSE LABORATORY

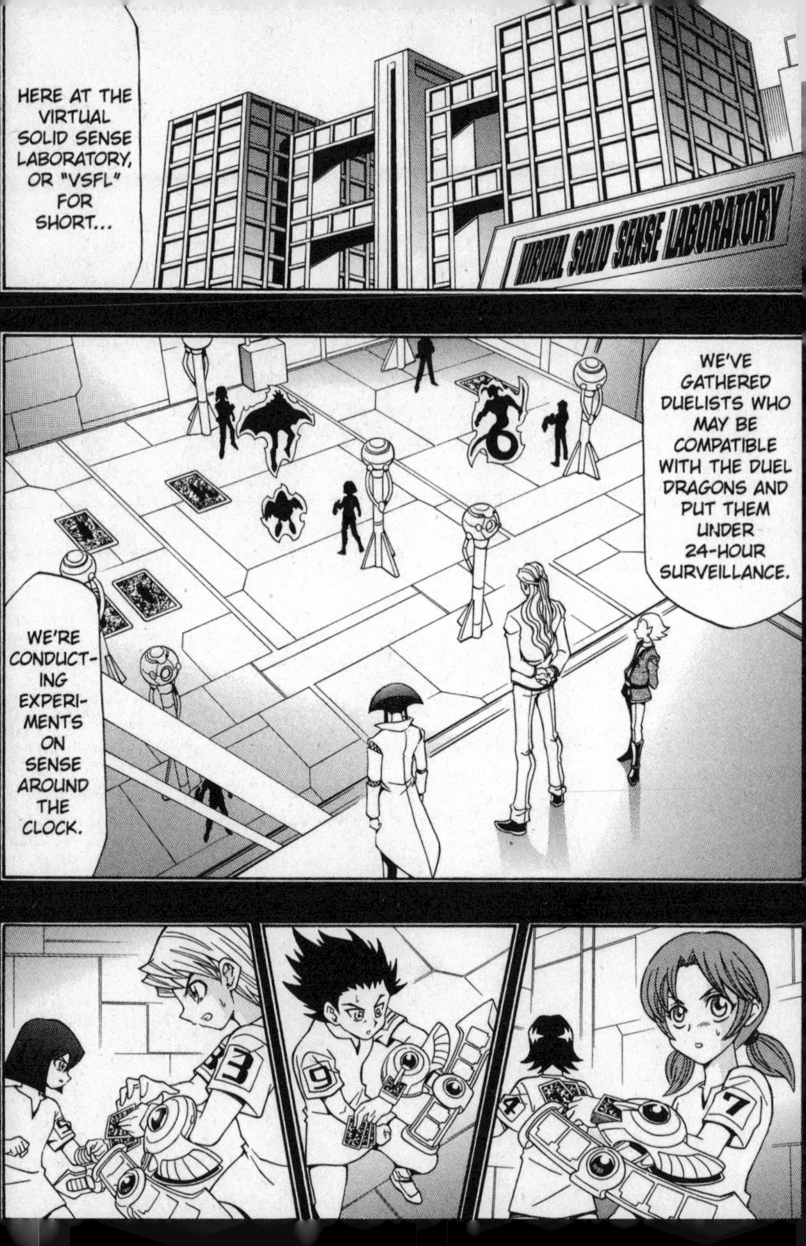
HERE AT THE VIRTUAL SOLID SENSE LABORATORY, OR "VSFL" FOR SHORT...
VIRTUAL SOLID SENSE LABORATORY
WE'VE GATHERED DUELISTS WHO MAY BE COMPATIBLE WITH THE DUEL DRAGONS AND PUT THEM UNDER 24-HOUR SURVEILLANCE.
WE'RE CONDUCTING EXPERIMENTS ON SENSE AROUND THE CLOCK.

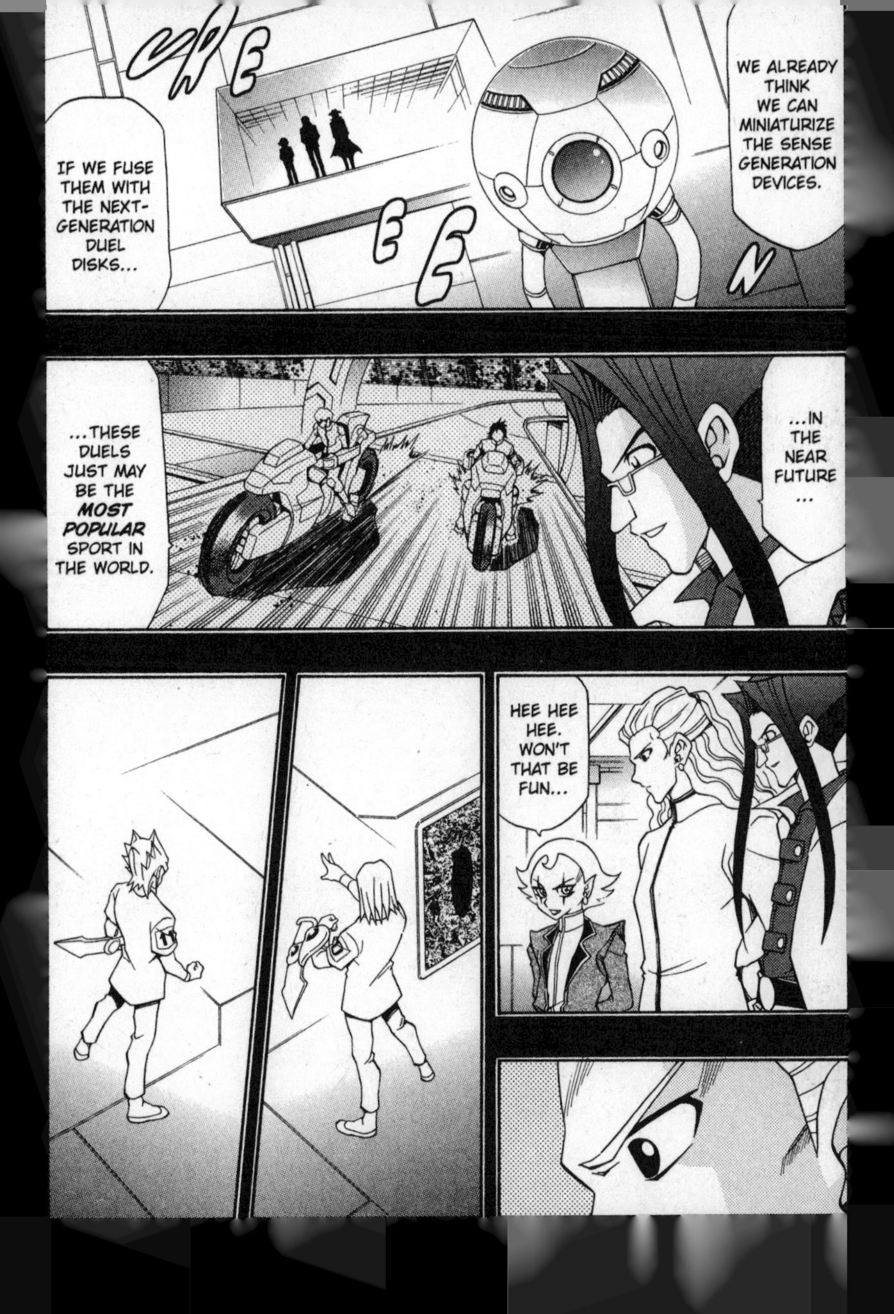
WE ALREADY THINK WE CAN MINIATURIZE THE SENSE GENERATION DEVICES.
IF WE FUSE THEM WITH THE NEXT-GENERATION DUEL DISKS...
...IN THE NEAR FUTURE...
...THESE DUELS JUST MAY BE THE MOST POPULAR SPORT IN THE WORLD.
HEE HEE HEE. WON'T THAT BE FUN...

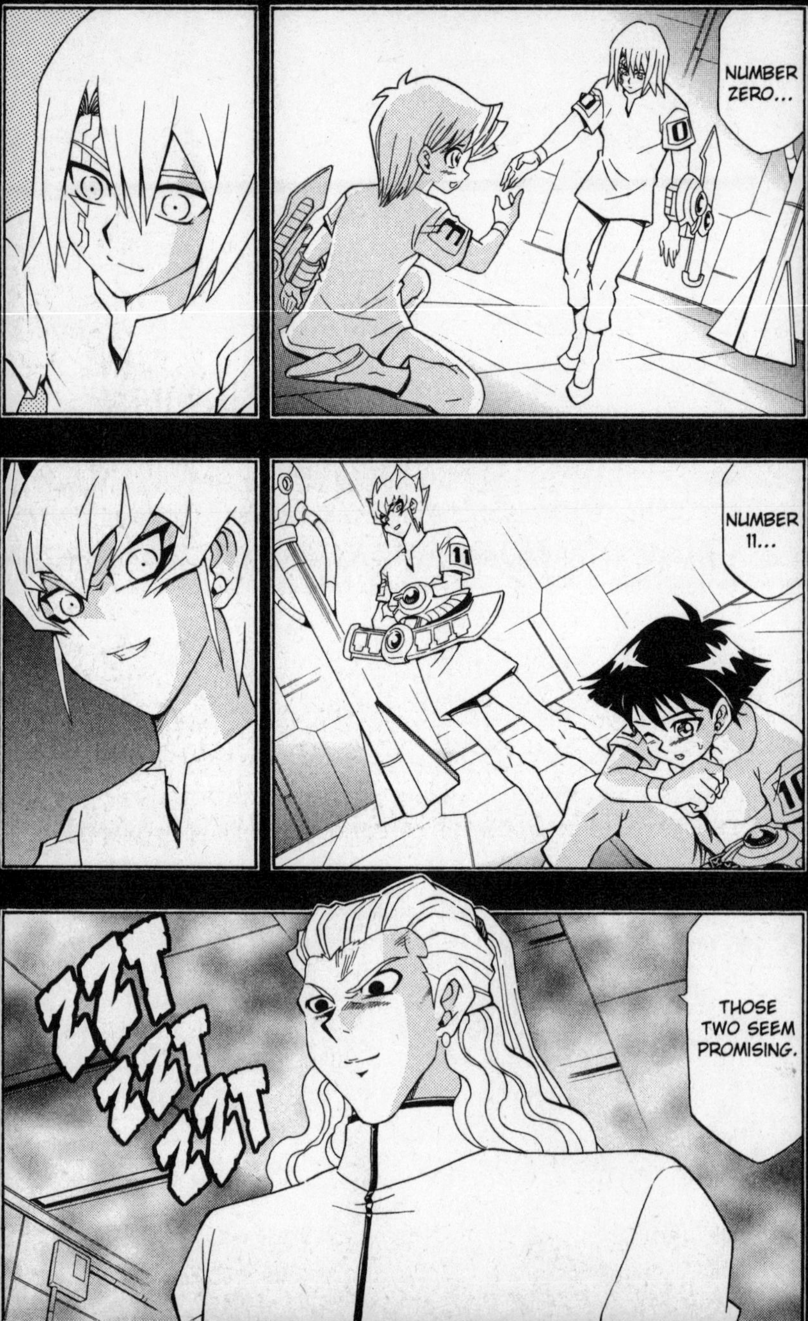
NUMBER ZERO...
NUMBER 11...
THOSE TWO SEEM PROMISING.
ZZZT ZZZT ZZZT

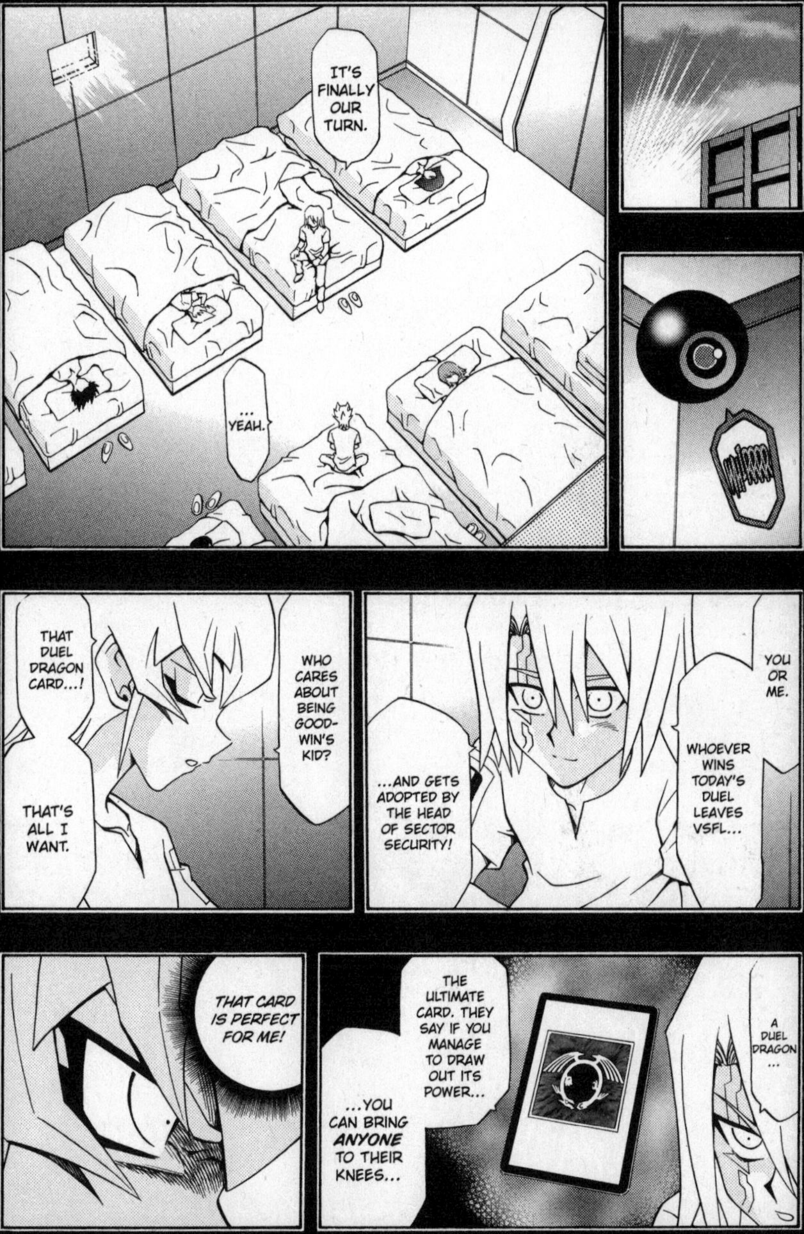
IT'S FINALLY OUR TURN.
... YEAH.
YOU OR ME.
WHOEVER WINS TODAY'S DUEL LEAVES VSFL...
...AND GETS ADOPTED BY THE HEAD OF SECTOR SECURITY!
WHO CARES ABOUT BEING GOOD-WIN'S KID?
THAT DUEL DRAGON CARD...!
THAT'S ALL I WANT.
A DUEL DRAGON...
THE ULTIMATE CARD. THEY SAY IF YOU MANAGE TO DRAW OUT ITS POWER...
...YOU CAN BRING *ANYONE* TO THEIR KNEES...
THAT CARD IS PERFECT FOR ME!

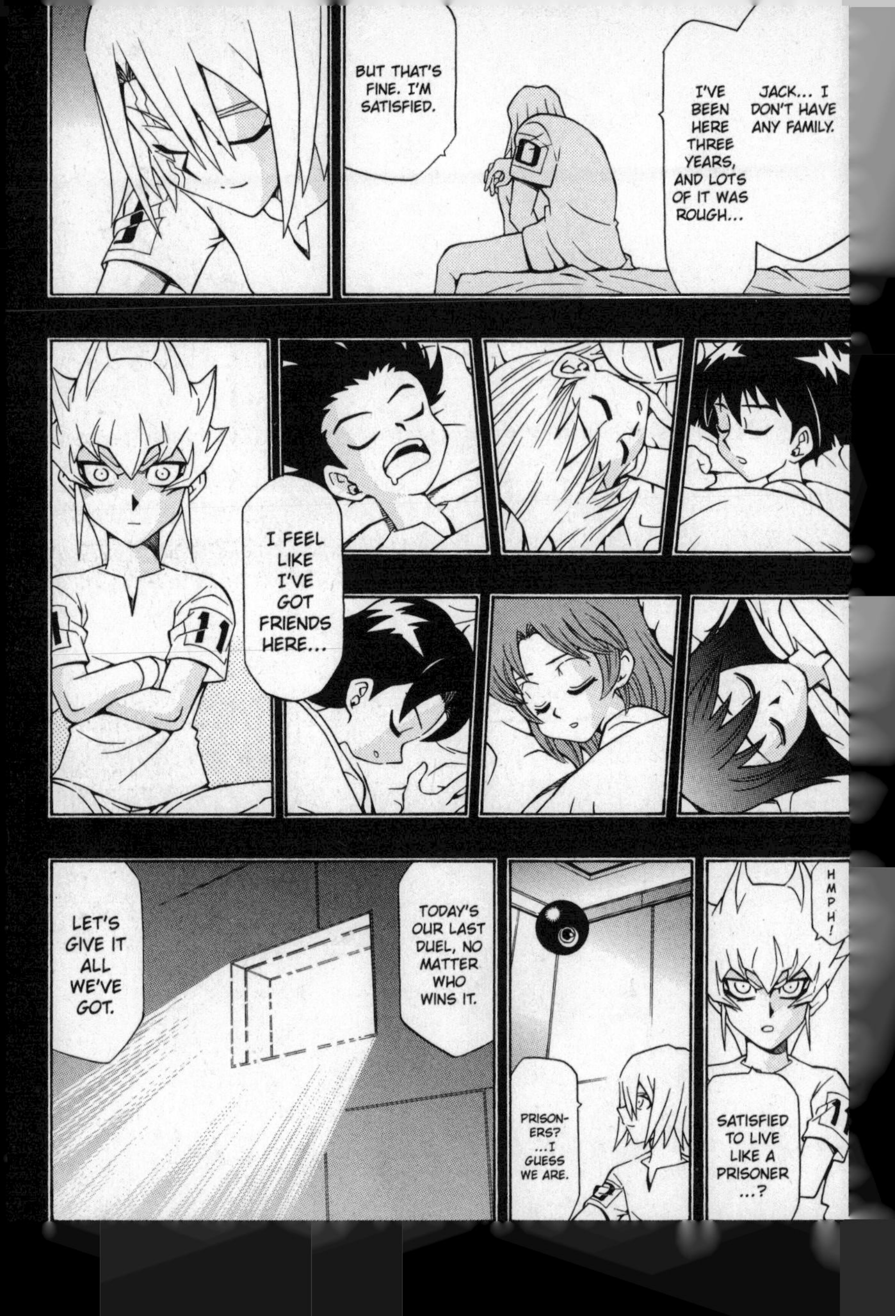
JACK... I DON'T HAVE ANY FAMILY.
I'VE BEEN HERE THREE YEARS, AND LOTS OF IT WAS ROUGH...
BUT THAT'S FINE. I'M SATISFIED.
I FEEL LIKE I'VE GOT FRIENDS HERE...
HMPH!
SATISFIED TO LIVE LIKE A PRISONER ...?
PRISONERS? ...I GUESS WE ARE.
TODAY'S OUR LAST DUEL, NO MATTER WHO WINS IT.
LET'S GIVE IT ALL WE'VE GOT.

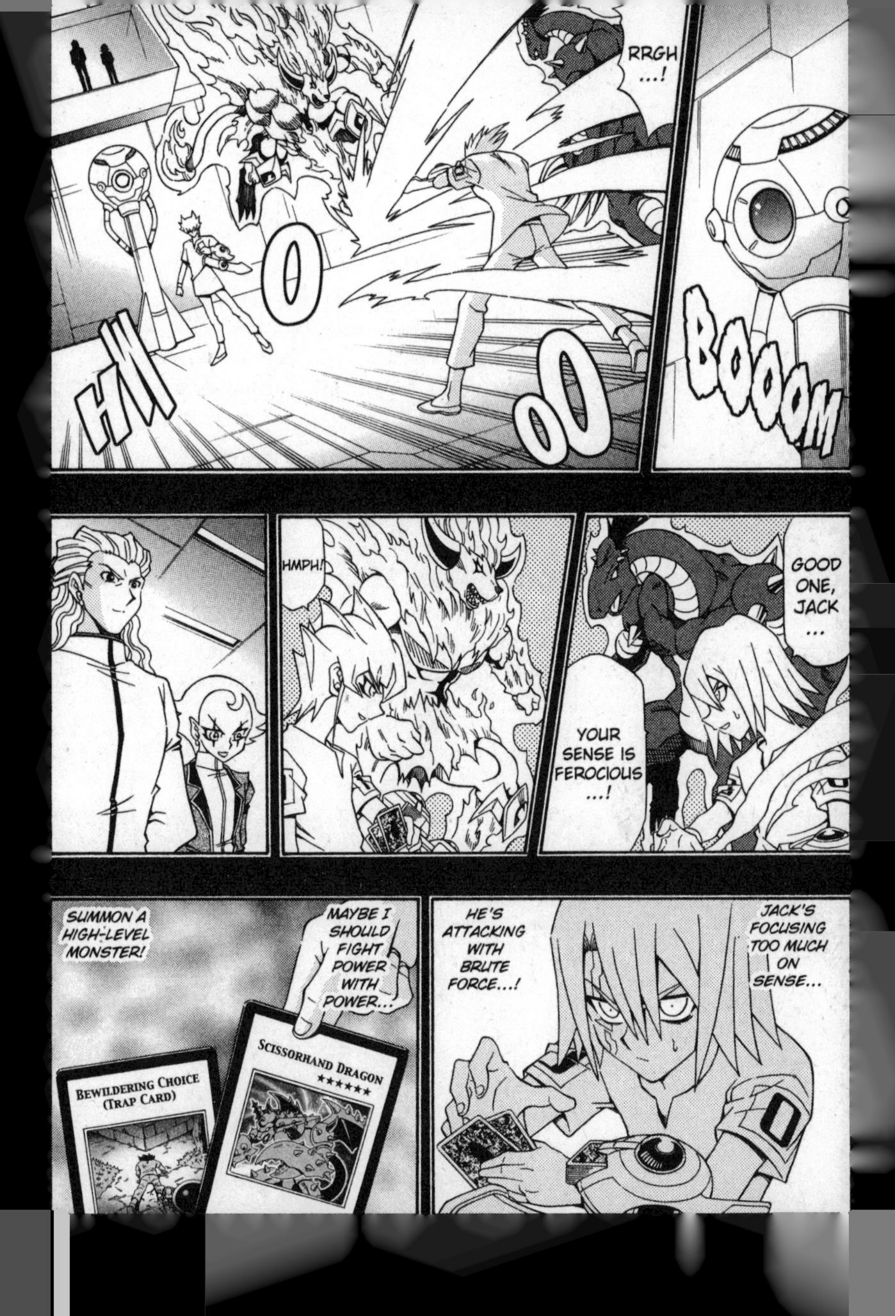
BOOOM
RRGH ...!
WHOOO
GOOD ONE, JACK ...
YOUR SENSE IS FEROCIOUS ...!
HMPH!
JACK'S FOCUSING TOO MUCH ON SENSE...
HE'S ATTACKING WITH BRUTE FORCE...!
MAYBE I SHOULD FIGHT POWER WITH POWER...
SUMMON A HIGH-LEVEL MONSTER!
SCISSORHAND DRAGON
BEWILDERING CHOICE (TRAP CARD)

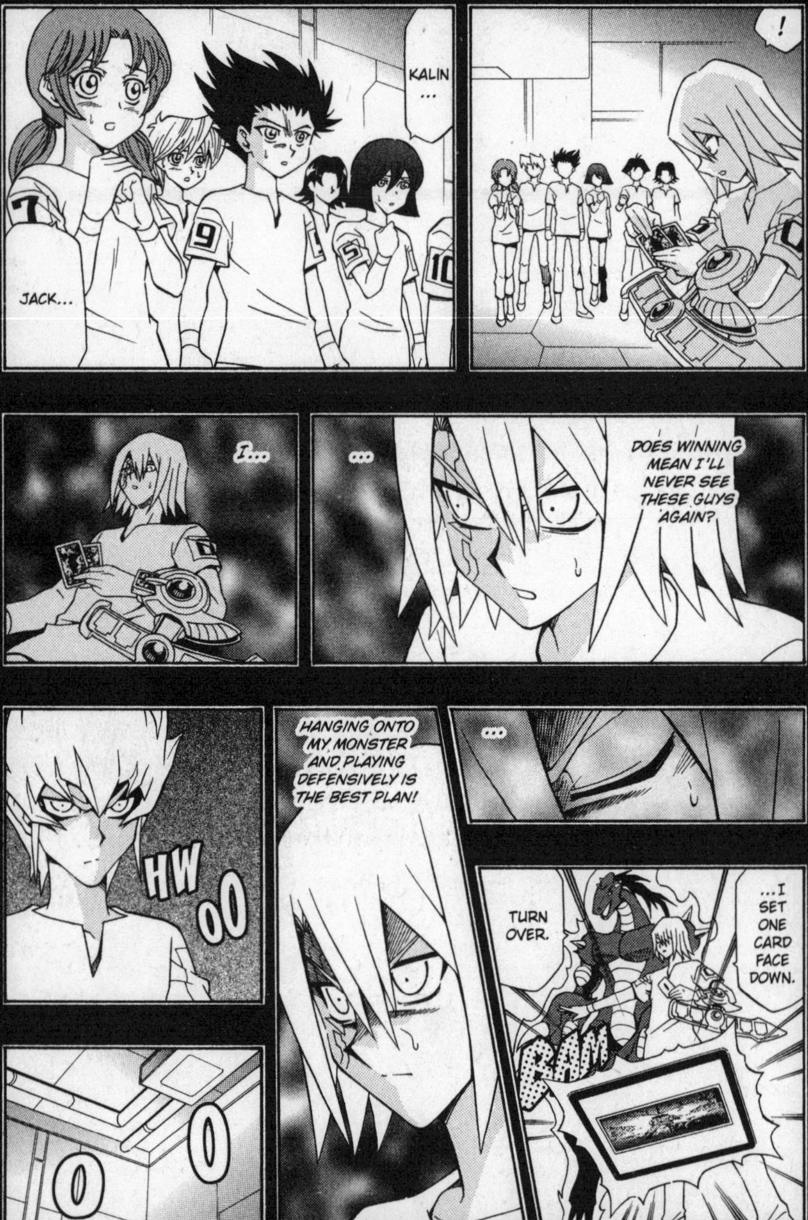

!
KALIN...
JACK...
DOES WINNING MEAN I'LL NEVER SEE THESE GUYS AGAIN?
...
I...
...
...I SET ONE CARD FACE DOWN.
TURN OVER.
BAM
HANGING ONTO MY MONSTER AND PLAYING DEFENSIVELY IS THE BEST PLAN!
HWOO
OO

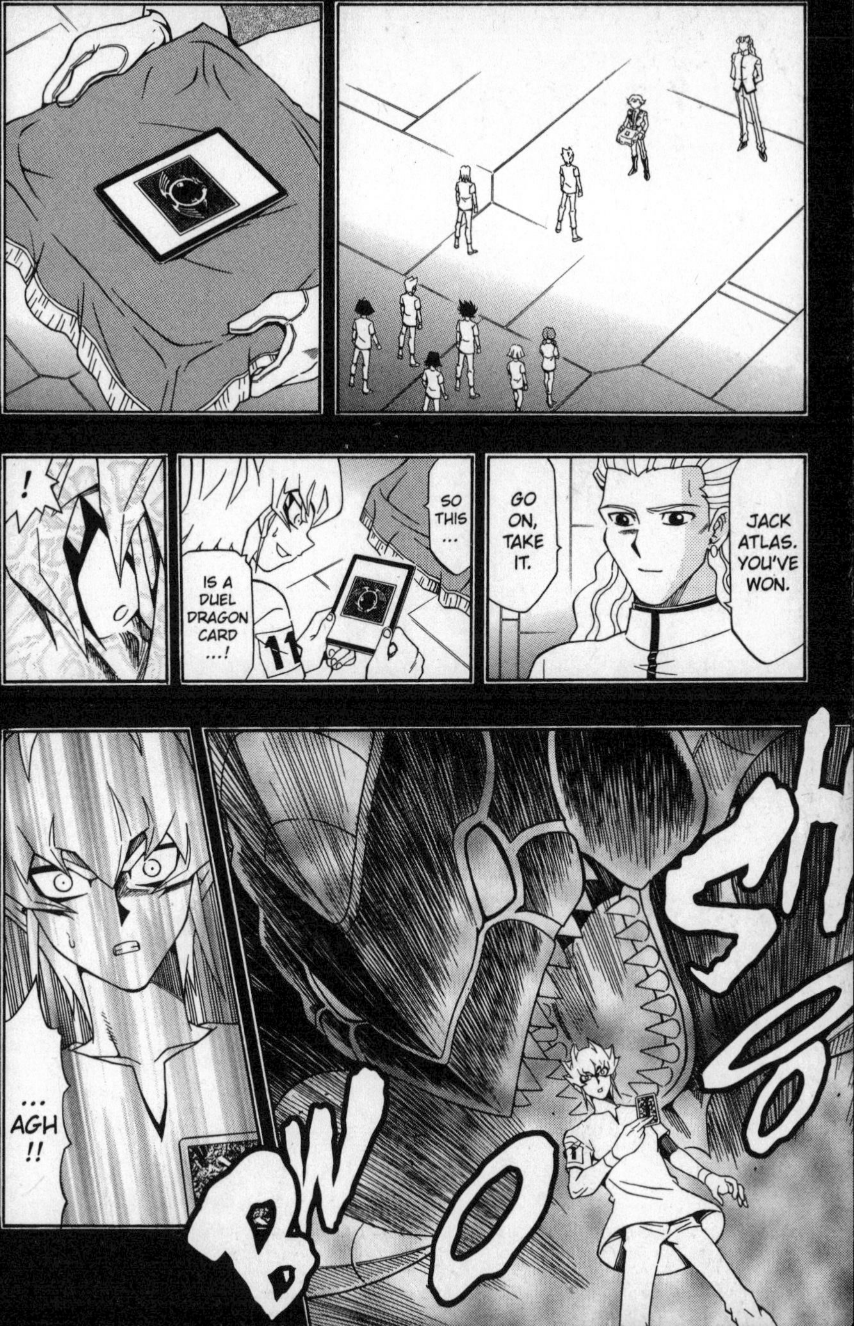
JACK ATLAS. YOU'VE WON.
GO ON, TAKE IT.
SO THIS...
IS A DUEL DRAGON CARD ...!
!
BWOOOSH
...AGH !!